Themes in Focus
Published titles

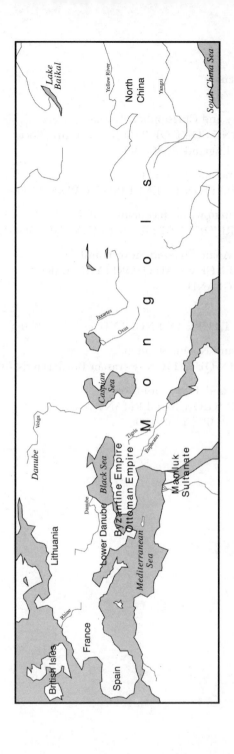

FRONTIERS IN QUESTION
Eurasian Borderlands, 700–1700

Edited by

Daniel Power

Lecturer in Medieval History
University of Sheffield

and

Naomi Standen

Assistant Professor of Asian History
University of Wisconsin-Superior

First published in Great Britain 1999 by
MACMILLAN PRESS LTD
Houndmills, Basingstoke, Hampshire RG21 6XS
and London
Companies and representatives throughout the world

A catalogue record for this book is available from the British Library.
ISBN 0–333–68452–4 hardcover
ISBN 0–333–68453–2 paperback

First published in the United States of America 1999 by
ST. MARTIN'S PRESS, INC.,
Scholarly and Reference Division,
175 Fifth Avenue, New York, N.Y. 10010

ISBN 0–312–21638–6 (cloth)

Library of Congress Cataloging-in-Publication Data

p. cm.
Includes bibliographical references and index.
ISBN 0–312–21638–6 (cloth)

CONTENTS

MAPS AND FIGURES

PREFACE

A new book on frontiers in history needs little justification. Frontiers are such a common and significant human phenomenon that there will always be room for a collection of regional studies which permit comparisons and contrasts between different frontiers to be made. Hence, given the vastness of this field of inquiry, the present volume confines itself to three aims. The first is to consider what makes a frontier explicitly a 'frontier'. This problem has received much attention from political scientists and geographers but rather less from historians, who, more often than not and with some justification, have regarded each frontier as unique and so have eschewed generalisation. Secondly, it is apparent that many frontiers do not simply 'exist' but are deemed to be 'frontiers' by their inhabitants, their rulers, or by later historians. Consequently this book also considers the different ways in which contemporaries and historians imagine frontiers, as well as the ways in which the frontier inhabitants' views of their environment differed from the understandings of the princes or governments who sought to control them. The third aim of this collection is to extend the geographical scope of comparison between political frontiers in history (as opposed to frontiers of settlement). Hence, as well as familiar frontiers in Western Europe, this book also includes examples from as far away as Mesopotamia and China, making hitherto untried comparisons possible.

Two further observations should be made here. Firstly, the use of the term 'frontier' in this work requires some explanation. The various meanings of the English word do not correspond exactly to terms in other languages, and in English the term can mean several different things; the two main ways in which historians use the term and its cognates are set out in the introduction. Hence the keen-eyed reader will notice a certain amount of latitude in the use of 'frontier' between the essays in this book; but by and large it is used for a major political division or zone of interaction. A North American audience in particular may find this confusing, since the European authors in this work often use 'frontier' to mean what a North American might be happier calling a 'boundary'. On the other hand, 'boundary' is both too specific, since it implies linear definition, and perhaps too belittling, since in British English it usually refers to a minor demarcation, such as a county or parliamentary constituency, rather than a major division. 'Border' is a more general term than 'frontier', as it ranges from the edge of a garden lawn to an international division, but it is too specific in character since it is primarily political or administrative. Both 'boundary' and 'border' imply division but they do not imply interaction in the way 'frontier' can. An alternative historical term, 'march', is too rooted in premodern history and, although sometimes used to denote a linear division in the Middle Ages, is likely to suggest a zone to a modern reader, whether or not this is appropriate in context. Hence 'frontier' is the only term that conveys adequately the many ways, both physical and imagined, in which societies separate themselves from and interact with one another.

The second observation concerns the timespan of this volume. It is implicit in this book that the modern state is capable of pervasive intrusion and control which was not possible before the rise of the nineteenth-century nation states. The subjects of the essays here are culled from the millennium preceding that epoch-making development: in other words, from the periods customarily known in the historiography of Europe as 'medieval' and 'early modern'. However, the geographical span of this book renders the usual European periodisation unsatisfactory, and consequently we have employed the word 'premodern' as a general term for the centuries covered in this book.

This book has come about with the help of a number of people. The articles concerning Spain, North China, Normandy, the Mediterranean, and the Ottomans were originally given as papers at a conference entitled *The Frontier in Question*, held at the University of Essex in April 1995: we are grateful to its organiser, Professor Hugh Brogan, for encouraging us to publish the premodern papers as a book, and also for allowing us to adapt the conference title for it. We have also received helpful advice and comments from Jonathan Steinberg, the members of the Department of History at the University of Sheffield, and Matthew Innes (DJP), and from Nicola di Cosmo, Marilynn Larew, Ruth Mostern, and contributors to H-ASIA and int-boundaries (NLS). Simon Winder and Jonathan Reeve of the Macmillan Press guided us through the difficulties of coediting a multi-author work and Penny Simmons through the copy-editing. The invention of e-mail made editorial collaboration unimaginably easier. The research for our contributions was carried out at Selwyn College and Trinity Hall, Cambridge (DJP), and the University of Durham (NLS), and the editorial work at the University of Sheffield (DJP) and St John's College, Oxford (NLS): the editors would like to thank all these academic insitutions for their support, both moral and financial. Several maps are reproduced with the kind permission of the following publishers: 4.1, 6.1, 6.2, and 6.3, Cambridge University Press; 7.1 and 7.2, Oxford University Press. The cover illustration is reproduced with the kind permission of the University Library, Uppsala, Sweden. Finally, Daniel Power wishes to express his gratitude to his family and to Clare for their undying patience. Naomi Standen wishes to thank Mike for reading and commenting on endless drafts and for generally putting up with the trials of living with an academic. The first editorial meeting for this volume took place in hospital (unexpectedly!), a fortnight before the birth of Naomi's son Sam, who has thus been around for as long as we have been compiling this volume. Naomi therefore dedicates her portion of the book to him.

DJP/NLS
September 1997

ABBREVIATIONS

ANS	*Anglo-Norman Studies (Proceedings of the Battle Conference)* [the date given is the date of the conference, not of publication]
AOASH	*Acta Orientalia Academiae Scientiarum Hungaricae*
AS	*Anatolian Studies*
BMFEA	*Bulletin of the Museum of Far Eastern Antiquities*
BMQ	*British Museum Quarterly*
BSOAS	*Bulletin of the School of Oriental and African Studies*
BTTK	*Belleten: Türk Tarih Kurumu*
BÜD	*Boğaz-içi Üniversitesi Dergisi – Beşeri Bilimler*
Cal. IPM	*Calendar of Inquisitions Post Mortem*
CFHB	*Corpus fontium historiae Byzantinae*
CFYG	*Cefu yuangui*
CHC	*Cambridge History of China*
CSHB	*Corpus scriptorum historiae Byzantinae*
DAI	*De Administrando Imperio*
EHR	*English Historical Review*
EI	*The Encyclopaedia of Islam*, ed. A. J. Wensinck et al., 4 vols and supplement, Leiden 1913–38
EI, new edn	*The Encyclopaedia of Islam*, new edn, ed. H. A. R. Gibb, Leiden 1953–
HI	*Humaniora Islamic*
HJAS	*Harvard Journal of Asiatic Studies*
HUS	*Harvard Ukrainian Studies*
JAOS	*Journal of the American Oriental Society*
JAS	*Journal of Asian Studies*
JRAS	*Journal of the Royal Asiatic Society*
JW	*Jiu Wudai shi [Old History of the Five Dynasties]*
LM6	*Lietuvos Metrika (1528–1547) 6-oji teismų bylų knyga (Kopija–xvi a. pabaiga)*, ed. S. Lazutka et al., Vilnius 1995
LM7	*Lietuvos Metrika knyga nr. 564 (1553–1567). Viešujų reikalų knyga 7*, ed. A. Baliulis, Vilnius 1996

LP Hen. VIII	*Letters and Papers, Foreign and Domestic, Reign of Henry VIII*
LS	*Liao shi [Liao History]*
MFS	*Medieval Frontier Societies*, ed. R. Bartlett and A. MacKay, Oxford 1989
MGH SS	*Monumenta Germaniae Historica: Scriptores*
MSOS	*Mitteilungen des Seminars für Orientalische Sprachen*
NH	*Northern History*
NLM AOM	National library of Malta, Archives of the Order of St John
NLM LIB	National Library of Malta, Library MSS
OsmAr	*Osmanlı Araştırmaları – The Journal of Ottoman Studies*
PVL	*Povest' Vremennykh Let*
QTW	*Quan Tang wen [Collected Prose of the Tang]*
REI	*Révue des Études Islamiques*
Rise	P. Wittek, *The Rise of the Ottoman Empire*, London 1938
SCIV	*Studii şi Cercetari de Istorie Veche şi Arheologie*
SRP	*Scriptores Rerum Prussicarum*, ed. F. Hirsch, M. Töppen, and E. Strehlke, 5 vols, Leipzig 1861–74, repr. Frankfurt-am-Main 1965
TJ	*Zizhi tongjian [Comprehensive Mirror to Aid in Government]*
TRHS	*Transactions of the Royal Historical Society*
WZKM	*Wiener Zeitschrift für die Kunde des Morgenlandes*
XW	*Xin Wudai shi [New History of the Five Dynasties]*
ZDMG	*Zeitschrift der Deutschen Morgenländischen Gesellschaft*

GLOSSARY

akra	Greek: 'the end', 'extremity', or 'limit'.
alp	Turkish: (in pre-Islamic Turkish societies) individuals noted for their heroic deeds and military valour. Cf. *ghāzī* (q.v.).
Amt	German: an administrative unit.
baba	Turkish: literally, 'father', 'head of a religious order'. Mendicant religious/dervish leader amongst the Islamicised Turkoman tribes of Anatolia and elsewhere.
ban	Old French (Latin: *bannum*): various forms of coercive power in medieval Western Europe; specifically, the control of blood-justice, military service, mills, and so on, which from the eleventh century were normally the prerogatives of castellans.
barīd	Arabic: Mamluk postal system based on horse relays.
beg/bey	Turkish: title (of Chinese origin) applied to a ruler. In Turco-Islamic usage synonymous with emir (q.v.).
beglik/beylik	Turkish: the territory under the control of a bey (q.v.). See emirate.
Boiar	Slavonic: (in Eastern Europe) a nobleman.
book	(To compile) a list of dependants for whose conduct the headsman or chief accepts responsibility.
boullotes	Greek: imperial officer, stationed in Constantinople where he regulated trade in controlled goods.
castelry	(Latin: *castellaria*, *castellania*). The area under the jurisdiction of a castle, normally its immediate surrounds.

xiii

Catholicus	Latin: title used to denote the spiritual leader of some Eastern Churches. Used here for the head of the Armenian church.
Central Plains	Chinese: *zhongyuan* 中原. Region of China proper (q.v.) between the Yellow and Yangzi (Yangtze) rivers. Traditional heartlands of Chinese civilisation.
China proper	Conventionally stretching from the Great Wall in the north to Hong Kong and Hainan islands in the south, excluding much of the present-day People's Republic: chiefly Yunnan, Tibet, Xinjiang, Inner Mongolia, and Manchuria (see Map 3.1).
Cilicia	Region in southern Anatolia, northwest of where the Syrian coast meets the coast of Anatolia. During time of Crusades and Mamluk-Mongol war, inhabited by Armenians who set up kingdom referred to as Lesser Armenia (see Map 6.1).
commandery	A convent belonging to a military religious order, and hence its basic unit of territorial and economic organisation.
dār al-ʿahd	Arabic: literally, 'abode of the pact or covenant'. In Muslim legal texts it refers to territories whose inhabitants are mainly Christians, Jews, or Zoroastrians who have agreed a treaty with the Muslims.
dār al-ḥarb	Arabic: literally, 'the abode of war'. The territories of the infidels, against whom Muslim rulers should enforce the Holy War (*jihād*, q.v.).
dār al-Islam	Arabic: literally, the 'abode of Islam'. The territories where Muslim laws and practices are enforced.
darb	Arabic: pl. *durūb*. Frontier; more specifically frontier regions of Arab states in Asia Minor, and between the Byzantine Empire and the Caliphate in the mountainous areas of the Tarsus.
dervish	Perso-Turkish: member of an Islamic mendi-

cant Sūfi order; a wandering religious enthusiast, generally with heterodox religious tendencies.

dynastic histories — Chinese: *zhengshi* 正史. Official histories compiled for each Chinese dynasty by its successor as a legitimating act, using contemporary records and preliminary histories compiled during the life of the dynasty.

ehl-i ḥudūa — Turco-Persian. Inhabitants of a Muslim border region, particularly those charged with its defence.

emic — Anthropological concept: the methodological approach which tries to describe a given human phenomenon by using the same categories which are implied within that phenomenon. See M. Harris, *Cultural Materialism: the struggle for a science of culture*, New York 1979, 32ff.

emir — Turkish: from Arabic *amīr*, 'one who commands'. A local or regional ruler (of a principality or of a larger, but less than imperial, entity).

emirate — Territory under the control of an emir. In the Ottoman/Anatolian context best translated as 'principality'.

encellulement — French: the disintegration of political power into tiny units, normally based around castles, in eleventh-century France.

eschatia — Greek: 'the furthest part' or 'a remote spot'.

Escorial taktikon — Greek: a precedence list, or list of imperial ranks and offices that pertained shortly after 976, and which would have been used to arrange the seating plan at an imperial banquet.

Five Dynasties — Chinese: *Wudai* 五代. Series of short-lived dynasties controlling part or all of north China from 907 to 960. Later Liang: 907–23, Later Tang: 923–36, Later Jin: 936–47, (Liao interregnum 947), Later Han: 947–50, Later Zhou: 951–60.

ghazā	Arabic: in Islam, war for the faith against unbelievers, carried out by *ghāzīs* (q.v.).
ghāzī	Arabic: a Muslim who fights for the faith on the frontiers of Islam.
Golden Horde	Mongol state north of the Black Sea (see Map 6.1).
Hebei 河北	Chinese: literally, 'north of the (Yellow) River'. Region of northeast China between the Yellow River and Manchuria, including a large area north of the Great Wall (see Maps 3.2 and 3.3).
Heerkönig	German: literally, 'army king'. Leader of an early medieval European warband or tribal grouping, invested with sacral qualities of kingship as ruler of the state formed around such a group. Applied by analogy to comparable figures in Turco-Islamic history.
horos, horia, horisma	Greek: 'boundary' or 'border'.
īlkhān	Arabic and Persian < Mongolian or Turkish: title of the Mongol ruler in Iran; often translated as 'subject *khān*' (q.v.).
imperial China	Period of Chinese history from the 'first unification' by Qin Shihuang to the republican revolution: 221 BC to AD 1911.
Jazīra	The area between the upper Euphrates and the Tigris, today comprising northern Iraq, northeastern Syria, and southeastern Turkey (see Map 6.2).
jihād	Arabic: the duty of a Muslim ruler to fight the unbelievers; in Islamic jurisprudence, the carrying-on of Holy War for the faith (cf. *ghazā*).
kerne	In Ireland and Scotland, a lightly armed foot-soldier.
khān	Mongolian and Turkish: Mongol ruler.
Kleinkrieg	German: ongoing petty warfare and skirmishing, specifically by local border forces on the frontiers of the Ottoman empire, particularly against the Habsburgs in Hungary, in the absence of a major cam-

paign by the central state forces of either side.

kleisurai   Greek: (in Byzantine use) the frontiers against the Muslims in Asia Minor. Military commanders in charge of these regions were called *kleisuraxai*.

kommerkiarios   Greek: imperial officer, monitored trade and extracted the sales tax (*kommerkion*) levied on all goods traded within the empire.

langue   French: literally, 'tongue' or 'language'. Regional organisation of the houses and estates of the Knights Hospitaller.

langue d'oc   French: the Romance language formerly spoken across most of southern France and still used in some districts there; also known today as Occitan or (less accurately) as Provençal (see Map 5.1).

langue d'oïl   French: the Romance language of northern France, also known as Old French, from which modern French is descended (see Map 5.1).

latifundia   Latin: large rural landholdings usually, in medieval Europe, under feudal tenure. Sometimes used by present-day Ottoman historians as a synonym for *wakf* (q.v.).

Lesser Armenia   See Cilicia.

limes   Latin: pl. *limites*. Usually a concept of a frontier as a strongly fortified, defensive line, based upon traditional, and now largely discredited, views of the Roman frontier. The various meanings of the term are numerous and complex. See the article by B. Isaac, cited in bibliography.

mamlūk   Arabic: 'owned'. A military slave.

Mamluk Sultanate   State established in Egypt and Syria, 1250–1517, by officers of *mamluk* origin (see Map 6.1).

Militärgrenze   German: 'military frontier'. The system of military colonisation and defence in depth developed from the sixteenth century by the

	Habsburgs, particularly on the Croatian-Hungarian frontier with the Ottomans.
mixobarbaros	Greek: 'half-barbarian'. Generally a (partially) Hellenised non-Greek living within the *oikoumene* (q.v.).
Mozarab	Arabic: 'half-Arab'. A Christian under Islamic rule since the fall of the Visigothic kingdom.
mutaṭāwwiᶜa	Arabic: volunteers who join Muslim campaigns against the infidels for the sake of practising Holy War.
notarios	Greek: imperial officer, a notary.
oikoumene	Greek: 'the inhabited world'. Used by Ancient Greeks to designate their own 'civilised' lands, and by Byzantines to designate their empire.
Ordenstaat	German: the state created on the southern shores of the Baltic by the Teutonic Order. After 1525, the heart of the Duchy of Prussia.
pagus	Latin: pl. *pagi*. A county in the Carolingian empire, later used more loosely for a district (hence French *pays*, country).
patrikios	Greek: imperial rank, very esteemed in the late tenth century.
Pays du Droit Coutumier	French: the area of pre-Revolutionary northern and central France where provincial customary law was used (see Map 5.1).
Pays du Droit Écrit	French: the area of pre-Revolutionary southern France where law was based upon 'written' (that is, Roman) law (see Map 5.1).
philotimiai	Greek: 'honour' or 'credit'. In this case an annual payment made to frontier communities from Constantinople.
presidio	Spanish: a fortified settlement, especially an outpost on the frontier with Islam.
qaraghul	Mongolian > Arabic *qarawul:* Mongol road or border patrols.
qāṣid	Arabic: pl. *quṣṣād*. Envoy; more specifically Mamluk intelligence agents.
Qipchaq	Turkish tribes living in the steppe north of the Black Sea; also applied as the name of this steppe.

Reconquista	Spanish: the long-term process of Christians fighting Muslims in medieval Spain in order to regain the territories lost after the Arab conquest of 711.
refugium	Latin: 'refuge'. Applied to specific areas of Inner and Central Asia which served as the command centre and residence for the rulers of successive nomadic steppe empires.
reive	Northern English and Scots dialect: to go on a raid for plunder (hence 'reiver').
renovatio imperii	Latin: 'renewal of empire'. Applied by analogy to the later seventeenth-century attempts at military and administrative reform and imperial renewal by Ottoman grand viziers of the Köprülü ministerial family.
repoblación	Spanish: the occupation by Christian immigrants of lands formerly deserted, or inhabited by conquered Muslim populations.
Rhomaios	Greek: 'Roman', as a Byzantine would have styled himself.
ribāt	Arabic: a garrisoned fortification whose occupiers devote themselves to the Holy War and to pious practices.
Rûm	Turkish: from the Arabic *bilād al-Rūm*, 'the lands of the Romans' = Byzantine Anatolia. After the Turkish conquest applied mainly to those parts of Anatolia forming part of the so-called Seljuq Sultanate of Rûm (1077–1308) (see Map 6.1).
Rumeli	Turkish: literally, 'the lands (*el*) of the Romans' = Byzantine Romania. In Ottoman usage referred to the lands of southeastern Europe brought successively under their rule from the mid fourteenth to the early sixteenth century (see Maps 9.1 and 10.1).
Sejm	Polish (Lithuanian: *seimas*). Parliament, council.
serhadd al-manṣūra	Perso-Arabic: 'the ever-victorious frontier'. A topos used by the Ottomans in relation to the outer limits of their state.

sharī'a	Arabic: Islamic law.
Shuowen 說文	Chinese etymological dictionary dating from the first century AD.
starosta	Polish: literally, 'elder'. Senior administrator of Polish and Lithuanian provinces.
strategos	Greek: Imperial officer, a provincial military commander.
surnames	Clan-like landowning families, especially in the far north of England, fourteenth to sixteenth centuries.
synoros	Greek: 'bordering on'.
termasi	Greek: 'edge' or 'end', in the plural means 'boundaries'.
thagr	Arabic: pl. *thugūr*. In a general sense can mean the whole area separating the *dār al-Islam* (q.v.) from the *dār al-ḥarb* (q.v.). In a more restricted sense can also be applied to a particular outpost in the frontier, like *thagr Sarqusta*.
tivun	Latinised Slavonic (Latin: *tivunus*; Lithuanian: *tijūnas*; Polish: *ciwun*; Russian: *tiiun*). Junior provincial administrator.
Turcomans	Muslim Turkish nomads in the Middle East.
tutejszy	Polish: from *tutaj*, literally, 'here'. Self-definition of local population.
uj	Turkish (Modern Turkish: *uc*). The limit or furthest extent of a thing. By extension, a frontier zone or marchland, especially Ottoman-Christian borders in the fourteenth and fifteenth centuries. Analogous with Arabic *thagr* (q.v.).
uj-begi	Turkish (Modern Turkish: *uc-beyi*). The usually semi-autonomous ruler (*beg*, *bey*, (q.v.)) of a frontier zone; a marcher lord.
ulemā	Arabic: pl. of *'ālim*. One versed in Islamic law.
Visitatio Liminum	Latin: formal visits by Roman Catholic bishops to Rome, instituted by Pope Sixtus V in 1585.
wāfidiyya	Arabic: refugees from the Ilkhanate to the Mamluk Sultanate.

wakf/wuqūf Arabic (Turkish: *vakıf*). In Islamic law, pious endowments devoted in perpetuity to the assistance of the needy, the maintenance of mosques, or the funding of the Holy War.

yasa Turkish < Mongolian *jasagh*. Command, decree or law. Also applied to the law code attributed to Chinggis Khan.

NOTES ON CONTRIBUTORS

Reuven Amitai-Preiss specialises in the late medieval history of the Middle East, with a particular interest in the states established by peoples originating from the Eurasian steppe. He has studied at the University of Pennsylvania, the School of Oriental and African Studies, and the Hebrew University where he received his Ph.D. in 1990. He has been a visiting research fellow at Princeton and Oxford. His book, *Mongols and Mamluks: the Mamluk-Ilkhanid war, 1260–1281*, was published in 1995 by Cambridge University Press. He is currently Senior Lecturer in Islamic History in the department of Islamic and Middle Eastern Studies at the Hebrew University of Jerusalem.

Steven G. Ellis is an Englishman who lectures in English and Gaelic on the history of the British Isles, 1300–1700, at the National University of Ireland, Galway, where he is Professor of History. He took his Bachelor's and Master's degrees at the University of Manchester, his Ph.D. at Queen's University, Belfast, and was awarded a D.Litt. by the National University for his published work which includes *Tudor Ireland: crown, community and the conflict of cultures, 1470–1603* (London 1985), and *Tudor Frontiers and Noble Power: the making of the British state* (Oxford 1995).

Colin Heywood is a historian working on the Ottoman Empire and aspects of the history of non-Ottoman western Asia in the later medieval and early modern period. He has degrees in History from the University of London, and taught in America before returning to the Department of History at the School of Oriental and African Studies. He has published in journals and collections from Britain, France, the USA, Germany, Austria, Hungary, former Yugoslavia, Greece, Turkey, Tunisia, and the Ukraine, and is the author of *The Turks* in Blackwell's 'Peoples of Asia' series.

Eduardo Manzano Moreno is a Researcher at the Centro de Estudios Históricos of the Consejo Superior de Investigaciones Científicas

(Madrid). He is also Associate Lecturer in the Department of Arabic of the Universidad Complutense of Madrid. As a medievalist who special-ises in the history of Muslim Spain, he has published in Spanish, French, and English periodicals, and is the author of *La frontera de al-Andalus en época de los Omeyas* (Madrid 1991) and of *Historia de las sociedades musulmanas en la Edad Media* (Madrid 1993).

Daniel Power works on the history of Northern France, especially Normandy, in the central Middle Ages. He is a lecturer in medieval history at the University of Sheffield, and was previously a Research Fellow at Trinity Hall, Cambridge. He took his BA in History and his Ph.D. at Selwyn College, Cambridge, and his doctoral thesis concerned frontier society on the borders of Normandy in the twelfth and early thirteenth centuries.

S. C. Rowell, MA, Ph.D. (Cantab) lives on the Balto-German frontier and conducts research at the Centre for West Lithuanian and Prussian History in Klaipeda, Lithuania. He is the author of *Lithuania Ascending: a pagan empire in East-Central Europe, 1295–1345* (Cambridge 1994).

Naomi Standen is a historian working on premodern China. She took a first degree in history at the University of London, then went to Taiwan to learn Chinese in order to do a Ph.D. on the phenomenon of frontier crossing in tenth-century China. Until 1997 she was a Junior Research Fellow at St. John's College, Oxford, and is now Assistant Professor of Asian History at the University of Wisconsin-Superior. She is the author of the chapter on the Five Dynasties (907–60) in the *Cambridge History of China*, volume 5 (forthcoming).

Paul Stephenson is a historian of Byzantium and the medieval Balkans. He took his first degree at Cambridge University, where he also wrote his doctoral thesis on the Byzantine frontier in the Balkans. Currently, he is a British Academy Postdoctoral Fellow and a Fellow of Keble College, Oxford.

Ann Williams was the Director of the Centre for Mediterranean Studies and Senior Lecturer in Mediterranean History at the University of Exeter until 1996. She currently holds an Emeritus Leverhulme Fellow-ship for research on the Hospital and charitable work of the Order of St

John in Malta, 1522–1798. She contributed the Mediterranean section to *Süleyman the Magnificent and His Age,* edited by Metin Kunt and Christine Woodhead (Longman 1995). She has just completed a constitutional and administrative history of the Order of St John, *Servants of the Sick: the Knights Hospitaller in Rhodes and Malta 1310–1631.*

1

INTRODUCTION

A. Frontiers: Terms, Concepts, and the Historians of Medieval and Early Modern Europe

Daniel Power

Anyone coming to the study of frontiers in history for the first time will be struck immediately by the diversity of the subject. Indeed, its geographical and chronological limits seem hardly less broad than those of History itself. Within a particular field of historical research, historians may have written about geographical, political, cultural, economic, linguistic, racial, or gender frontiers, to name only some of the more popular types.[1] The perceptive student may well ask three basic questions. Firstly, why do there appear to be so many different types of frontiers in historical writing? After all, at first glance a frontier appears to be a very mundane phenomenon. Secondly, how valid are comparisons between different frontiers, whether from the same or different periods of history? For much of the attraction to historians of the idea of 'frontiers' rests on the assumption that frontiers can be compared profitably with one another; yet some historians write of frontiers as political divisions between states, whereas to others a frontier is the margin of settled land in a wilderness, or is an entirely cultural division between peoples. Thirdly, how did people view frontiers and frontier societies in the past? Like all historical phenomena, contemporary and subsequent views of the frontier often diverge widely; but the ways in which people envisaged frontiers can tell us much about their concepts of identity and political control.

1

The nine essays in this book consider 'frontiers' that were separated widely in space and time, ranging from Western Europe to China and from the eighth to the eighteenth centuries. This introduction will place these essays in their historiographical context. The first half is a general examination of the terms and concepts associated with frontiers: it classifies the main sorts of frontiers that the student will encounter in historiography. The second half considers the themes that are common to the nine chosen frontiers in this book, and shows why this field is an important area of historical inquiry.

Classifying Frontiers

The diversity of frontiers in historiography requires some discussion. Although it is now widely accepted that each frontier is intrinsically unique and so defies simple categorisation, there have been various attempts to classify so-called 'frontiers'.[2] As early as 1907 Lord Curzon, no doubt reflecting on his experience as Viceroy of India, distinguished between 'frontiers of separation' and 'frontiers of contact', a contrast that geographers subsequently developed.[3] More recently, German geographers have differentiated 'converging frontiers' (*Zusammenwachsgrenzen*) from 'frontiers of separation' (*Trennungsgrenzen*); while Eduardo Manzano Moreno's paper in this volume contrasts 'unstable', 'enclosing', and 'expanding' frontiers.[4] Classification is impeded, however, by the fact that there are two quite distinct notions of what a 'frontier' comprises, corresponding more or less to a European and a North American frontier concept. The reader will be spared much confusion if this dichotomy is grasped at the outset, especially as many historians refer to 'frontiers' without defining the term – although some have carefully noted its different meanings on opposite sides of the Atlantic.[5] These two categories shall be referred to here as *political frontiers* and *frontiers of settlement*.[6]

The British English term 'frontier' and its European cognates normally mean a political barrier between states or peoples, often militarised. The European frontier is sometimes envisaged as linear, sometimes as a zone; its political exigencies may provoke the tightening of political control in comparison with the hinterland, or conversely, it may sometimes be necessary to appease the inhabitants to retain their loyalty. In contrast, the American 'frontier' is not a barrier but a zone of passage and a land of opportunity, involving conflict with the natural environment rather than neighbours. It is a region where the challenges of the wilderness encourage self-reliance and so individual freedom. It has occupied an important place in American history and historiography, but it has influenced the study of frontiers far beyond the shores of North America.[7]

In the English language, then, the word 'frontier' can be employed for two quite separate ideas. However, historians have sometimes applied the term in its European sense to the political borders of North America, and others have repeatedly used the American concept to study European societies. These two types of frontier often share many characteristics, such as clashes of identity, militarised institutions, or weak political control; but these should not obscure the fundamental distinction between the two types of frontier in the historiography. The essays in this book deal with primarily political frontiers, and so the term is employed in this book first and foremost in its European sense. However, the influence of the American concept upon the study of premodern frontiers will also be apparent in several essays in this volume.

European Concepts: Frontiers as Political Barriers

As might be expected, the study of political frontiers, so important in international affairs, has not been confined to historians alone. Geographers and political scientists have defined and categorised frontiers and boundaries, which they distinguish from one another: frontiers are the zones that evolve organically between states or societies, and boundaries are the artificial lines of separation which those states eventually demarcate within these zones.[8] Although the insights of geography are of utmost importance for understanding modern frontiers and have generally had some basis in historical analysis, they cannot be easily applied to political frontiers before the modern era, for in general they require the existence of sovereign states with relatively strong central control. They also ignore the fact that potent concepts often become attached to frontiers with time, as well as the ways in which frontiers and boundaries have changed in history – except by seeing boundaries as the end result of the narrowing of a frontier. In regarding frontiers as organic and boundaries as artificial, and boundaries as a consequence of frontiers, geographers are forgetting the interplay between the two. Boundaries can take on a life of their own: the history of the border in Ireland since 1922 is an obvious example.

Historians, on the other hand, have noted that political frontiers in the past were sometimes very different from the modern state frontier, beginning with the co-founder of the *Annales* School, Lucien Febvre. Febvre traced the history of both the terms and the concepts for frontiers in European tradition; he was influenced by geographers such as Friedrich Ratzel and used their distinction between boundaries and political frontiers (in French, *limites* and *frontières*), but by unravelling the origins of the word *frontière* and its associated concepts, he showed the historical relationship between frontiers and boundaries, which, he demonstrated, had originally been distinct phenomena.[9] He was also keen to point out that the terms used for frontiers have their own history, and since their meanings vary from language to language, they cast much light upon the varied historical experiences of different peoples and regions. In the light of his and subsequent research we can construct a history of political frontiers, which demonstrates that they did not evolve in a simple fashion from zones into lines or from being divisions of minor to divisions of major significance. The linear boundary could function as a political division in very ancient times, and often possessed great social significance in the past; but its transition to a major state border has been very interrupted.[10]

In Classical Antiquity there was no notion of frontiers as linear state borders. Local administrative boundaries certainly did exist and, indeed, were often hallowed with a sacral function; although sometimes defined by a broad natural feature such as a forest, these were often linear, marked by lines of boundary stones or rivers. In the more Romanised provinces of the Empire such as Gaul, these local boundaries survived as the limits of Merovingian and Carolingian dioceses and *pagi*. Even the great military works which the Romans constructed on the fringes of their empire were not imbued with the defensive significance with which we have been accustomed to view them; instead, the Romans' universalist creed divided the world into lands already conquered and lands to be conquered, rather than into the empire and its neighbours, an outlook which was essentially expansionist and ideological rather than defensive and territorial.[11] The very term *limes*, which historians have become accustomed to use as a paradigm for the fortified linear defences of the Empire, had a quite different meaning for most of the Roman period.[12] Our familiar picture of the Roman Empire's solid military defensive frontiers owes more to the influence of nineteenth-century Western imperialism than to the policies of the Emperor Augustus. It is worth noting that at the other end of the

Eurasian land mass, another imperial frontier usually seen as a defensive barrier, the Great Wall of China, appears never to have existed as a single wall at all.[13]

Although the Western Roman Empire disappeared as a political entity in the late fifth century, the non-territorial, frontierless concept of a universal Christian empire persisted in the Eastern (Byzantine) Empire and was revived in Western Europe by the Carolingians; like the Romans before them, Frankish rulers sought to achieve hegemony and clientage rather than to seal off their territory against their neighbours.[14] As the political division of Christendom became an established fact, however, a stronger sense of territorial division did emerge, including amongst the Byzantines, as Paul Stephenson's essay demonstrates (see Chapter 4). Yet even the concept of *regnum* was less than territorial, signifying not so much 'realm' as 'rulership', whether the domination of a people or, by the Central Middle Ages, the dominion or bundle of rights which a king or prince exercised by virtue of his position.[15] Linear administrative boundaries were no more absent from early medieval society than they had been from the imperial Roman world – in any case, the transition from the latter to the former was a very drawn-out process – but their significance was generally very localised; borders of greater political import were invariably ambiguous, often defined in a linear fashion but in fact functioning as a zone because jurisdictions were usually fragmented, royal or princely control was usually constrained by magnate power, and rulers were as concerned with their inherited rights as with fixed notions of territory.[16] Across western Europe, there are frequent references to 'marches' but these could be both local divisions or broad, sometimes militarised zones of competing control.[17] With the disappearance of the Carolingian empire political power became far more diffused, while the proliferation of castles across much of the continent from the turn of the millennium onwards also tended to break power down to a very local level. The political frontiers of sorts that did exist were a far remove from modern concepts of a linear sovereign state border.[18]

From the later Middle Ages onwards, however, a growing concept of territorial sovereignty conferred a more territorial definition upon political borders, which gradually heightened the importance of the boundaries of kingdoms at the expense of other divisions; local, pacific boundaries eventually merged with militarised state frontier defences into a single concept of sovereign divisions between states. In the seventeenth and eighteenth centuries, the concepts of just 'natural frontiers' and of 'scientific frontiers' had a powerful influence upon the statesmen of the time, not least because of the development of scientific cartography, although the opportunities for expansion which such frontiers offered were also influential.[19] In fact, it is now recognised that 'natural' frontiers are as unrealistic on the ground as they are attractive on maps.[20] Then, from the nineteenth century, historic, natural and scientific frontiers, all imperfect, had to contend with the newest idea of all for state borders, the national frontier. This concept triumphed at the Treaty of Versailles in 1919 and has dominated the history of the twentieth century; but the development of the political frontier into a 'major, national, inter-state demarcation' has been very tortuous.[21]

European Frontier Terms

It will be apparent from this brief survey that the changing concepts of political frontiers reveal a great deal about the societies which they served. Moreover, as Febvre noted, the terms describing these frontiers have evolved accordingly, and tell us much about notions of frontiers in the past. For instance, most of the different European words now corresponding to our 'frontier', such as *frontière* and *Grenze*, did not appear until the late Middle Ages, just when territorial borders were growing in importance. The word 'frontier' is not found in English before the early fifteenth century; in French it had appeared somewhat earlier, but not before the end of the thirteenth century. In both languages, its significance was originally military; the figurative sense now so prevalent in English dates from a much later period.[22]

The French word *frontière* provides an interesting example of how a term for a political border could change in meaning as ideas of frontiers evolved. Febvre posited that the term *frontière* is both etymologically and semantically a military term, distinct from the more pacific *limite(s)*, or boundary, which it absorbed at a surprisingly recent date. The popularity of *frontière* as a term for political borders, especially the borders of the kingdom of France, seems to have arisen in the sixteenth century as military exigencies forced the Valois kings to put much effort into fortifying the boundaries (*fins* or *limites*) of their kingdom; and so the term used to describe these defences, *frontières*, began to absorb the words for lesser administrative divisions. *Fins* disappeared altogether, and *limite* came to mean almost the same as *frontière*. That word was increasingly associated with the expansionist policies of Henri II, Henri IV, and Richelieu; when French expansion halted for a time in the eighteenth century, *limites* became the preferred Enlightenment term for political borders precisely because it was less militaristic than *frontière*. However, *limite* gave way once more to *frontière* as the chief term for a major border in the great upheavals that followed the formation of the French national state in 1789.[23] A *frontière* was and is a political frontier *par excellence*, embracing most 'borders' but with less of the figurative sense that 'frontier' enjoys in English generally, and none of the American notions of a frontier of settlement. It is chiefly with ideas of a political, often militarised border that French studies of frontiers have been pursued.[24]

In some other languages, the equivalent terms have fewer military connotations, reflecting different historical experiences. For instance, the German term *Grenze* evolved through the *Drang nach Osten*, during which the Teutonic Knights adopted the Slavonic word for boundary-marker (*granica*) in the thirteenth century; only with Luther did it spread to the rest of the German-speaking world, including the Low Countries, replacing the older *mark*.[25] It was not that political borders in German-speaking lands were necessarily more peaceful than those of France; indeed, the Austrian military border with the Turks became one of the most heavily fortified barriers in Europe, defended by fearsome military colonists or *Grenzer* ('borderers').[26] *Grenze*, though, is as symbolic of the historical disunity of Germany as *frontière* reflects the rise of the French state: the German language continues to use *Grenze* for both local boundaries and state borders without distinction, probably because local, manorial boundaries remained the chief political divisions of the Holy Roman Empire into the nineteenth century.[27] Only then did the term acquire a wider political significance and consequently terms such as 'frontier zone' (*Grenzgebiet*) had to be coined; but its local, administrative and pacific meaning was by then well established.[28] Some Slavonic languages may reflect the instability of political borders in eastern Europe, for the words for 'country' and 'borderland' appear to be closely related, and the name of a whole country, the Ukraine, means simply 'the march' (*ukrajina*), testimony to its status as the borderland of first Poland-Lithuania and then Muscovy with the Tartars.[29] The same name has been given to two historical border regions of Southeastern Europe, Krajn (or Carniola, now part of Slovenia and once part of the Imperial border with Hungary) and

Krajina (Western Croatia, formerly a section of the Austrian military border), and the latter has proved itself a fiercely disputed borderland even in the 1990s.

Terms for frontiers have many derivations and appeared at different times, and it is not always easy to trace their changing meanings over time; nevertheless, some common patterns do emerge from the terms discussed in the essays in this volume. As we might expect, many terms suggested demarcation, such as Latin *terminus*, Slavonic *granica* and hence German *Grenze*, and Greek *horos* ('marker'), or a fringe or outer limit, such as Greek *akra* and Latin *fines* (hence Old French *fins*). Several seem to have passed from the meaning of a local boundary to that of a whole border territory: examples are found as far apart as Chinese *jing* 境, Germanic *mark*, Turkish *uj* and the Slavonic *krai* discussed above. These terms all imply some concept of territorial division or control. Perhaps more surprising to the modern mind are those terms which imply passage and contact, such as Arabic *thagr* ('mouth', 'breach') and Chinese *guan* 關 ('gate' or 'passage'), while an early meaning of the Latin *limes* was a road, albeit usually in a military context.[30] Some words for frontier seem to have come to relate to specific natural features: in Old French *marche* ('march') also meant the entrance to a forest in 1200,[31] and a further meaning of the Slavonic *krai* was likewise 'forest'. Moreover, some terms for borders and borderlands acquired very specific connotations or resonance. Although the importance of the term *limes* in Classical Roman history has recently been disputed, Michael Bonner has shown how the Arabic term *thughūr* came to be applied chiefly to the great zone of conflict between the Muslims and the Christian Byzantine Empire, and was popular in an age of chronic Muslim division because it harked back to a time of Islamic unity against the infidel. As Bonner notes, 'disagreements over names point[ed] to deeper conflicts'.[32] The Spanish term *frontera* also gradually acquired the notions of a militarised borderland through Spain's situation as a permanent battleground, at least in Reconquista ideology, between Christians and Muslims.[33] It is surely no coincidence that one of the earliest attested appearances of *frontière* in French concerned the 'Saracen frontier' (*frontière de Sarrizins*) in Spain.[34] The term 'march' came to be especially important on the Anglo-Welsh borders, where between the eleventh and sixteenth centuries, the 'Marches' had their own customs and a strong sense of 'Marcher' identity.[35] In all these instances, a general term for a borderland was developing a particular significance.

We can conclude that political frontiers before the modern era have a far more intricate and evolved history than simply the evolution of linear state barriers from vague border zones; and the terms and concepts relating to these frontiers are as susceptible to change – and historical interpretation – as the realities on the ground. The essays in this volume examine nine regions at various stages in this development and illustrate a number of ways in which contemporaries and historians have viewed these borders and borderlands.

North American Concepts: Frontiers of Settlement

Many of the 'frontiers' encountered in historiography cannot be easily classified amongst the political frontiers discussed so far. These generally correspond much more closely to North American ideas of frontier, namely a sparsely populated zone located between a metropolitan culture on one side and a wilderness on the other. These three zones are not independent of each other: the wilderness influences the frontier, which in turn affects the metropolis. This American frontier-type, or *frontier of settlement*, is best known from the work of Frederick Jackson Turner, who in 1893 drew attention to the dynamic role of an 'open' frontier of settlement in the formation of American society. Historians have comprehensively summarised the implications, strengths and weaknesses of his thesis, which will not be reconsidered in detail here; but all discussion of the Turner thesis, whether favourable or hostile, focuses attention upon American ideas of the frontier as a zone of settlement and struggle with nature, rather than as a political division.[36]

Turner wished to point out that the American 'frontier', hitherto 'open', was now 'closed', and explicitly stated that this frontier experience was a uniquely American historical phenomenon; however, he admitted that his thesis had comparative potential in the conclusion to his paper,[37] and historians eventually began to apply his theories to other periods and continents. Soon they also used the notion of a frontier of settlement for colonisation amongst established populations as well as in empty territory; once divorced from the specific context of environmental struggle, this American frontier-type mingled with and was reinforced by the strongly figurative connotations of 'frontiers' in modern English. American notions of frontiers have other attributes. The frontier has often been given a moral quality: Turner, for instance, described it as 'the meeting point between savagery and civilization'. It was also generally an expanding phenomenon, since the settlers had an overwhelming superiority over indigenous populations. Recently, however, the belated recognition of the presence of the Native Americans in the American 'wilderness' has reoriented historiography towards the more stable phases in the American frontier's history, such as the late seventeenth and eighteenth centuries, when a 'middle ground' developed between Native Americans and Europeans. Since these two cultures were then in relative equilibrium, the middle ground was characterised by what Richard White calls 'creative misunderstandings' which enabled the two societies to overcome their cultural differences. The concept of the 'middle ground' as a zone of interaction to be considered in its own right is the latest notion to flourish in frontier historiography.[38]

How has the concept of a frontier of settlement been used to interpret premodern Europe? There does not seem to have been any contemporary term for such a frontier; the nearest equivalent in medieval western Europe was probably 'waste' (for example, *vastum, gast*). Nevertheless, the concept has had profound implications for medieval European historiography, on both sides of the Atlantic.[39] Studies of frontiers in this sense may be divided for our purposes into three main groups: those which consider the frontier of settlement literally; those which consider the expanding 'frontier' of a society, such as Latin Christendom as a whole; and those which have reinterpreted political borders as zones of passage and contact rather than as merely fortified lines.

The first, perhaps most direct use of ideas from the American West assesses the effects which the conquest of the great wildernesses wrought upon medieval European society. For instance, the taming of the Dutch boglands between the tenth and fourteenth centuries triggered an agricultural revolution that radically altered the society and culture of Northwest Europe, encouraging huge increases in population, in contrast to the Mediterranean lands where there were fewer opportunities for internal colonisation.[40] The effects of the presence of an untamed wilderness have been discerned in regions as far apart as Kievan Russia and South Wales, and in the early modern period in the steppe corridor north of the Black Sea, where the Cossacks, as heralds of settled, agricultural society, had some interesting parallels in their lifestyle with American frontiersmen.[41] More specific comparisons are also possible; one such study has compared ranching in the Spanish frontier zone with later American experiences.[42]

The second group is not concerned primarily with the effect of the natural environment upon the development of society, but borrows from the American West the themes of colonisation, settlement, and cultural interaction, which, it has recently been suggested, were intrinsic features of all medieval frontier societies.[43] It concentrates in particular upon the sharp clash at the fringes of expanding societies. Medieval European examples include the *Drang nach Osten* of German settlers and knights into the Slavonic and Balt peoples of Eastern Europe,[44] the activities of the Normans from the British Isles to Syria in the eleventh century,[45] and the Spanish frontiers between Christians and Muslims, at once political, cultural, and economic frontiers as well as frontiers of settlement.[46] Robert Bartlett has recently drawn together these various fringes of Latin Christian society into a single 'frontier' experience, apparently as formative in the moulding of Western Europe before 1500 as Turner believed his frontier was in the shaping of American society. In contrast to Turner, though, Bartlett considers the effects of the metropolis (the Franks' homelands) on the frontier (the fringes of Latin Christendom) more than the reverse, although he does assert that this common experience forged a distinctive European society and identity.[47] This notion of a single Latin 'frontier' allows Bartlett to make fruitful and informative comparisons of specific social traits, such as language or personal laws, from Ireland to Poland, and from Scandinavia to Spain and Outremer. In stressing the unity of this shared European experience, Bartlett was prefigured by A. R. Lewis (1958), who portrayed the halt to Western European expansion from the late thirteenth century onwards as the 'closing of the medieval frontier', as opportunities for colonisation on the fringes of Latin Christian society were apparently exhausted.[48]

To see Latin Christendom as a single expanding 'Frankish' society marginalises political frontiers *within* Western Europe where, for all its religious unity and shared aristocratic culture, society was in many ways still deeply fragmented. However, the third group of studies arising from American ideas of frontier does not restrict itself to the limits of whole societies, but reinterprets political borders, some of which indeed coincided with deep cultural divisions whereas others cut across populations that were broadly very similar to each other in their history and culture, but separated by political organisation and often by a 'rhetoric of identity'. In some cases, such as Wales after 1066 (as well as several of the regions discussed in this volume), political borders overlapped with frontiers of settlement: regions of competing political control were therefore also regions of colonisation and often of cultural interaction.[49] But even in fairly densely populated areas, the idea of a frontier as a zone of passage and interaction rather than as a barrier can show a political border in a rather different light, offering opportunities for reinterpretation. In effect, such a frontier zone is a hybrid of the two different concepts of frontier.

Frontier zones of interaction between political units may be found in many parts of Europe. Some were quite stable regions of passage and contact. The 'land of war' in fourteenth-century Ireland was in many ways a frontier zone between two metropolitan cultures, the Gaelic kingdoms in the west and the Anglo-Norman Pale;[50] as such, it bears a striking similiarity to the militarised borderlands between the Byzantines and Arabs some centuries earlier, which were likewise locally unstable and prone to violence but regionally stable.[51] Others, like Turner's frontier, were dynamic and expanding; the 'frontiers' of the Carolingian empire have recently been depicted as regions in this mould, comprising not merely the empire's external borders with Slavs or Muslims but also a ring of subject groups within the empire, such as Aquitanians, Saxons, and Bavarians, who dwelt around the Frankish heartlands and who had previously been subjected to a rather looser Merovingian hegemony.[52] So the historiographical distinction between European and American concepts of the frontier is often blurred where a political division is concerned. In both sorts of frontier, questions of identity arise; in both, state control and its effectiveness is often an important dimension, usually with military considerations. Settlement, a prerequisite for the American type of frontier, can also be a feature of the European frontier type. Nevertheless, a basic distinction between frontiers which are zones of settlement and frontiers which constitute political barriers is apparent in most frontier historiography.

This brief survey demonstrates the breadth of research into premodern frontiers, and it is clear that terms and concepts as well as the realities of the frontier vary from language to language, region to region, and period to period. Yet it is precisely in this diversity that the opportunities for illuminating comparisons and contrasts lie. Students who are aware of the various concepts behind the innocuous word 'frontier' and its equivalents will not only avoid making invalid comparisons, but also discover fascinating parallels between frontiers widely separated by time or space.

B. Nine Case Studies of Premodern Frontiers

Naomi Standen

Political geographers believe that premodern zonal frontiers developed into modern linear boundaries and draw a clear distinction between the two. Much to their chagrin, the lay audience treats 'frontier', 'border' and 'boundary' as synonyms, while retaining a profoundly persistent conception that all three are linear. Thus we are accustomed to thinking of a 'frontier' as an enforceable boundary line that not only marks the territorial limit of a particular state's authority, but also divides that state peacefully from its neighbouring states. However, neither the clear separation made by geographers nor the popular conflation of terms that they deplore does justice to the complexity and fluidity of premodern frontiers.

This part of the introduction will survey the nine essays presented here, and then draw out some common threads which illustrate the importance to contemporaries, both of defining the frontier and of blurring that definition. Frontier inhabitants had their own conceptions of where the divisions between them and their neighbours lay. Rulers wishing to maintain or extend their control over their frontiers had to work with these local understandings in a highly flexible and creative manner. Historians, however, along with modern geographers and lay people, have had a tendency to 'tidy up' the processes involved so that the complexities and manifold nature of the frontiers are obscured.

*

Eduardo Manzano Moreno opens this volume (see Chapter 2) with a discussion of several issues that will recur in subsequent chapters. Manzano uses the case of the frontier between Muslim and Christian in Spain to argue that such simple dichotomies are so misleading that the notion of 'frontier' as a category of analysis is thrown into question. We cannot ignore the fact that there are divisions between groups of people, but these require a detailed and sophisticated analysis which they have not always received. Manzano states clearly the important point that frontiers will always exist because there will always be antagonisms between groups with different values, languages, religions, allegiances, and so on, and these antagonisms will create limits that will be apparent to those who live with them. He also emphasises that this awareness did not create homogeneous or distinctive groupings, nor did it result in a clear differentiation between groups such as that implied by a bounding line drawn on a map. Yet this is the view purveyed by many previous students of medieval Spanish frontiers: that we are discussing a phenomenon that clearly divided one group from another, and that accordingly it had a linear manifestation as a boundary. This general perception is mirrored by the subject divisions within academe, which lead to the Christian side of the border being the province of medieval historians, while the Arab side of the border is the terrain of Area Studies specialists. This disciplinary boundary reinforces the commonplace perception of frontiers as clear-cut lines, when in reality neighbours, although conscious of being from different groups, were still able and willing to find accommodations and exploit opportunities that cut across any kind of neat and mappable boundary line. Although the Arab and Christian rulers established ideological barriers through their respective rhetorics of *jihād* and *reconquista*, the social and political realities of the peninsula were far more complex, and were played out despite and not because of religious differences.

The second essay (see Chapter 3) looks at a somewhat different situation. The author sees the regimes of tenth-century north China as a collection of poorly bounded units – ill-defined and somewhat unstable, both socially and politically – in which the strength of ever-present antagonisms varied in significant ways. The north China frontier developed from a highly confused and complex zone, such as that described by Manzano in Spain, towards a much more clearly defined entity that could be conceptualised as a line, and agreed as such in a treaty that went on to keep the peace for a century. The transformation of the frontier from a zone of political volatility, local control, and ever-changing allegiances into a relatively neat division between neighbouring centralised regimes was obviously something that rulers of these nascent states desired and worked towards: the clarification and simplification of the frontier into a border both contributed to and arose from an increase in effective central authority. In the early part of the tenth century the emperor's position depended upon the tacit support of powerful provincial governors, who could place their allegiance with various competing or neighbouring regimes if they were not kept happy. Such changes of allegiance were made without reference to other markers of identity such as culture or ethnic orgin, so that a Han Chinese could serve a nomadic Kitan without concern on either side. However, the later historical records for this period tend to make the early-tenth-century frontier appear clearer than it actually was, emphasising aspects of individual stories that suggest those concerned were more governed by their perception of their ethnic identity than the earlier records show. The historiography thus conceals the flexibility of early-tenth-century frontier inhabitants, who, while clearly understanding the differences between Chinese and non-Chinese, did not turn this awareness into insurmountable antagonism.

Paul Stephenson's essay (see Chapter 4) on the Byzantine frontier at the Lower Danube illustrates a central authority's response to the problem of maintaining control at the frontiers of a geographically large empire that is not increasing its control as in north China, but gradually losing it. A militaristic approach that focused on strong points along natural barriers – that is, fortified towns along the Danube – was effective when the empire was strong, but it required a large investment of resources. Byzantium's 'civilian emperors' saved themselves enormous expense by deliberately not maintaining defences against their nomadic neighbours. Instead they spent what were probably far smaller sums on paying annual subsidies both to the Byzantine townsfolk on the Danube, and to their Pecheneg neighbours. Stephenson argues from archaeological, largely numismatic, evidence that these payments were intended to shore up the loyalty of the Byzantine citizens, and to provide the Pechenegs with incentives to replace raiding with trade and employment in the frontier towns of the Lower Danube. This policy was a remarkably intelligent and tolerant approach, and it proved at least as effective as the military alternative. This example shows that we cannot simply assume that premodern governments were always bound to behave in a reactive and crudely, ideologically driven manner, but could sometimes display a sophisticated understanding of what made their neighbours tick, and an imaginative approach to handling this in terms of frontier policy. However, when the emperors ceased to maintain their chosen methods – fortifications or subsidies – both approaches failed, and Byzantine authority in the frontier was diminished or lost. The frontier here, as in China and elsewhere, had centrifugal tendencies that could only be overcome through continuous effort on the part of the central authorities.

All the essays in this volume are at some level asking the question 'what is a frontier?' but Daniel Power's chapter (see Chapter 5) on the frontier between Normandy and its neighbouring provinces focuses on this explicitly. Modern French historiography has tended to focus attention on the external borders of France, whereas in fact the internal divisions were far more politically significant. At the same time, the external borders had a changing meaning which could be far from negligible. But the question 'what is a frontier?' arises particularly clearly from the curious position of Normandy. The militarised nature of the borderlands of Normandy and her neighbouring principalities, and the close coincidence of administrative, legal, and ecclesiastical boundaries create what has appeared to historians to be a remarkably well-defined frontier, and Power agrees that indeed the term is justified in this case. In examining whether it is applicable, however, Power reveals, once again, the complexity and multiplicity of what is usually depicted as a linear boundary. In fact, the vagaries of lordship combined with a conception of the frontier that, once again, stressed particular fortifications rather than some abstract border line, producing even here the characteristic medieval European frontier of enclaves and exclaves belonging to a variety of lords. Furthermore, as in China, and indeed in the rest of France, it was not clear just how far beyond any given fortification the occupier's writ actually ran. Coexisting with a fairly clear sense – ideological, practical, or simply conventional – of where the limits of one lord's jurisdiction met the limits of his neighbour, there was an immensely complex, greatly varied, and highly localised collection of rights, duties, and privileges. As in Spain, this tangled web defies the drawing of neat boundary lines, but because the sources allow us to achieve such a level of detail, it is a particularly useful example of what constituted a premodern frontier in reality.

Reuven Amitai-Preiss's contribution on the Mamluk-Mongol frontier (see Chapter 6) provides a clear illustration of the way in which a linear frontier – initially defined in this case by military means – could be reinforced by ideological divisions based on religious differences and particularly on the concept of Holy War. This case illustrates at greater length a phenomenon that is mentioned briefly in other chapters, such as the Chinese and Norman examples: that groups, not least among them centralised regimes, will go to considerable lengths to develop or maintain antagonisms that will help to reinforce the political boundary, even if those antagonisms are based on features that in other circumstances would tend towards greater unity and co-operation. Hence the common steppe origins of Mamluks and Mongols did not prevent them being implacable foes, and after the Mongols converted to Islam, the Mamluks maintained the religious divide between the two groups by denigrating the Mongols' Islam as inferior. This makes clear the important point that frontiers, and the mechanisms by which they are created and maintained, are wholly and absolutely constructions made by human beings. Where groups within a frontier have differences, these can be overcome; where groups divided by a frontier have similarities, differences can be found. Expediency is all.

The British example (see Chapter 7) is of a state already formed, centralised, and relatively strong, but which still had problems with its frontiers. Instead of the successful move from militarised border to 'frontier of peace' that we have seen in north China, the Lower Danube, and Syria – all under central guidance – the English borderlands saw increased state involvement *reducing* the effectiveness of frontier control. Steven Ellis argues that the Tudor crown brought most of these problems upon itself through an impatience with the apparent laxity and local disruption that characterised decentralised marcher methods of handling its land frontiers. The Tudors feared the threat posed to the crown by the overmighty wardens, who traditionally superintended the frontier regions, and so attempted to replace the familiar set of accommodations and regular frontier breaches with a centralised system of local government, in the belief that this would automatically produce a situation of 'English civility' in their Scottish and Irish borderlands as it had in Wales. In fact, the wardens' frontier defences proved to have been essential to maintaining any semblance of law and order in the borders; without them, the military situation on both Scottish and Irish frontiers deteriorated, leading, in Ireland, to the English conquest of the whole island. The Tudor crown had a clear vision of its frontiers, but the attempt to impose that vision took no account of the realities and uniqueness of different frontier situations, nor of the fact that the frontier inhabitants saw things differently. It was difficult to impose frontiers on an unwilling population, at least for any length of time. The techniques and resources which, for instance, maintained the Iron Curtain for four decades, were simply unavailable.

Even where frontiers divided groups who agreed that they were different, communication across the divide was always necessary. S. C. Rowell's discussion of the Lithuano-Prussian frontier (see Chapter 8) provides a highly detailed picture of how this local accommodation influenced, and was influenced by, the existence of an agreed boundary line. Operating under conditions of peace, the inhabitants and rulers of this frontier zone nevertheless sought to extend their grip on the area, less in terms of control judged militarily than of 'ownership and occupation'. Such gradual extension was possible because the agreed definition of the overall boundary line was actually rather vague when it came to certain details on the ground. At the same time, questions of ownership were of crucial importance when it came to deciding who had what rights to exploit which resource, so at a minute level very precise divisions could be agreed when economic advantage was at stake. The Lithuanian case shows particularly clearly the functioning and importance of the frontier as a location of crossings and points of access, in both the absence and presence of effective central control. It also shows the effects created by the imposition of a borderline across what could, politics aside, easily have been a geographically unified region.

According to Ann Williams (see Chapter 9), the Mediterranean frontier, defended for Christendom chiefly by the Order of St John, was another militarised frontier not only reinforced, but created by a strong ideological-religious division between Christianity and Islam. Often under the implicit or overt direction of the papacy, the efforts of the Order were expended on defending their holdings in the Mediterranean or trying to win control of larger possessions, but the Order, with or without allies, was never able to sustain the military effort required. This was partly because of a lack of coherent policy and of adequate logistical support from its *Langues* (regional organisations) in mainland western Europe, but mostly because of the special nature of the sea as a frontier, and the position of the Knights within that sea. The Order's 'centre' on its tiny island homes was also its frontier, and at the same time constituted the frontier of (Catholic) Christendom. The Order was perpetually pushing out against the ever-encroaching sea-borne perils represented by the maritime arms of the Islamic powers bordering on the Mediterranean. While strategically important, the islands of Rhodes and Malta were nevertheless isolated, and even though Islamic maritime strength fluctuated, the Order was rarely in a position to dominate the sea effectively. Unlike many other small border powers working to retain their autonomy in the frontier zone, the Order did not have the option of placing its allegiance with the other side – the ideological frontier was too strong for that – although it did resort to indiscriminate piracy on grain ships, Christian and

Muslim alike, when the supply situation was particularly desperate. Still, the Order fell unequivocally on the Christian side of the border; but it was not only a frontier outpost imposing a Christian presence to challenge the Muslims for control of the sea, it was also, during its extended periods on Rhodes and Malta, an enclave struggling for survival. The necessarily uncompromising nature of the Order's mission in the Mediterranean contributed greatly to its problems, but the Order did not have the resources to follow this rigid line through to its logical, military conclusion.

The strength of an ideological frontier is also the issue underlying Colin Heywood's discussion of the historiography of the Ottoman frontier (see Chapter 10). The 'traditional' view expressed by Paul Wittek was that the Ottomans' empire was a frontier polity, founded upon a *ghāzī* ideology that demanded an ongoing Holy War against the infidel. This frontier ideology affected the whole state: policy, military organisation, and sociopolitical structure. It contrasts with the notion of centralised 'civility' on which the Tudor state was based. Wittek also felt that Ottoman frontier society, in constant contact with the infidels, partook of so much cultural influence that it became almost as 'uncivilised' as the infidels themselves; without careful handling, the mixed society could contaminate the hinterland and drag down its culture. The ghazis, though, were so devoted to their mission of Holy War that they preserved their own purity while driving the boundaries of the empire outwards. As the empire grew so the expanding frontier was repeatedly peripheralised by the centre, both institutionally and ideologically, but to Wittek the ghazis remained holy heroes. In such a situation the relationship between the state and its frontier was particularly vital. Critics of Wittek have questioned whether the ghazis really played such a crucial role on the frontier, and also whether the Ottoman state really did depend for its justification on the ideology of Holy War. The Turkish frontier lords, who were 'contaminated' by their accommodations with neighbouring cultures, appear to have been more significant than ghazi activity, and the Ottoman Empire continued to exist for over two centuries after it accepted a demarcated borderline that denied subsequent 'ghazis' a legitimate zone of operations. Heywood's historiographical emphasis reminds us how much frontiers are constructions not only of those in the past, but of subsequent accounts and analyses that may, like Wittek's, owe as much to the circumstances of the writer as to any kind of recoverable historical reality.

Human Frontiers

These essays reinforce our understanding that frontiers will always exist because there will always be antagonisms between groups, but there is an ever-shifting relationship between: (a) the real differences between groups of people; (b) the degree of antagonism they feel towards each other; and (c) the extent to which they nevertheless interact peacefully. It is worth emphasising that this will be so regardless of the strength of rulers or governments at any given time, and that although language and ecological factors such as the pastoral-sedentary divide created differences it was hard to ignore, other aspects of culture became important only because human beings decided that this would be so.[53]

The most striking of these 'human frontiers' is religion. Different categories of religion could be grounds for major antagonism, as in the medieval Spanish peninsula. These same differences could be overlooked when it was convenient: in Spain, Muslims lived voluntarily under Christian rule and vice versa. What is more, similarities of religion were not necessarily enough to bind two groups together: the antagonism between Mamluks and Mongols did not diminish when the Mongols converted to Islam, and a shared Christianity did not prevent conflicts in central medieval France. Ethnic identity could also be ignored or brought into play as circumstances required. Hence the 'ethnic affinity' between Mongols and the Turkish Mamluks – both originally nomadic – could become an argument used to entice Turks over to the Mongol side, but it did not prevent a Mamluk of Mongol origin from abandoning family and high status with the Mongols for a return to Mamluk allegiance.

Antagonisms could be created and maintained on a local level,[54] but, as is now well known, they always coexisted with a need for interaction, mostly for purposes of trade. The societies that developed on the frontiers had their own leaders who understood how to work with the ambiguities of their particular frontier situation in order to maintain their own authority over their own communities, as well as the crucial command of the resources – chiefly people – from which that authority was derived. This meant striking a balance between defence and accommodation, between encroachment from outside and their own people's needs for economic exchange. It also meant serving as the intermediary between the leader's own district and any neighbouring powers: centralised regimes, would-be centralisers, or other border leaders. This role was highly significant.

Frontier Leaders and 'Superior' Authorities

Before the modern era we cannot always make a clear distinction between the 'centre' and the 'frontier', and levels of political control cannot always be clearly distinguished either. The political centre did not have to be physically located in the middle of the territory it sought to control, but could easily be in the frontier zone, rendering it open to attack. Even where the political hub was distant from the borderlands, ideology could still give the frontier a central role, as with the ghazi ideology of the Ottoman empire. If the political 'centre' might actually be located in the periphery, so, too, the levels of authority might not be as clear-cut as the terminology of 'centre' and 'periphery' might suggest. The distributed nature of power is very clear in the Lithuano-Prussian border region, where authority in any one place rested on what rights a particular nobleman held there; but it is also a feature of north China and of the Tudor land frontiers. In these places governors and marcher lords could hold so many *de facto* powers that they sometimes had to be treated almost as if they led independent regimes. Frontier lords acknowledged the overlordship, however nominal, of one (or more) 'central' ruler, whom they thus acknowledged as their superior, but they remained under 'superior' control only while it suited them; their allegiance could change if it seemed advantageous. In some cases, such as tenth-century north China, frontier lords were distinguished from their superior rulers by little more than title: an 'emperor' might be able to exercise no more practical authority than a 'governor'.

Such a situation shows the validity of treating the frontier zone as a distinct area. However, although the culture, customs, and economic arrangements of frontier societies can profitably be studied with little or no reference to their relationship to the central – or superior – authorities between which they sat, the same is not true when those societies are regarded as political entities. Frontier lordships, by definition, were not politically self-sufficient. They could not exist without the presence of superior authorities. Hence the relationship between frontier lords and superior authorities was a crucial factor in maintaining the superior authorities' claims to the frontier region. This could give the frontier leaders far more bargaining power with their overlords than their formal relationship implied. The very fact that such local leaders were located on the frontier immediately gave them more leverage than a local leader in the interior, because a disgruntled frontier leader could provoke disturbances in a vulnerable area, which at worst could result in the complete loss of that region (along with the people and resources that made it a desirable possession) to a neighbouring power. Accordingly, rulers could rarely risk trying to impose their will on the frontier lords by force. The military effort required to bring them or their territories under closer control was too great to be worthwhile, even if victory were feasible. In order to maintain their claims to the frontier, rulers were forced to persuade and negotiate.

Methods of Frontier Control

Since persuasion had to play such a large role in superior authorities' handling of their frontier regions, it is no surprise that symbolism and ideology were important tools of frontier control. At the same time, the idea of the frontier was itself an important contributor to the establishment or development of regimes that attempted to transcend the personality of a particular ruler and develop into more powerful, centralised polities. Clearly defined frontiers showed that a ruler was strong enough to enforce his will at the border (and even beyond), and thus demonstrated a greater degree of political control. The ruler aimed to define the frontier so as to include the territories of the frontier lords, and then to persuade those lords to accept this definition. In the essays collected here we repeatedly see would-be statebuilders seeking to create or maintain a virtuous circle in which they define the borders of their regime more clearly, thereby exhibiting their own legitimacy and attracting more loyalty from the frontier inhabitants and their leaders, which has the effect of defining the borders more clearly, and so on. Although the discussion below relates to superior authorities, frontier lords could also attempt to employ at least some of the same methods in their own districts.

There were various concrete ways in which rulers attempted to tighten their control over their borderlands, and thus to clarify the division between their spheres of authority and those of neighbouring rulers. Most of the rulers discussed here made treaties with their neighbours, which often demarcated a linear boundary as depicted in Figure 1.1(a). Defences, though, were always established independently of any agreed borderline at discretely located strategic spots, many of which were some distance from any agreed lines. They indicated what was to be protected (Figure 1.1(b)). Rulers also instituted communications

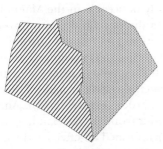

(a) Linear frontier agreed by treaty

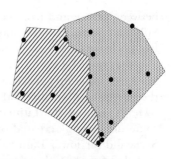

(b) Frontier fortifications

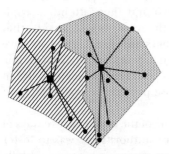

(c) Communication between centre and frontier

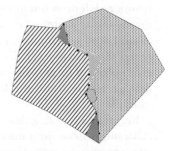

(d) Boundary markers, showing evolution of frontier

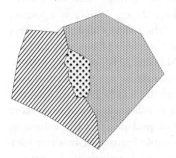

(e) Frontier wasteland

Fig. 1.1   Methods of frontier control and definition.

between centre and frontier – particularly noticeable in the Mamluk Sultanate – which was a way of asserting direct central control over frontier-based institutions such as fortifications and frontier lordships, and thus denying such control to neighbouring rulers (Figure 1.1(c)). Some rulers set up border markers, which attempted to make concrete the provisions of treaties, although they often also took on a life of their own, as seen on the Lithuano-Prussian border (Figure 1.1(d)). And some deliberately created or maintained a frontier wasteland, as in Syria and the lower Danube region, which formed an effective divide and defence, but also denied either contiguous regime the use of the territory and resources involved (Figure 1.1(e)). These methods tended to produce rather diffuse frontiers, but these were by no means insignificant: frontier inhabitants noticed the positive effects of frontier defences (including wastelands) and their attendant com- munications systems in preventing the cross-border raids that could paralyse economic life. Geographers and social scientists have noted the dynamic relationship between a boundary or frontier line given physical form – 'border landscapes' – and the people who live in that landscape,[55] and the Lithuanian case provides a straightforward example.

Beyond such practicalities, however, one of the most effective ways of clarifying where the limits to the ruler's authority lay was to foster antagonism towards the neighbouring group or groups, chiefly through the creation, revival, and maintenance of ideologies, with their accompanying myths and symbols, that emphasised the uniqueness of the in-group and a negative picture of the out-group,[56] and most of the cases here show rulers doing precisely these things. Where religious or cultural distinctions were less apparent, 'rhetorics of difference' were developed which overcame the similarities between Normandy and her neighbours, and between Mongol and Mamluk.[57] By contrast, Lithua- nia offers some fine examples of complaints by central authorities, political and religious, that the frontier inhabitants lacked any ideology of separation, even though cross-border conflicts at a local level were commonplace. The ideologies thus developed masked the ethnic or social confusions which are such a noticeable feature of frontier soci- eties. Rulers sought to harness differences – real, accentuated, or imag- ined – for divisive ends, exposing the ambiguities of the frontier society and trying to force its inhabitants to choose clearly which side they were on. The complex interplay of frontier accommodations and antagonisms were overlaid with a much simplified rhetoric which stressed the unity of Us as against the parallel unity of Them. Hence the regular recurrence of the idea of 'our' country as civilised, in opposition to 'the barbarians' on the other side of the frontier.

Although in many ways it was in the government's interests to define the frontier as unambiguously as possible within the logistical limitations of the time, at the same time it could not afford to make that definition too inflexible, as the early Tudor crown found to its cost. The trick for rulers was to define the frontier sufficiently closely that its existence served to bolster the government's justification for ruling, chiefly through ensuring the safety of the frontier inhabitants, while allowing enough slack for those same inhabitants to carry on their daily lives in a profitable manner. Most strikingly in north China and on the Lower Danube, government action, direct or indirect, not only prevented raids but also established markets, and sometimes even supplied the cash to spend there. While these things were done, both frontiers enjoyed peace. As soon as governments neglected their frontier provisions they disrupted the delicate equilibrium of the frontier; they could never afford to relax.

The question remains, however, of whether different forms of polity and different methods of state formation affected the frontier situation. The regimes discussed here range from princely fiefs to bureaucratic states with imperial ideologies, but their frontier experiences, while they contain many comparable features, do not seem to fall into categories according to type of polity any more than they fall into groupings based on religious, ecological, ethnic, or cultural criteria. Nevertheless, comparison of frontiers in terms of political organisation is an area which has been scarcely touched upon, at least in the historical literature, and it would be a fruitful area of enquiry.

Historiography and the Imagining of Frontiers

It is clear that the historian, past or present, plays a vital role in representing what we know of any particular frontier, and in several of the cases here it is argued that the conception of the frontier as derived from the records is an invention. All too often, the chroniclers' records were at least partly intended to bolster the vision of the frontier that a contemporary ruling power was trying to impose, and subsequent historians have had agendas of their own. Modern historians, too, have sometimes been greatly influenced by current political situations, as is most striking in the case of Paul Wittek. Even where historians have no particular axe to grind, frontiers can still be viewed somewhat anachronistically.

But the problem is more complicated still. We have seen that frontiers could be clarified without recourse to modern concepts such as nationalism, but the fact remains that our current structures for thinking about historical issues are still constructed on remarkably strict national grounds, taking the modern nations of the world as the basis for dividing up the history of the world into slightly less unmanageable chunks. We mark ourselves as historians of China, France, Spain, and so on. British frontiers have been shared out amongst historians of England, Ireland, Scotland, and Wales, while the Byzantine Lower Danube is split between scholars from different modern nations, chiefly Romania and Bulgaria. The divisions are not just between historians of or from different regions, but between academic disciplines too. The Danube frontier is divided between historians, classicists, and archaeologists. The Christians in Spain have been studied by European medievalists, but the Arabs in Spain have been studied by language specialists with a distinctly philological bent. Normandy is one of the few places that might be said to have benefited from divisions between modern nations: it is studied by medievalists, some of whom focus on France and others on England, providing an unusually rich selection of approaches.

These modern divisions can make it hard to see, let alone begin to think about, frontiers that may or may not have existed in previous times, as several of the essays in this volume make clear. Looking from within our modern states, under the pervasive (even if unwanted) influence of nationalism, it can be hard to dislodge ourselves from the teleological view that all of history was leading to this moment when we can call ourselves a citizen of this state, or a historian of that state. But in fact, there is nothing inevitable or permanent about the situation we have arrived at. England was once a possession of dukes of Normandy, Spain was divided between Arab and Christian rule, Beijing is now the capital of the People's Republic of China but for hundreds of years was under non-Chinese rule, what we now call the Middle East was once divided up very differently, while the Byzantine and Ottoman empires straddled the traditional division, and thus formed a long-lasting join between Europe and Asia. Many of these situations obtained for hundreds of years – for much longer, in fact, than the current arrangement of 'nation-states'. The problem (and its cause too) is that the idea of the nation-state was dominant at precisely the time that the relevant academic disciplines were born, so that not only were the divisions between nation-states particularly clear, but they also appeared particularly inevitable and appropriate, and were duly enshrined in the structuring of the academy. Interdisciplinary efforts are slowly becoming more popular, and several of the contributors here have made deliberate efforts to cross the disciplinary boundaries in their particular area.

Conclusion

We are looking at premodern frontiers through the eyes of people accustomed to national frontiers, which may help to explain why this subject is so difficult to grasp. Our present-day conceptions of frontiers are firstly as lines, and the ramifications of their existence flow from that: the line is drawn and then border functions are applied there.[58] In the premodern case government functions – such as defence and the facilitation of trade – came first, and, in practice if not in theory, were all based upon discrete places. Though there often was a line, it was secondary to other considerations, even though, as in Lithuania, it could have an impact of its own. In the modern world it has been possible to divide communities with concrete and barbed wire regardless of the inhabitants' views. The ability to create such clear lines, coinciding with the rise of nationalism, has shifted the priorities of states away from the premodern necessity of achieving the best accommodation with the manifold realities of the frontier situation, and onto a concern to force those realities to conform to the rigid line of the state boundary.[59]

To say exactly when and why this happened is, however, beyond the scope of a mere nine essays covering a millennium of Eurasian history, although the themes explored here may hold some clues. What our cases do show is that each individual frontier was subject to change over relatively short periods of time, and that change could increase the vagueness of frontiers as well as their clarity. Above all, a frontier was not a singular entity, but was formed from the conjunction of many coexisting institutions, practices, ideologies, and so on. It was conceived by contemporaries in both linear and zonal terms – often simultaneously – but furthermore, as whole sets of lines and zones amongst which frontier inhabitants and rulers could pick and choose according to circumstances. Teasing out the empirical details and theoretical implications of such complexity is a task which is still far from complete.

NOTES

1. For example, *Shifting Frontiers in Late Antiquity*, ed. R. W. Mathisen and H. S. Sivan, Aldershot 1996, examines a variety of frontiers in the period AD 200–700.

2. S. B. Jones, *Boundary-Making: a handbook for statesmen, treaty editors and boundary commissioners*, Washington 1945, 7, 9–11, sees every boundary as unique; L. K. D. Kristof, 'The nature of frontiers and boundaries', *Annals of the Association of American Geographers*, XLIX (1959), 273, depicts 'frontiers' (of settlement) as unique but 'boundaries' (including political frontiers) as artificial and hence open to generalisation.

3. See J. R. V. Prescott, *Boundaries and Frontiers*, London 1978, 17–18, 20.

4. Kristof, 'Nature of frontiers', 259, n. 27; see in this volume, 35–6.

5. For instance, J. L. Wieczynski, *The Russian Frontier: the impact of borderlands upon the course of early Russian history*, Charlottesville, Virginia 1976, 6–7; T. F. X. Noble, 'Louis the Pious and the frontiers of the Frankish realm', *Charlemagne's Heir: the reign of Louis the Pious*, ed. P. Godman and R. Collins, Oxford 1990, 334. Cf. A. Hennessy, *The Frontier in Latin American History*, 54–109, esp. 106–9. The third, figurative meaning of the term now so prevalent in English needs no discussion here.

6. Cf. Prescott, *Boundaries*, 33–48.

7. See in this volume, 9–12.

8. Kristof, 'Nature of frontiers', 269–82. For a useful summary of geographical analysis of boundaries and frontiers, see Prescott, *Boundaries*, 13–32.

9. L. Febvre, '*Frontière*' [1928], trans. as '*Frontière*: the word and the concept', *A New Kind of History: from the writings of Lucien Febvre*, trans. K. Folca, ed. P. Burke, London 1973, 208–18; 'The problem of frontiers and the natural bounds of states', in L. Febvre, *A Geographical Introduction to History*, trans. E. G. Mountford and J. H. Paxton, London 1932, 296–314.

10. For what follows, see R. J. W. Evans, 'Frontiers and national identities in Central Europe', *International History Review*, XIV (1992), 480–502; P. Sahlins, *Boundaries: the making of France and Spain in the Pyrenees*, University of California 1989, 1–7; *idem*, 'Natural frontiers revisited: France's boundaries since the seventeenth century', *American Historical Review*, XCV (1990), 1423–51; C. R. Whittaker, *Frontiers of the Roman Empire: a social and economic study*, Baltimore and London 1994; cf. D. H. Miller, 'Frontier societies and the transition between Late Antiquity and the early Middle Ages', *Shifting Frontiers*, ed. Mathisen and Sivan, 158–71.

11. Whittaker, *Frontiers of the Roman Empire*, 1–97.

12. B. Isaac, 'The meaning of the terms *limes* and *limitanei*', *Journal of Roman Studies*, LXXVIII (1988), 125–47.

13. A. Waldron, *The Great Wall of China: from history to myth*, Cambridge 1990.

14. For Carolingian frontiers, see J. M. H. Smith, 'The *fines imperii*: the marches', *The New Cambridge Medieval History*, II (*c. 700–c. 900*), ed. R. McKitterick, Cambridge 1995, 169–89; for recent case studies, *idem*, *Province and Empire: Brittany and the Carolingians*, Cambridge 1992; C. R. Bowlus, *Franks, Moravians, and Magyars: the struggle for the Middle Danube, 788–907*, Philadelphia 1995; cf. M. Innes, 'Franks and Slavs,

c. 700–1000: European expansion before the millennium?', *Early Medieval Europe*, VI (1997), 201–15.

15. Noble, 'Louis the Pious', 337–8; C. T. Wood, '*Regnum Francorum*: a problem in Capetian administrative usage', *Traditio*, XVI (1967), 117–47.
16. Evans, 'Frontiers and national identities', 481–3.
17. Smith, '*Fines imperii*', 176–7; see in this volume, 111–12.
18. See in this volume, 109–12.
19. Sahlins, 'Natural frontiers revisited', 1424–43.
20. Jones, *Boundary-Making*, 7–9; 108–33 advises that river boundaries should not be used as political borders wherever possible; cf. Evans, 'Frontiers and national identities', 489.
21. Evans, 'Frontiers and national identities', 480–1.
22. 'Frontier' in a territorial sense is first recorded in English in 1413, but its figurative meaning only in 1672–73 (*OED*, VI, 218). The English word originally meant 'front part of an army' (*c.* 1400).
23. Febvre, '*Frontière*', 208–11; Sahlins, 'Natural frontiers revisited', 1435–43.
24. Fèbvre, '*Frontière*', 216–17; M. Foucher, *L'invention des frontières*, Paris 1986, 97–110. Like its English counterpart, *frontière* had previously meant 'front part of the army', attested as early as 1213.
25. *Deutsches Wörterbuch von Jakob und Wilhelm Grimm*, 1935 edn., Leipzig, IV, cols. 124–5; Febvre, '*Frontière*', 217; Evans, 'Frontiers and national identities', 481. For its spread into Dutch (*grens*) through Luther's Bible, see *Woorderboek de Nederlandsche Taal*, 37 vols, The Hague and Leiden 1882–1956, V, col. 661.
26. G. E. Rothenberg, *The Austrian Military Border in Croatia, 1522–1747*, Urbana 1960; Evans, 'Frontiers and national identities', 490–1.
27. *Ibid.*, 481–4.
28. *Deutsches Wörterbuch von Grimm*, IV, col. 161.
29. *Ukrainian-English Dictionary*, ed. C. H. Andrusyshen and J. N. Krett, 2nd edn, Toronto 1957, 1069; Kristof, 'Nature of frontiers', 269, n. 7. Cf. Polish *kraj* ('country'). I am grateful to Neil Bermel of the Department of Slavonic Studies, University of Sheffield, for his assistance in this matter. For Ukraine as both a defensive march (that is, a political frontier) and a frontier of settlement, see W. H. McNeill, *Europe's Steppe Frontier 1500–1800*, Chicago 1964, for instance 111–23.
30. Isaac, '*Limes*', 126.
31. *Très Ancien Coutumier*, ed. E.-J. Tardif, 1 vol. in 2, Rouen and Paris 1881–1903, I:II, 25, *c.* XXXIII. Cf. *OED*, IX, 377.
32. Isaac, '*Limes*'; M. Bonner, 'The naming of the frontier:*ʿawāsim, thughūr*, and the Arab geographers', *BSOAS*, LVII (1994), 17–24.
33. The early history of *frontera* is very contested. *The Poem of My Cid*, ed. and trans. P. Such and J. Hodgkinson, 2nd edn, Warminster 1991, line 840 (written in 1207?), mentions the 'Moors of the frontiers', but P. Linehan, *History and the Historians of Medieval Spain*, Oxford 1993, 263, dates the term's adaptation to the divide between Muslims and Christians to the 1220s. Cf. *ibid.*, 205–9, for the ideological context of the Reconquest; for the complexities of the Spanish 'frontier' in reality, see Eduardo Manzano Moreno's essay, Chapter 2 in this volume.

34. F. Godefroy, *Dictionnaire de l'ancienne langue française*, 10 vols, Paris 1881–92, IV, 163.

35. See the many works of R. R. Davies, including 'The Law of the March', *Welsh History Review*, V (1971), 1–30; *Lordship and Society in the March of Wales 1282–1400*, Oxford 1978; 'Kings, lords and liberties in the March of Wales, 1066–1272', *TRHS*, 5th ser. XXIX (1979), 41–61. For Marcher identity, see R. Bartlett, *Gerald of Wales*, Oxford 1982, 20–6.

36. The first century of Turnerism has produced an immense bibliography, beginning with his paper (1893), reprinted as F. J. Turner, 'The significance of the frontier for American history', *The Frontier in American History*, New York 1921, 1–38.

37. *Ibid.*, 38.

38. R. White, *The Middle Ground: Indians, Empires, and Republics in the Great Lakes Region, 1650–1815*, Cambridge 1991, for instance x–xiv.

39. For Turnerism and medieval studies, see R. I. Burns, 'The significance of the frontier in the Middle Ages', *MFS*, 307–30.

40. W. H. TeBrake, *Medieval Frontier: culture and ecology in Rijnland*, Texas University 1985.

41. Wieczynski, *Russian Frontier*, 17–25; L. H. Nelson, *The Normans in South Wales*, Austin, Texas 1966, 60–1, 76–8, 176–84; McNeill, *Europe's Steppe Frontier*, 111–15.

42. C. J. Bishko, 'The Castilian as plainsman: the medieval ranching frontier in La Mancha and Extremadura', *The New World Looks at its History: Proceedings of the Second International Congress of Historians of the United States and Mexico*, ed. A. R. Lewis and T. F. McGann, Austin, Texas 1963, 47–69.

43. *MFS*, V–VII. Another common feature mentioned was the development of military institutions.

44. See the articles by P. Knoll and F. Lotter in *MFS*, 151–74, 267–306.

45. See in this volume, 105.

46. See Chapter 2 by Eduardo Manzano Moreno in this volume.

47. R. Bartlett, *The Making of Europe: conquest, colonization and cultural change 950–1350*, London 1993, esp. ch. 11; cf. R. L. Reynolds, 'The Mediterranean frontier', *The Frontier in Perspective*, ed. W. D. Wyman and C. B. Kroeber, Madison 1957, 33.

48. A. R. Lewis, 'The closing of the mediaeval frontier, 1250–1350', *Speculum*, XXXIII (1958), 475–83.

49. D. Walker, 'The Norman settlement in Wales', *ANS*, I (1978), 131–43; for the Anglo-Scottish border, see G. W. S. Barrow, 'Frontier and settlement: which influenced which?', *MFS*, 3–21.

50. P. M. Duffy, 'The nature of the medieval frontier in Ireland', *Studia Hibernica*, XXII–XXIII (1982–83), 21, but cf. 36–8, where he doubts the utility of the frontier for interpreting medieval Irish history. See also *Colony and Frontier in Medieval Ireland: essays presented to J. F. Lydon*, ed. T. Barry, R. Frame, and K. Simms, London 1995, and Chapter 7 by Steven Ellis in this volume.

51. J. F. Haldon and H. Kennedy, 'The Arab-Byzantine frontier in the 8th and 9th centuries: military organisation in the Borderlands', *Recueil des travaux de l'Institut d'Études Byzantines*, XIX (1980), 79–116.

52. Noble, 'Louis the Pious'; cf. Smith, *'Fines imperii'*, 169–71.
53. The discussion that follows has been greatly influenced by J. A. Armstrong, *Nations before Nationalism*, Chapel Hill 1982, which sets out a broadly based, formal, theoretical framework for premodern frontier studies from a social science perspective. It should be compulsory reading for any historian interested in this topic.
54. For instance, Sahlins, *Boundaries*, ch. 4, shows how Pyreneans adopted French and Spanish identity for their own ends.
55. J. R. V. Prescott, *Political Frontiers and Boundaries*, London 1987, ch. 6; Armstrong, *Nations before Nationalism*, esp. ch. 2, 51–2; and in this volume, 26–7.
56. For an exhaustive survey of the available methods for doing this, see R. A. LeVine and D. T. Campbell, *Ethnocentrism: theories of conflict, ethnic attitudes and group behavior*, New York 1972.
57. The 'myth-symbol complex' underlying ethnic identity is discussed at length by A. D. Smith, *The Ethnic Origins of Nations*, Oxford 1986, and also by Armstrong, *Nations before Nationalism*.
58. Prescott, *Political Frontiers and Boundaries*, 80–1.
59. Cf. Evans, 'Frontiers and national identities', 480–502.

2

THE CREATION OF A MEDIEVAL FRONTIER: ISLAM AND CHRISTIANITY IN THE IBERIAN PENINSULA, EIGHTH TO ELEVENTH CENTURIES

Eduardo Manzano Moreno

Would-be historians of the Spanish Middle Ages have to make an important decision before starting their careers: they have to choose to study either the Muslim or the Christian side. In so choosing, they will affiliate themselves with one of two distinct academic traditions which, over the last hundred years of Western scholarship, have developed clear-cut disciplinary divisions. In short, they will become either Arabists or Medievalists. As Arabists they will be mainly concerned with the history of al-Andalus, the land formerly known as Hispania, which the Arabs conquered in 711. As Medievalists, our would-be historians will deal with the kingdoms that originated in the aftermath of that conquest in the mountainous and inaccessible areas of the north.

Depending on the period in which they specialise, these Arabists or Medievalists will have to look at a larger or smaller territory, since the different kingdoms that emerged in the north during the eighth and ninth centuries began to expand southwards at the expense of the shrinking land of al-Andalus, in what is known – very inappropriately, as we shall see – as the *Reconquista*. Conceived as the process of recovering a territory usurped by foreign invaders, the Reconquista advanced gradually throughout the centuries, and was concluded only in 1492 when the Reyes Católicos conquered Granada, the last redoubt of Arab rule in al-Andalus. Moving at the same pace, the 'fields' (in the literal sense) of the Medievalist or the Arabist also gradually shift because the

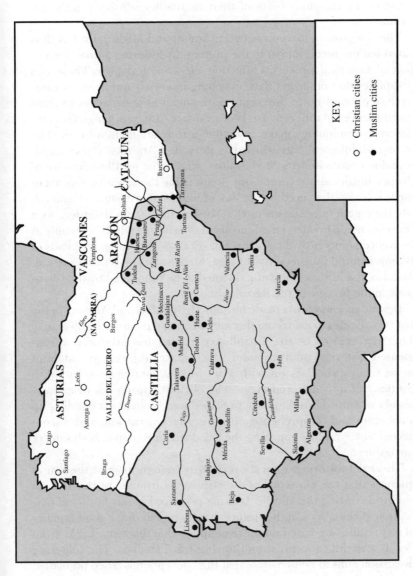

Map 2.1 The Iberian Peninsula in the ninth and tenth centuries. Drawing by María Jésus Moreno (CSIC).

distinction between them derives from the systematic antagonism between Islam and Christianity, usually presumed to be in conflict because of the incompatibility of their mutually exclusive creeds and
civilisations.

The disciplinary division between Arabist and Medievalist has thus
extended the medieval rift to the present, by fostering a dual perception of historical processes affecting the same territory. These two
disciplines do not always have matching interests, and in many cases
have developed quite different epistemological approaches to their
specific subjects: different kinds of evidence, different languages and
different terminology make any attempt to relate them difficult. The
strong philological bias which has pervaded Arabists' works on al-
Andalus is criticised by Medievalists, who insist on the necessity of
deeper historical interpretations. Reasonable though it is, this argument is counterbalanced by the lack of interest that Spanish Medievalists have generally shown in the Muslim side of the frontier. As a
consequence, Christian kingdoms seem to exist in Arabists' eyes only as
reference points providing a chronological context, or as recipients of
Islamic cultural transfers. By contrast, Medievalists tend to consider al-
Andalus as a historical vacuum doomed to be conquered by the Christians in the process of the Reconquista.

Despite serious efforts made by both Medievalists and Arabists in the
last two decades to overcome this state of affairs, the breach still exists.[1]
The 'gap' created by the disciplinary frontier has produced a fragmented historical interpretation which makes difficult any attempt
to correlate processes on both sides of the frontier or to establish
continuities in conquered areas. The obvious approaches of military
history or cultural studies have prevailed over attempts at building up
a coherent and comprehensive historical reconstruction, and disconnected bibliographies epitomise the failed attempts to span both sides of
the border.

This brief historiographical overview is enough to show the consequences that the existence of a conspicuous frontier in the Iberian
peninsula during the Middle Ages has produced in our historical perception. A closer look at this historiography reveals that a good number
of its premises are based on the assumption that this remarkable 'frontier' is a useful conceptual tool for historical analysis. The following
discussion aims to demonstrate that this conception is based on blatant
essentialism and an uncritical assessment of available evidence. As I
hope to show, the case of the Iberian peninsula in the Middle Ages as a

frontier territory *par excellence*, the arena for confrontation between two opposing civilisations, hides what in fact seems to have been an ambiguous and problematical frontier.

Frontiers and 'the Frontier'

As Daniel Power has shown in the Introduction to this volume, frontier studies have produced different 'models' of characteristic frontiers, which have been described for different times and places. The obvious question is, what kind of 'frontier' has produced the traditional historiography of medieval Spain outlined above?

In frontier studies three divergent notions of frontiers can be discerned. The first is what I will call the 'unstable frontier', meaning those frontiers whose limits change constantly depending on political, military, or diplomatic factors. The shaping of modern European states is full of disputes concerning portions of their highly volatile frontiers, which nevertheless tended to be more and more precise – though not necessarily more homogeneous or universally recognised – as those states consolidated.[2] The second model is that of the 'enclosing frontier', a limit separating two distinctive and well-defined political, economic, social, or cultural areas. Both areas are mutually exclusive, for the same political, economic, social, or cultural reasons, and their limits tend to be highly stable unless sudden events (like invasions or migrations) rip them open. When described from a political point of view, these frontiers usually have strong military implications and consequently their limits become a defensive or offensive line where hostile contacts take place. Perhaps the best example of an 'enclosing frontier' is the imperial Roman system of the *limes*, as portrayed by traditional historiography.[3] The third model is that of the 'expanding frontier'. These are frontiers of potential colonisation, where the extension of limits may be achieved by military means, but whose main feature is the occupation of land by settlers, so as to make the frontiers' limits broadly coincide with those of settlement. Obviously, the model of the expanding frontier is one sided, as it is always described from the settlers' perspective, thus implying that the colonised territories were either deserted or inhabited by trifling populations, which quite 'naturally' disappeared, or were absorbed or removed during the process. F. J. Turner's description of the western American frontier in the nineteenth century – described not as a limit but as an access – remains the paramount example of an expanding frontier characteristically associ-

ated with cultural values such as individualism or 'love of freedom', and
to broad historical interpretations which stress the 'manifest destiny' of
the people who forged it.[4]

These three basic models of frontier have one thing in common: they
always define a fringe, whose territorial shaping is determined by a
number of natural or human elements. These overlap, producing a
neat borderline which, in turn, can be either 'unstable', 'enclosing', or
'expanding'. The idea of premodern frontiers as borderlines is sometimes criticised as a transposition of today's concept of state boundaries
on to societies which lacked the means of territorial control available to
present-day states. Nevertheless, frontiers are still basically viewed as
fringes or outer boundaries.[5] Febvre's assertion, that historians should
look more for frontier regions and less for rigid boundaries, has not
always been taken into account since the notion of boundaries provides
for easier historical interpretation than the inextricable, paradoxical,
and confusing idea of commingled areas.[6] In this way, frontiers in
history have become artificial lines drawn in order to recognise distinctive patterns of human experience.

These general considerations are particularly relevant for the study
of frontiers in the European Middle Ages. In principle, there are a
good number of medieval frontiers which seem to be well defined.
Frontiers between kingdoms, frontiers against foreign peoples, or
frontiers between contending civilisations (for instance, Christianity
and Islam) are commonly described in contemporary accounts, openly
portraying cultural perceptions of difference or antagonism. However,
things are not so simple. By using the word 'frontier' we are automatically accepting two ideas implicit in it: on the one hand, the existence
of distinctive, homogeneous, and clearly differentiated political,
economic, or cultural realms and, on the other, the recognition of a
more or less open antagonism or violence between them. The latter
premise is easily recognisable, but the former hardly fits in the medieval
world.

It is frequently forgotten that one of the essential features of the
medieval European landscape was its lack of cohesion and unity; its
discontinuity and disordered character. This ambiguity meant that the
whole territory of medieval Europe was, in itself, a frontier. One can
find this pervasive frontier in feudal enclaves, which fragmented and
divided the territory in such a way that crossing from one to another
meant passing through the jurisdictions of different lords; in the limits
between towns and rural areas, with the former often having their own

laws and enjoying special privileges; or even in the political arena, where stability, a basic constituent of a homogeneous realm, was always greatly under threat, since it depended on a lord recognising the authority of someone above him. Lack of such recognition meant immediately the formation of an internal frontier, a development rarely perceived by contemporaries as less relevant than the threat posed by 'external' enemies to the frontiers of a given kingdom.

None of these frontiers, examples of which could be multiplied, is likely to be reflected in the textbook political map of the Middle Ages. Nevertheless, they show how difficult it is to draw a homogeneous picture of the kingdoms girdled by conventional medieval frontiers. The prevalence of violence or personal ties of dependence, to name just two key elements of medieval society which tended to create frontiers of their own, renders impossible a clear-cut definition of the realms which those frontiers created. Therefore, the emphasis laid upon the 'external' frontiers in medieval historiography merely reflects convention; frontiers are a convenient tool for historical interpretation, which demarcates fields of analysis by over-simplifying a richer reality, and by stressing the most apparent, political, level to the detriment of other aspects.

The Case for the Frontier in the Iberian Peninsula

Interestingly, the two historiographical traditions which have been mentioned above – Medievalist and Arabist – have developed different models of 'frontier' for the Christian kingdoms and for al-Andalus. The Christian frontier clearly fits the model of the expanding frontier, whereas the 'Muslim frontier' can be portrayed as a typical enclosing frontier. Furthermore, frontiers between Christian kingdoms correspond to the model of unstable frontiers described above.

The characterisation of the Christian frontier as an expanding line is best portrayed in the works of Sánchez Albornoz, one of the most influential historians of the Spanish Middle Ages. According to him, the creation of the frontier against Islam was the crucial event in the history of Spain in general, and of Castile in particular. It was indeed a very special frontier. As early as the mid eighth century the lands lying south of the mountains that sheltered the kingdom of Asturias, and more particularly the Duero river valley, became a desert: a no-man's land consciously created as a buffer area by the kings of Asturias in order to protect their territories. The rapid consolidation of this kingdom raised the population in a mountainous area, and encouraged a southward flow of people who started a process of colonisation known as *repoblación*. The massive movement of population which constituted the colonisation of these lands produced a distinctive society in which the prospect of empty lands attracted peasants from the north, who were prepared to endure the dangers of a frontier always exposed to Muslim raids. In these conditions the acute need for a workforce in such hazardous areas inhibited the emergence of a feudal society, as kings were unable to draw settlers to these lands unless they were granted privileges and freedom. These freeholders were partly responsible for strengthening the frontier from the Christian side as they combined colonisation duties with military expansion.[7]

The dynamics created by the *repoblación* of the Duero valley became a distinctive feature of the Christian frontier in the following centuries. Once the Duero valley had been occupied there was no further need for a buffer zone, but by then the Reconquista had become closely associated with *repoblación*. The declared aim of the Christians was the expulsion of the infidel intruders, and therefore the Muslim populations of the lands of al-Andalus conquered by the Christians were either expelled or greatly reduced. The demographic vacuum left by Muslim emigrants was filled by waves of northern immigrants, attracted by the prospects of new lands. When the Reconquista came to an end in 1492, the process was temporarily interrupted, but the spirit of the Castilian as a frontiersman did not die out, as a new frontier was found in the continent discovered the same year.

Although there is no clear evidence that Sánchez Albornoz was acquainted with Turner's ideas, the picture he drew of the Christian medieval frontier in the Middle Ages bears a clear resemblance to the American historian's view of his country's western frontier. Ideas such as individual freedom (for instance, the absence of feudal social structures) or 'manifest destiny' (the Castilian frontiersman as the ancestor of the *conquistador*) are perfectly interchangable between the western American frontier and medieval Spain. This conception has also proved to be extremely successful, as a long historiographical tradition has stressed the uniqueness of medieval Spain on account of the pecularities imposed by the frontier, and by the necessity of constant warfare against the Muslims.[8]

In contrast with the Christian frontier of expanding limits, its Muslim equivalent is an illustrative case of an enclosing frontier. *Thagr* (plural, *thugūr*) is the most common word used to refer to it in medieval Arab sources. Although the word also has other meanings, like 'mouth' or 'breach', 'frontier' is the most frequent. Arabic dictionaries clearly specify that *thagr*, when meaning 'frontier', is the area which separates the *dār al-Islam* (literally, the 'abode of Islam') from the *dār al-ḥarb*, (literally, 'the abode of war').[9] In other words, *thagr* is the territory that marks the limits of the Muslim lands, beyond which lies the land of the unbelievers.

There is strong evidence showing that this neat dichotomy was only formulated once the early Arab conquests had come to a halt and the new Islamic empire had been consolidated. It was then, in the first half of the eighth century (second century Hegira), that Muslim legal theorists elaborated on the dichotomy by defining the conditions which had to prevail for a given territory to be considered as *dār al-Islam*. Abū Ḥanīfa (d. 767/150*H*), one of the leading jurists of this period, set forth three cases in which *dār al-Islam* became *dār al-ḥarb*: enforcement of non-Muslim laws, proximity to *dār al-ḥarb*, and a lack of security for the life and safety of Muslims. The model for this definition was based on the life of the prophet Muḥammad himself, who also had his own *dār al-Islam* in his city of Medina, in conflict with the *dār al-ḥarb* of his Meccan enemies.[10]

This particular formulation of the dichotomy had a strongly militant character, which is also reflected in the works of Islamic political theorists. According to these theorists, prominent among the duties of any Muslim ruler was the sustenance of religion, the maintenance of a fair fiscal administration, and also the safeguarding of the *thugūr al-muslimīn*, the frontiers of the Muslims. Moreover, the *thagr* also marked a line of political behaviour, because once the frontier had been breached the Holy War (*jihād*) became an unavoidable obligation for the ruler.[11] Hence, in medieval Islam *thagr* had a wider meaning than mere territorial demarcation, because its militant character served as a means of political legitimisation for Muslim rulers.

The concept of *thagr* was elaborated in the Islamic East, but was rapidly transferred to al-Andalus, a region of close contact with the 'unbelievers'. The deep meaning of the notion of *thagr* was taken up by Andalusian writers who worked in the service of the Umayyads and can be assessed in the chronicle accounts that describe the efforts and energies devoted by Umayyad rulers to the defence of their frontiers. In this connection, Arab sources written in Umayyad Cordoba never fail to note the importance and success of the military campaigns against the Christian kingdoms, the fortification of frontier enclaves, or the concern shown by Cordoban rulers over the issue of Muslim captives in the north, a recurrent topic closely associated with the necessity of frontier defence.[12]

Despite the much more sophisticated definition of the idea of frontier on the Andalusian side in comparison to its Christian counterpart, the *thugūr al-Andalus* lack a comprehensive historical interpretation similar to the one set out by Sánchez Albornoz and other Spanish medievalists. One thing, however, seems to be certain: after the defeat at Poitiers in 732, the Muslim land frontier never expanded again. The defensive character of the al-Andalusian *thagr* clearly appears in the Umayyad period, when numerous military expeditions against the north never produced a significant territorial expansion of the *dār al-Islam*. Accordingly, most studies of the Andalusian frontier have stressed its defensive disposition and have suggested, more or less openly, the existence of a line of fortifications against the expanding Christian frontier. The main characteristics of these fortifications were the primacy of the military administration, due to the defensive function of these territories, and lower taxes than in other areas of al-Andalus, owing to the preponderance of warfare in these regions.[13]

Although this line successfully resisted Christian expansion throughout the Umayyad period, it gradually broke down after the collapse of the Caliphate in 1031. Later efforts by the North African dynasties – the Almoravids (1086–1118) and Almohads (1147–1212) – to reverse this trend failed resoundingly after some initial, short-lived successes. Its survival throughout the fourteenth and most of the fifteenth centuries was more the result of the political complexities of the period than of the line's effectiveness.

The Ambiguities of the Frontier

The historiographical perception of the Christian frontier as 'expanding' and of the Muslim frontier as 'enclosing' has provided the general framework for historical interpretations of the Iberian Middle Ages. Furthermore, this frontier had a militant and legitimising ideology behind it as medieval writers, both Arab and Christian, widely referred to and justified the conflict by resorting to notions such as *jihād* or Reconquista, and to contentious confrontations of a religious kind.

Few will deny that this picture lacks coherence, even though it corresponds to a long-term trend ending in the last decade of the fifteenth century. Moreover, a closer scrutiny of its premises and a critical approach to the evidence upon which it lies reveals serious inconsistencies, which should lead us to rethink the whole framework.

These inconsistencies can first be grasped at the ideological level elaborated on each side of the frontier. At a basic level, the notion of *jihād* is conveniently simple: it makes clear the duty to fight the unbelievers in obedience to God's commands. In fact, if we were to believe the Arab chroniclers, then all the wars waged by Muslim rulers against infidels were Holy Wars, prompted by the necessity of fulfilling a religious command. However, present-day historiography would hardly agree that the objective of all Islamic wars was always to wipe every infidel off the face of the earth, and would instead maintain that such wars served to demonstrate the just and divinely inspired nature of the rulers' actions. Although it is true that there were specific moments when the spirit of *jihād* played an important role in fostering military expansion or defence, it would seem more reasonable – at least from a secular historical viewpoint – to assume that at each historical juncture there was an interplay of political, economic, and ideological conditioning factors, and that it was these which were decisive in producing confrontations with the Christians.[14]

Besides, the general idea of *jihād* had practical applications, and these did not always correspond to the strict principles from which they sprang. In al-Andalus the notion of *jihād*, though widespread, never developed any further. Andalusian legal theorists consistently repeated the same definitions and legal enforcements associated with this concept, exactly as they had originally been formulated by their peers in the Muslim East. This lack of innovation in a notion supposedly everpresent in Andalusian society is noteworthy. It has been suggested that it mirrors the considerable distance existing between an imported militant theory and a complex and difficult reality.[15]

This distance can be perceived in some revealing details. The Umayyads never encouraged the use of elements typically associated with the Holy War. Fortifications which sheltered pious Muslims devoted to praying, ascetic exercises, and the practice of the Holy War, the so-called *ribāṭs*, are almost completely absent from the map of the *thugūr al-Andalus*, a situation that was in strong contrast with the Islamic frontiers in the contemporary Near East. Geographical and historical accounts describe the frontier against the Byzantine Empire as bristling with *ribāṭs* sustained from the incomes of inalienable foundations (*wuqūf*). Although sources from the Umayyad period in al-Andalus do contain mentions of individuals who were eager to settle in the 'frontier' in order to practise the Holy War and eventually to find martyrdom, such references are relatively few and never allow us to construe that their initiative was encouraged by the central government.[16]

The prevalence of the idea of Holy War associated with the need of defending the frontiers is also closely associated in the East with the enrolling of 'volunteers' (*mutaṭawwi'a*) imbued with the idea of religious expansion through Muslim campaigns. In al-Andalus there is ample evidence of the presence of these volunteers, who joined the regular army out of religious zeal and were not regularly paid, but had a right to a share of the booty in the campaigns against the North.[17] However, these volunteers never seem to have played an important role in the campaigns – the chief burden rested on the regular troops and the frontier inhabitants who agreed to take part – and sometimes they even seem to have been considered as cannon fodder by unscrupulous military commanders.[18]

Accordingly, Andalusian *jihād* was not so impressive as a mere theoretical disquisition would lead us to believe. It was conditioned by the specific circumstances which prevailed in al-Andalus. As will be made clear below, these circumstances did not allow the theoretical principles which backed the idea of Holy War to be easily implemented. It was only at some particular junctures – like the campaigns of al-Manṣūr (end of the tenth and beginning of the eleventh centuries), the first moments of Almoravid and Almohad expansion (twelfth and thirteenth centuries), or at the time of strong military pressure by the Christians – that this idea seems to have imbued cohesive force into and acquired paramount importance in Andalusian society.[19]

The concept of Reconquista is equally misleading. As early as the second half of the ninth century, Latin chroniclers remarked on the continuity between the defeated kingdom of the Visigoths and the new kingdoms which had emerged in the north and were portrayed as the natural successors of the defeated. These chroniclers conferred a providentialist spirit on the enterprise of recovering the lost land of their ancestors by considering the Saracens as invaders, who would be expelled with the aid of God.[20] However, modern Spanish scholarship has demonstrated that what is commonly called the Reconquista originated in a very different way and that it is hard to see these northern kingdoms as the successors of the Visigoths. The northern parts of the peninsula where the Reconquista is said to have primarily begun were occupied by peoples (in particular, the Astures) who had persistently opposed Roman and Visigothic rule. The resistance that Arab conquerors met here was similar to the difficulties that their predecessors had encountered in subduing these areas. The battle of Covadonga (725), usually considered as the starting point of the Reconquista, was probably nothing more than a successful skirmish which convinced the Arabs of the difficulties of an effective occupation of these marginal areas. A century and a half later, the Asturian kingdom had consolidated and its rulers sought to legitimise their rule. How better to do this than to establish a link of continuity between them and the Visigoths? Ecclesiastical writers working in the royal court proclaimed that their frequent struggles with the Muslims were guided by God, who was ready to forget the sins committed by the Visigoths and help their successors to recover their land.[21]

These remarks should warn us against applying indiscriminately categories which seem to be well founded in the written sources. Obviously, it would be absurd to deny the existence of an ideology of the Reconquista throughout the Middle Ages or to reject the impact of the idea of Holy War in particular circumstances. What is at stake here is to what extent these ideological notions, when taken at their face value, provide an accurate framework for historical interpretation. The preceding discussion has clearly shown that they do not provide such a framework, unless we consider the historian's task as merely the reiteration of the contents of their sources. Reducing medieval Spanish history to a long enterprise aimed at recovering a lost land is no less misleading than framing historical interpretation on the Muslim side within the notion of *jihād*.

If the contemporary ideological understandings of the frontier cannot withstand a serious critique, the same goes for further assumptions partly derived from them. This is the case with the association between Reconquista and *repoblación* which lies at the core of the idea of a Christian 'expanding frontier'. As we have seen, Sánchez Albornoz considered that this process originated at a very early stage, when the kings of Asturias started the occupation of the areas of the Duero valley which their predecessors had consciously depopulated in the middle of the eighth century. But were those areas really depopulated?

In a celebrated article, R. Menéndez Pidal challenged the view of his former student, arguing the practical infeasibility of a purposeful depopulation of such a huge area by the feeble kings of Asturias, which is what Sánchez Albornoz had suggested. Menéndez Pidal thought that

the information gleaned from two Latin sources, describing a campaign
by the king Alfonso I (739–57) in the course of which he 'depopulated'
this region, should not be taken literally.[22] In fact, it is difficult to
imagine how Alfonso I was able to uproot such a huge population from
their dwellings and to bring them with him to the kingdom of Asturias.
Both texts are likely to be embellishments by the chroniclers of a
particularly successful campaign. What this campaign probably produced was disarray in the administrative organisation of the area which
neither the rulers of al-Andalus nor the northern kingdoms were able
to control for more than a century. This would explain why this area
virtually disappears from our sources throughout this period. When it
appears again in Christian documents of the tenth century, landholders
occupying these areas are said to be 'populating' them (Latin: *populare*).
However, Menéndez Pidal held that this verb should not be understood
as describing the colonising of hitherto deserted lands, but as portraying a process of bringing back to political and social control lands which
had hitherto remained out of bounds. This would explain why many
documents which mention the 'population' of the Duero Valley refer to
water mills or fisheries in areas which otherwise are described as deserted.[23]

Despite Sánchez Albornoz's efforts to answer these criticisms, the
origins and true character of the *repoblación* of the Duero Valley remain
highly controversial.[24] Neither archaeology nor analysis of place names
has demonstrated the existence of a population vacuum which would
justify the conclusions of the Spanish medievalist. In fact, if we accept
that the population remained in place, it would be necessary to explain
how it was integrated into the political and social structures of the
northern kingdom.[25]

In the last two decades, Spanish historiography has ignored what
Sánchez Albornoz used to consider the cornerstone of his interpretation
of the Spanish Middle Ages, and has tried to answer some of the
implications of this question by demonstrating that the social processes
in the Iberian peninsula had their own dynamics, notwithstanding the
existence of a frontier against the infidels. The spread of links of
dependence as the general form of social organisation followed a variety of patterns, resulting in the widespread adoption of feudal forms of
production. In this way, the idea of a Castilian free peasantry as the
vanguard of the frontier expansion has also been put into question.
This leaves the Christian frontier denuded of one of its most conspicu-

ous features: far from being the expanding line of a colonising and enterprising movement, the *repoblación* is now considered a typical example of feudal expansion which can be compared with similar cases of expanding societies in the rest of medieval Europe. Under this new light Christian expansion is considered a by-product of feudal conflicts which set dominant groups in mutual opposition for the control of limited resources. The need for new lands to increase the availability of such resources was the main aim of an expansion actively encouraged by kings eager to reduce internal strife in their domains.[26]

The Muslim 'enclosing frontier' also reveals numerous inconsistencies when carefully analysed. One of these inconsistencies is related to the very notion of a *thagr* that neatly divides the territory into two distinctive parts. As mentioned above, the quest for homogeneous realms in the medieval world is an attempt doomed to fail, due to the lack of internal coherence in medieval polities. This is also true for Islamic political formations, despite the fact that they tend to be defined within an ideological construct, in this case Islam. However, Muslim medieval theorists were aware that this ideology was not completely dominant and had to recognise that the lands of the *dār al-Islam* were far from constituting a homogeneous realm: this is why they elaborated the notion of *dār al-ʿahd* (literally, 'abode of the pact') which designates the 'abode' which had been conquered by the Muslims, but whose populations had established a pact by which they had submitted to the conquerors, and had kept their properties and creed in exchange for the payment of certain taxes. *Dār al-ʿahd* was included within the *dār al-Islam*, but was clearly differentiated from it, because breach of the existing pact led immediately to its transformation into *dār al-ḥarb*, and consequently liable to attack by Muslim armies.[27]

These subtle distinctions indicate that *thagr* cannot be taken as a simple boundary. Pacts with non-Muslim populations living under Muslim rule were a constituent part of Islamic political formations. It was not so much territorial dominion as recognition of rule by conquered communities that engendered political limits. The definitions of Muslim theorists identified this rule with Islam, but obviously this was a legitimating device, by virtue of which the dominant political formation that ruled the *thagr* defined itself in ideological-religious terms. These terms allowed the existence of non-Muslim communities within the 'abode of Islam', but also defined the exclusion of other non-Muslim communities by stressing the militant character of the frontier. This dual attitude is well attested in al-Andalus where there is evidence showing that Christian communities lived under Muslim rule in regions of the *thagr* that bordered the Christian kingdoms.[28] In this connection, A. K. S. Lambton's remarks on the nature of Islamic political formations are particularly enlightening. According to Lambton the basis of the Islamic state was essentially ideological, 'not political, territorial or ethnical [*sic*]'.[29]

That the Arab *thagr* embodies a broad, ill-defined meaning of territory may also be traced to the etymology of the word. It is noteworthy that the root of the word *th.g.r.* appears in other Semitic languages with the meaning of 'opening', 'gate', and 'pass'. We do not know exactly how it came to mean 'frontier' in Arabic, but I think it is significant that the Latin word for frontier, *limes*, also originally meant 'military road' or 'pass'.[30] Arab authors in the East used the word *thagr* in relation to the frontier separating the Byzantine Empire and in particular, when referring to the mountainous regions of the Taurus and the Anti Taurus, which constituted the dividing line between Arabs and Byzantines. Curiously enough, the Byzantine authors used a term with a very similar meaning, *kleisurai*, to refer to these areas. This word is originally found meaning 'pass' or 'defile' and at least until the tenth century it served to designate the fortifications built at a frontier mountain pass.[31] Another word used in Arab sources to refer to the frontier regions in Asia Minor was *darb* (plural, *durūb*). The origins of this word are obscure: it could have come from a local dialect, or was perhaps borrowed from Persian. Whatever the case, the important thing is that this word developed two meanings: the idea of 'gate', 'way', or 'pass'; and a meaning synonymous with *thagr*.[32]

This brief incursion into philology reveals a perception of frontier which is clearly linked with the idea of 'pass' or 'opening'. It is significant that this coincidence occurs both in a Semitic language (Arabic) and in Indo-European languages. The reason behind this is simple: a frontier was not a line, a distinctly defined demarcation; instead, it consisted of a series of strategic points which all provided access to the territory. It is not at all surprising therefore to find that, for example, the word *thagr* sometimes refers to a single castle or a particular city (for instance, *thagr Saraqusṭa*: frontier of Zaragoza). The *thugūr* were perceived as a series of 'passes' which controlled the access to a given territory. This perception fits well with the character of the frontier described above, as it highlights the discontinuity and irregularity of the frontier landscape.

The al-Andalus Frontier at the Time of the Umayyads (755–1031)

The aim of the Andalusian Umayyads in regard to these *thugūr* or 'passes' was twofold: on the one hand, to control them in order to check the advances of the Christians, and on the other, to portray themselves as defenders of the Muslim community sequestered behind the *thagr* in order to legitimise their own rule. The latter was easier to achieve than the former. The frontiers of al-Andalus were always rife with political instability, and Cordoba was not always able to exert its authority on the peripheral areas which were supposed to be the defending walls of the *dār al-Islam*.

The frontier regions were in fact the quintessence of al-Andalus' internal divisions, as is demonstrated in the numerous references in the sources to 'rebellions' against central authority in these areas. When describing such revolts these sources, written from a pro-Umayyad perspective, usually portray them as 'separations of obedience' or as 'breaches of existing pacts', expressions which bring us back to the ideological basis of Islamic political formations as described by Lambton.

In some cases these internal rebellions were particularly persistent. This was the case with Toledo, the former capital of the Visigoths, located in a strategic area of the Andalusian frontier. Toledo led constant uprisings against the authority of the Umayyad amirs between the eighth and tenth centuries. The precise causes of these rebellions are never explicitly attested in the sources, but we can infer from some scattered references that the Toledans refused the fiscal duties that the Umayyads tried to impose upon them. Be that as it may, revolts in the city were persistent and sometimes attracted military support from the northern kingdoms. The growing threat that these rebellions posed to Umayyad rule in the central peninsula in the mid ninth century forced the Cordoban amir Muḥammad I (852–86) to fortify a series of enclaves (Madrid, Peñafora, Talamanca, Calatrava, and Talavera) which ultimately constituted a formidable ring around the city. The aim of this internal frontier was twofold: to protect the crucial routes which crossed the central plateau of the peninsula from Toledan expeditions, and to prevent Toledan communications with the north.[33]

Other sectors of the *thugūr al-Andalus* were in the hands of aristocratic families who, from the eighth to the tenth century or even beyond, managed to seize and hold most of the key strongholds of these areas and to carve themselves a strong position *vis-à-vis* the Umayyads.

Against a background of ill-defined boundaries, these families built up
a complex network of political alliances and personal loyalties which ran
across both sides of the frontier, much to the despair of the Umayyad
rulers. These networks need to be carefully analysed in order to understand the significance of the frontier.

The ethnic origins of these families were not homogeneous. Some of
them belonged to indigenous stock, others were of Arab or Berber
descent. Nevertheless, they came to find themselves in very similar
situations, and having similarly troublesome relations with the
Umayyads. Part of the indigenous aristocracy had managed to survive
the Arab conquest, thanks to pacts with the conquerors and conversion
to Islam. These agreements secured their social position, probably in
exchange for political recognition entailing fiscal payments to Cordoba.
Some of these indigenous families were settled in the frontier areas.
This was the case with the Banū Qasī, the Banū ʿAmrūs, and the Banū
Šabrīṭ, who played a prominent military and political role during the
ninth and tenth centuries in the frontier regions of the Ebro valley. The
complex history of each of these lineages turns on two fundamental
axes: on the one hand, their relations with the other local powers
(including the Christian kingdoms), and on the other, their relations
with the Umayyads. The complex – and not always clear – network of
alliances or enmities into which these families entered helped to create
ambiguous situations, in which more complex factors than mere religious affinities played a prominent role.

The case of one of these frontier families, the so-called Banū Qasī,
illustrates the intricacies of this situation well. They were the descendants of a certain Casius, a military commander who had been in charge
of the system of frontier defences that the Visigoths were compelled
to set up against the restless Basque populations of the northern
peninsula. At the time of the Arab conquest Casius surrendered to
the newcomers and converted to Islam. The conquerors probably
allowed him to keep the same territories he had been ruling up until
then. These fortresses were Arnedo, Olite, Viguera, and Calahorra,
all of them well documented in the Visigothic period as part of the
defences against the Basques, and all of them firmly in the hands of
members of the Banū Qasī lineage until its disappearance in the tenth
century.

In the aftermath of the conquest an interesting development took
place: in the first half of the ninth century, the Banū Qasī entered into
an alliance with the Basque family of the Arista, who ruled the neigh-

bouring city of Pamplona, the embryo of the future kingdom of Navarra. The alliance lasted more than seventy years and resulted in joint political and military actions, and in a series of marriages between the families. It only came to an end when the Arista were overthrown by the rival family of the Jimenos in 905.

The ambiguous loyalties of the Banū Qasī were a constant source of trouble for the Umayyads. The chronicles describe countless rebellions by members of this family against the Cordoban rulers and ambitious attempts to extend their territories against other frontier families. These rebellions always followed a similar pattern: one of the descendants of Casius takes over a stronghold or a city, or defies the authority of the Umayyads by refusing to take part in a military campaign; an expedition is sent from Cordoba; and the rebel finally agrees to acknowledge Umayyad rule once more. Sometimes sources inform us that this surrender – at least from the Cordoban perspective – is accompanied by the former rebel taking a new oath of allegiance. It is also worth mentioning that these rebellions never resulted in the dispossession of the Banū Qasī of their original lands: the family was so firmly rooted through its control of strategic enclaves in their sector of the *thagr* that the Umayyads had no choice but to have dealings with them.

In fact, the Banū Qasī disappeared from the frontier only when the rival Arab family of the Tujībids emerged at the end of the ninth century. The Tujībids were initially backed by the Umayyads, who used them as allies to counteract the growing power of the Banū Qasī. This policy proved successful, and during the tenth century the Tujībids became masters of the frontier section which had previously belonged to their rivals. They were even able to extend their control considerably. Not surprisingly, perhaps, relations with the Umayyads became increasingly strained due to the reluctance of members of this family to comply with fiscal and military demands from Cordoba, and the caliph ʿAbd al-Raḥmān III had to face a number of rebellions led by them.

The most important of these rebellions ended in 937 when Zaragoza, the main city in the hands of the Tujībids, surrendered to the army of the Cordoban caliph after a long siege. Despite this surrender the Tujībids were not overthrown; instead a treaty was concluded between ʿAbd al-Raḥmān III and Muḥammad b. Hāshim al-Tujībi, the leading member of the family at that time. The latter was obliged to swear an oath of allegiance (*bayʿa*) to the caliph, to take part in his military campaigns, to send fiscal contributions to Cordoba, and to refuse any alliance with the Christians. In exchange for this he was granted full authority in his domains for his lifetime, and permission to bequeath them to his descendants.[34]

Berber groups in al-Andalus tell a different story, though with a similar ending. At the time of the conquest they settled in areas of the Levante, Spain's central plateau, and the valleys of the Guadalquivir and Guadiana. We do not know exactly what their social structures were, but judging from the vocabulary of the sources it has been suggested that tribal structures were prevalent among them at this early period. However, in the aftermath of conquest, at least some of these structures disintegrated. A good example of this process is provided by the Banū Zannūn, a Berber group which settled in the frontier region of Santaver. In the middle of the ninth century these Berbers arabised their name, thus becoming the Banū Ḏī l-Nūn. This coincided with the emergence of a chieftain, named Sulaymān b. Ḏī l-Nūn, who came to terms with the Umayyad amir of Cordoba. In exchange for political recognition Sulaymān was granted the whole territory under his rule.

If there was a tribal component in the internal organisation of this Berber group, this quickly disappeared in the following years as Sulaymān's succesors established a well-defined territorial domain. This included a certain number of castles and fortifications which impeded the entrance of the amirs' armies, and related rural settlements where the Banū Ḏī l-Nūn exercised 'oppression over the people'. Our sources also inform us that the Banū Ḏī l-Nūn could raise an army of 20 000 soldiers in their territories, a figure probably exaggerated, but which corroborates the strength of their resources.[35]

Despite their different ethnic backgrounds, all these families reached a similar degree of power in the sectors of the frontier they controlled. However, the pre-eminence of these (and many other) frontier lineages was tested during the first third of the tenth century, when the Umayyad caliph ʿAbd al-Raḥmān III tried to curtail their power in the frontier after having defeated a number of rebellions in the interior regions of al-Andalus. In 939 this policy suddenly came to an end. In that year the caliph suffered a severe defeat while campaigning in Christian territory. Part of his army was annihilated and he narrowly escaped death. Arab sources speak of treason among the caliphal ranks and point to frontier chieftains as the main culprits, since they left the camp when the attack against the Umayyad column was at its fiercest. In the aftermath of this disaster ʿAbd al-Raḥmān III took a bold decision: he would campaign no more, and decided to entrust the defence of the frontier to the local aristocracy who 'inherited their tracts from their ancestors, the brave and tough Tujībids, Banū Zirwāl, Banū Gazlūn, Banū al-Ṭawīl, Banū Razīn and others'.[36]

ʿAbd al-Raḥmān III's acknowledgment of his defeat amounted to recognition of the total impossibility of adapting the frontier to the theoretical requirements of the Holy War. If we are to believe the vocabulary of the Cordoban sources written under Umayyad patronage, the caliph's aim was a *thagr* geared to the Holy War and bristling with *ribāṭ* foundations full of volunteers seeking martyrdom on the path of God. Reality was a quite different matter. Whole sectors of the frontier were in the hands of powerful families with very different backgrounds, but with a common aversion to political control exerted from Cordoba. In fact, some of these families, for instance the Tujībids or the Banū Ḏī l-Nūn, managed to survive after the fall of the Umayyads and governed some of the Taifa kingdoms which succeeded them.

Conclusion

In examining the formation of the frontier between Islam and Christendom in the Iberian peninsula, several points have been clarified. First is the necessity of abandoning ideological premises drawn from contemporary accounts. The uncritical acceptance of these premises has led historians to draw a linear demarcation in which political boundaries mirror the clear-cut ideological division of our sources. This *emic* (see Glossary) approach hinders any attempt at rational historical interpretation because it overlooks an important fact: that it was easier for medieval political formations to set out their ideological and exclusive legitimation than it was for them to exert control on a frontier reality full of unholy alliances, rebellions, and internal strife.

The traditional notions of the Christian frontier in Spain as 'expanding' and the Muslim as 'enclosing' also cannot withstand a serious critique. The Christian frontier was not an autonomous historical entity, but rather the by-product of a strong feudal society which sought to resolve its own contradictions through expansion, a process which bears strong similarities with well-known processes of feudal expansion like the Crusades or the German *Drang nach Osten*. The Muslim frontier was not a neat line of division between believers and unbelievers, but a complex abode of mixed loyalties and aristocratic rule, with which the central government had to deal in order to attract its leaders into the centre's political sphere.

However, it is important to bear in mind that these conclusions do not attempt to deny the existence of a difference, of an antagonism or a confrontation between the realms of Christianity and Islam in the Iberian peninsula. More or less continuously, more or less apparently, conflict did exist, and took a variety of forms throughout the eight centuries of Muslim rule. It is obvious that this strife produced frontiers, but it seems clear that these frontiers cannot be assessed by projecting present-day notions of borders on to the Middle Ages. Medieval society was heterogeneous and diverse, and frontier areas were no exception to this. In fact, their complex peculiarities increased their fragmented character: loyalties swung, territorial control was always highly unstable, and religious or ethnic ascription never meant much when confronted with other factors, including material ones. From this perspective it is difficult to see how borders can be considered as a useful tool for historical analysis. The result of such a view is an essentialist discourse which rests upon seemingly coherent premises, but lacks a sound historical basis.

NOTES

1. See esp. T. H. Glick, *Islamic and Christian Spain in the Early Middle Ages: comparative perspectives on social and cultural formation*, Princeton 1979. Interestingly, Glick does not believe there was a permanent confrontation along the border, but rather an 'ecological frontier', 103–5.
2. M. Foucher speaks of a 'sacralisation' of boundaries in modern states, *L'invention des frontières*, Paris 1986, 27.
3. This standard conception has provoked considerable debate among historians of the ancient world, C. R. Whittaker, *Frontiers of the Roman Empire: a social and economic study*, Baltimore and London 1994; B. Isaac, *The Limits of Empire*, revised edn Oxford 1992.
4. F. J. Turner, 'The significance of the frontier in American history', *The Frontier in American History*, New York 1920, 1–38.
5. J. C. Hudson, 'Theory and methodology in comparative frontier studies', *The Frontier*, ed. D. H. Miller and J. O. Steffen, Oklahoma 1977, 5–35.
6. L. Febvre, *A Geographical Introduction to History*, trans. E. G. Mountford and J. H. Paxton, Westport, Conn. 1932, 296–315.
7. Sánchez Albornoz's ideas are summarised in C. Sánchez Albornoz, 'The frontier and Castilian liberties', *The World Looks at its History: Proceedings of the Second International Congress of Historians of the United States and Mexico*, Austin 1963, 27–46.
8. S. de Moxó, *Repoblación y sociedad en la España cristiana medieval*, Madrid 1979; M. González Jiménez, 'Frontier and settlement in Castile (1085–1350)', *MFS*, 49–74.

9. Ibn Manẓūr, *Lisān al-ʿarab*, Beirut 1935, IV, 103–4.

10. R. Peters, *Islam and Colonialism: the doctrine of 'jihād' in modern history*, The Hague 1979, 11–12.

11. A. K. S. Lambton, *State and Government in Medieval Islam. An Introduction to Islamic Political Theory: the jurists*, Oxford 1981, 18–19, 91.

12. Occasionally this was accomplished through the incorporation of literary *topoi* which bore little relation to fact, E. Manzano Moreno, 'Oriental *topoi* in Andalusian historical sources', *Arabica*, XXXIX (1992), 42–58.

13. J. Boch Vilá, 'Algunas consideraciones sobre el Ṯagr en al-Andalus y la división político administrativa de la España Musulmana', *Etudes d'Orientalisme dediées à la mémoire de Lévi Provençal*, Paris 1962, 23–33; P. Chalmeta, 'El concepto de Ṯagr', *La Marche Supérieure d'al-Andalus et l'Occident Chrétien*, ed. P. Sénac, Madrid 1991, 23.

14. Peters, *Islam and Colonialism*, 6.

15. D. Urvoy, 'Sur l'évolution de la notion de Gihād dans l'Espagne Musulmane', *Melanges de la Casa de Velazquez*, IX (1973), 335–71.

16. E. Manzano Moreno, *La frontera de al-Andalus en época de los Omeyas*, Madrid 1991, 60–9.

17. C. Bosworth, '*mutaṭāwwiʿa*', *EI*, new edn.

18. P. Chalmeta, 'Simancas y Alhándega', *Hispania*, XXXVI (1976), 359–444.

19. Al-Manṣūr's campaigns: E. Lévi Provençal, *Historia de la España Musulmana*, *Historia de España Menéndez Pidal*, IV, Madrid 1950, 410–29. Almoravids and the Almohads: ed. M. J. Viguera *El retroceso territorial de al-Andalus: Almoravides y Almohaes, siglos XII–XIII*, Menéndez Pidal, VIII–IX, Madrid 1997.

20. *Crónica de Albelda*, ed. E. Gómez Moreno, 'Las primeras crónicas de la reconquista: el ciclo de Alfonso III', *Boletín de la Real Academia de la Historia*, C (1932), 601.

21. A. Barbero and M. Vigil, *Sobre los orígenes sociales de la Reconquista*, Barcelona 1974, and *La formación del feudalismo en la Península Ibérica*, Barcelona 1978.

22. *Crónica de Albelda* and *Crónica de Alfonso III*, 'Primeras crónicas', 601ff.

23. R. Menéndez Pidal, 'Repoblación y tradición en la cuenca del Duero', *Enciclopedia Lingüística Hispana*, Madrid 1960, i, xxix–lvii.

24. C. Sánchez Albornoz, *Despoblación y repoblación del valle del Duero*, Buenos Aires 1966.

25. Barbero and Vigil, *La formación del feudalismo*, 224–8. The remarkable occurrence of Arab personal and place names in the tenth-century Latin documents of this area may be due not to the immigration of Mozarabs, as traditionally thought, but to a process of arabisation of the local populations, a hypothesis given some support by an Arab source: E. Manzano Moreno, 'Christian-Muslim frontier in al-Andalus: idea and reality', *The Arab Influence upon Medieval Europe*, ed. D. A. Agius and R. Hitchcock, Reading 1994, 95.

26. A. Rodríguez López, *La consolidación territorial de la monarquía feudal castellana: expansión y fronteras durante el reinado de Fernando III*, Madrid 1994, 15.

27. Peters, *Islam and Colonialism*, 11.

28. Manzano Moreno, 'Christian-Muslim frontier', 92.

29. Lambton, *State and Government in Medieval Islam*, 13.
30. B. Isaac, 'The meaning of the terms *limes* and *limitanei*', *Journal of Roman Studies*, LXXVIII (1989), 125–47.
31. Procopius, *De aedificiis*, III, 3:2; III, 7:5.
32. R. Hartmann, '*darb*', *EI*.
33. Ibn Ḥayyān, *al-Muqtabis min anba⁻ᶜ āhl al-Andalus*, ed. Maḥmūd ʿAlī Makki, Cairo 1390/1971, 132, repeated in the late chronicle of Ximenez de Rada, *Historia Arabum*, ed. J. Lozano Sánchez, Seville 1993, 43.
34. Ibn Ḥayyān, *al-Muqtabis*, ed. P. Chalmeta, F. Corriente, and M. Sobh, Madrid 1979, V, 275–9.
35. Ibn Ḥayyān, *al-Muqtabis – fī taʾrīj rijāl al-Andalus*, ed. M. Martínez Antuña, Paris 1937, 17–18.
36. Ibn Ḥayyān, *al-Muqtabis*, ed. Chalmeta et al., V, 296.

3

(RE)CONSTRUCTING THE FRONTIERS OF TENTH-CENTURY NORTH CHINA

Naomi Standen

The northern frontier of China is frequently equated with the Great Wall. The line of the Wall is widely regarded as delimiting 'China proper' (see Map 3.1), separating 'civilisation' from the 'barbarian' lands of the steppe nomad since the third century BC.[1] In fact, the Wall tourists visit today was not built until the Ming 明 dynasty (1368–1644), and a recent book by Arthur Waldron argues that it represents a uniquely sustained effort at creating long-term, static, linear defences, contrasting sharply with earlier Chinese wall-building, which tended to happen in brief bursts, producing only short sections of wall which were generally not maintained.[2] For most of its history then, China's northern frontier has *not* been marked by a physical wall, and although the *idea* of a Great Wall crops up from time to time in the sources, it is far more common to find references to fortifications of quite specific kinds than to a generalised 'Great Wall'. In the absence of a Wall or even references to it, how were the northern frontiers of China defined and maintained? The tenth century provides examples of frontier construction and maintenance, both real and theoretical, and, as we shall see, extending beyond the tenth century itself to the vital question of the depiction of the northern frontier in later historical records.

Both the frontier events and the record of them must be seen in the context of the state-building efforts of the regimes that competed for control of north China in the tenth century. The words used to signify the frontiers suggest their essential relationship with a 'central' government, and this chapter begins with a discussion of the terminology. I then argue that in the early tenth century the breakdown of central

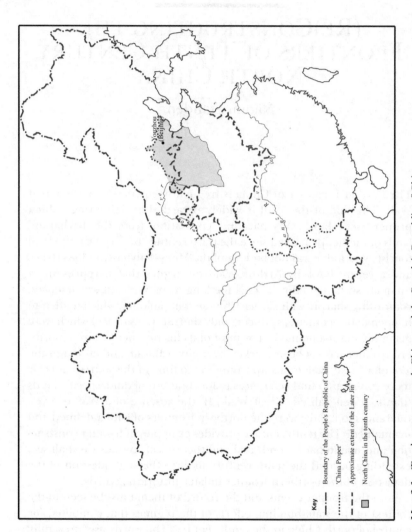

Map 3.1   Tenth-century north China and the People's Republic of China.

control meant that the location and nature of the frontier was decided by leaders based in the frontier zone, who had a relatively free choice as to where they placed their allegiances. By mid century these leaders had lost their influence over the course of events at the centre, such that it became possible for a pretender to the throne to determine where the frontier should lie without reference to those who had hitherto controlled the territory involved. Subsequently, the central authority consolidated its control of the actual frontier not least through an emphasis – both at the time but especially in the historical writings produced later – on the distinctions between the Chinese 'us' and the non-Chinese 'them'. In the tenth century, instead of the tidy line on a map that we in the present day expect, and that the myth of the Great Wall implies, there were instead multiple, simultaneous ways of regarding and defining the frontier. A line by itself was neither necessary nor sufficient to create a frontier.

Terminology

Chinese, like other languages, has several words for 'frontier' (so many, in fact, that only a selection will be covered here), whose range of meanings reflects the various functions, characteristics, and perceptions of a complex phenomenon, but above all the intimate relationship between frontiers and governments.[3] Three characters with an ancient meaning of 'boundary', 界 *jie*, 疆 *jiang*, and 境 *jing*, are all used to define each other in the first-century etymological dictionary, the *Shuowen* 説文, and are very much concerned with the delineation of boundaries. For instance, the ancient graph for *jiang* shows two fields 田 delimited by three boundary lines 一.[4] After the most ancient period the thing defined is no longer fields but usually a polity of some kind, with the implication of territory spreading towards designated limits, as represented most clearly by *jing*, early meanings of which also include 'end' or 'limit', although the sense of delimitation by lines is absent except by implication. *Jiang* and *jing* both added 'territory' or 'region' to their meanings, and paralleling this notion of more or less delimited territory is the idea that the region marked out has to be under some kind of rule or government.

域 *yu* originally conveyed this sense of governance very well: the original Zhou 周 (*c*. 1050–249 BC) graph 或 showed a 'dagger-axe' 戈, signifying an army, and a mouth 口, meaning 'command',[5] which together meant 'territory' or 'state', and only later came to mean 'bound-

ary' as well. Hence the primary meaning here seems to be of organisation and protection rather than delimitation. Nevertheless, central authority cannot go on forever, so borders are always implied in the
concept of a state. In later times, a boundary □ was added to the
original form of the character 或 to make 國 *guo*, meaning 'country', that
is, a centrally organised state.

Several of the Chinese words for 'boundary' thus have at their core
the implication of some kind of 'central' control. At the same time, one
of the spatial implications of states spreading to borders was recognised
in the use of 邊 *bian* for 'boundary', which conveys a sense of liminality
or marginality through its equally old meanings of 'side' or 'edge'. *Bian*
is the most commonly used word for 'frontier' to be found in the six
dynastic histories that cover the tenth century,[6] suggesting that the
peripheral nature of the frontier was predominant at least in the minds
of historians.

Another implication of bounded states is that they have neighbours,
and this can be seen already in the Zhou meanings of *jie*, which include
'inserted between' and 'contiguous to'; the word was commonly used in
later times to mean 'having a common boundary'. 關 *guan* also acknowl-
edges the existence of neighbours, if somewhat indirectly. Its Zhou
meaning appears to have been 'bar', 'barrier', 'doorway', or more specifically, 'frontier gate', from which rapidly developed the meaning of
'fortress' or 'fortification', and the sense of 'to close (a gate)'. The
northern edge of China proper is marked by a range of mountains
which begin just north of present-day Beijing 北京 , and which are
pierced by a number of passes. These were naturally the focus of
northern defence preparations in imperial China, and the fortified
passes came to signify the northern borders of China. However, meanings with roots in the sense of 'doorway' coexisted, so *guan* could be
used as a verb meaning 'pass through' and 'traverse'. Perhaps the most
telling usages are those meaning 'customs collection point' and 'customs
duty', both of which go back to the earliest surviving Chinese writings.
Guan were not only strongholds that could be closed off, but could also
be places of peaceful entry for necessary and profitable purposes. This
word was the second most commonly used for 'frontier' in the six
relevant histories – since *guan* also came to mean 'pass', it occurs in
many place-names – suggesting that perhaps those using it were
thinking of their frontiers less in terms of lines than as a series of
fortified points of ingress and egress: defensive when the need

arose, but at other times allowing for passage back and forth, and for exchange.

A more diffuse view of frontiers was also encouraged by the tendency of government to focus on the control of people rather than on territory for its own sake. Although territorial authority was crucial in the pre-imperial period ending with China's first unification in 221 BC, by 150 years later, a 'fief' no longer conferred territory but a number of households on which the lord could levy taxes.[7] Land was only involved inasmuch as people needed it to grow the grain with which to pay their dues. Hence, as reflected in the vocabulary, Chinese rulers were perpetually concerned with extending central authority over the inhabitants of their frontier zones.

Thus Chinese words for 'frontier' were of very early date, and offered many options for ways of seeing the border and borderlands. In the tenth century AD the words most commonly used for 'frontier' were those suggesting the idea of a peripheral region, a place defensible, but also one of (carefully controlled) contact with outsiders. Although terminology for the idea of a delineated frontier remained available, in this period it was less often used.

North China at the beginning of the Tenth Century[8]

The period of Chinese history from the mid eighth to the mid eleventh centuries – the 'Tang-Song transition' – was a crucial period of change. The basic trends of the period are a shift in the basis of political and social power from aristocratic to bureaucratic, with an accompanying rise in imperial authority; agricultural developments bringing a 'commercial revolution' and technological advance in their wake; a 'civilianising' of a culture and administration that formerly had strong martial elements; and the development of an intellectual orthodoxy which spread down from the elite to popular level, and was to remain in place for the remainder of the imperial period. The tenth century – from the last years of the Tang 唐 (618–907), through the Five Dynasties 五代 (907–60), and into the founding reigns of the Northern Song 北宋 (960–1126) – is particularly important in the process of change, and had many parallels with early medieval Europe.

The Five Dynasties stands at the end of a long period during which military interests were dominant. In the last years of the seventh century, the defence needs of the northern frontier led to the

establishment of a system of frontier governors who controlled large
provinces, and who wielded civil as well as military authority: a departure from the Chinese imperial tradition of separation of powers.[9] A
major rebellion in 755 led to a fragmentation of authority, formalised at
the beginning of the tenth century when the Tang empire split into a
number of independent states coexisting in the south, and a succession
of regimes – the Five Dynasties – in north China which claimed to be
continuators of the imperial tradition. North China was itself fragmented, especially in the first quarter of the century (see Map 3.2),
between provincial governors exercising full civil and military authority, and with extensive powers of appointment. Emperors were heavily
reliant upon their support, and in many cases were little more than
glorified provincial governors themselves. 'Internal' borders could thus
be just as important as 'external' frontiers, if not more so. However, it
was the 'external' frontier between just two parties – the Chinese and
the Kitan 契丹 – that came to be of more significance in the course of the
tenth century.

The north China governors and the people they led were of several
different ethnic categories, notably the Kitan, the Shatuo Turks 沙陀,
and the 'Han' 漢 Chinese. Differences between the Shatuo and the Han
are minimised in the sources because three of the Five Dynasties were
led by Shatuo. The Kitan were more distinctive. They founded a
Chinese-style dynasty, called Liao 遼 (907–1125), and became one of the
major powers in tenth- to twelfth-century east Asia. The Chinese
sources stereotype the Kitan as 'barbarians' constantly waiting for
China to be weak enough to conquer; feared because of their nomadic
way of life. Most Kitan were indeed pastoralists who followed
their sheep, cattle, and horses from one grazing area to the next in
accordance with the season. However, many of them grew crops during
some of these sojourns, they hunted and fished, and they practised
certain crafts. Their diet naturally included a great deal of meat and
dairy products.[10] By contrast, the majority of Chinese were accustomed to a settled life in villages close to towns, with a diet consisting
largely of grain (millet in the north, rice in the south) and vegetables,
with meat only as a luxury and no dairy products. Urban life played a
significant role, with towns acting primarily as administrative centres
for the government, but also as centres for artisans and the educated
elite, and for the distribution of agricultural surpluses via a network of
markets. Dress and dwellings also reflected these differing economic
bases.

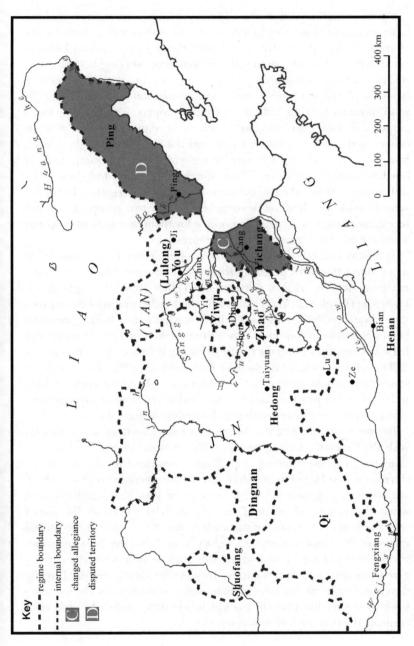

Map 3.2 North China in 907.

Yet these marked differences did not preclude contact, indeed, there is an argument that these specific economic differences actively *require* contact.[11] Certainly the Kitan had been dealing with various Chinese courts since at least the sixth century, sometimes seeking help in internecine conflicts, sometimes posing a military threat, and sometimes being employed in Chinese armies. It was common for Kitan leaders to send missions bearing 'tribute' to Chinese courts, whether they be of emperor or local governor, and to receive in return generous 'gifts': in other words, they conducted trade, and not only at this highest level, but also with ordinary Chinese and government representatives at border markets, whenever Chinese emperors permitted these. The differences between the two cultures should not be forgotten, but at the same time the depth of the cleavage between the two groups should not be exaggerated: it was perfectly possible for them to coexist throughout a remarkably large range of circumstances.[12]

Everyday contacts across a relatively open frontier were significant in enabling this, and probably the most important location for such exchange was the region north of the Yellow River (*Huanghe* 黃河), known as Hebei 河北, and particularly the northernmost of these provinces, Youzhou 幽州. This was centred on what is now Beijing, and had been essentially autonomous since the rebellion of 755. Through the lives of Youzhou's governors, and particularly that of one Zhao Dejun 趙德鈞, who governed Youzhou for over a decade (925–36), we can see something of how the northern frontiers of early tenth-century China were defined in practice, and how the realities of frontier management related to and interacted with the theoretical definitions.

Between 706 and 822 the Tang court had negotiated seven treaties with the Tibetans, paying considerable attention to border demarcation, and probably drawing maps.[13] But a century after the last treaty, during the first half of the tenth century, it had become rare for 'central' authorities to express any such opinion (at least that survives) as to where the frontiers *should* lie. There appear to have been no discussions over the demarcation of existing borders, nor of restoring the territorial extent of the Tang dynasty in its glory days. Nevertheless, contemporaries seem to have known whose side they or others were on at any given moment, and to this extent frontiers are clearly visible. It is the development from this unmappable conceptualisation of the frontiers back to the notion that they could be centrally defined – and thus controlled – that we will now trace.

Administrative boundaries and actual authority

A claim to authority over certain areas did not always equate with real control; it merely expressed an ideal, and perhaps an intention. Furthermore, it is not always as easy as it seems to determine the exact extent of the area in question. Perhaps the most obvious way of defining the north China frontier is to take Chinese territory as being coterminous with the extent of its prefectures and counties.[14] This appears easy to do, as the dynastic histories always include a section on administrative geography, listing every district and the changes in its relative status and constituent sub-districts due to natural events, conquest, or administrative reorganisation. In fact, the listings are always given in terms of the names of the towns which acted as the administrative centre for this or that district, but there is almost no information about the actual extent of the territory administered from the town. It is, however, not uncommon for the records to note the number of households registered for taxation in the district: an excellent example of the priority of people over territory. The result is that cartographers have to use educated guesswork in drawing the boundaries of administrative districts.

Even if one could accurately plot the boundaries decreed by a central administration, the places and populations actually under the control of a representative of the central authority might be quite different. Hence Zhao Dejun is praised in some texts for recovering control of the area immediately around his provincial seat (also called Youzhou).[15] The northern part of the province had been abandoned by the garrison troops, enabling the Kitan to plunder it annually. Despite military escorts, supply convoys were often ambushed by the Kitan; one work says the governor's writ ran only to about three miles east of the city and beyond that the land had been abandoned for fear of raids.[16] Amongst other activities, Dejun fortified the favourite ambush spot, and built and garrisoned a number of fortified towns and a section of wall, allowing the local population to resume farming and herding, and enabling provisions to be transported safely. Modern maps of the province make no distinction between the situations before and after the improvements, and naturally, it was in the interests of government, both local and central, to play down any lack of control.

While minimising the extent of control difficulties, emperors also tried to maximise the apparent extent of their power by granting individuals a form of provisional authority in territory which, for instance, had been taken over by a rebel. If a governor rebelled, then the emperor might well give the leader of the expeditionary forces supervisory powers over that province. The expeditionary commander was marked as the imperial representative, and once the rebel was put down, imperial jurisdiction could be restored instantaneously. Hence when Wang Yanqiu 王晏球 was sent to crush a rebel northern governor he was, concurrently with his expeditionary command, placed 'in charge of the affairs of the . . . expeditionary army and prefectures'.[17] The ideal was clearly set out: making it real was another matter altogether.

Fortification and accommodation

Unsurprisingly, fortifications played an important part in securing the frontier (from within as well as without), but non-military methods had their place too. In the early tenth century, as in the Tang, fortifications were discrete structures defending 'strategic places' such as passes, river crossings, and so on. It seems from the terminology that these defences were mostly fortified towns. This implies a civilian population living alongside the soldiery and, doubtless, trading with their neighbours regardless of whether or not they came under Chinese imperial authority. Zhao Dejun's defences seem typical, including as they did the walling of existing towns and the establishment of new walled towns with garrisons. Although nothing on the scale of the Ming Great Wall was built in the tenth century, northern Chinese governors such as Zhao Dejun constructed short sections of wall, as did the Liao.[18] Dejun's wall section shows that they could be effective defences in certain circumstances, although how they were actually used against a mounted enemy which could surely have easily ridden around them is a matter which remains to be researched.

A series of such varied defences could give an idea of where a central authority felt its jurisdiction had its limits, but it should not be taken as an indication that the centre was trying to define a frontier *line* as such; such fortifications formed, at best, a disconnected chain located according to strategic considerations rather than an attempt to draw a line around 'China'. On those rare occasions when treaties were agreed, as between Tang and Tibet, the defence provisions for particularly problematical frontier locations often included the creation of a dead zone – not only demilitarised but also depopulated – between opposing fortifications.[19] These were thus sited away from any notional limits on authority, and within the territory under the jurisdiction of one side or the other. Dejun's fortifications all lay well within the notional boundaries of his province, but were clearly regarded as frontier defences nevertheless. In an important sense provisions like this constituted a defence in depth, but given that a defining characteristic of a Chinese town is that it has a wall, such urbanised defences should not be seen as part of any kind of 'frontier policy', but simply the use of the town wall for its original purpose.

Dejun's defences illustrate another factor: although they were built to defend the population of Youzhou against external threats, such protective measures were also an important way in which Dejun secured his administrative authority *within* his own province. Dejun's defences clearly improved the security and confidence of the common people in particular, which would naturally have benefited Dejun's local government by increasing tax revenues, while giving the central authority more of the frontier security it sought.[20] He also argued at court for central measures which would help to prevent raids, adding his voice to those against the release of some 50 Kitan commanders captured while aiding a rebel governor, believing that their retention was preventing major Kitan incursions.[21]

But military measures were not the only means to this end. At the same time that Dejun was improving his anti-Kitan defences and arguing the case for keeping hostages, he was also in formal contact with the Kitan central authorities through the exchange of envoys. In 926 Dejun informed the court that the Kitan ruler had given him a mink robe, and subsequently he passed on another Liao envoy's report of the same ruler's death.[22] In January 932 he received 'an edict' from Liao, and in August he sent them 'the fruits of the season'.[23] These were perfectly normal exchanges at a time when the various regimes of the region were accustomed to exchanging envoys, and thus gifts.[24] It seems that Dejun acted as the formal channel to the Chinese court for the Liao, and this fits with earlier evidence that Kitan embassies en route to the Central Plains courts always stopped off at Youzhou, leaving behind most of their personnel to trade until the remainder of the party returned.[25] Hence the Liao-Youzhou envoy contacts were probably intended not least as another method of improving frontier security. Dejun was presumably trying to encourage the Liao emperor to keep his tribesmen in check (something the emperor could not always achieve). The Liao emperors quite possibly sought to persuade Dejun not to retaliate with counter-raids (which certain Youzhou governors had done in the past), and probably more importantly, to keep open channels for cross-border trade. Although in the latter part of the century Chinese emperors increasingly tried to control such trade, both they and frontier governors like Dejun always recognised its value, particularly in keeping the peace. The frontier was thus maintained at a local level, through a mixture of military and peaceful, political and economic methods.

The individual practice of personal loyalty

Despite the vital importance of arrangments on the ground for the creation and maintenance of a frontier between neighbouring powers, for the central authorities of north China in the early tenth century (as earlier) what mattered were not the details of how the frontier was maintained, but whether there was a frontier at all. In other words, whether the frontier governors gave their individual allegiances to the imperial court or to one of its enemies. This was a period when 'emperors' could not hold their positions without the support of powerful and semi-autonomous regional governors, and also one in which alternative sources of legitimating authority were readily available just across the many political borders that existed at the time. In such a climate the decisions of an individual – who could be far more junior than a provincial governor – could have significant, even dramatic, effects on the frontiers between the state to which he owed allegiance and its neighbours. Numerous examples in the histories for the first half of the tenth century show that a leader with administrative authority could take his population with him whomever he served.[26] 'Central' authority over the territory was removed from one regime and granted instead to a (usually) adjacent regime. Hence when a leader decided to offer his allegiance to a different ruler, his change of master affected not just him and his immediate entourage, but the border line between the two powers concerned. An individual leader could effectively take the border line with him as he crossed from one allegiance to another. Loyalty in the early tenth century was a major defining factor in determining where a political border ran at any given moment, and could thus have effects which could determine the course of events at the centre of the 'empire'.

Here are just two examples. The independent frontier prince of the Taiyuan Jin 太原晉 (895–923) appears to have made an agreement with the Kitan Liao court in 916, but Jin and Liao were driven into conflict when a Jin official, Lu Wenjin 盧文進, killed his governor and took his army over to Liao allegiance.[27] Wenjin became a frontier governor under the Liao, but ten years later took his province and a huge army back to Chinese allegiance.[28] The Kitan and Chinese emperors agreed a peace, but the Liao still retook the province by force.[29] During the war between the Liao and the Five Dynasties regime of Later Jin 後晉 (936–47), one Sun Fangjian 孫方簡 established an independent power in the small province centred on Dingzhou 定州, then technically part of the Liao regime. The Kitan held the Jin responsible for Fangjian's actions, and launched a new attack. Fangjian placed himself, and thus his province, under the Liao, but when they tried to transfer him from Dingzhou he returned once again to Chinese allegiance, helping to bolster the newly established Later Han 後漢 (947–50), the fourth of the Five Dynasties.[30] These examples give some idea of the extent to which the changing allegiances of individuals operating in frontier territories acted as a driving force in the 'central' politics of the time by modifying the line of the political border. As they crossed and recrossed what we might call the 'loyalty frontier', so in a very real sense were they responsible for creating the political border in all its volatility.

Changing Conceptions of the Frontier

However, this situation was about to change. While being instrumental in creating and locating the political and loyalty frontiers, governors simultaneously had responsibilities arising from their chosen position on one side of the 'line' or the other. To a significant extent the centre was reliant on its frontier governors to maintain the external security of the entire regime. Imperial armies could be dispatched in response to particularly serious raids, or 'pacification commissioners' appointed, but in the early tenth century it was almost always the case that such armies were led, and such posts were held, by frontier governors. However, the corollary of gubernatorial military power and independence was that internal security depended on them too. Frontier governors had the responsibility of keeping raiders and invaders out of the Central Plains, but had to be kept happy enough that they did not use their military might to seek the throne for themselves. When courts failed to do this, emperors could fall and, as new leaders sought military backing and political legitimation, not only the line but the definition of and attitude towards the frontiers could change too. The replacement of the Later Tang 後唐 (923–36) with the Later Jin illustrates some such changes.

By 929 the Five Dynasties' regime of Later Tang had greatly reduced

the number of autonomous powers operating in north China, and by
932 both Youzhou and Hedong 河東 (west of Youzhou) were governed
by long-standing members of the emperor's retinue, Zhao Dejun and
Shi Jingtang 石敬瑭. Between them they controlled the whole of the
Later Tang's northern frontier. In 933 the emperor died, and his
eventual replacement was suspicious of the frontier governors he had
inherited. In 936 he tried to transfer Jingtang from Hedong, and
Jingtang rebelled, seeking help from the Kitan in a bid for the throne.
Jingtang's allies besieged the Later Tang expeditionary army, and
Dejun was made commander-in-chief of a relief force. The besieged
army eventually surrendered, after which the Liao emperor Taizong 太
宗 invested Jingtang as emperor of Later Jin. In return Jingtang promised annual payments and handed over title to several frontier districts.
Dejun meanwhile tried to extract a governorship for his son from the
Tang court and when this failed, he too turned to the Liao, seeking the
north China throne. Despite his commitment to Jingtang, Liao Taizong
was tempted by Dejun's offer, which included more military muscle
than Jingtang could muster, but in the end he stuck to his agreement
with Jingtang. Dejun died in Liao captivity, a broken man.[31]

These events illustrate the practical effects of changing understandings of the frontier. To the end of his life, Dejun continued
to live by the understanding with which he and Jingtang had grown up.
Dejun's political loyalties, like those of most of his contemporaries, were
focused chiefly on personal relationships with more or less charismatic
leaders, some of whom became emperors. If this relationship had any
beneficial effects for the empire, this was largely a coincidence of service
to the lord. Hence Dejun's defence of his province secured the frontier
of the empire and was thus of general benefit to the regime, but only
because Dejun's lord happened to be the emperor. Dejun himself
clearly did not feel enough attachment to the empire itself, let alone
anything we might call 'China', to prevent him from seeking foreign
help if the situation demanded it. While loyalties based on personal
relationships were often maintained through the original lord's descendants, the political 'line' of the frontier was something that could be
disregarded if circumstances required. When it became clear that the
Later Tang would collapse, Dejun could reasonably expect, under the
old dispensation, that at the very least he could offer his allegiance, and
thus his province of Youzhou, to the Liao, and that he would remain as
governor under his new masters, having taken the frontier line with
him. Unfortunately for Dejun, by the time he tried to do this the world

had already begun to change around him, and central to that change was a redefinition of what constituted the frontier.[32]

That redefinition came about because Jingtang had changed the rules. Seeking help from the Kitan was unexceptional enough, but this was usually in the form of hiring cavalry in relatively small numbers, not the 50 000 or more which placed Jingtang on the throne and left his own forces sitting on the sidelines. More important was Jingtang's gift of the frontier districts known as the Sixteen Prefectures (highlighted on Map 3.3), which included the whole of Youzhou.[33] The effect on Dejun was to deprive him of legitimate authority, so that instead of being able to carry the border line with him as he took his allegiance northwards, he found that the line had already been moved over his head. Hence when he offered his allegiance to the Liao, he did so, unknowingly, as an individual.

But the ramifications of Jingtang's action went far beyond its effects on a particular governor. Giving away the Sixteen Prefectures was not the same as the standard practice of granting provisional administrative authority to a general sent to recover a rebel district on the emperor's behalf. Nor was it the same as giving up strategically significant but otherwise dead territory. The gift of the Sixteen Prefectures was effected by the handover of the population registers, showing that Jingtang was surrendering full control of the districts in question; in other words, control of populations, together with the tax revenue they provided. Unlike in the long-standing relationship between Chinese imperial courts and their provincial governors, there was no question of Jingtang attempting to undermine Kitan authority in their new possessions by appointing his own officials wherever he could.[34] Unlike in the granting of a fief, the Kitan emperor had no obligation of loyalty towards Jingtang, and it was clear that Jingtang was not going to recover authority over these districts once his allies had taken them. He handed over administrative districts, complete with officials and the populations that gave the land its value, and gave them to someone acknowledged to be outside the control of the 'Chinese' world. In this Jingtang was doing something apparently new: he was surrendering *territory* in the fullest sense of the word. But he might not have realised initially the import of his action; in any case he changed his mind shortly after ascending the throne, because he tried to buy the Prefectures back with extra annual payments, an offer which Liao Taizong refused.[35] If Shi Jingtang regretted the change he had initiated, it was already too late to turn back.

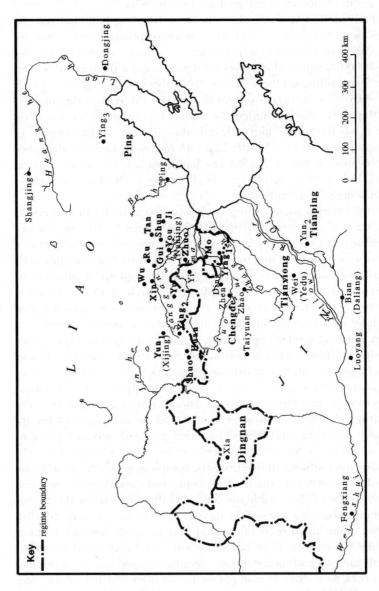

Map 3.3 North China in 938, showing the Sixteen Prefectures.

The court definition of the frontier

Thereafter we can trace an increasing consciousness of the frontier as something which divides; a consciousness that parallels the increasing authority of the Chinese state. The continuing alliance between the Liao and Later Jin removed the major source of alternative authority which could have brought success to the many rebels against Jingtang's rule, and was thus a major factor not just in bringing Jingtang to the throne, but also in keeping him there. This was cross-border accommodation on a wholly other level. Nevertheless, there were misgivings, and certain interests at court were keen to provoke war with the Liao as soon as Jingtang died. That war ended in the brief Liao conquest of the Central Plains in 947, after which there begins to be evidence that issues of identity were growing in importance such that a new 'ethnic frontier' was created where previously there had been none.[36] Liu Zhiyuan 劉知遠 lamented that 'the barbarians have invaded and insulted us, . . . they have made the provincial governors give their adherence to foreigners',[37] and went on to found the Later Han under a banner of shared identification in the Central Plains. The Later Zhou 後周 (951–59) and Northern Song emperors encouraged the perception of difference between 'Chinese' and 'barbarians' as part of their efforts to strengthen their own states from within by defining their boundaries more clearly. Hence Zhou Shizong 周世宗 banned his people from raiding the Liao borders for profit, and continual discussion of how to handle the problem of the northern 'barbarians' accompanied the Zhou and Song conquests of the south China states.

This discussion of the north while actually dealing with the south became increasingly curious. The Zhou emperors divided their fighting time between their neighbours to north and south, the Northern Han 北漢 (951–79, a continuation of the Later Han) and the Southern Tang 南唐 (937–76). By contrast, the founding emperors of the Song concentrated first on bringing the south back under central control, while almost ignoring the northern frontier. Thus they effectively stated where they believed China *should* be. There were practical economic reasons for this policy, but the Liao also posed a real threat, through backing the aggressions of the Northern Han. The Song focus on the south reflects a significant change in attitude and approach to the northern frontier, already noticeable in the growing emphasis on the 'foreignness' of peoples such as the Kitan. More tangibly, institutional changes initiated by the emperors of Later Tang and Later Jin had by now begun to bear fruit, with military power increasingly removed from the hands of provincial, and particularly frontier, governors, and vested instead in the hands of the emperor himself, or of his intimates at court.[38] The fact that the first four of the Five Dynasties were established by governors or princes from the frontier, while the last of the Five, and the Song, were founded by commanders-in-chief of the imperial armies, speaks volumes for the change that took place. Yet even as the manifold real frontiers, and those who lived there, were being denied their former significance as the engines of political events within the Chinese regimes, the *idea* of 'The Frontier' was coming to be of more importance to those – at court – who now held actual political power. Gradually the centre managed to reify its own conception of the frontier to the exclusion of all others; this reflected a general increase in central control, but was also significant in bringing it about. In some sense then, we can say that whoever had control of the northern frontiers – whether locally or conceptually – was the dominant force in tenth-century north China politics.

The culmination of this reification process was the treaty of Shanyuan 澶淵, agreed in 1005, that ended the long wars between Liao and Song. The treaty has been described as establishing 'a genuine international frontier in the modern sense, something unprecedented in China's history',[39] but it also shares certain features with some of the Tang-Tibetan treaties of the eighth and ninth centuries. Like the earlier agreements, Shanyuan laid down a mappable frontier line that clarified under whose jurisdiction inhabitants of the frontier zone should live. The division was probably still based on populations rather than on a more arbitrary line of demarcation; it was not possible to draw a boundary line that divided a settlement between administrative districts. Yet the 1005 treaty also marks a change in conceptions of the frontier, not least because it lasted: Song and Liao enjoyed a century of peace, maintained through regular envoy exchanges.[40] The treaty included a statement that both sides would return fugitives from justice, as had the earlier treaties, but whereas continual war between Tang and Tibet made a nonsense of such promises, the same provision in Shanyuan was adhered to right from the start, preventing the return home of the captured Song general, Wang Jizhong 王繼忠.[41] The treaty thus sealed the frontier through an effective and lasting agreement between two central powers that necessarily acknowledged the other's legitimate and permanent existence. At the same time, the treaty sought to prevent future raids by granting annual payments to the Kitan, and also made provision for official border markets. These markets were essential to maintaining peace, but they also pierced the neat dividing 'lines' established by other provisions. The border was closed to those who would cross it permanently, even as it opened portals for the peaceful prosecution of trade. Yet this may not have been a problem. The fact that Wang Jizhong asked to go home illustrates a strong sense of 'belonging' on one side or the other, contrasting with the easy side-changing of a century before. Such identification with a 'homeland' meant the political line was easier to define and maintain because it chimed with the feelings of significant groups in the population.

The border produced by the treaty was still the frontier of discrete defended places allowing ingress and egress suggested by the vocabulary discussed above, and in many ways the old frontier mechanisms had simply been institutionalised. But this institutionalisation also constituted the difference from the early-tenth-century understandings of the frontier. Institutionalisation meant not only permanence but centralisation, and the frontier had now come under close central control in a way that would have been impossible less than a century before. Furthermore, in theory it was now unnecessary to maintain the kind of internal defences to be found in Youzhou and other places. While the treaty held, both sides kept a careful eye on the frontier troop movements of the other. Repair and maintenance of border fortifications was permitted, but any new building was interpreted as a sign of aggression. However, such activity was now met not with the dispatch of an expeditionary force, but of diplomatic envoys.[42] It is possible that in the long term, these new arrangements brought further changes in the understanding of the frontier. A hint comes from the peaceful renegotiation of the treaty in 1074–76, when the Liao attempted to push their boundary incrementally southwards, provoking intensive discussion of whether the previously agreed border line actually ran along the foot of a mountain range, or its ridge.[43] Any such negotiations between Tang and Tibet would have ended in war. In the tenth century they would have been not only impossible but beyond comprehension. By the eleventh century two central authorities could negotiate their border line secure in the knowledge that their agreement really would determine practice at the frontier.

Historiographical Definitions of the Frontier

Efforts to define the frontier did not stop with the practical and political: historians played a crucial role too. The records used to construct the above picture of the various frontiers found in tenth-century north

China are almost entirely official written histories. These are usually at
least two recensions from the directly contemporaneous material, none
of which now survives.[44] The oldest account of the period to 960 comes
from one such 'dynastic history', the *Jiu Wudai shi* 舊五代史 [*Old History
of the Five Dynasties*] completed in 974.[45] Although dynastic histories
were intended to provide the definitive account of a dynasty, a strongly
revisionist tendency amongst China's official classes during the second
half of the eleventh century produced dissatisfaction with the *Old History*, and it was rewritten as the *Xin Wudai shi* 新五代史 [*New History of the
Five Dynasties*] (1073), with an emphasis on passing clear moral judgments.[46] At about the same time, the same material was taken as the
basis for part of a court-sponsored universal history, also written from
within the new moralising mindset. This work, the *Zizhi tongjian* 資治通
鑑 (1084), is beautifully written and provides a clear narrative.[47] It is
highly influential, being used in the compilation of many later works,
and its versions of events, as well as its judgments, have frequently been
accepted at face value. Doing this overlooks the ways in which the
process of rewriting altered the accounts, and thus the effect these
alterations can have on the understanding of events as conveyed by the
text. Such changes were not merely matters of collation or cosmetics,
but had a significance of their own: they could alter the story, and
sometimes even create it.

   This is particularly apparent when we consider the question of loyalty, for which the *Old History* of 974 presents a far more nuanced view
than the later works. Loyalty was one of the cardinal Confucian vir-
tues,[48] but as we have seen, in the early tenth century it appears to have
been defined individually and pragmatically, and had nothing to do
with ethnic groupings: Han Chinese could serve Kitan or Shatuo without concern on either side. During the second half of the century there
appears to be a shift in perceptions among the elite themselves as to
where their allegiances should lie, encouraged, if not initiated, by central government, as discussed above. Han Chinese now felt decidedly
uncomfortable at the prospect of taking service with the Kitan 'Other',
and Chinese identity began to be a consideration in an individual's
decision-making process. This is exemplified by the case of the unfortunate Wang Jizhong, trapped in Liao by the terms of the treaty he
helped to negotiate. The Song elite, at least, was increasingly conscious
that loyalty was due to that dynasty and none other. Oddly, though,
there is some reason for supposing that the common people were
consistently more interested in maintaining their allegiances than were

members of the ruling groups. The latter could be tempted by choices or possibilities that commoners never faced.[49]

This attitudinal shift is revealed by the *Old History*, which provides the strongest evidence that those taking service with the Liao in the early tenth century were not concerned about any Han Chinese identity they may have had. It seems that they probably were conscious of possessing such an identity (and one even declares it), but this awareness does not become a factor influencing their actions (although it could be useful when negotiating terms and conditions). In the eleventh-century texts, however, the authors have edited and altered their sources for the early tenth century so as to emphasise those aspects of individual stories suggesting their subjects' continued identification as Han Chinese, even though they have transferred all other allegiances to the foreign court.[50] This represents an effort to explain actions which were, by the eleventh century, incomprehensible to court-based officials.

Hence although the earliest empirical evidence records the messy realities of frontier life fairly faithfully, and shows the fluidity and indeterminacy of the boundaries around the north China regimes, the later texts illustrate efforts to convert this into something more like the clearly defined picture that theory had come to require. Accordingly, most of the historiography assumes that there were neat lines, and proceeds to put everybody on one side of the line or the other, regardless of the actual situation. Much subtlety, not to mention accuracy, is lost by this approach. The shift in the historiographical attitude towards the frontiers reflects the increased strength of Chinese central authority by the time the eleventh-century texts were written. Whereas the earlier material shows that real people, and especially those living on the frontier, were relatively relaxed about the frontier 'line' in the early part of the century, but became more concerned to maintain it by the end, in the eleventh century the centre demanded tidy definitions, and tidy, easily categorised behaviour to match, and these were applied to the whole of the tenth century, as if no change had occurred.

Thus, if it were not for the historiography drawing ever clearer distinctions between who was loyal and who was not, then we would not have anything like such a clear picture of where the frontier lay in this period. It might appear, for instance, that Youzhou was in fact more independent than it is generally taken to be, thus forming a greater continuity with its eighth- and ninth-century history. More significantly, the strength and independence of the Taiyuan Jin is downplayed by present-day historians, and yet their power is unavoidably apparent even in the eleventh-century sources. It was in the interests of even the earliest historians of the tenth century to conceal such independence because all the Five Dynasties, not to mention subsequent regimes, were concerned to claim the northern frontier zone as their own. Hence we might argue that, in several real senses, it is the historiography that creates the frontier.

Conclusion

During the tenth century north China had multiple frontiers defined by accommodation, negotiation, personal relationships, local treaties, and defences. Frontiers founded on such bases were essentially ephemeral because they depended on relations between individuals and so were subject to constant change. Nevertheless, contemporaries in the frontier zones lived their daily lives according to these definitions, without regard for ideology. Such frontier praxis is reflected in the terminology that existed to name the frontier. Developments at the north China frontier and in the Chinese state fed each other: as the state exercised more real control, so the existence of the frontiers came more to the fore, and as consciousness of the frontiers grew such that people began to act upon it, so the state had more justification for increased control within the limits defined by those frontiers. Furthermore, as the Chinese state recovered strength, so it developed a theoretical under-pinning – reflected in much of the surviving record of this period – to justify its increased control. But in the end, the image of the frontier conveyed by its historiographical construction and reconstruction is infinitely more lasting than any picture we can painstakingly build of the real complexities involved. The myth of a clear and continuous frontier of separation between 'China' and her northern neighbours – the myth of the Great Wall – lives on.

NOTES

1. The ecological basis for this division is stressed by O. Lattimore, 'Origins of the Great Wall of China: a frontier concept in theory and practice', *Geographical Review*, XXVII, 4 (1937), repr. *Studies in Frontier History: collected papers 1928–58*, London 1962, 97–118.
2. A. Waldron, *The Great Wall of China: from history to myth*, Cambridge 1990.
3. Etymologies derived from *GSR*; *Shuowen jiezi zhu* 説文解字注 , comp. Xu

Shen 許慎, Shanghai 1981; *Hanyu da cidian* 漢語大詞典, ed. Meng Zhufeng 夢竹風 et al., Shanghai 1986–94.

4. 田 *tian* itself shows enclosed and divided spaces. J. Needham, *Science and Civilisation in China*, III. *Mathematics and the Sciences of the Heavens and the Earth*, Cambridge 1970, 497.

5. *GSR*, 244; Needham, *Science and Civilisation*, 498, thinks this mouth refers to 'eaters'.

6. Excluding *feng* 封, which most commonly referred to granting control of territory or households in return for service.

7. J. Gernet, *A History of Chinese Civilisation*, trans. J. R. Foster, Cambridge 1982, 54–5, 116.

8. *CHC*, V. *Five Dynasties and Sung*, ed. D. Twitchett, Cambridge (forthcoming), will provide the first full narrative of the whole century. The 'Introduction' in *CHC*, VI. *Alien Regimes and Border States 907–1368*, ed. D. Twitchett and H. Franke, Cambridge 1994, gives a flavour of the period. Chapter 1 of my doctoral thesis, N. Standen, 'Frontier crossings from north China to Liao, *c.* 900–1005', University of Durham 1994, narrates Chinese-Kitan interaction during the whole century. Wang Gungwu, *The Structure of Power in North China During the Five Dynasties*, Stanford 1963, covers institutional changes to 947; E. H. Worthy, Jr., 'The founding of Sung China, 950–1000: integrative changes in military and political institutions', Ph.D. diss., Princeton 1976, covers later changes. The Chinese works are similarly split between the dynasties.

9. *CHC*, III. *Sui and T'ang China 589–906, pt. 1*, ed. D. Twitchett, Cambridge 1979, ch. 8.

10. K. A. Wittfogel and Feng Jiasheng, *History of Chinese Society: Liao (907–1125)*, Philadelphia 1949, 115–20, 126n, 141–2.

11. S. Jagchid and J. Van Simmons, *Peace, War and Trade along the Great Wall*, Indiana 1989; T. J. Barfield, *The Perilous Frontier: nomadic empires and China, 221 BC to AD 1757*, Oxford 1989. Xiongnu and Kitan economic bases may not have been as similar as these authors imply, see N. Di Cosmo, 'Ancient Inner Asian nomads: their economic basis and its significance in Chinese history', *JAS*, LIII (1994), 1092–1126.

12. See J. A. Armstrong, *Nations before Nationalism*, Chapel Hill 1982, ch. 2.

13. Pan Yihong, 'The Sino-Tibetan treaties in the T'ang dynasty', *T'oung Pao*, LXXVIII (1992), 116–61.

14. As in *Zhongguo lishi ditu ji* 中國歷史地圖集 [*The Historical Atlas of China*], ed. Tan Qixiang 譚其驤 et al., V–VI, Shanghai 1982.

15. The fullest account is *XW*, 72:892.

16. *TJ*, 278:9076.

17. *JW*, 39:538.

18. *LS*, 1:3.

19. Pan, 'Sino-Tibetan treaties', 139–40.

20. Any increase in revenues may not have been passed on to the court. Wang, *Structure of Power*, 139–40.

21. *JW*, 43:591; *TJ*, 277:9067.

22. *CFYG*, 980:23a, 24a–b, reprod. *QTW*, 849:15b.

23. *LS*, 3:33–4.

24. Lin Ronggui 林榮貴 and Chen Liankai 陳連開, 'Wudai Shiguo shiqi Qidan, Shatuo, Hanzu de zhengzhi, jingji he wenhua jiaoliu' 五代十國時期契丹、沙陀、漢族的政治、經濟和文化交流 [The political, economic and cultural contacts between the Kitan, Shatuo and Han during the Five Dynasties and Ten Kingdoms], *Liao Jin shi lunji* 遼金史論集, III, ed. Chen Shu 陳述, Beijing 1987, esp. 168–70.

25. *CHC*, VI, 50.

26. Standen, 'Frontier crossings', Table 1, lists all moves to Liao service.

27. *TJ*, 269:8811–270:8819; *JW*, 28:389–90, 137:1828–9; *LS*, 1:11–12.

28. *TJ*, 275:8994; *JW*, 37:511.

29. *TJ*, 276:9013; *JW*, 39:533.

30. *TJ*, 285:9303–4, 287:9371–2, 288:9389; *JW*, 84:1115, 100:1336, 1347–8; *LS*, 4:57.

31. *JW*, 32:445, 43:596, 44:610–46:631, 47:659–48:668; 75:983–92; 98:1308–10; *XW*, 72:893–4; *TJ*, 273:8930, 278:9079–80, 9095–102, 279:9103–16, 9131–7, 280:9138–61; *LS*, 3:38–9, 76:1247.

32. Dejun's case is the subject of Standen, 'Frontiers without maps: loyalty and historiography in the life of a Chinese governor', forthcoming.

33. The Sixteen Prefectures were You 幽, Ji 薊, Ying$_1$ 瀛, Mo 莫, Zhuo 涿, Tan 檀, Shun 順, Xin 新, Gui 媯, Ru 儒, Wu 武, Yun$_1$ 雲, Ying$_2$ 應, Huan 寰, Shuo 朔 and Yu 蔚 (*TJ*, 280:9154).

34. Cf. Wang, *Structure of Power*, ch. 7.

35. *LS*, 3:41.

36. N. Standen, 'The disappearance of a frontier region: the Liao and the borders of tenth-century north China', *Selected Papers of the 10th Biannual Conference, European Association for Chinese Studies*, Prague 1996, unpaginated.

37. *TJ*, 286:9339.

38. Wang, *Structure of Power*, Worthy, 'Founding of Sung'.

39. *CHC*, VI, 110. Also C. Schwarz-Schilling, *Der Friede von Shan Yüan (1005 n. Chr.)*, Wiesbaden 1959.

40. M. Ang, 'Sung-Liao diplomacy in eleventh- and twelfth-century China: a study of the social and political determinants of foreign policy', Ph.D. diss., University of Pennsylvania 1983; D. C. Wright, 'Sung-Liao diplomatic practices', Ph.D. diss., Princeton University 1993.

41. Standen, 'Frontier crossings', ch. 7.

42. Ang, 'Sung-Liao diplomacy'.

43. K. Tietze, 'The Liao Song border conflict of 1074–1076', *Studia Sino-Mongolica: Festschrift für Herbert Franke*, ed. W. Bauer, Wiesbaden 1979, 127–51.

44. D. C. Twitchett, *The Writing of Official History under the T'ang*, Cambridge 1992; Yang Lien-sheng, 'The organisation of Chinese official historiography: principles and methods of the standard histories from the T'ang through the Ming dynasty', *Historians of China and Japan*, ed. W. G. Beasley and E. G. Pulleyblank, London 1961, 44–59.

45. *Jiu Wudai shi* 舊五代史, comp. Xue Juzheng 薛居正 et al., Beijing 1976.

46. *Xin Wudai shi* 新五代史, Ouyang Xiu 歐陽修, Beijing 1974.

47. *Zizhi tongjian* 資治通鑑 [*Comprehensive Mirror to Aid in Government*], Sima Guang 司馬光 et al., Beijing 1956.
48. Standen, 'Frontier crossings', ch. 8, surveys practical definitions of loyalty up to the early Song.
49. *Ibid.*, 91.
50. *Ibid.*, 280–3.

4

THE BYZANTINE FRONTIER AT THE LOWER DANUBE IN THE LATE TENTH AND ELEVENTH CENTURIES

Paul Stephenson

The Byzantine frontier in the Balkans appears on modern maps as a line of demarcation.[1] The linear frontier in the textbook joins the furthest points where, at a given time, the emperor could exercise his political will, and where his right to do so was recognised. It represents an attempt by modern scholars to measure the extent of the Byzantine empire at a given point in time, and to represent this in a manner intelligible to a modern audience. The spatial and political qualities of the linear frontier are familiar to both scholars and their audience, and therefore certain ideas can be transmitted with the minimum disruption to the historical narrative. The linear frontier can advance or retreat according to the prevailing political circumstances, graphically underlining the twists and turn of fate that are outlined by the sources. Moreover, scholars may legitimately believe that they are recreating the situation as it was perceived by the subjects of their narratives. Sources often refer to peace treaties, and, although not in the case of the lower Danube, the texts of treaties have survived which refer to areas of political influence and, very often, to a negotiated, linear division between them. Therefore, much scholarship has proceeded from the justifiable, although rarely explicitly justified, premise that linear frontiers are common to medieval and modern societies, and that consequently 'the frontier element [in any situation can] speak for itself'.[2] The reader will be aware that one purpose of this volume is to question that premise, to explore the notion of what constitutes a frontier, how it was perceived by the characters in our histories, and how their perceptions differ from our own.

The Frontier in Byzantine Sources

Byzantine authors often refer to frontiers, but do not attempt a definition.[3] The only definition of which I am aware is contained in the Byzantine dictionary, the *Souda*, which states that 'the zones near the edges (*termasi*) of the lands are called *eschatia*, which are bounded by a mountain or the sea'.[4] Although compiled in the tenth century, this is a record of the situation which prevailed in the later third century.[5] Further specific terms appear to have been formulated in the seventh and eighth centuries to describe the empire's eastern borders.[6] This was a period of retrenchment in Byzantium, and the terms are essentially defensive. Significantly, they suggest that the frontier was perceived both as a region and as a political boundary which defined the limits of imperial territory in relation to the Muslim lands beyond.[7] Three notable terms are used in the *De Administrando Imperio*, which was compiled shortly after 950, and written for the most part in Greek as it was spoken in the tenth century.[8] The first term, *synoros*, means simply 'bordering on'.[9] The second, *akra*, is most plainly translated as 'the extremity', although it can also mean the top of a hill, and hence came to mean a citadel.[10] The third term, *horothesia*, describes the action of fixing the boundary, *horos* or *horion*, often by setting up stones.[11] Both *horos* and *horion* are used frequently by Anna Comnena, writing in the mid twelfth century, to refer to a fixed linear border, such as a river, or in the context of a peace treaty.[12] In a similar context Anna also uses *horisma* to refer to the boundaries of the empire.[13]

The term *akra* is used regularly in sources of the tenth century and later. The author of the *De velitatione bellica* offers several pieces of advice on the defence of *akra*, as does the anonymous author of the tenth-century treatise *On Skirmishing*.[14] However, the author of a contemporary treatise, *On Camp Organisation and Tactics*, uses *akra* to refer to the edge of a fortified encampment, as well as to the edge of the empire.[15] The frequent use of *akra* suggests that Byzantines, or at least Byzantine military strategists and tacticians, conceived of the frontier spatially. That is, the frontier was a region at the edge of the empire where particular defensive techniques were practised against those settled beyond the limits of the empire. This was the realm of the border guards, or *akrites*, celebrated in a genre of Byzantine poetry which has distinct parallels with the western *chansons de geste*. The most famous poem is Digenes Akrites, and the genre known as *akritic*.[16] The term *eschatia* is virtually synonymous with *akra*. It was used frequently in the sixth century by Procopius when he referred to the edges of the *Rhomaion ge*, the Roman lands.[17]

We can deduce from this brief, and far from comprehensive survey, that Byzantine authors acknowledged that the empire, the sixth-century *Rhomaion ge* or medieval *oikoumene*, had political limits which were defined by a fixed linear border (*horos* or *horion*), which might be defined physically by the erection of boundary stones (*horothesia*). The frontier was also conceived of in spatial terms, as a region which might border upon (*synoros*) another where peculiar institutions and practices were required to prevent incursions from without. However, perhaps the most interesting perceived quality of a frontier in Byzantine literature is that it was marginal and peripheral.

Frontier regions (*akra* or *eschatia*) were by definition remote from Constantinople where the vast majority of the Byzantine authors lived and wrote. This peripheral status was not merely geographical, but also cultural. For the literate elite of the capital, civilisation was the preserve of the imperial court, since the imperial household and courtiers were both the patrons and audience for their work. Thus, the terms employed to signify the frontier were not merely descriptive, but also conveyed a value judgement by the Constantinopolitan elite. Moreover, this picture is further distorted by the Byzantine practice of composing contemporary history in classical Greek, imposing an additional linguistic and cultural boundary between the signified object or feature and the chosen word or signifier.[18] For example, the Byzantine authors Michael Attaleiates and Anna Comnena both describe people dwelling at the lower Danube in the later eleventh century as *mixobarbaroi*, 'half-barbarians'.[19] Not only does this demonstrate an obvious value judgement on the part of the authors, but the deliberate use of a classical Greek word used by Euripides, Xenophon, and Plato to describe a hellenised barbarian living within the jurisdiction of Greek law.[20] This obscures the fact that the medieval distinction between *barbaroi* and *Rhomaioi*, as the Byzantines styled themselves, was no longer ethnic. According to Obolensky 'the true, distinctive mark of the *Rhomaios* was his membership of the Orthodox Church and allegiance to the emperor'.[21] As we will see below, eleventh-century *mixobarbaroi* fulfilled both these criteria of 'citizenship'. Therefore, many of the documentary sources to which we must turn for a Byzantine perspective on the empire's frontiers and frontier populations offer us a peculiarly elitist Constantinopolitan perspective further distorted through the deliberate employment of classical terminology.

The limitations of Byzantine documentary sources for studying the empire's frontiers have been exacerbated by the nature of scholarship in the Balkans. To date, there is no synthetic history of the Byzantine Balkans. Instead we must rely on occasional monographs dealing with aspects of life in medieval Rumania, Bulgaria, Serbia, Montenegro, Bosnia, Croatia, Macedonia, Albania, and Greece.[22] Academic scrutiny of the lower Danube has taken the form of a protracted debate between Bulgarian and Rumanian historians and archaeologists. For this reason, current interpretations owe more to which side of the modern frontier they were formulated than to medieval conditions. Attempts at an overview or synthesis are further inhibited by the jealously guarded borders between distinct disciplines within Byzantine studies. In the following analysis I will make use of documentary sources, as well as archaeological, numismatic, and sigillographical evidence in an attempt to cross the many modern boundaries which have delimited our knowledge of the Byzantine frontier at the lower Danube.

Byzantine Authority in the Balkans, 963–76

For the first part of the tenth century Byzantium was only the second power in the Balkans. The Bulgarian empire of Tsars Symeon (893–927) and Peter (927–69) dominated the peninsula from the Black Sea to the Adriatic (see Map 4.1). From the start of Peter's reign Byzantine-Bulgarian relations were generally harmonious, and the emperor paid the tsar an annual tribute in recognition of his efforts to prevent bands of nomadic Magyars from crossing the Danube and raiding imperial lands.[23] However, the situation beyond the Danube was often turbulent and difficult to police. In the later years of Peter's reign Magyars began, once again, to cross the river and penetrate through Bulgaria as far as Byzantine lands.

Early in his reign the emperor Nicephorus I Phocas (963–69) determined to end tribute payments to Bulgaria, and in 965 he not only dismissed a Bulgarian embassy which demanded the tribute, but scourged the ambassadors.[24] In June 967 Nicephorus moved to estab-

Map 4.1 The Balkans in the tenth century.
Reproduced by kind permission of Cambridge University Press from *Cambridge Medieval History*, 4:1, ed. J. Hussey.

lish a defensible border with Bulgaria. He made a thorough inspection of the fortifications in Thrace as far as the 'great ditch', before writing to Tsar Peter warning him not to allow further Magyar raids to reach Byzantine lands. Peter did not, or could not comply, and Magyar raids penetrated Byzantium in both 967 and 968, reaching Macedonia and the environs of Thessalonica where 500 hostages were taken.[25] Liudprand of Cremona records that 200 Magyars pressed on towards Constantinople itself.[26] Since Nicephorus was intent on returning to the East, he devised an inventive plan to punish the tsar: he raised a certain Kalokyras to the exalted rank of *patrikios* and despatched him to Cherson to bribe the Rus to attack Bulgaria with the promise of 'gifts and honours in abundance'.[27] The Rus were warrior merchants who had come to dominate the lands bordering the north coast of the Black Sea. From 911, if not 907, they had made annual journeys as far as Constantinople to sell the wares, principally slaves, they had gathered from their tributaries. By 944 the volume of trade had increased dramatically, and detailed agreements were drawn up to regulate the process of exchange.[28]

The events that followed have been the subject of much scholarly debate which I will not reprise here.[29] However, the plan backfired spectacularly when the Russian prince, Svyatoslav Igorevich, decided to settle on the lower Danube and forged an alliance with the Bulgarians. This almost certainly resulted in the assassination of Nicephorus Phocas on 11 December 969.[30] The new emperor John I Tzimiskes (969–76) committed Byzantium to the occupation of Bulgaria.

In Easter week 971 John Tzimiskes personally led his troops through the passes in the Haemus (Balkan) mountains, taking the Bulgarian defenders by surprise. Resistance evaporated in the face of the Byzantine advance, allowing the emperor to advance rapidly to the Danube, where he besieged the Rus in the city of Dristra.[31] Eventually Svyatoslav was forced to sue for peace. The *Russian Primary Chronicle* purports to present a copy of the treaty concluded at Dristra in July 971, where the Russian prince undertook to return to Kiev.[32] In fact Svyatoslav did not make it home, but was captured by Pechenegs at the Dnieper rapids: 'The nomads took his head, and made a cup out of his skull, overlaying it with gold, and they drank from it.'[33] Nevertheless, Tzimiskes took extensive precautions against a further Russian attack, instigating an active frontier defence policy at the lower Danube which replaced the failed understanding with the Bulgarian tsar.

Tzimiskes occupied and renovated Dristra, which had suffered from his protracted siege and assault. Excavations at the site have been limited by the topography of the modern city of Silistra. However, an inscription has survived which attests to the reconstruction of a church, probably between 976 and 979.[34] Clearly, a place of worship was required for the newly installed garrison, as well as the native population of the city. Tzimiskes also undertook the restoration of several late antique fortifications on the southern bank of the Danube that had long since fallen into disrepair. Excavations have uncovered his handiwork at many sites, including Capidava, Dervent, Dinogetia, Noviodunum, and Pereyaslavets (see Map 4.2).[35]

Pereyaslavets, also known as Theodoropolis, was an established centre for trade and exchange.[36] The *Russian Primary Chronicle* records that Svyatoslav had determined to settle there because 'all riches are concentrated there: golds, silks, wines and various fruits from Greece, silver and horses from Hungary and Bohemia, and from Rus, furs, wax and honey'.[37] Ongoing excavations lend conclusive support to Oikonomides's contention that we should locate Pereyaslavets at Nufărul on the St George arm of the Danube delta. Vestiges of medieval buildings have been found 800 metres from the riverbank, including the foundations of ramparts on a promontory which overlooks the Danube. At the eastern end of the promontory archaeologists have identified a semi-circular tower. The site is littered with sherds of pottery (glazed and unglazed). Both jewellery and utensils have been uncovered. However, the most significant finds are five Byzantine lead seals, and more than seven hundred Byzantine coins.[38] As an outpost of Byzantine authority and a rich entrepôt Pereyaslavets was central to the Byzantine frontier policy that I will elaborate upon below.

The most impressive development at the lower Danube was the construction of an entirely new fortified complex on the island known today as Păcuiul lui Soare, the Island of the Sun. Excavations have revealed a huge landing stage at the southeast corner of the site, above which rose a tower gateway.[39] This suggests that the complex was designed as a naval base to police the lower Danube and prevent further Russian invasions. It has been argued that the monumental structure and extensive use of marble was to symbolise an age of reconquest. However, it is possible that this signalled little more than an abundance of late antique *spolia*.[40] There is much evidence that Păcuiul lui Soare became a trading centre to rival Pereyaslavets in the eleventh century.

The chronicler Yahya of Antioch records that the emperor installed generals from his field army as military governors, or *strategoi*, in the renovated citadels.[41] This is corroborated by lead seals struck by several of the commanders. Several seals prove that the 'Domestic of the *hikanatoi* of the West', Leo Sarakinopoulos, was appointed *strategos*

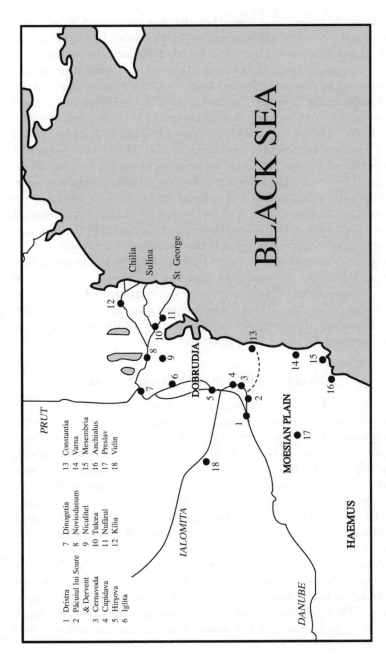

Map 4.2 The Lower Danube, 900–1100.

at Dristra.[42] At the same time, the otherwise unattested Sisinios was appointed *strategos* of Theodoropolis (Pereyaslavets). Further evidence proves that Tzimiskes's efforts to consolidate Byzantine authority at the lower Danube involved the creation of two new administrative districts (themes). The first incorporated Dristra and the former capital of the Bulgarian empire, Preslav.[43] Further seals of Leo Sarakinopoulos reveal that he was first to hold this command.[44] However, by the time the *Escorial taktikon* was compiled, between 976 and 979, the command had disappeared. Instead, Preslav was associated with the established command of Thrace, which lay to the south of the Haemus mountain range. This reveals that Tzimiskes was intent on integrating the frontier district within the existing hierarchy of themes, and suggests that resources under the command of the *strategos* of Thrace, both cash and manpower, were to be deployed when necessary north of the Haemus. The *Escorial taktikon* also records the existence of a second district, known as Mesopotamia ('between rivers') of the West.[45] Oikonomides has convincingly demonstrated that this designated the region of the Danube delta.[46] Not only is the designation 'between rivers' appropriate, but the Danube was compared by the Byzantines with the Euphrates, their ancient border in the east which, with the Tigris, encompassed the original Mesopotamia.

Byzantine Activity in the Balkans, 976–1025

The fear of further Russian invasions which provoked Tzimiskes's extensive programme of reforms and renovations proved false. Instead, immediately upon the emperor's death in 976, four sons of the governor of Macedonia rebelled. By 986 the youngest rebel, Samuel, had captured Preslav and set himself up as the successor to Symeon and Peter.[47] The expansion of Samuel's empire was facilitated by civil wars in Byzantium, and the renewed threat of the Fatimid Caliphate in the east prevented an effective imperial response.[48] By 997 Samuel held most of the lands which Symeon had ruled at the height of his power.[49]

Between 1001 and 1018 the Byzantine emperor Basil II (976–1025) masterminded a systematic and bloody recovery of strongholds and territory in the Balkans which earned him the epithet 'the Bulgarslayer'. The northern limit of Basil's empire stretched from the Black Sea as far as Sirmium on the middle Danube, and his authority was

recognised in all the lands of the Slavs settled within the Balkan peninsula. Whereas Tzimiskes had considered the Rus to be the principal
threat to Byzantine domination of the lower Danube, Basil II was
confronted by a new menace: the Pechenegs.

In the years before the *De Administrando Imperio* (*c.* 950) was compiled,
the Pechenegs had occupied the region between the rivers Don
and Prut, south of Kiev and directly north of Cherson.[50] However,
around 1015 the first wave of Pechenegs arrived north of the mouth
of the river Danube. In 1017 Basil II despatched a trusted senior
commander, Tzotzikios the Iberian, to Dristra to direct negotiations
with the nomads.[51] Excavations demonstrate that Basil simultaneously
established garrisons at strategic sites the length of the river. The
most telling evidence is the discovery of large numbers of class A2
anonymous *folles*, Byzantine copper coins struck between 976 and 1025.
In Byzantium coin was struck and circulated to facilitate public
expenditure. Although it might then go on to perform a secondary
function as a medium of private exchange, this was not its primary
function. In most periods at least 75 per cent of public expenditure was
military. This figure must have been higher still during Basil's reign.
Therefore we can conclude that the presence of large numbers of Basil's
coins, particularly low value coins, in a far-flung region must indicate
the dispersal of coin to pay troops stationed in that region. Recent
numismatic research has distinguished four distinct issues of class A2
anonymous *folles*, and demonstrates that the largest number discovered
at sites on the lower Danube were of Basil II's third issue, struck
between 1010–15 and 1020–25. Thus we can conclude that Basil II
established greater numbers of troops at Capidava, Noviodunum,
Păcuiul lui Soare, and Pereyaslavets (Nufărul) as a direct response to
the increased Pecheneg threat.[52]

The New Frontier System on the Ground:
Natural Barriers, Defence in Depth

Basil II's garrisoned outposts were intended to monitor and police
activity beyond the river. However, the river was not regarded as an
impermeable barrier. Although crossing the river could be problematical, it was certainly possible. In 1064 'the entire nation of Ouzes', a
nomadic people who followed the Pechenegs across the south Russian
steppe, 'crossed the frozen Danube in long wooden boats and

sharp-prowed vessels of branches lashed together'.[53] A century later some Cumans, another people closely related to the Pechenegs, tried sitting on straw-filled cushions and clinging to the tails of their horses.[54] Alexander Kazhdan has noted that of the 21 references to the Danube in the work of the chronicler John Skylitzes, most are associated with crossings.[55] Clearly, the river alone was not, and was not perceived to be, a sufficient natural barrier to raids. Therefore raids were further discouraged by maintaining additional geographical deterrents.

To the south of the Danube lay the vast and uninhabited Moesian plain which reached to the foothills of the Haemus mountain range. John Cinnamus recorded that in 1148 the emperor Manuel I Comnenus hunted on this plain, 'for a great quantity of wild beasts dwell in herds there since the [plains] have lain entirely deserted and uninhabited for many years'.[56] A second Byzantine author, Nicetas Choniates, recorded similarly that in 1186 the emperor Isaac II Angelus was: 'hindered from making his way through Moesia by the vast wilderness. Most of the cities in that territory are in the vicinity of the Haemus mountains'.[57] The region is naturally arid, and has only been widely cultivated since advances in irrigation during the nineteenth century. It is interesting in this context to note an observation by the Latin historian William of Tyre that in the twelfth century, the Byzantine emperor did not allow settlement or cultivation in the Velika Morava river valley or surrounding mountains (in modern Serbia) so that a thickly wooded buffer zone prevented access to the rich central Balkan lands.[58] The barren Moesian plain, although unwooded, performed a similar function: invaders could not support themselves from the land, and would therefore be hampered by their own provisions. The need to cross a vast and barren tract of land only to reach a range of mountains must also have acted as a psychological deterrent to potential invaders. Finally, if invaders reached the Haemus mountains, they would have found the passes which allowed access to the rich lands beyond heavily fortified and manned.

The network of frontier defences established by John Tzimiskes, then restored and developed by Basil II, utilised and augmented a series of natural physical barriers which acted as a buffer between the steppe and the rich lands of the central and southern Balkans. Maintaining this system required substantial reserves of cash and manpower. However, such a distribution of resources was not acceptable to Basil II's successors.

The Frontier 1025–81: Imperial Strategies and Responses

Inexplicably, when Basil died in 1025 he left no provision for his succession. Hence the military champion was succeeded by a series of civilians. George Ostrogorsky, author of the paramount political history of Byzantium, has characterised the years between the deaths of Basil II and Constantine IX (1042–55), as 'a period of decline, during which in its foreign policy Byzantium lived on the prestige won in the previous age and at home gave free play to all the forces making for disintegration'.[59] This notion, and the tension between military and civilian elements in eleventh-century Byzantium, has been the subject of an important discussion among Byzantine historians. Recently, scholars have done much to restore the reputation of the civilian emperors.[60] Imperial efforts to contain the Pechenegs in the mid eleventh century might also be considered more sympathetically than Ostrogorsky allowed, and lend the insights of peripheral vision to a period hitherto perceived predominantly from Constantinople through documentary sources.

After Basil II's death Pecheneg invasions had become increasingly frequent and destructive, bringing the efficacy of Basil's defence strategy into question. Between 1032 and 1036 a series of raids penetrated as far as Thessalonica on the Aegean coast, laying waste much of Thrace and Macedonia.[61] In spring 1036 the suburbs of both Noviodunum and Dinogetia were razed, and the fortified settlements of Dervent and Capidava were both destroyed, never to be restored.[62] The persistent nomad menace inspired a complete reappraisal of imperial policy in the region and inspired the adoption of practices diametrically opposed to those implemented by Basil II.

The emperor Michael IV (1034–41) recognised that the motivation for nomad raids was principally the acquisition of booty, and therefore determined to remove several potential targets. The sacked settlements of Capidava and Dervent were not rebuilt; instead the inhabitants were moved en masse to purpose-built housing which was constructed at Păcuiul lui Soare and Dinogetia. Excavations at both sites have uncovered distinctive levels of surface-level dwellings of regular construction, unlike other houses which were semi-subterranean. Such a systematic enterprise can only have been an imperial initiative to concentrate populations at a few well-defended strongholds.[63] Rationalisation also extended to the administrative structure of the region: a new commander was appointed in Dristra with authority over the whole lower

Danube, which was known, for the first time, as Paristrion. The first
man to hold this office was Katakalon Kekaumenos.[64] No attempt was
made to integrate the lands north of the Haemus in this command, and
excavations have demonstrated that the once mighty district of Preslav
was allowed to decline, further exacerbating the barrenness of the
Moesian plain.[65]

With many troops withdrawn from the frontier, a greater emphasis
was placed on diplomacy among the empire's nomadic neighbours as a
means to direct their activity and prevent further destructive raids. The
general ethnonym 'Pecheneg', which I have used thus far without
qualification, masked a loose confederate structure, and it is clear that
except for migrations and other extraordinary expeditions, activities
were conducted by small semi-autonomous bands.[66] This suited the
preferred methods of Byzantine diplomats, who could exploit and
foment internecine tensions to neutralise larger threats to the empire,
and periodically to purchase the services of individual groups for particular imperial projects.[67] In 1046 the Byzantine commander in
Dristra, Michael son of the Logothete, saw an opportunity to exploit a
Pecheneg feud. Skylitzes provides a detailed account of the rivalry
between Tyrach, the blood overlord of the Pechenegs, and his brilliant
general, Kegen, which saw the latter flee to an island near Dristra. He
was received by Michael, who swiftly informed the emperor of his
charge. Kegen was escorted to Constantinople, baptised, and returned
to the lower Danube where he and his followers were to act as roving
border guards between the scattered Byzantine strongholds on the
river.[68] However, the scheme backfired. First, Kegen could not resist
harrying Tyrach, and provoked a massive Pecheneg invasion, probably
in the winter of 1046–47. Fatefully, a plague decimated the huge force,
and many of the survivors were allowed to settle within the empire and
enrolled in the Byzantine army. However, this precipitated a second
crisis. A group of Byzantine provincial military aristocrats, led by
Leo Tornikios, had plotted to rebel against the civilian regime in Constantinople, and seized upon the enrolment of nomads at a time when
traditional Greek divisions were being disbanded.[69] The situation north
of the Haemus was not resolved until 1053, when the united Byzantine
eastern and western armies were besieged by Pechenegs at Preslav,
forcing the emperor to negotiate and sign a 30-year peace.[70]

The historical coverage of the Pecheneg wars is remarkable for its
richness and detail. It is also wholly typical of the tendency of Byzantine
authors to elaborate on the extraordinary, and completely to ignore the

mundane. So far, I have also emphasised these more striking episodes, which would support Ostrogorsky's notion of 'disintegration'. However, to understand Byzantine policy in this period fully we must rely far more on a careful interpretation of the material evidence, in particular numismatic data accumulated during excavations at the lower Danube.[71]

Archaeological Evidence for Byzantine Frontier Policy

I have already noted that abundant finds of class A2 anonymous *folles* in fortresses at the lower Danube attest to the presence of Basil II's troops. It will be clear from Figure 4.3 that finds of low-value coins struck after the death of Basil II are even more abundant. The figure illustrates the numbers of coin finds averaged to represent a total for each year of each imperial reign. At each site there is a remarkable surge in the 1030s which continues until the 1070s, the period of 'disintegration'. As I have outlined above, Byzantine coin did not circulate freely, but rather was distributed to meet the fiscal demands of the administration. Therefore such vast numbers of coins cannot have reached the lower Danube independently, and must have been the result of a deliberate imperial policy which channelled coin struck in Constantinople to sites on the lower Danube. This appears to be at odds with the testimony of several sources that troops were withdrawn from the frontiers and fortresses were decommissioned. We must therefore find a convincing explanation for the abundance of coin.

There is much evidence from elsewhere in the Balkans that during the mid eleventh century large sums of coin were despatched to local rulers to secure their loyalty to the emperor. Byzantine control of Dyrrachium (in modern Albania), the principal port on the Adriatic coast, was secured through the backing of the city's leading family, the Chryselioi. 'Piles of gold and silver' were sent into Serbia and Bosna (which are located in, but do not correspond with, modern Serbia and Bosnia) to secure the support of native warlords.[72] The ruler of the Dalmatian city of Zadar, known alternatively as Gregorius or Dobronja, was twice rewarded with cash and titles from Constantinople. Significantly, we know that a similar policy was pursued at the lower Danube. The historian Attaleiates records that annual subsidies (*philotimiai*) were despatched to the citizens (*enchorioi*) of the towns beside the Danube.[73] He also reveals that it was an imperial decision in 1072 not to pay the *philotimiai* that resulted in a general rebellion in

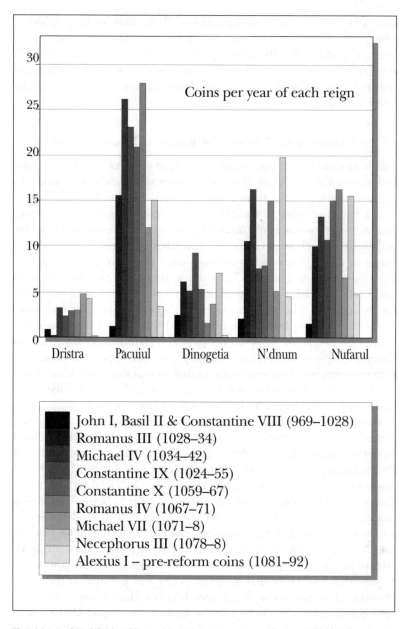

Fig. 4.3   Isolated finds of low-value Byzantine coins at the Lower Danube.

Paristrion. Consequently, the townsfolk allied with the neighbouring Pechenegs and handed over vital citadels, including Dristra, to their chieftains.[74]

The alliance of the townsfolk and the Pecheneg suggests that they had long been co-operating to ensure harmony at the lower Danube. Moreover, after an intial period of disturbance, which is illustrated by a series of coin hoards, both parties seem to have lived peacefully in Paristrion.[75] The *Alexiad* records that afterwards there followed 'a period of peace when they [the Pechenegs] tilled the soil and sowed millet and wheat'.[76] It seems clear that the Pechenegs, who might have seized the paristrian citadels and land at any time, only did so in 1072 because they too had been deprived of their share of the *philotimiai*.

The citizens of Dristra and other cities had almost certainly used much of their *philotimiai* to buy the Pechenegs' goods and services. This practice had a precedent. The *De Administrando Imperio* records that when the Pechenegs were settled near Cherson, on the Crimean peninsula north of the Black Sea, a scheme operated whereby the nomads received 'from the Chersonites a prearranged remuneration . . . proportionate to their labour and trouble in the form of pieces of purple cloth, ribbon, loosely woven cloths, gold brocade, pepper, scarlet or "Parthian" leather, and other commodities'. It added that the Pechenegs were 'free men . . . and never perform any service without remuneration'.[77]

The Pechenegs' desire to acquire luxury goods would have made the emporia on the lower Danube peculiarly attractive. It seems certain that they were granted access to the markets at Dristra, Păcuiul lui Soare, Dinogetia, Noviodunum, and Pereyaslavets where they could purchase such wares. It is equally certain that the Byzantines both promoted and monitored this process of exchange. Besides providing low-value coins to facilitate exchange, many goods which originated in Constantinople have been uncovered in excavations. Trade between the capital and lower Danube clearly was flourishing in this period. Excavations have unearthed many amphorae which would have been used to export, among other commodities, Byzantine wine and olive oil. Furthermore, copious green-glazed ceramics and some examples of sgraffito ware which were produced in Constantinople have been uncovered at many sites.[78] A rare written reference to trade along the Black Sea coast in the mid eleventh century can be found in the *Life of St Cyril the Phileote*.[79] The discovery of lead seals proves that Byzantine officials known as the *kommerkiarioi* were present at both Dristra and Pereyaslavets to monitor this trade, and perhaps to extract the *kommerkion*, a sales tax imposed on all goods traded within the empire.[80] Moreover, a seal discovered at Noviodunum was struck by a certain 'Niketas, *notarios* and *boullotes*'.[81] The *boullotes* was a dignitary based in Constantinople who applied an official seal to regulated merchandise, and his seal provides incontrovertible evidence for officially sponsored trade in controlled wares between the capital and the frontier.[82]

When examined together, the numismatic and documentary evidence therefore suggests that although the civilian emperors of the mid eleventh century withdrew troops from the towns of the lower Danube, they determined to secure the loyalty of the citizens through the distributing of annual stipends. The numismatic evidence demonstrates that an element of this was paid in low-value coin, deliberately to facilitate the process of exchange in the regional emporia. Locals who received payments would, in turn, employ many of the nomads as border guards and offer them access to their rich markets. The new scheme successfully prevented nomad raids on the scale of the regular invasions which had taken place in the 1020s and 1030s, and only faltered in 1072 when a decision was taken to withhold the *philotimiai*. Thereafter, authority in the region was lost to the Pechenegs for almost two decades, and only restored by a protracted and bloody series of encounters under the emperor Alexius I (1081–1118). Ultimately, he defeated the Pechenegs at the battle of Levunium in April 1091.

Conclusion: Disintegration or Assimilation?

It will be clear from the foregoing discussion that Byzantine policy towards the frontier at the lower Danube can be divided into two distinct phases. In the first period, between the accession of John I and the death of Basil II, a military ethos prevailed which favoured the renovation of late-antique fortifications at strategic locations and the deployment of garrisons. In the second period, while civilian government prevailed in Constantinople, emperors sought to guarantee stability through the distribution of subsidies and the promotion of carefully controlled trade. Contrary to Ostrogorsky's claim, this policy did not lead inevitably to 'disintegration', but was remarkably successful in preventing destructive nomad incursions for several decades.

Under both military and civilian regimes the aim of imperial frontier policy was to guarantee the security and integrity of the empire's productive heartland, which lay south of the Balkan mountain ranges.

Although for defensive purposes the river Danube was only one element in a more complex frontier system, it was clearly regarded as the empire's appropriate, and perhaps 'natural frontier'. The *Souda* definition of *eschatia*, which I have cited in full above, contains not only the notion of limitation and marginality, but also associates the frontier with natural geographical boundaries. Yet we must question how natural a frontier the Danube was for the empire in the eleventh century. The Haemus mountains formed a more obvious boundary between the sparsely populated Moesian plain and the heavily populated and cultivated lands of Thrace. Moreover, at these mountains the continental climate of the steppe and northern Balkan plains gave way to the Mediterranean climate of the south. However, the notion of what constitutes a 'natural frontier' is a deeply ideological issue which owes less to geography and climate than to historical precedent and political expediency.[83] In this regard, John Tzimiskes could certainly claim to have restored the empire, whose subjects still regarded themselves as Romans, to its ancient and therefore natural limits. This is a view which has been unconsciously adopted by modern scholars. For example, in the recently published *Oxford Dictionary of Byzantium* the Euphrates and Danube are said to have formed the empire's 'natural frontiers to the east and west respectively'.[84] A conscious case can also be made that the river did indeed constitute a natural boundary to the medieval empire, since (excepting distant Russia) it marked the limits of Orthodox Christianity, and increasingly of Orthodox material culture.

The Bulgarian tsars Symeon and Peter had endeavoured to establish the Orthodox faith between the Haemus mountains and the lower Danube in the first half of the tenth century. Their Byzantine conquerors continued this policy with the construction of stone churches in the paristrian towns. In these same settlements many seals of Byzantine clerics have been discovered. Moreover, sealed imperial decrees (*sigillia*) of Basil II and episcopal lists of the late eleventh century demonstrate that Orthodox bishops, who were subject to a metropolitan of Dristra, were present at several sites on the lower Danube throughout the period under discussion.[85]

Byzantine attitudes towards the Pechenegs reinforce the notion that the Danube was deemed to be the frontier of Orthodoxy. The confederate structure of Pecheneg society dictated that potential settlers arrived at the Danube in small, organised groups which could, for the most part, be absorbed into the Byzantine army and settled elsewhere in the empire. The Byzantine author Zonaras refers to a groups of Pechenegs established at Moglena in Bulgaria. Skylitzes records that Pecheneg prisoners were rearmed and transferred to the eastern front in the late 1040s. However, before they were allowed to settle within the empire they were required to receive baptism. John Mauropous records that in the late 1040s, despite their fierce nature, many Pechenegs converted.[86] Similarly, the *Life of St. Cyril the Phileote* records that after Alexius I's victory at Levunium in 1091: 'the Scyths [Pechenegs] who were otherwise wolves [were] transformed with God's aid and favour, into lambs and gathered to the Lord's flock with the bath of regeneration.'[87]

Thus, the eleventh-century perception of the empire required that those settled within its perceived limits entered the community of Orthodox Christians, and that the lower Danube was deemed to be the limit of the empire in the north. This was in spite of the fact that many of the ethnically diverse inhabitants of the frontier region were regarded as *mixobarbaroi* by the literary elite of Constantinople. Moreover, these 'half-barbarian' Christians increasingly began to absorb Byzantine cultural ideas.

Urban imposition – the establishment of a resident population, for example a garrison, in an existing centre – is one of the most likely methods by which cultural ideas are transmitted from one people to another. A second, closely related process is implantation, the establishment of a colony at a previously unsettled site within a region occupied by another society. The Byzantine occupation of Dristra and Pereyaslavets, the renovation of Capidava and Dervent, and the development of Păcuiul lui Soare, are examples of both categories.[88] The arrival of soldiers from other regions of the empire must therefore have served as a catalyst for the process of transmission, which we might call 'Byzantinisation'. However, it does not appear to have suffered by their withdrawal. In fact, subsequent imperial reliance on local elites probably accelerated the process. In some societies increased contact with alternative cultural ideas leads to the ritualistic preservation of certain norms as a means of expressing identity.[89] In this instance, the absence of a large imperial military presence allowed the native elite to receive Byzantine gifts without their being associated with an oppressive regime. Moreover, the enlightened trade policy ensured that an abundance of Byzantine wares reached the markets on the lower Danube. The subsequent emulation of Byzantine models must reflect a regional demand for such products, demonstrating that appreciation of Orthodox material culture was not restricted to the regional elite.

Despite the tendency in Byzantine scholarship to establish borders between cognate disciplines, and the trend in Balkan scholarship to impose further national barriers to our understanding of prenationalist societies, it is possible to construct a fairly comprehensive picture of Byzantine policy at the lower Danube which also gives an enlightening 'peripheral', but far from insignificant, perspective on both military and civilian regimes. We have seen that the changed emphasis in frontier policy during the mid eleventh century was not a factor in the empire's 'disintegration', but was a rational response to the dynamic situation at and beyond the frontier, and was sensitive to the local interests. In the face of considerable pressure it was also remarkably successful. Ultimately, it is clear that despite the literate Byzantine notion that the empire's frontiers were marginal and semi-barbaric, imperial policies ensured that the society at the lower Danube grew richer and increasingly 'Byzantine' during the eleventh century.

NOTES

1. See for example, *Cambridge Medieval History*, IV:1, ed. J. Hussey, Cambridge 1966, 512; G. Ostrogorsky, *History of the Byzantine State*, trans. J. Hussey, 2nd edn, Oxford 1968, 289; D. Obolensky, *The Byzantine Commonwealth: Eastern Europe, 500–1453*, London 1971, 100, 268–9.
2. *MFS*, V.
3. 'Frontier', *The Oxford Dictionary of Byzantium*, ed. A. Kazhdan, Oxford 1991, II, 807.
4. *Suidae Lexicon*, ed. A. Adler, Leipzig 1935, I, 432.
5. B. Isaac, 'The meaning of the terms *limes* and *limitanei*', *Journal of Roman Studies*, LXXVIII (1988), 125–47.
6. J. Haldon and H. Kennedy, 'The Arab-Byzantine frontier in the eighth and ninth centuries: military organisation and society in the borderlands', *Zbornik Radova Vizantoloskog Instituta*, XIX (1980), 79–116; W. Kaegi, 'The frontier: barrier or bridge?', *17th International Byzantine Congress, Major Papers*, New York 1986, 279–305.
7. Similarly, medieval Arabic sources uses several terms to indicate limits or frontiers, including *afaq, hudud, and tukhum*. However, the most common, applied particularly to the Arab-Byzantine frontier, was *thugur*. See M. Bonner, 'The naming of the frontier: *'Awāsim, thughūr*, and the Arab geographers', *BSOAS*, LVII (1994), 17–24.
8. *DAI*, ed. G. Moravcsik, trans. R. J. H. Jenkins, *CFHB*, 2nd edn, I, Washington DC 1967. For some perceptive comments on frontiers in the *DAI*, see J.-P. Arrignon and J.-F. Duneau, 'La frontière chez deux auteurs byzantins:

Procope de Césarée et Constantin VII Porphyrogénète', *Geographica Byzantina*, ed. H. Ahrweiler, Paris 1981, 17–30.

9. *DAI*, 140, 144, 154, 212, 214.

10. *DAI*, 228, 236, 238.

11. *DAI*, 266, 270. Similarly, Tsar Symeon of Bulgaria erected inscribed stones to mark his border with Byzantium in the early part of the tenth century. See J. Shepard, 'Symeon of Bulgaria – peacemaker', *Annuaire de l'Université de Sofia 'St. Kliment Ohridski'*, LXXXIII (1989) [1991], 9–48.

12. For example, *Anne Comnène, Alexiade*, ed. and trans. B. Leib, Paris 1937, I, 138, where the river Drakon is referred to as the *horos* with the Turks; *ibid.*, II, 43, where, as a term of the peace treaty of Devol, Bohemond, the leader of the Normans, agrees to withdraw from the region of Dyrrachium (in modern Albania) to beyond the *horia* of the empire. For an English translation see E. R. A. Sewter, *The Alexiad of Anna Comnena*, London 1969, 130, 182.

13. *Alexiade*, ed. Leib, III, 128 (trans. Sewter, 426).

14. *Le traité sur la guerilla de l'empereur Nicéphore Phocas (963–969)*, ed. and trans. G. Dagron and H. Mihaescu, Paris 1986, 41, 45, 49, 51; *Three Byzantine Military Treatises*, ed. and trans. G. T. Dennis, *CFHB*, XXV, Washington DC 1985, 152, 154, 156, 160, 162, 202.

15. *Three Byzantine Military Treatises*, 254, 264 (camp), 320 (empire).

16. A valuable introduction in English is presented by D. Ricks, *Byzantine Heroic Poetry*, Bristol 1990.

17. Procopius of Caesarea, *Wars*, ed. and trans. H. B. Dewing, Cambridge, Mass. 1961–68, I, 150–1, 184–5, 196–8, 294–5; IV, 443–57; V, 21–3, 96–7.

18. C. Mango, *Byzantine Literature as a Distorting Mirror: an inaugural lecture delivered before the University of Oxford on 21 May 1974*, Oxford 1975, 5–6.

19. *Michaelis Attaliotae Historia* (hereafter Attaleiates), ed. I. Bekker, *CSHB*, Bonn 1853, 204–5; *Alexiade*, ed. Leib, II, 117–18, 194, 201; III, 14–15, 41, 154, 192, 205–7.

20. N.-Ş. Tanaşoca, 'Les mixobarbares et les formations politiques paristriennes du XIᵉ siècle', *Revue Roumaine d'Histoire*, XII (1973), 67.

21. D. Obolensky, 'The principles and methods of Byzantine diplomacy', *Actes du XIIᵉ congrès international des études byzantines*, I, Belgrade 1963, 56, repr. D. Obolensky, *Byzantium and the Slavs*, New York 1994, 13.

22. J. V. A. Fine, *The Early Medieval Balkans*, Ann Arbor 1983, has limitations, and the best general survey from a Byzantine perspective is still Obolensky's *Byzantine Commonwealth*.

23. For concise analyses of their origin and migrations, see P. B. Golden, *The Cambridge History of Early Inner Asia*, ed. D. Sinor, Cambridge 1990, 242–8, 270–5.

24. *Leonis Diaconi Caloensis historiae libri decem*, (hereafter Leo the Deacon), ed. C. B. Hase, *CSHB*, Bonn 1828, 61–2.

25. *Ioannis Skylitzae synopsis historiarum*, (hereafter Skylitzes), ed. J. Thurn, *CFHB*, V, Berlin and New York 1973, 276–8.

26. Liudprand of Cremona, *Legatione*, in Liuprand of Cremona, *Opera*, ed. I. Bekker, *MGH SS in usum scholarum*, Hanover and Leipzig 1915, 564

(English trans. F. A. Wright, *The Works of Liutprand of Cremona*, London 1930, 262).

27. Skylitzes, 277.

28. *PVL*, 36–7 (English trans. S. H. Cross and O. P. Sherbowitz-Wetzor, *The Russian Primary Chronicle*, Cambridge, Mass. 1953, 73–8). For the expansion of trade, see J. Shepard, 'Constantinople – gateway to the north: the Russians', *Constantinople and its Hinterland*, ed. C. Mango and G. Dagron, Aldershot 1995, 243–60.

29. See the select bibliography in *Cambridge Medieval History*, IV: 1, 963–4. The classic English analysis is A. D. Stokes, 'The Balkan campaigns of Svyatoslav Igorevich', *Slavonic and East European Review*, XL (1962), 466–96. Also see now, S. Franklin and J. Shepard, *The Emergence of Rus 750–1200*, London and New York 1996, 143–51.

30. Skylitzes, 279. See also Michael Psellus, *Historia syntomos*, ed. W. J. Aerts, *CFHB*, XXX, Berlin and New York 1990, 100–5.

31. Skylitzes, 297–309; Leo the Deacon, 130–4.

32. *PVL*, 52 (trans. Cross and Sherbowitz-Wetzor, 89–90).

33. *PVL*, 53 (trans. Cross and Sherbowitz-Wetzor, 90).

34. I. Ševčenko, 'A Byzantine inscription from Silistra reinterpreted', *Revue des Études Sud-Est Européenes*, VII (1969), 591–8; M. Salamon, 'Some notes on a medieval inscription from Silistra (*c.* 976)', *ibid.*, IX (1971), 487–96.

35. I. Barnea, 'Dinogetia et Noviodunum, deux villes byzantines du Bas-Danube', *Revue des Études Sud-Est Européenes*, IX (1971), 343–62.

36. The location and identity of the city of Theodoropolis has been disputed. Leo the Deacon, 157–8, states that Dristra was renamed Theodoropolis in recognition of the miraculous intervention of St Theodore the *stratelate* on the Byzantine side against the Rus. However, current consensus favours the identification of Theodoropolis with Little Preslav, which in turn can be identified with Pereyaslavets. See N. Oikonomides, 'Presthlavitza, the Little Preslav', *Südost-Forschungen*, XLII (1983), 1–9; I. Jordanov and V. Tăpkova-Zaimova, 'Quelques nouvelles donnés sur l'administration byzantine au bas-Danube (fin du Xe–XIe s.)', *Géographie historique du monde méditerranéen*, ed. H. Ahrweiler, Paris 1988, 120; V. Tăpkova-Zaimova, 'L'administration byzantine au Bas Danube (fin du Xe–XIe s.)', *Byzantinoslavica*, LIV (1993), 96. Cf. P. Diaconu, 'De nouveau à propos de Presthlavitza', *Südost-Forschungen*, LXVI (1987), 279–93; V. B. Perhavko, 'Gde že nahodilsiya dunaiskii grad Pereyaslavec?'[Where was the city of Pereyaslavets located?], *Byzantinoslavica*, LV (1994), 278–90.

37. *PVL*, 48 (trans. Cross and Sherbowitz-Wetzor, 86).

38. Pottery: S. Baraschi and O. Damian, 'Considerations sur la céramique émaillée de Nufăru', *Dacia*, XXXVII (1993), 237–8; Seals: I. Barnea, 'Sigilii bizantine inedite din Dobrogea' [Unpublished Byzantine seals from the Dobrudja], 1; *Pontica*, XVI (1983), 263–72; 3, *Pontica*, XXIII (1990), 315–34; I. Barnea, 'Sceaux byzantins inédits de Dobroudja', *Studies in Byzantine Sigillography*, 3, ed. N. Oikonomides, Washington DC 1993, 61–5; Coins: G. Mănucu-Adameşteanu, 'Circulaţia monetară la Nufăru în secolele X–XIV' [Monetary circulation at Nufărul in the 10th to 14th centuries], *Peuce*, XXIV (1991), 497–554.

39. P. Diaconu and D. Vîlceanu, *Păcuiul lui Soare, cetatea bizantină*, I, Bucharest 1972, 47–58. Their conclusions have been challenged by the Bulgarian scholar, D. Ovčarov, 'La fortresse protobulgare sur l'île danubienne de Pacuiul lui Soare', *Dobrudža – études ethno-culturelles*, ed. D. Ovčarov, Sofia 1987, 57–68, who maintains that the Byzantine complex replaced a ninth-century Bulgarian fortress.

40. Diaconu and Vîlceanu, *Păcuiul lui Soare*, I, 27–46, note that the walls were built of irregular blocks, which is consistent with the use of *spolia*. We can assume that carved stone was available locally, because blocks were used as the foundations of humble dwellings in the later eleventh century (*ibid.*, 217). The use of *spolia* even extended to the mortar which bound the blocks. Two of the three types of mortar contain fragments of late-antique brick.

41. *Histoire de Yahya-Ibn-Sa'ïd d'Antioche*, ed. and trans. J. Kratschkovsky and A. A. Vasiliev, *Patrologia Orientalis*, XVIII (1924), 833.

42. I. Mititelu and I. Barnea, 'Sigilii de plumb bizantine din regiunea Dunării de Jos' [Byzantine lead seals from the lower Danube region], *SCIV*, XVII (1966), n. 5; I. Jordanov, 'Pečati na Leo Sarakinopul ot Veliki Preslav' [Seals of Leo Sarakinopoulos from Great Preslav], *Arkeologiya*, 1982:1, 12–23; I. Jordanov, *Pečatite ot strategiiat v Preslav, 977–1088* [Seals from the military command of Preslav, 977–1088], Sofia 1993, 94–7, 105, 118.

43. Skylitzes, 298.

44. Jordanov, *Pečatite*, 136–7.

45. *Les listes de préséance byzantines des IXᵉ et Xᵉ siècles*, ed. and trans. N. Oikonomides, Paris 1972, 268–9.

46. N. Oikonomides, 'Recherches sur l'histoire du Bas-Danube aux Xᵉ–XIIᵉ siècles: la Mésopotamie d'Occident', *Revue des Études Sud-Est Européenes*, III (1965), 57–79.

47. For general coverage of this event, see Obolensky, *Byzantine Commonwealth*, 176–9; Fine, *Early Medieval Balkans*, 188–97.

48. Michael Psellus, *Chronographia*, ed. E. Rénauld, Paris 1928, I, 1–24, provides a colourful sketch of these episodes. English trans. E. R. A. Sewter, *Michael Psellus. Fourteen Byzantine Rulers*, London 1966, 27–49.

49. Fine, *Early Medieval Balkans*, 193; Ostrogorsky, *Byzantine State*, 301–2.

50. *DAI*, 48–9. See also, *Marvazi on China, the Turks and India*, ed. and trans. V. Minorsky, London 1942, 20–1 (Arabic), 32–3 (English).

51. Skylitzes, 356.

52. V. Ivaniševič, 'Interpretation and dating of the *folles* of Basil II and Constantine VIII – the class A2', *Zbornik Radova Vizantološkog Instituta*, XXVII–XXVIII (1989), 19–42; Mănucu-Adameştenau, 'Circulaţia monetară la Nufăru', 497–554.

53. Attaleiates, 83.

54. *Nicetae Choniatae historia* (hereafter Choniates), ed. J. Van Dieten, *CFHB*, XI: 1, Berlin 1975, 94.

55. A. Kazhdan and G. Constable, *People and Power in Byzantium: an introduction to modern Byzantine studies*, Washington DC 1982, 38–9.

56. *Ioannis Cinnami epitome rerum ab Ioanne et Alexio Comnenis gestarum*, ed. A. Meineke, *CSHB*, Bonn 1836, 93.

57. Choniates, 373.
58. *Historia rerum in partibus transmarinis gestarum, recueil des historiens de croisades, historiens occidentaux*, Paris 1844, I, 946–7. English trans. E. A. Babcock and A. C. Krey, *William of Tyre: history of deeds done beyond the sea*, London 1943, II, 348–9.
59. Ostrogorsky, *Byzantine State*, 320.
60. The interested reader should start with P. Lemerle, *Cinq études sur le XIᵉ siècle byzantin*, Paris 1977.
61. Skylitzes, 385, 397–9.
62. P. Diaconu, *Les Pétchènegues au Bas-Danube*, Bucharest 1970, 43–9; G. Ştefan et al., *Dinogetia*, Bucharest 1967, I, 22–9.
63. Diaconu and Vîlceanu, *Păcuiul lui Soare*, I, 59–69; Diaconu, *Petchénègues*, 48–9.
64. Skylitzes, 433.
65. I. Jordanov, 'Établissement administratif byzantin à Preslav aux Xᵉ et XIᵉ siècles', *Jahrbuch der Österreichischen Byzantinistik*, XXXII (1982), 35–44; E. Malamut, 'L'image byzantine des Petchénègues', *Byzantinische Zeitschrift*, LXXXVIII (1995), 127, suggests that this change in policy did not take place until 1051–52.
66. *DAI*, 166–71.
67. Obolensky, 'Principles and methods of Byzantine diplomacy', 6–7.
68. Skylitzes, 455–7.
69. Skylitzes, 465; M. Angold, 'Archons and dynasts: local aristocracies and the cities of the later Byzantine empire', *The Byzantine Aristocracy, IX–XIII Centuries*, ed. M. Angold, Oxford 1984, 242; J.-Cl. Cheynet, *Pouvoirs et contestations à Byzance (963–1210)*, Paris 1990, 59–61, 220.
70. Skylitzes, 476; Attaleiates, 43.
71. The figure is based on data provided by: I. Jordanov, 'Dobrudža – selon les données de la numismatique et de la sphragistique', *Dobrudža*, ed. Ovčarov, 203–7; G. Mănucu-Adameşteanu, 'Tomis – Constantia – Constanţa', *Pontica*, XXIV (1991), 324–5.
72. *Letopis Popa Dukljanina*, ed. F. Šišič, Belgrade and Zagreb 1928, 346.
73. Attaleiates, 204–5.
74. *Alexiade*, ed. Leib, II, 81–2 (trans. Sewter, 212).
75. Coins were often concealed for security during periods of unrest. See N. Conovici and N. Lungu, 'Un nou tezaur de monede bizantine descoperit la Păcuiul lui Soare' [A new parcel of Byzantine coins discovered at Păcuiul lui Soare], *SCIV*, XXXI (1980), 397–402; D. M. Metcalf, *Coinage in South-Eastern Europe, 820–1396*, London 1979, 75.
76. *Alexiade*, ed. Leib, II, 82, 82 (trans. Sewter, 212).
77. *DAI*, 52–3.
78. Ştefan et al., *Dinogetia*, I, 229 (green-glazed ware), 246–7 (sgraffito), 249–76 (amphorae); Diaconu and Vîlceanu, *Păcuiul lui Soare*, I, 71–119. Baraschi and Damian, 'Céramique émaillée de Nufăru', 237–78. For the latest comprehensive classification of Constantinopolitan ceramics, see J. Hayes, *Excavations at Saraçhane in Istanbul*, II., *The Pottery*, Princeton 1992.
79. *La vie de Saint Cyrille le Philéote moine byzantin (d. 1110)*, ed. E. Sargologos, *Subsidia hagiographica*, XXXIX, Brussels 1964, 63, 284–5.

80. I. Jordanov, 'Neizdedani vizantijski olovni pečati ot Silistra (III)' [Unpublished Byzantine leads seals from Dristra, III], *Izvestija na Narodnija Muzej Varna*, xxiv [xxxix] (1990), 88; *Catalogue of Byzantine Seals at Dumbarton Oaks and in the Fogg Museum of Art*, i, ed. J. Nesbitt and N. Oikonomides, Washington DC 1991, 151, 178–9; Oikonomides, 'Presthlavitza', 3–4.

81. Barnea, 'Sceaux inédits de Dobroudja', 60–1.

82. *Listes de préséance*, ed. Oikonomides, 21.

83. P. Sahlins, 'Natural frontiers revisited: France's boundaries since the seventeenth century', *American Historical Review*, xcv (1990), 1423–51.

84. *Oxford Dictionary of Byzantium*, iii, 1797–8.

85. H. Gelzer, 'Ungedruckte und wenig bekannte Bistümerverzeichnisse der orientalischen Kirche', *Byzantinische Zeitschrift*, ii (1893), 42–6; *Notitiae episcopatuum ecclesiae Constantinopolitanae*, ed. J. Darrouzès, Paris 1981, 344–50.

86. *Ioannis Euchaitorum metropolitae quae in cod. Vat. gr. 676 supersunt*, ed. P. Lagarde, Göttingen 1882, 142–7.

87. *La vie de St. Cyrille*, ed. and trans. Sargologos, 230, 465.

88. C. Renfrew, 'Trade as action at a distance: questions of integration and communication', *Ancient Civilization and Trade*, ed. J. A. Sabloff and C. C. Lamberg-Karlovsky, Albuquerque 1975, 3–59; D. B. Saddington, 'The parameters of Romanization', *Roman Frontier Studies*, ed. V. A. Maxfield and M. J. Dobson, Exeter 1991, 413–18.

89. I. Hodder, 'Pottery distributions: service and tribal areas', *Pottery and the Archaeologist*, ed. M. Millet, London 1979, 7–23; I. Hodder, *Symbols in Action: ethnoarchaeological studies of material culture*, Cambridge 1982, 215–20.

5

FRENCH AND NORMAN FRONTIERS IN THE CENTRAL MIDDLE AGES

Daniel Power

In a well-known article Karl Ferdinand Werner described eleventh-century Western Europe as 'a world of princes'.[1] By extension it was a world of principalities, for most of these princes claimed to rule over large tracts of territory; and as they sought to assert their hegemony over their lands, rulers naturally tried to define and control their borders. In general, provincial borders in medieval France have not received the attention they deserve from historians, for they dwindled in importance in the later Middle Ages with the growth of the French state. Yet these borders and borderlands are worth studying both for their own sake and for their place in the evolution of political frontiers in general. This article will consider one of the most powerful French principalities in the central Middle Ages, the duchy of Normandy.[2]

French historians frequently mention *la frontière normande* without feeling the need to define or justify this term.[3] However, English-speaking historians may be reluctant to talk of the Norman 'frontier' without explanation or definition; as I have set out in the introduction to this volume, Part A, there are significant semantic variations between the different European cognates for 'frontier', and the term has two widely different meanings in English.[4] In the eleventh century there was an important Norman 'frontier' in the American sense of the term, as the limit of expansion and settlement, and indeed it extended from the British Isles to Anatolia.[5] However, the Norman 'frontier' will be considered here as a major political division in the European sense of the word. The political border of the duchy of Normandy will be examined to see whether such borders merit being described as 'frontiers', and how far there was a concept of 'frontiers' in the central Middle Ages.

The Frontiers of the Kingdom of France

The nature of medieval French provincial borders is best seen in the context of the external borders of the kingdom itself, where the very concept of *frontière*, as a fortified barrier protecting a state, evolved from the late Middle Ages onwards.[6] The most significant of these external 'frontiers' was the border with the Empire: not only was the eastern border of France an abiding preoccupation of the rulers and historians of France until the failure of the Maginot Line in 1940, but the northern end also had significant implications for the history of the Low Countries.[7] This *frontière* originated in the divisions separating two of the three portions of Charlemagne's Empire by the treaty of Verdun (843), namely those assigned to Charles the Bald (to its west) and Lothar (to the east). In French historiography the treaty of Verdun consequently lies 'at the very origins of French national history'.[8] Although the treaty was just one of a series of dynastic arrangements of this type and was soon superseded by fresh divisions, the lines fixed at Verdun were used again on several occasions over the next hundred years; and as the Saxon kings of the East Franks welded all the Carolingian lands to the east into a revived 'Empire', the boundary of 843 came to form the border between their empire and the kingdom of France.[9] In this basic form, the Franco-Imperial border (*fines imperii et regni*) survived for several centuries: it was not superseded in the region of the Rhône until the fourteenth century, and in the district of the Meuse it persisted for another two hundred years.

The significance of this boundary was far from constant. Its original whereabouts were sometimes even forgotten: it had been assigned to the limits of various Carolingian *pagi* in 843, but by the Central Middle Ages the rivers Scheldt, Meuse, Saône, and Rhône were generally taken to be the limits of the kingdom of France, generally somewhat to the east of the original demarcation.[10] Not surprisingly, some lordships slipped the net completely, for instance in both Champagne and the Namurois, and elsewhere the frontier comprised a vague zone rather than a fixed line.[11] In the tenth century the Saxon kings sometimes asserted their hegemony westwards over the West Frankish kingdom;

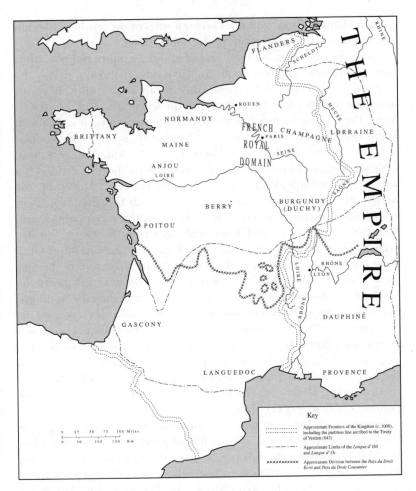

Map 5.1 The kingdom of France in the Central Middle Ages.

conversely, from the fourteenth century onwards, the antiquity of this line did not prevent the Capetian and Valois kings of France expanding their *regnum* east of the Rhône into imperial territory, first to Lyon and Dauphiné and later into Provence and Lorraine. In addition, the political interests of both lay and ecclesiastical magnates frequently straddled the Franco-Imperial border: families such as the Bosonids in the ninth and tenth, the counts of Flanders, Champagne, and Toulouse in the twelfth, or the dukes of Burgundy in the fourteenth century all acquired lands, offices, and titles on both sides of the border, although this rarely led to modifications in the border itself.

The political border between France and the Empire did not correspond to several important cultural divisions. It did not match the linguistic frontiers of the region, since it ran almost entirely across Romance territory and cut across both the *langue d'oïl* and *langue d'oc*: hence the Empire included French-speaking regions such as Brabant, Hainault, Lorraine, and the county of Burgundy, as well as the Occitan-speaking county of Provence. However, as the kingdom of France embraced most of Flanders, the Franco-Imperial border divided the western Flemish-speaking districts from the eastern.[12] Moreover, the border of 843 frequently did not coincide with the already ancient ecclesiastical divisions of Gaul, for it bisected the metropolitan provinces of Reims, Lyon, and Trier, and numerous dioceses;[13] this discrepancy swelled as the diocesan boundaries increased in importance from the tenth century onwards.[14] The gradual relocation of the *fines regni et imperii* along the Four Rivers over the next few centuries resolved this disjunction in some districts but exacerbated it in others, particularly along the Rhône where nearly all the dioceses traversed the river. Sometimes where royal power was weak, the political border was eventually adjusted to suit the more effective diocesan framework,[15] but in general the political border of the kingdom remained at odds with the ecclesiastical boundaries until the sixteenth century. Only then did the Valois and Habsburgs reorganise diocesan structures to match the political division between them.

Nevertheless, although often insignificant and sometimes forgotten, the Franco-Imperial border was not negligible. Sometimes it symbolised the authority of the two rulers: when the Emperor Henry II met Robert II of France in 1023, their counsellors advised them to confer by boat in the middle of the River Meuse, 'the border of both kingdoms' (*limes utriusque regni*), since if one crossed the river to meet the other, it would imply subordination.[16] If it was normally a 'cold' political frontier, it was liable to 'heat up' in times of rivalry between the kings of France and the emperors. For instance, the papal schism of 1159–78 focused attention upon the limits of the jurisdictions of Louis VII of France, a supporter of Alexander III, and of the Emperor Frederick Barbarossa, who nurtured a succession of antipopes, and this gave the Franco-Imperial border a greatly heightened political significance for a while.[17] The border also remained in folk memory long after it had been superseded: in the nineteenth century the boatmen along the Rhône were still referring to the riverbanks as *Riau* ('the Kingdom') and *Empi* ('the Empire').[18]

So the Franco-Imperial frontier was primarily a political and administrative border, marking the ultimate spheres of influence of the two chief powers in Western Europe. In the Middle Ages the kings and emperors did not maintain it as a fortified line and it did not function as the border of a sovereign state, but it was a division of both political and cultural significance. The other external borders of the kingdom also rarely troubled the kings of France before the late thirteenth century because they were so remote from the royal domain; only the cataclysmic Franco-Aragonese wars of the late thirteenth century, for instance, highlighted the fact that the king of Aragon possessed the Val d'Aran on the northern slopes of the Pyrenees, an anomaly which was never resolved but simply ignored once the crisis had passed.[19] France was not unique in possessing such 'frontiers'. The external borders of other medieval kingdoms could remain extraordinarily stable even though they generally did not match linguistic or cultural divisions: to take one example, the Imperial (and later Austrian) border with the kingdom of Hungary cut across German-speaking populations and yet remained unaltered for eight centuries until 1918.[20]

Frontiers within the Kingdom of France

However, the border between the kingdom of France and the Empire was by no means the only French 'frontier' in the twelfth century. There were also important political and cultural divisions within the kingdom of France. The most notable of these were the two great fissures between Northern and Southern France: the linguistic divide between the *langue d'oc* and *langue d'oïl*;[21] and the legal contrast between the *Pays du Droit Écrit*, which used forms of Roman Law, and the *Pays du Droit Coutumier*, where oral customary law prevailed and tended to tighten into highly regionalised customs in the late twelfth and thirteenth centuries.[22] Some way to the north, the middle and lower course of the Loire, which long before had served as the southern limits of the Frankish kingdoms and later of Carolingian Neustria,[23] continued to function as a notional divide between Northern France and the rest of the kingdom, even though the river no longer formed a political boundary. Hence the continental dominions of the Plantagenet

(Angevin) dynasty, extending in the late twelfth century from Normandy to Gascony, were sometimes reckoned for convenience as 'this side of the Loire' and 'beyond the Loire'.[24]

Moreover, until the Capetian kings added a series of spectacular annexations to their domains in the thirteenth century, political power and influence lay as much with the great principalities, such as the duchies of Normandy, Burgundy, and Aquitaine, or the counties of Flanders, Champagne, and Toulouse, as with the king of France.[25] The Capetian royal domain in *Francia* (the Île-de-France and surrounding districts) was just one of these principalities, and in the eleventh century in particular it was set apart from the others by little more than its ruler's royal title. In other words, the realm of France was deeply divided into smaller territorial units, each with its own borders which French historians have tended to call *frontières*. Only the most ardent believer in the French national myth would dismiss these provincial divisions as ephemeral or inconsequential.[26] Whereas disputes about the borders of the kingdom were exceedingly rare and tended to emerge from exceptional political crises, the provincial borders were a daily concern of kings and princes in France alike.

Can we regard these provincial borders as 'frontiers', that is, as major political barriers between territorially established political units? Often they were not defined even by natural features or landmarks, and frequently appear to be zones of diminishing control, comprising enclaves and exclaves, and competing or overlapping rights, rather than fixed linear borders. These features also characterised the Franco-Imperial border,[27] but the internal provincial borders of France were even less permanent and were far more prone to fluctuate or vanish entirely. For instance, in the twelfth and thirteenth centuries the count of Champagne was wont to parley with his neighbours at certain places at the fringes of his lands such as bridges, as if these fixed points, hallowed by tradition, demarcated the border of his territory; and in the minds of contemporaries the River Armançon formed the western border of Champagne with the county of Auxerre. Yet in spite of these notionally linear borders, in practice the limits of the county of Champagne shifted constantly.[28]

Quite apart from their impermanence, there was another reason why 'frontier' may seem an inapposite term for these provincial borders. Just as royal authority fragmented in the tenth century, in the course of the next hundred years the power and authority of the princes disintegrated in many parts of the kingdom, until local lordship came to be as important as any wider political organisation. This fragmentation (*encellulement*) meant that the castle and its *banlieue* or castelry – the area which the castellan commanded with his *ban* – became the primary unit of political power in many parts of France for much of the eleventh and. twelfth centuries.[29] The Carolingian court system was largely superseded by the conventions of settling disputes at the fringes of these castelries, normally through raids and counter-raids which served to deny a neighbour's lordship.[30] Rights of jurisdiction became an intrinsic dimension of lordship: for instance, lords took tolls at almost every town gate or river crossing. Were strong notions of frontiers' between provinces possible in this milieu? Some historians think not, and have found lordship a more attractive concept than frontiers for analysing and comparing medieval societies.[31] If collections of rights over individuals were more significant than territorially rooted political organisation, by extension contemporaries must have found the concept of political frontiers difficult or impossible to grasp, or else insignificant.

Yet two factors suggest that there are grounds for treating the borders of principalities as political 'frontiers'. Firstly, the power and authority of the princes did not fragment throughout France in the eleventh century, and where they did break down, many princes soon reasserted their authority, either by taking castles back into their own hands, or by establishing the right to enter and use the fortresses in time of need.[32] New administrative systems based on castles sprang up. At the fringes of their lands, where their power was likely to be disputed by a neighbour, princes paid particular attention to their fortresses, and so their lands often appeared to be girded by a series of fortifications. But fixed lines of demarcation could not match the realities of political control based upon fortresses, and inevitably these new, fortified borders were studded with enclaves and exclaves.

A second factor for treating these borders as frontiers is the frequency of contemporary references to them as important divisions, usually either as 'limits' (*fines*) or 'marches' (*marchie*). These inherently imprecise terms always implied a concept of political division, but could mean militarised borderlands as well as simple territorial demarcations. In terms of lordship, the borders of Champagne and Burgundy consisted of a bewildering mass of enclaves and competing rights, and the duke of Burgundy was lord of the count of Champagne for the count's prize possession, the county of Troyes. Nevertheless, there was a clear concept that there was a 'march' between the two provinces, for the count performed 'homage in the march' to the duke for Troyes.[33] In western France, the counties of Anjou, Brittany, and Poitou were in chronic competition to the south of the Loire until the mid twelfth century; yet the borderlands where the three provinces met were likewise termed *marches*. One twelfth-century chronicler described the fortress of Thouars as 'on the border of the Poitevins and Angevins' and the abbey of Fontevraud as 'on the edge of Angevin and Poitevin soil',[34] and a complex set of arrangements evolved to resolve the competing jurisdictions of the three principalities, in a series of villages known as the *Marches Séparantes*.[35] The fixed points in such 'marches' could have great political significance: they influenced contemporary views of the borders, since they seemed to symbolise political divisions, and they thereby became the customary sites for colloquies between the rulers or inhabitants of neighbouring principalities. In some regions these negotiations were occasional events, but they could also be veritable institutions, as in the *Marches Séparantes* or the Namurois.[36]

So provincial borders certainly existed in France in the eleventh and twelfth centuries, but they cannot be depicted satisfactorily on a map. Even where a province's exact geographical limits were defined by natural features or artificial markers, its political frontiers tended to comprise a broad zone of conflicting control, often eluding precise territorial definition, but within which there would be minute definition (in characteristic medieval fashion!) of rights over parcels of land, forests, waterways, castles, churches, people, and livestock.[37] Although a far cry from our sovereign-state frontiers, these 'marches' nevertheless marked out the main political units of the day.

The Frontiers of Normandy

It is now possible to examine the political frontier of Normandy. This border came into existence in about 911 when Rollo, the leader of a Scandinavian warband, made the treaty of Saint-Clair-sur-Epte with King Charles the Simple of France. The territorial extent of Rollo's principality was probably restricted to eastern (Upper) Normandy, where the rivers Epte and Eure were used from an early period to delineate the province. Since the early history of Normandy is shrouded in obscurity, however, it is difficult to say much more than this before the late tenth century. By the reign of Duke Richard II (996–1026), the 'Normans' were calling their land 'Normandy', and their rulers, now often calling themselves dukes, were building castles at the fringes of their territorial control.[38] At the same time, they succeeded in preventing the political disintegration of their duchy which afflicted so many other regions of the kingdom. Moreover, since castles were as aggressive as they were defensive, the dukes used their fortresses as springboards for further expansion southwards until the reign of Henry I of England as duke of Normandy (1106–35). Although Henry temporarily subjugated the neighbouring lordship of Bellême (1113), his defeat by the count of Anjou at Alençon (1119) effectively ended the southward expansion of the Normans.[39] Indeed, Normandy itself was conquered by the next count of Anjou in 1144. The political frontier of Normandy continued to exist, however; indeed, it came to be of prime importance to the whole of Western European politics by the late twelfth century as the chief battleground for the dynastic rivalry of the Plantagenets and Capetians. Even after the king of France annexed Normandy in 1204, the duchy's frontier did not vanish: the 'march' of Normandy was still worthy of note in Froissart's day, and this border retained administrative, legal, and at times political significance until the French Revolution.[40]

Historians of medieval France have had particular reasons for analysing the limits of Normandy. Whereas medieval political borders often seem like fluid zones of competing control, by the late twelfth century Normandy appears to have had an exact and definitive 'frontier', a militarised line which excluded the authority of the kings of France and within which the Norman 'state' enjoyed political, legal, and ecclesiastical unity, and sovereignty, until the sudden end of the duchy's independence in 1204. This view is based on the apparently close coincidence of the ecclesiastical, legal, and administrative limits of Normandy: the linear diocesan boundaries of the metropolitan province of Rouen, the district where the customs of Normandy were followed, and the area demonstrably under ducal fiscal and judicial administration in the twelfth century.[41] In fact, much of the evidence for the supposedly linear administrative boundary dates from the late Middle Ages, and the boundary of the Coutume has been deduced mainly from sixteenth-century inquests.[42] The ecclesiastical province never matched the duchy exactly: the French Vexin and Perche lay in the 'Norman' dioceses of Rouen and Sées respectively but beyond the borders of the duchy; on the other hand, the dukes exerted fluctuating control over the district called the Passais, although it lay in the diocese of Le Mans and metropolitan province of Tours, whose sees were outside the duchy, and

there were other, more minor variations besides.[43] Nevertheless, the
border of Normandy certainly was demarcated in a linear fashion in
some places in the twelfth century, notably where it lay along the
courses of the rivers Bresle, Epte, Eure, Avre, Sarthe, and Couesnon.
Along much of the southern border, Henry II is said to have constructed a series of earthworks, the *Fossés Royaux*, 'between France and
Normandy' according to one contemporary observer; they followed the
Sarthe and Avre and traversed the broken and wooded terrain between
those two river valleys.[44] Elsewhere the Normans had adopted the
boundaries of the dioceses or Carolingian counties (*pagi*) as the limits of
their territory in some districts, and set up boundary-posts (*mete*) or
chosen natural landmarks in others.[45]

However, can a linear border be understood without also considering
the surrounding region? Studies of the Roman walls and *limes*, Offa's
Dyke, and the Great Wall of China, to take only the most famous
'frontiers' of this genre, all suggest that borders defined in linear
fashion need to be viewed in the context of the regions they bisect.[46]
The Norman frontier was no exception. When we examine the political
arrangements made on the fringes of Normandy, it is apparent that
fortresses mattered far more than linear boundaries. It was the border
castles which drew the attention of chroniclers, especially when they
changed hands between the duke and his neighbours, or else, as frequently happened, between the duke and his own barons. In moments
of ducal weakness, such as the war of succession for Normandy between
Stephen of Blois and Geoffrey of Anjou (1135–44) or the Plantagenet
succession crisis of 1199, castellan families might be tempted to recover
the fortresses which the duke had seized from them or their ancestors
and which dominated their localities. Ducal power and authority consequently ebbed and flowed across a broad area, sometimes creating
enclaves and exclaves in its wake, especially along the southern borders.
Once the king of France began trying to overrun the eastern and
southeastern Norman borders, from 1193, this uncertainty increased,
but it had never been wholly banished from the districts at the fringes
of ducal authority.[47] When the duke seized a neighbour's castle, it has
been usual to see the entire territory around them as attached to the
duchy of Normandy, and historians' maps echo this. But it may well be
that sometimes garrisons alone were established in a fortress, with all
the attendant symbolism of political control and subjection which this
entailed, in the midst of a district whose ordinary administration belonged elsewhere.[48] At a given moment we may state the castles

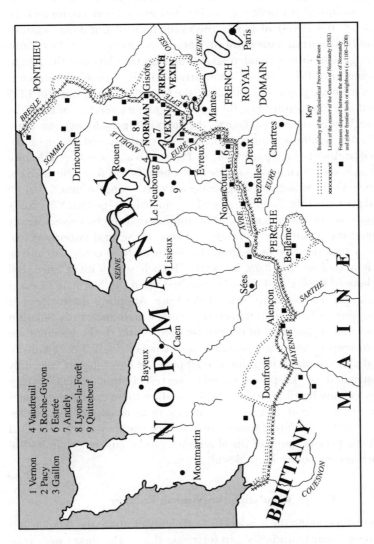

Map 5.2 The Frontiers of Normandy in the twelfth century.

1 Vernon
2 Pacy
3 Gaillon
4 Vaudreuil
5 Roche-Guyon
6 Estrée
7 Andely
8 Lyons-la-Forêt
9 Quittebeuf

Key

⋯⋯⋯ Boundary of the Ecclesiastical Province of Rouen

xxxxxxxxx Limit of the *ressort* of the Custom of Normandy (1583)

⋯⋯⋯ Fortresses disputed between the duke of Normandy and either frontier lords or neighbours (c. 1100–1200)

■

under ducal control far more easily than the exact limits of ducal jurisdiction.

Linear boundaries served a rather different purpose, not as sovereign and definitive political barriers but as practical landmarks. In England, the Forest of Lyme, the lower limit of Cheshire's eastern uplands, demarcated the authority of the earls of Chester in the county, although Cheshire extended some miles up the slopes of the neighbouring hills. Primarily an administrative limit, it could nevertheless take on a more political significance: the Cheshire Magna Carta of 1215 stated that the county knights owed no military service 'outside the Lyme'.[49] In Normandy, of course, the limits of the duchy were far more politically significant but the rulers of Normandy used linear or notional landmarks in a similar way. In 1206, soon after the king of France had annexed Normandy, Guy de la Roche, a baron from the adjacent French Vexin whom the king suspected of treason, promised that he would not cross the Rivers Epte or Eure 'in order to go into Normandy (*causa eundi in Normanniam*)'.[50] This implies that the two rivers neatly formed the frontier of Normandy. However, several important fortresses traditionally held from the duke of Normandy, including Vernon, Gaillon, and Pacy, lay on the 'French' side of River Eure, and the king of France had often encroached upon the Norman Vexin, a district on the 'Norman' side of the Epte. Adopting these rivers as approximate limits was therefore a very rough-and-ready solution rather than a statement of the precise border, and the king's intention was to keep a ready check on Guy whose chief castle, La Roche-Guyon, stood only two miles from the River Epte. The *Fossés Royaux*, allegedly constructed to 'keep out raiders', served a similar demarcatory purpose: any hostile warriors found north of these earthworks would receive short shrift.[51] Such lines, natural or artificial, offered a pragmatic means of defining spheres of influence, but they rarely coincided with the precise limits of ducal administration, custom, ecclesiastical structures, or political loyalties all at once.

Regulating the Norman Frontier

Negotiations along the borders of Normandy illustrate the relationship between linear boundaries and fortresses there. The dukes were conscious of the need to regulate and define the borders of their territory. As early as 968 Normans and French were meeting at Gisors on the Epte to regulate their affairs,[52] and in later years the dukes often held parleys with neighbouring princes 'in the march'. These meetings were frequently accompanied by the performance of homage, which became an important recognition of reciprocal rights between the duke and his neighbours.[53] Almost as ritualistic as these peaceful processes were the cross-border raids in wartime, a convention so common to marcher societies.[54]

The most detailed recorded statements about the Norman border formed part of two treaties during the wars of Philip Augustus of France with the last two Plantagenet dukes of Normandy, namely the kings of England, Richard I (1189–99) and John (1199–1216). King Philip's version of the Treaty of Louviers (1196) included the following provisions:

> Be it known that markers (*mete*) are to be placed midway between the fortress of Gaillon and the fortress of Vaudreuil, and from that marker in one direction as far as the Seine and in the other as far as the Eure, whatever shall be towards Gaillon shall be ours, and whatever shall be towards Vaudreuil shall be King Richard of England's.[55]

Four years later King Philip made even more precise terms with Richard the Lionheart's successor, King John, which included the following statement:

> Markers have been placed midway between Évreux and Le Neubourg, and everything within these markers towards France shall be ours, and everything on the other side towards Le Neubourg shall be the king of England's. And we shall have as much land towards Conches and Acquigny as we do towards Le Neubourg, by the same measurement in the direction of the abbey of La Noë as the river Iton flows. He has given Quittebeuf to us, wherever it may be.[56]

At first glance these statements suggest that the Norman frontier was to be an exact line enclosing a sovereign territory. Yet the treaties themselves reveal that the new border comprised more than a line of boundary-markers. In ecclesiastical terms, the treaty of Le Goulet affected a much larger region than the new borderline, for all the regalia of the bishopric of Évreux fell to the king of France, even though only a third of the diocese was in his hands. Moreover, despite the demarcation of new boundary lines, the prime concerns of the treaties were not precise

lines but the castles on either side, as well as the allegiances of the lords
of the disputed districts. Indeed, both treaties established an unfortified
border zone between the most disputed castles, in which existing fortifications were to be destroyed and no new ones were to be built.
Besides, in some places the contested fortresses were so valuable that
the new boundary lines were simply ignored. In 1196, the Treaty of
Louviers stipulated that Andely, a manor of the archbishop of Rouen,
was to remain unfortified and neither king could claim any fief or
domain there, although it lay within a district awarded to the king
of France: it was considered too fine a defensive site to be granted
to either party. Disregarding these terms, however, Richard I soon
seized Andely, built his famous Château-Gaillard and a series of lesser
fortifications there, and compensated the indignant archbishop with
property elsewhere; the treaty of 1200 therefore acknowledged that
Andely had now become an enclave of the duke of Normandy within
the French king's territory.[57] In 1200, as the text cited above shows,
the manor of Quittebeuf became a French enclave within the duke's
territory. The princes would accept linear divisions of territory only as
long as there were not more pressing considerations of defence, power,
or wealth.

Contemporary Views of the Norman Frontier

For all their inconsistencies, these agreements demonstrate that contemporaries recognised the existence of a militarised, territorially
defined frontier at the limits of ducal power. Records of ducal government reflect this, devoting much attention to a militarised 'march'.
Although 'march' could have more peaceful connotations as a local
jurisdictional limit, payments for defence of the Norman 'march' give it
much greater political and military significance. Taxes were levied 'to
keep men-at-arms in the March', orders and money were sent to the
'constables of the March' and their castles, and throughout Normandy
knight-service was organised to defend the duchy's marches.[58]

More often the sources refer simply to the 'limits of Normandy'
(confinium Normannie, fines Normannie). This description does not necessarily imply a militarised border: when a charter for the lazarhouse of
Grand-Beaulieu at Chartres – that is, in 'France' – described the ducal
fortress of Nonancourt as 'on the limits of France and Normandy' (in
finibus Francie et Normannie), this did not necessarily imply anything
more than the recognition of a local boundary, possibly mentioned for

its legal significance.[59] But the narrative sources often explicitly depict the *fines Normannie* as a fortified region. The greatest ducal fortress of all, Gisors, lay 'on the border of France and Normandy' (*in confinio Francie et Normannie*); but the context in which we learn this from the commentator, namely the disastrous betrayal of the fortress to the king of France in 1193, shows that this location was no mere geographical detail.[60] One chronicler stated that the county of Aumale had been 'established long before to safeguard the *fines Normanniæ*'.[61] In the 1130s Orderic Vitalis, writing close to the Norman frontier, stated that the 'Manceau and Norman borderers' (*finitimi Cenomannenses et Normanni*) dwelling near the castle of Saint-Cénery were plagued by constant wars.[62] His view of the *fines Normannie* was echoed by the other chief Norman commentator of the day, Robert of Torigny, prior of Bec and later abbot of Mont-Saint-Michel, a close associate of Henry II (d. 1189) in Normandy. Torigny described the fortifying activities of Henry I (d. 1135) on the 'margin of his duchy and the neighbouring provinces', as if this were a single policy. The 'margin' that Torigny imagined was a broad district rather than a single line, for the castles included Drincourt, some fifteen miles into Normandy from the River Bresle, the supposed limit of the duchy and the diocese of Rouen.[63] Torigny later added to his list Évreux and Lyons-la-Forêt, likewise some distance from the boundary along the rivers Eure and Epte respectively.[64] His comments suggest that the frontiers of Normandy were less linear than historians have supposed, but the rulers of Normandy nevertheless treated them as a single military concern.

From the other side of the Norman border these fortresses also appeared as a barrier. The monastic commentator most closely associated with Louis VI of France, Abbot Suger of Saint-Denis, shows the significance of such fortresses to the French. Gisors, he said, was situated at the 'common boundary' (*utrumque terminum*) between the French and Normans, and it 'offers easy entry for the Normans to rush into France while it hinders a French approach'.[65] His perceptive comment is not so different from an observation of the great French military engineer Vauban five centuries later, who noted the need to fortify the external frontier of France 'in such a way that it closes the enemy's way into our country and facilitates our entry into his'.[66] Suger also referred to 'almost the whole march of Normandy' and 'the march of the Normans'.[67] A later monk of Saint-Denis, Rigord, noted that in 1193 Philip Augustus, the king of France, subdued 'the whole march of Normandy'.[68] The earliest French royal accounts (1202–03) made

separate provisions for the revenues of the 'Marches', chiefly
the castelries which King Philip had conquered from the duke of
Normandy since 1193.[69]

The Permeable Frontier

So contemporary rulers and chroniclers certainly recognised the existence of a Norman political frontier. Yet there is much evidence that the
inhabitants of the frontier regions themselves viewed their localities in
a rather different light from either the courts of Rouen and Paris or the
chroniclers. Many aspects of daily life were hardly affected by the
presence of the frontier. Trade passed in and out of Normandy, from
the fair of Montmartin in the Côtentin to Brittany, and up and down
the Rivers Seine and Sarthe.[70] Charters of exemption from customs, our
best guide to these, show that there were customs posts throughout the
duchy, not merely on the borders, erected at the limits of many a lord's
ban. Travelling up the Seine, a merchant would have probably encountered no officials of the duke of Normandy after Pont-de-l'Arche, but
thirty miles upstream he would have still been paying tolls to barons
who owed allegiance to the duke of Normandy, namely the lords of
Vernon. The merchant would then have passed the customs posts of
the lords of Roche-Guyon and Rosny, who owed allegiance to the king
of France, but only at Mantes would he have met the French king's
officials, the first manifestation of direct Capetian authority.[71] This
trade persisted even in time of conflict: in 1202 King John guaranteed
that wine merchants could come down the Seine from *Francia* into
Normandy, even though he was at war with the king of France.[72]

The economic unity of the districts divided by the Norman borders
is visible in other ways. For instance, at the abbey of Estrée, on the
'Norman' bank of the boundary River Avre, donors might assess
the grain they were giving in alms from their 'Norman' lands using the
weights and measures of towns which all lay beyond the 'French' bank
of the Avre, such as Chartres, Dreux, or Brezolles.[73] One benefactor of
Estrée, who held lands on both sides of the Avre, promised that in
wartime he would provide an escort for the grain, which he had assigned to the abbey from his 'French' lands, to the safety of either
Brezolles (on the 'French' side of the Avre) or Nonancourt (the major
ducal fortress on the 'Norman' side). In other words, the local aristocracy would protect the abbey's livelihood when war between rulers
divided this local society.[74] As in so many frontier regions, the inhabit-

ants here had to disregard political divisions in order to survive through commerce and contacts with their neighbours, but were rarely free of the perils of living along a militarised frontier.

As may be expected, there were many cross-border lordships and ties of association between Norman landowners and their neighbours. In the Norman Vexin, one of the most contested border regions, the four main families all had close ties of land and kinship with the French Vexin beyond the River Epte, although these varied significantly from family to family.[75] The same could be said of most of the main aristocratic families along the borders of the duchy. These families reinforced bonds of kinship and homage with communal actions, such as the foundation and endowment of abbeys. Nor were such ties restricted to the greater aristocracy; they can also be traced for knights and burgesses.[76] Family links across the border leave us wondering what the criteria were by which the aristocracy came to regard themselves as 'Norman' or 'French', if indeed they did at all. The narrative sources employ a clear 'rhetoric of difference' to distinguish the Normans from their neighbours, but the reality on the ground must have been far more difficult to discern.[77]

The Norman Frontier after 1204

The border of Normandy, then, may be termed a 'frontier', in that it linked territorial political organisation with military institutions and a concept of the March as a military concern. It was just one example of a common sort of *frontière* within the kingdom of France, but it enjoyed unusually precise notional and jurisdictional limits compared with other provincial frontiers. Yet the Norman frontier also functioned as a zone of contact, for it was crossed by traders, aristocratic estates, and increasingly by the rights of the king of France. The Norman state had certainly no chance to develop sovereign territorial *frontières*, such as became common in France in the Late Middle Ages, before the king of France destroyed the chief political significance of the Norman frontier in 1204.

Yet the extinction of the duchy's power and the expulsion of its dukes in 1204 did not put an end to the Norman frontier: for the English Channel was transformed from being primarily a highway between England and Normandy into a major political barrier, creating a whole new set of frontier problems.[78] In some ways, this Norman frontier was as complex as the earlier landed border, retaining many political, administrative, ecclesiastical, and legal ambiguities. For a generation or so after 1204 Norman ships aided the kings of England in their abortive expeditions to reconquer their lost French lands.[79] Besides, the Channel Islands, an integral part of ducal Normandy, remained under ducal control and have been separated politically from Normandy ever since. Yet they also formed part of the metropolitan province of Rouen and the diocese of Coutances until the late fifteenth century, and again, at least in the eyes of the Catholic Church, from the Reformation until the Concordat with Napoleon.[80] Norman abbeys retained their properties on the islands. The islanders continued to follow Norman law, not a version fossilised in 1204 but one which remained abreast of developments in Norman custom in succeeding centuries. The Channel now became the militarised border across which sporadic raids took place but coexistence and commerce were also normal; the new fortified enclaves in the Norman frontier were the Channel Islands, their jurisdictions abounding in ambiguities.[81] Thanks to the islands' persisting anomalous status, the political legacy of the medieval Norman frontier in some forms remains with us today.

NOTES

1. K. F. Werner, 'Kingdom and principality in twelfth-century France', *The Medieval Nobility*, ed. and trans. T. Reuter, Amsterdam 1978, 243.

2. For the Norman frontier, see J.-F. Lemarignier, *Recherches sur l'hommage en marche et les frontières féodales*, Lille 1945; L. Musset, 'Actes inédits du XIᵉ siècle. III: Les plus anciennes chartes normandes de l'abbaye de Bourgueil', *Bulletin de la Société des Antiquaires de Normandie*, LIV (1957–58), 15–54, esp. 36–47; *idem*, 'Considérations sur la genèse et le trace des frontières de la Normandie', *Media in Francia, Recueil . . . K. F. Werner*, Maulévrier 1989, 309–18; J. Yver, 'Philippe Auguste et les châteaux normands: la frontière orientale du duché', *Bulletin de la Société des Antiquaires de Normandie*, LIX (1967–89), 309–48. For reassessment of Lemarignier's thesis, see J. Le Patourel, *The Norman Empire*, Oxford 1976, 3–12; D. J. Power, 'What did the frontier of Angevin Normandy comprise?', *ANS*, XVII (1994), 181–201.

3. For example J. Boussard, *Le Gouvernement d'Henri II Plantegenêt*, Paris 1956, 19, 92; A. Chédeville, *Chartres et ses campagnes*, Paris 1973, 41, 59; P. Contamine, *La guerre au moyen âge*, Paris 1980, 370.

4. Cf. the introduction to this volume. Part A. For German references to the Norman frontier (*die Grenze zur Normandie*), see D. Lohrmann, 'St-Germer-de-Fly und das Anglonormannische Reich', *Francia*, I (1973), 193–4.

5. Cf. the introduction to this volume, 9–12.

6. Cf. the introduction to this volume, 3–6.

7. See P. Sahlins, 'Natural frontiers revisited: France's boundaries since the seventeenth century', *American Historical Review*, XCV (1990), 1423–51, including the Maginot line (1450).

8. R. Dion, 'À propos du traité de Verdun', *Annales: Économies, Sociétés, Civilisations*, V (1950), 464.

9. For the events and division of 843, see R. Dion, *Les frontières de la France*, Paris 1947, 71–85; F. L. Ganshof, 'The significance of the treaty of Verdun (843)', *The Carolingians and the Frankish Monarchy: Studies in Carolingian History*, trans. J. Sondheimer, London 1971, 289–302; P. Classen, 'Die Verträge von Verdun und Coulaines, 843, als politische Grundlagen des westfränkischen Reiches', *Historische Zeitschrift*, CXCVI (1963), 1–35; J. L. Nelson, *Charles the Bald*, London 1992, 1–4, 132–5. None discusses the exact course of the chosen line.

10. Sahlins, 'Natural frontiers revisited', 1425–30. For the Franco-Imperial border in the Low Countries, see F. Lot, 'La frontière de la France et de l'Empire sur le cours inférieur de l'Escaut du IXᵉ au XIIIᵉ siècle', *Bibliothèque de l'École des Chartes*, LXXI (1910), 5–32; Lemarignier, *Homage en marche*, 13 n. 12; L. Génicot, 'La ligne et zone: la frontière des principautés médiévales', *Études sur les principautés lotharingiennes*, Louvain 1975, 172–85; also n. 12 below. For its character along the upper Meuse, see M. Bur, 'La frontière entre la Champagne et la Lorraine du milieu du Xᵉ siècle à la fin du XIIᵉ siècle', *Francia*, IV (1976), 237–54; *idem*, 'Recherches sur la frontière dans la région mosane aux XIIᵉ et XIIIᵉ siècles', *Actes du 103ᵉ Congrès National des Sociétés Savantes (Nancy-Metz, 1978): principautés et territoires et études d'histoire lorraine*, Paris 1979, 143–60; but cf. Lemarignier, *Hommage en marche*, 168–9, for the border separating the counties of Bar (in the Empire) and Champagne (in the kingdom of France). For the border in Burgundy, see J. Richard, *Les ducs de Bourgogne et la formation du duché du XIᵉ au XIVᵉ siècle*, Paris 1954, 44, 46–7. For the Rhône, see F. Braudel, *The Identity of France*, trans. S. Reynolds, 2 vols, London 1988–90, I, 281–8.

11. Bur, 'frontière mosane', 151; Génicot, 'ligne et zone', 178, 183.

12. J. Dhondt, 'Essai sur l'origine de la frontière linguistique', *L'Antiquité Classique*, XVI (1947), 261–86. The medieval frontier between French and Flemish ran somewhat to the west and south of the present linguistic frontier, across Artois.

13. *The Historical Atlas of Modern Europe*, ed. R. L. Poole, Oxford 1902, Plates LIII, LV, LVII, together provide a basic if rather simplistic picture of these discrepancies.

14. M. Bur, *La formation du comté de Champagne*, Nancy 1977, 84–5.

15. Bur, 'frontière entre Champagne et Lorraine', 254.

16. Rodulfus Glaber, *Opera*, ed. and trans. J. France, Oxford 1989, 108–10.

17. G. Duby, *La société aux XIᵉ et XIIᵉ siècles dans la région mâconnaise*, 2nd edn, Paris 1971, 405–9.

18. Dion, *frontières*, 82.

19. P. Lauer, 'Une enquête au sujet de la frontière française dans le val d'Aran sous Philippe le Bel', *Comité des Travaux Historiques et Scientifiques: Bulletin de la Section de Géographie*, XXXV (1920), 17–38.

20. R. J. W. Evans, 'Frontiers and national identities in Central Europe', *International History Review*, XIV (1992), 497.

21. F. Brunot, *Histoire de la Langue Française des origines à nos jours*, new edn, 13 vols in 23, Paris 1966–72, I, 304–9; for the main dialects within the *langue d'oïl*, see 309–31. It is very difficult to know the extent and location of the divisions between these dialects in the twelfth century.

22. See, for instance, J. Yver, *Égalité entre héritiers et exclusion des enfants dotés*, Paris 1966; P. Ourliac, 'Législation, coutume et coutumiers au temps de Philippe Auguste', *La France de Philippe Auguste: le temps des mutations*, ed. R.-H. Bautier, Paris 1982, 471–88.

23. Cf. Classen, 'Verträge von Verdun', 5–6.

24. *Chronica Magistri Rogeri de Hovedene*, ed. W. Stubbs, 4 vols, London 1868–71, III, 259 (Plantagenet-Capetian truce of 1194); *Œuvres de Rigord et de Guillaume le Breton*, ed. H.-F. Delaborde, 2 vols, Paris 1882–5, II, 167–9, for King John of England's promise not to take his imprisoned nephew Arthur across the Loire (towards Normandy).

25. H. Wolfram, 'The shaping of the early medieval principality as a form of non-royal rulership', *Viator*, II (1971), 49–51; Werner, 'Kingdom and principality'.

26. Cf. R. Fossier, *L'enfance de l'Europe (X–XII siècles): aspects économiques et sociaux*, 2 vols, Paris 1982, I, 293–4.

27. Génicot, 'ligne et zone', e.g. 183; Bur, 'frontière mosane', 143–60.

28. Lemarignier, *Hommage en marche*, 126–54; for the Armançon, see 142 and n. 61; and Bur, *formation de Champagne*, 163.

29. J.-F. Lemarignier, 'La dislocation du «pagus» et le problème des «consuetudines» (Xᵉ–XIᵉ siècles)', *Mélanges d'histoire du Moyen Âge dédiés à la mémoire de Louis Halphen*, Paris 1951, 401–10, is the classic analysis of the disruption of the Carolingian administrative system and the rise of bannal lordships. For *encellulement*, see R. Fossier, *Enfance de l'Europe*, I, 288–595; Duby, *La région mâconnaise*, 137–262; G. Devailly, *Le Berry du Xᵉ Siècle au milieu du XIIIᵉ*, Paris 1973, 168–76, 317–49; J.-P. Poly and E. Bournazel, *The Feudal Transformation 900–1200*, trans. C. Higgitt, New York and London 1991; T. Bisson, 'The "Feudal Revolution"?', *Past and Present*, CXLIV (1994), 6–42. Chédeville, *Chartres*, 268–307, and D. Barthélemy, *La société dans le comté de Vendôme de l'an mil au xivᵉ siècle*, Paris 1993, 333–64, both challenge the extent of this disintegration.

30. S. D. White, 'Feuding and peace-making in the Touraine around the year 1100', *Traditio*, XLII (1986), 195–263.

31. For example J. M. H. Smith, *Province and Empire: Brittany and the Carolingians*, Cambridge 1992, 2–3; P. M. Duffy, 'The nature of the medieval frontier in Ireland', *Studia Hibernica*, XXII–XXIII (1982–83), 21–38, esp. 36–8.

32. For the custom of right of entry to castles, see C. L. H. Coulson, 'Rendability and castellation in medieval France', *Château-Gaillard*, VI (1973), 59–67; idem, 'Fortress-policy in Capetian tradition and Angevin practice: aspects of the conquest of Normandy by Philip Augustus', *ANS*, VI (1983), 13–38.

33. Lemarignier, *Hommage en marche*, 155–76. For the various homages given to the duke of Burgundy in the 'marches' of his duchy, see Richard, *ducs de Bourgogne*, 24–49.

34. *Chronique de Robert de Torigni*, ed. L. Delisle, 2 vols, Paris 1871–72, II, 169, 189.

35. É. Chénon, 'Les marches séparantes d'Anjou, Bretagne, et Poitou', *Nouvelle Revue Historique du Droit Français et Étranger*, XVI (1892), 18–62, 165–211; XXI (1897), 62–80.

36. J. Balon, 'L'organisation judiciaire des marches féodales', *Annales de la Société Archéologique de Namur*, XLVI (1951), 5–72.

37. For precise definition of Plantagenet and Capetian rights at Tours in 1190, see *Recueil des actes de Philippe Auguste*, ed. H.-F. Delaborde et al., 4 vols, Paris 1916–79, I, no. 361.

38. For contrasting interpretations of the early history of Normandy, see D. Bates, *Normandy before 1066*, London 1982; E. Searle, *Predatory Kinship and the Creation of Norman Power*, University of California 1988.

39. *The Ecclesiastical History of Orderic Vitalis*, ed. M. Chibnall, 6 vols, Oxford 1969–80, VI, 178–82, 204–8; *Chroniques des comtes d'Anjou et des seigneurs d'Amboise*, ed. L. Halphen and R. Poupardin, Paris 1913, 155–61. For fluctuating control of this southern border, see Power, 'Frontier of Angevin Normandy', 186–9.

40. Jean Froissart, *Chroniques*, ed. G. T. Diller, 4 vols to date, Geneva 1991–, e.g. III, 234.

41. Lemarignier, *Hommage en marche*, 18–23.

42. Power, 'Frontier of Angevin Normandy', 191–3.

43. Lemarignier, *Hommage en marche*, 47–55, 61, 65 n. 152; Le Patourel, *Norman Empire*, 10; Power, 'Frontier of Angevin Normandy', 191.

44. *Chronique de Robert de Torigni*, II, 13 (1169); Contamine, *La guerre*, 369–70.

45. Lemarignier, *Hommage en marche*, 11–19 (*pagi*), 103–5 (elm of Gisors).

46. C. R. Whittaker, *Frontiers of the Roman Empire: a social and economic study*, Baltimore and London 1994, who also (62 and notes) discusses recent historiography of Offa's Dyke; O. Lattimore, 'Origins of the Great Wall of China: a frontier concept in theory and practice', *Studies in Frontier History*, Oxford 1962, 97–118, esp. 113–17; A. Waldron, *The Great Wall of China: from history to myth*, Cambridge 1990. See also the introduction to this volume, 4–5. Cf. P. Sahlins, *Boundaries: the making of France and Spain in the Pyrenees*, University of California 1989, 4–5.

47. Cf. Power, 'Frontier of Angevin Normandy', 186–90.

48. *Ibid.*, 189 (Bellême).

49. *The Charters of the Anglo-Norman Earls of Chester*, ed. G. Barraclough et al., Chester 1988, no. 394 (cf. nos 266, 395); cf. *The Place-Names of Cheshire*, ed. J. McN. Dodgson, 5 vols, Cambridge 1970–81, I, 2–6.

50. *Layettes du Trésor des Chartes*, ed. A. Teulet et al., 5 vols, Paris 1863–1909, I, no. 799.

51. *Chronique de Robert de Torigni*, II, 13.

52. *Recueil des actes des ducs de Normandie de 911 à 1066*, ed. M. Fauroux, Caen 1961, no. 3.

53. Lemarignier, *Hommage en marche*, 73–125. The count of Perche did homage to the duke of Normandy in 1113 and 1158, but it is not known where: Orderic, VI, 182; *Chronique de Robert de Torigni*, I, 315.

54. See J. Gillingham, 'War and chivalry in the *History of William the Marshal*', *Thirteenth-Century England: Proceedings of the Newcastle-upon-Tyne Conference 1987*, ed. P. R. Coss and S. D. Lloyd, Woodbridge 1988, 1–13. For Irish and Welsh parallels in raiding and parleys, see Duffy, 'frontier in Ireland', 23–4; R. R. Davies, 'Frontier arrangements in fragmented societies: Ireland and Wales', (*MFS*), 77–100, esp. 83–9; for raiding practices along the Franco-Spanish Pyrenean border in the early modern era, see Sahlins, *Boundaries*, 17–18.

55. *Diplomatic Documents 1101–1272*, ed. P. Chaplais, I, London 1964, no. 6; King Richard's version is *Layettes du Trésor des Chartes*, I, no. 412. For parallels from other parts of France, see P. Bonenfant, 'À propos des limites médiévales', *Éventail de l'histoire vivant: hommage à Lucien Febvre*, 2 vols, Paris 1953, 76–9.

56. *Diplomatic Documents*, no. 9; King John's version is *Layettes du Trésor des Chartes*, I, no. 578. F. M. Powicke, *The Loss of Normandy*, 2nd edn, Manchester 1961, 168–70, attempts to map the new boundary.

57. *Diplomatic Documents*, no. 6; Powicke, *Loss of Normandy*, 114–17, 136.

58. See the references collected in Power, 'Frontier of Angevin Normandy', 185 n. 13.

59. *Cartulaire de la léproserie du Grand-Beaulieu*, ed. R. Merlet and M. Josselin, Chartres 1909, no. 52 (*c.* 1160).

60. *Itinerarium Peregrinorum et Gesta Regis Ricardi*, ed. W. Stubbs, London, 1864, 176.

61. *The Historical Works of Ralph de Diceto*, ed. W. Stubbs, 2 vols, London 1876, II, 3.

62. Orderic, IV, 156.

63. Robert of Torigny, interpolations to William of Jumièges, *Gesta Normannorum Ducum*, ed. E. M. C. van Houts, 2 vols, Oxford 1992–95, II, 250 (my translation differs slightly); cf. 92, where William of Jumièges likewise envisaged the Norman borders as a troubled zone, a century earlier.

64. *Chronique de Robert de Torigni*, I, 196.

65. Suger, *Vie de Louis le Gros*, ed. H. Waquet, Paris 1929, 102. I follow the translation in *The Deeds of Louis the Fat*, trans. R. C. Cusimano and J. Moorhead, Washington DC 1992, 71.

66. S. de Vauban, *Mémoire des places frontières de Flandres* (1678), quoted by L. Febvre, '*Frontière*: the word and the concept', *A New Idea of History (from the Writings of Febvre)*, trans. K. Folca, ed. P. Burke, London 1973, 210.

67. Suger, 110, 184.

68. *Œuvres de Rigord*, I, 123.

69. F. Lot and R. Fawtier, *Le premier budget de la monarchie française*, Paris 1932, eg. CLXV, CLXXV, CLXXXVII, CCIV; cf. 154–6, 196–205.

70. Powicke, *Loss of Normandy*, 179.

71. For numerous exemptions along the Seine, see the cartularies of Fécamp and St-Georges-de-Boscherville (Rouen, Bibliothèque Municipale, Y 51, Y

52); *Cartulaire de l'abbaye royale de Notre-Dame de Bonport*, ed. J. Andrieux, Évreux 1862; F. Lot, *Études critiques sur l'abbaye de Saint-Wandrille*, Paris 1913 (2ᵉ partie); *Chartes de l'abbaye de Jumièges*, ed. J. J. Vernier, 2 vols, Rouen and Paris 1916.

72. *Rotuli Litterarum Patentium*, ed. T. Duffus Hardy, London 1835, 15.

73. Évreux, Archives de l'Eure, H 319 (Estrée Cartulary), eg. fol. 14v.–15, no. 25 (Chartres); fol. 57, no. 129 (Dreux); fol. 16, no. 28 (Brezolles).

74. Estrée Cartulary, fol. 16, no. 28 (Richard de Courteilles).

75. J. A. Green, 'Lords of the Norman Vexin', *War and Government in the Middle Ages*, ed. J. Gillingham and J. C. Holt, Woodbridge 1984, 47–61.

76. Cf. Power, 'Frontier of Angevin Normandy', 193–8. See my forthcoming book on the Norman frontier.

77. For Norman identity in the southern frontier districts, see Power, 'Frontier of Angevin Normandy', 199–200; for the complexities of Norman identity, see R. H. C. Davis, *The Normans and their Myth*, London 1976; G. A. Loud, 'The *Gens Normannorum* – myth or reality?', *ANS*, IV (1981), 104–16. The phrase 'rhetoric of difference' is adapted from Smith, *Province and Empire*, 3, who refers to a 'rhetoric of ethnic difference' between ninth-century Franks and Bretons; the term 'ethnic' appears inappropriate for the distinctions between the Normans and their neighbours in the twelfth century.

78. W. Stevenson, 'England and Normandy, 1204–59', unpub. Ph.D. thesis, 2 vols, University of Leeds 1974.

79. For aid of the men of Dieppe and Leure (near modern Le Havre) to Henry III's expedition to Brittany and Poitou in 1230, see *Patent Rolls (Henry III) 1225–32*, ed. HMSO, London 1903, 370–5.

80. A. J. Eagleston, *The Channel Islands under Tudor Government 1485–1642: a study in administrative history*, Cambridge 1949, ch. 6.

81. For the Channel Isles after 1204, see J. Le Patourel, *Feudal Empires: Norman and Plantagenet*, ed. M. Jones, London 1984, nos. II–IV; Stevenson, 'England and Normandy', II, 238–319.

6

NORTHERN SYRIA BETWEEN THE MONGOLS AND MAMLUKS: POLITICAL BOUNDARY, MILITARY FRONTIER, AND ETHNIC AFFINITIES[1]

Reuven Amitai-Preiss

On Friday, 3 September 1260, the apparently relentless advance of the Mongols into the Muslim world was halted at ʿAyn Jālūt in northern Palestine by the Mamluk rulers of Egypt. The Mongol conquest of the Islamic Middle East had begun with the campaigns of Chinggis (Genghiz) Khan into northeastern Iran in 1219–23. In subsequent decades, Mongol-controlled territory expanded to include almost all of present-day Iran, the area south of the Caucasus, and most of Anatolia. During the early 1250s, Chinggis Khan's grandson, Hülegü, was dispatched by his brother, the Great Khan (Qaʾan) Möngke, to reorganise previously conquered territory in the Islamic countries, and to continue expansion to the west and south. A milestone in this campaign was the taking of Baghdad in 1258 and the subsequent execution of the Caliph; the Mongols thereby put an end to a moribund political institution, which yet had remaining symbolic importance to most Muslims. By the beginning of 1260, the Mongols were ready to move into northern Syria. To the majority of the local population and rulers, not to say the Mongols themselves, it was clear that no one was capable of stopping this march.[2]

What the Mongols had not counted on was an opponent as capable and determined as the Mamluks, who had taken control of Egypt in 1250. The Mamluks not only defeated the Mongols in 1260 at ʿAyn Jālūt, but over the next 60 years successfully withstood repeated Mongol aggression against their kingdom, now including Syria. An important aspect of this war was the fighting on the frontier in northern Syria and along the Euphrates. The Mamluks adopted a realistic and coherent frontier strategy and made concerted efforts to implement it, thereby strengthening their hold on these outlying regions and affording greater protection to the Syrian heartland. The Mongols, on the other hand, appear not to have conceived any consistent policy for their side of the frontier and maintained at best an intermittent presence there, thus indirectly contributing to the integrity and security of the Mamluk marches. The military frontier was paralleled by a generally clear political boundary, delineated to a large degree by geography, and emphasised by religious and ideological elements. Paradoxically, together with this long-term and often intense military struggle, there are many similarities, even commonalities, between the military-political elites of the two states, engendered by their common origin, the Eurasian steppe. Yet, in spite of this ethnic and linguistic closeness – recognised by the participants themselves – and the occasional blurring of political and cultural identities, the struggle between these two ruling groups, fuelled by religion and other beliefs, continued until around 1320. Behind the military and political frontier was a clear dichotomy of identity and ideology.

Background: The Mamluk Institution

The success of the Mamluk Sultanate in withstanding Mongol aggression, not least on the frontier, was due largely to the nature of the Mamluk military society which led it. The Mamluks were military slaves (*mamlūk* literally means 'owned'), mainly hailing from the Turkish tribes then nomadising in the steppes north of the Black Sea. The importing of Turkish slaves to serve in the Muslim armies had begun in the early ninth century, if not before. Mamluk units, almost invariably composed of mounted archers, soon became the backbone of Muslim armies. The underlying principles of the Mamluk system were that boys and young men would be taken out of their normal nomadic – and pagan – environment, and imported as slaves, whereafter they were converted to Islam and underwent years of training. Upon its completion, they were enrolled in the army of their patron (a ruler or senior officer), to whom they were expected to show great loyalty, as they were to each

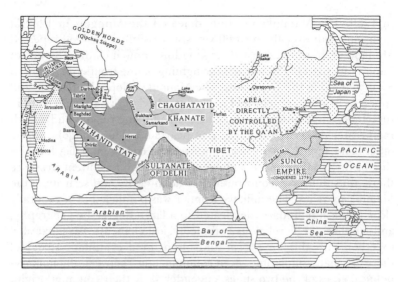

Map 6.1   Asia after 1260, showing territory under Mongol control (divided into the various Khanates), as well as the Mamluk Sultanate.
Reproduced by kind permission of Cambridge University Press from Reuven Amitai-Preiss, *Mongols and Mamluks: the Ilkhanid-Mamluk war, 1260–1281.*

other. The sons of Mamluks were not generally considered as Mamluks; in other words, the Mamluk system was a one-generational military elite, constantly replenished by fresh young recruits.[3]

It is worth stressing the importance of the Turkish element in this revolution in military manpower, which eventually led to the Arabs (bedouin and urban) and Iranians being supplanted as the dominant military element in most of the medieval Muslim world. The young Turks of the Eurasian steppes were imported because they were excellent raw material for soldiers. The harsh environment of Inner Asia, as well as the rigours of the pastoral nomadic lifestyle, made for strong and hardy inhabitants. Pastoral nomadism also demanded and cultivated the use of the horse. From a very young age, Inner Asian nomads grew accustomed to riding, and essentially all were potential cavalrymen. The weapon of choice in Central Asia was the composite bow, wielded with great skill on horseback. But the nomads of Inner Asia were not only hardened horsemen and proficient archers: from early times, the traditional tactics of Inner Asian armies were based on large and disciplined masses of lightly armoured and highly mobile mounted archers.[4]

The idea of the Mamluk system, then, was to take these Inner Asians, meaning primarily Turks, at an age when they had been formed enough by their original environment and culture to be hardy and competent horseman, and perhaps had picked up the rudiments of archery and other useful skills, but when they were still young enough to be transformed by their new society into faithful Muslims and loyal servants of their patrons. With all its problems, the system seemed to work well enough: the institution of military slavery spread rapidly from its original abode in Iraq to most of the Islamic world and lasted, albeit in a somewhat altered form, for 1000 years. More to the point in the present context, it was to prove itself in the wars fought against the Crusaders and, more importantly, the Mongols.

The Mamluk-Mongol War and the Beginnings of the Frontier

The first decade of Mamluk rule (1250–60), initially limited to Egypt, was one of instability and infighting.[5] Yet, with the approach of the Mongols, the Mamluks under Quṭuz were able to achieve a modicum of unity, and in the summer of 1260 set out for Syria to confront the relatively small army then occupying Syria, the main Mongol force having moved further east to Azerbaijan. The Mamluk victory at the battle of ʿAyn Jālūt in 1260 was due to several reasons: spirited and capable leadership; high morale owing to a win-or-die attitude, as compared to a feeling of complacency among the Mongols; the apparent numerical superiority of the Mamluks; and the death of the Mongol commander in the battle.[6] Perhaps the most important factor, however, was the similarity in the fighting methods of the Turkish Mamluks and the Mongols, both based on disciplined masses of mounted archers, deriving from the common steppe origin of both sides. This fact was not lost on contemporary writers, most notably the Damascene Abū Shāma (d. 1267), who wrote: 'Among the amazing things is that the Mongols were defeated and annihilated by members of their own race (*jins*) from among the Turks.'[7] I will return to this sense of ethnic similarity and even commonality below.

Given the smallness of the Mongol force involved at ʿAyn Jālūt, the Mamluk victory may have been only of limited importance from a purely military point of view. But its psychological significance was great, showing that the invincible Mongols could be defeated, and providing the young Mamluk regime with much-needed legitimacy.[8] It also gave the Mamluks control over Syria, for the Mongols had eradicated the Ayyūbid rulers there. In the weeks after the battle, Mamluk forces were to move into northern Syria, advancing as far as the Euphrates and the foothills of the Taurus mountains. In actuality, it was to be several months until the areas of north and northeast Syria were firmly incorporated into the newly enlarged Mamluk state, and in some areas it was even a matter of several years. This consolidation process was also punctuated early on by a large-scale Mongol raid in late 1260, repulsed by a second Mamluk victory north of the central Syrian city of Homs.

In the aftermath of these battles, the frontier zone became more and more defined, certainly to the northeast, along the Euphrates. Due east, Mamluk direct control faded into the expanses of the Syrian desert, but Mamluk suzerainty was generally recognised by the bedouins in that area up to the Euphrates, at times even beyond. To the north, the border was less delineated, but after the repulsion of several raids from the Armenian kingdom of Cilicia (known as Lesser Armenia), there too a frontier zone under Mamluk control became increasingly clear.[9] With the exception of most of the coast, which was in Crusader hands (until 1291), and a few residual enclaves controlled by local Muslim potentates, Syria was now under direct Mamluk rule, and remained so until the Ottoman conquest in 1516. The heartland of Mamluk Syria – meaning the major cities of north and central Syria (Aleppo, Homs, Hama, Tripoli, and Damascus), and various smaller cities (Jerusalem, Safad, and so on), together with their agricultural hinterlands – was relatively far from the frontier region.

The Mamluks leaders were aware that their victory at ʿAyn Jālūt had not ended the Mongol danger, and increasingly it became clear to them that it was only a matter of time before Hülegü (d. 1265), who had taken the title *īlkhān*,[10] and his successors would launch another invasion of Syria; whatever imperialistic designs the Mongols would have harboured were exacerbated by their desire to revenge their defeats in 1260. The Mamluks, led by their energetic sultan Baybars (1260–77), conceived a two-pronged strategy to meet this challenge. First, was the expansion and strengthening of the army, accompanied by the creation or reorganisation of communications systems, espionage networks, transportation infrastructure, and fortifications. Second, was the

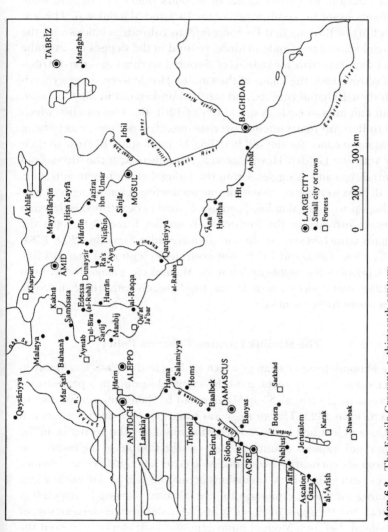

Map 6.2 The Fertile Crescent, c. thirteenth century.
Reproduced by kind permission of Cambridge University Press. From Reuven Amitai-Preiss, *Mongols and Mamluks: the Ilkhanid-Mamluk war, 1260–1281*.

adoption of a coherent and determined policy in the frontier region, primarily to repel the frequent Mongol incursions over the border, but also to bring the war into Mongol-controlled territory.

In addition, one other aspect of Mamluk policy was to have huge implications for the continuation of the Ilkhanid-Mamluk war. This was the effort of Baybars and his successors to cultivate relations with the Mongol state of the Golden Horde, centred in the steppes north of the Black Sea. Primarily for reasons of disputed territory and the distribution of revenues, the khans of the Golden Horde were at loggerheads with their Ilkhanid cousins, and war had broken out in the Caucasian Mountain area as early as the winter of 1261–62. This conflict, which was to flare up intermittently over the next few decades, was to be of great significance for the still fledgling Mamluk state. Because of their war with the Golden Horde, as well as conflicts with the Mongols of Central Asia and struggles within the Mongol elite of their own state, the Ilkhans were rarely able to devote themselves for any length of time to the war with the Mamluks, and usually had to be satisfied with trying to make inroads on the frontier with smaller forces.[11] In total, the Ilkhans launched only six major offensives into Syria (in 1260, 1281, 1299, 1300, 1303, and 1312). But, with the exception of that in 1299, the Mongols were unable to defeat the Mamluks in a major battle. Even in 1299 after a victory near Homs, the Mongols withdrew from Syria after about three months.[12]

The Mamluk Frontier: Coherent Policy

The Mamluk frontier strategy which evolved in the 1260s was to stay in force for some sixty years, until the eventual signing of a peace treaty between the Sultan al-Nāṣir Muḥammad b. Qalāwūn and the Ilkhan Abū Saʿīd in 1323. This strategy was based on the following elements: castles and fortified towns at selected points along the border or in the hinterland; rapid communications to tie the frontier to the centre; use of nomads (primarily bedouins) as couriers, scouts, reconnaissance forces, and skirmishers; incursions across the border for raiding and scouting purposes; espionage to give advance warning of impending attacks by Mongols or their allies; the deliberate destruction of grasslands before a Mongol campaign; and swift response to even the rumour of a Mongol raid or campaign into Syria, by dispatching a relieving force from Syria and, if necessary, from Egypt.

On the Euphrates, there were two large and impressive forts, al-Bīra and al-Raḥba. The former, farther to the south, was actually on the eastern side of the Euphrates in what could be called a small enclave of Mamluk-controlled territory in the Jazīra (the 'island' between the Tigris and the Euphrates, combining areas from the north of modern Iraq, the southeast of Turkey, and northwestern Syria). Both forts guarded important river crossings, and served as early warning posts against Mongol incursions, staging points for Mamluk raiders, scouts and spies, and symbols of Mamluk authority in this frontier region. These two forts were attacked time after time, both as part of larger Mongol campaigns to invade Syria and as the target of individual operations. Due to the strength of their fortifications, the determination of their defenders, and the timely arrival of reinforcements, neither castle was ever taken. Even the knowledge that reinforcements were on their way was at times enough to convince the Mongols to give up their siege and beat a hasty retreat. No less important, the certainty which the defenders, military and civilian, had of being relieved was highly significant in raising their morale. Ibn ʿAbd al-Ẓāhir (d. 1292), personal secretary of Sultan Baybars and author of his semi-official biography, wrote:

> The people were reassured that the Sultan did not neglect an act, [but rather] carried it out, and he did not abandon his servants. The hearts of the castle defenders (or inhabitants: *ahl al-qilāʿ*) were calmed at this, and they said: 'The Sultan moves quickly to our aid, and his armies reach the besieging enemy before news [of his approaching armies] comes.'[13]

In spite of the panegyric tone, the point is well made. The particular importance of al-Bīra, which bore the brunt of the attacks in the early period of the war (up to 1281), when the fighting on the border was particularly intense, is emphasised by another biographer of Baybars, Shāfiʿ ibn ʿAlī (d. 1330), who writes that it was 'the lock of Syria'.[14]

Of course, a rapid and appropriate response from the centre to any threat from across the border was predicated on the existence of a system of rapid communication which could convey the necessary information to the Sultan or at least the governors in the major Syrian cities. In fact, al-Bīra and al-Raḥba were the termini of two communications networks: a pigeon-post relay system and a chain of bonfires (smoke by day, flames at night).[15] Further towards the interior, connecting the provincial cities with each other and the capital in Cairo, was the system of postal horse relays (al-barīd), which theoretically (and initially in practice) was for important government business only. It would appear that Baybars, in resuscitating this old caliphal institution, was inspired by a parallel Mongol institution, the yam.[16]

Whatever the ultimate influence, it would seem that the necessity for quick communications between Egypt, where the main Mamluk army was generally based, and the Syrian provinces were the impetus for the establishment of such a horse-relay system, together with the other communications networks; not only was there an ever-present danger of Mongol incursions, but until 1291 the Crusader presence on the Syrian coast represented a real peril, and there was also the threat of internal dissension among the Mamluk officers in Syria.

The situation in the far north was in many ways much more precarious than that in the northeast. In the latter there was generally a clear-cut divide – the Euphrates – between Mongol- and Mamluk-controlled territory, and the distance between the frontier region and the heavily inhabited heartland was great and in places (especially to the south) composed of desert or semi-desert, thereby making passage difficult even for raiders. But to the north, because of the relative closeness of Lesser Armenia, the ever-loyal ally of the Mongols,[17] there would be little advanced warning of an Armenian or Mongol incursion. This was a particularly acute problem before Baybars was able to gain control over several castles in the frontier region, such as Bahasnā and al-Darbassāk, in the aftermath of complex negotiations following a devastating Mamluk raid on Lesser Armenia in 1266.[18] The capture of Antioch from the Franks in 1268, and the subsequent abandonment of nearby Baghrās, further increased Mamluk control and security in the area.[19] It would appear, however, that Mamluk control over these farthest reaches of the northern frontier was far from absolute or permanent: in 1292 Bahasnā was again ceded to the Sultan after a Mamluk campaign to the north, in which the Qalʿat al-Rūm, the seat of the Armenian Catholicus, was taken, and before a projected invasion into Lesser Armenia was carried out.[20] However, the fact that two cities unmentioned in the agreement of 1268 are now named (Marʿash, and Tall Ḥamdūn near Adana) may indicate that in the long run Mamluk influence in the area was expanding. Here, too, establishing control was easier said than done: a Mamluk army had to conquer these two castles by siege some five years later.[21]

In spite of this amelioration, there could be no absolute security from

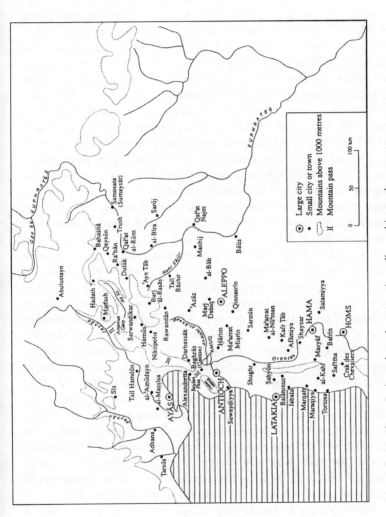

Map 6.3 Northern Syria and southeastern Anatolia, c. thirteenth century.
Reproduced by kind permission of Cambridge University Press from Reuven Amitai-Preiss, *Mongols and Mamluks: the Ilkhanid-Mamluk war, 1260–1281.*

this direction, nor even full confidence of receiving an early alert. Defence, however, was somewhat improved by the presence of two fortified towns north of Aleppo: ʿAyn Tāb and ʿAzāz. Ibn Shaddād al-Ḥalabī (d. 1285), a highly placed official and important writer, observed that the former was 'a watchpost (raṣad) for fresh developments coming from the land of the Armenians and Anatolia (bilād al-rūm)'.[22] While Mamluk forces were maintained at other cities in northern Syria (Tall Bāshir, Burj al-Raṣāṣ, and Ḥārim), their fortifications, which had been destroyed by the Mongol invasion of 1260, were not repaired, at least not during the reign of Baybars.[23] Mamluk troops appear to have been few and far between in the northern Syrian frontier, but this was partly alleviated by yearly patrol in the region by a corps of the Syrian army.[24] In the long run, the best protection for the very north of Syria was provided by the deterrent effect of repeated Mamluk raids into the territory of Lesser Armenia, effectively dissuading its king from launching independent raids over the frontier.[25]

Of fundamental importance for the stability of the border region was the *modus vivendi* worked out early on between the Mamluk sultans and the bedouin tribes of northern Syria. The bedouins acted as scouts, couriers, and raiders, and played a not-insignificant role in several pitched battles. No less important, their joining of the Mamluk camp meant that a potentially highly disruptive element in the sensitive frontier area and beyond was largely neutralised. Most prominent of these tribes was the Āl Faḍl federation, whose leaders had already been cultivated by Sultan Quṭuz. Compliance with the emerging Mamluk order in Syria was achieved by largesse in the distribution of gifts, subsidies, titles, and appanages, although on occasion a judicious use of force by the Sultan or his representatives was necessary. Although there were some nomadic elements in Syria who sometimes aggravated the Mamluk authorities, even going over to the Mongol side, on the whole, in the sixty-year war with the Ilkhanids, the bedouin as well as the Turcomans of northern Syria sided with the Mamluks.[26] More than once the Mamluks were also successful in garnering some support among the bedouins of Iraq, thereby bringing about disruption in Mongol-controlled territory, and not only in the frontier zone.[27]

In order to impede any Mongol advance into northern Syria, the Mamluks appear to have developed a scorched-earth strategy to deny pasturelands to their enemy. The Mongol army, composed mainly of cavalrymen, each leading a string of sturdy steppe horses, was dependent on local pasturage and crops for foraging its mounts.[28] With news of an impending invasion or raid, Mamluk operatives were dispatched to ignite the grasslands of northern Syria and even beyond the border into Mongol territory, where they were assisted and hidden by local sympathisers.[29]

A final element of this frontier strategy were incursions launched across the Euphrates or to the north. The obvious goals of such campaigns were to bring the war into the enemy camp, disrupting life, military preparations, and economics there, with the additional advantages of gathering intelligence and booty, as well as giving troops experience and strengthening their morale. There were occasions when these raids were intended to draw attention from a Mamluk campaign elsewhere. At times, the territory under Mamluk control could even be extended. These Mamluk raids start in the mid 1260s and continue intermittently until the 1310s.[30] Perhaps the most famous, and certainly the largest, is Baybars's campaign into Anatolia in 1276, in which he led most of his army. Having defeated a medium-sized Mongol force at Abulustayn (Elbistan, in southwest Turkey today), he marched with great pomp to the Seljuq capital of Qaysariyya before turning back to Syria. The aim of this campaign was not conquest: the permanent occupation of Anatolia was beyond his reach. But by flexing his muscles, he humiliated the Mongols, disrupted their rule in the country, trained his troops, and gained great prestige at home and abroad.[31]

In fact, the activities of Baybars and his successors on the border and beyond are an important component of the image of the ruler as holy warrior which these rulers sought to project. An examination of the titles used repeatedly in the epigraphy of the early Mamluk sultans, which harks back to earlier models, shows the importance of the theme of Holy War (*jihād*), especially on the frontier. Prominent among these titles are *mujāhid* (fighter in the Holy War), *muthāhir* (warrior on the frontier, *thaghr*) and *murābiṭ* (warrior on the border fortress, *ribāṭ*),[32] which recall an earlier period of frontier war enshrined in Muslim tradition: that against the Byzantines in the early ʿAbbāsid period (late eighth and ninth centuries).[33]

It should be clear from the above survey that the Mamluks devoted much thought and energy, and a great deal of resources, to define and defend their frontier region. These efforts reveal the extreme significance which the Sultan and his senior officers attributed to the frontier in the general strategy of their war against the Mongols. It would appear that to the Mamluk mind, any defeat or setback, even on the far-flung northern borders of their state, would have had major, and even fatal, consequences for their regime. The resources devoted to the war in the frontier, as with the efforts made in enlarging and strengthening the Mamluk army as a whole, as well as their efforts devoted to espionage (on which more below), show that the Mamluks took the Mongol threat very seriously.

The Mongol Frontier: Malign Neglect

The Mongol attitude towards their adversaries to the west was somewhat different. There is no doubt that the Ilkhans and the Mongol elite harboured great animosity towards the Mamluk regime, and would have been very happy to eradicate it by conquering Syria and Egypt. This bitter hostility was fuelled firstly by an imperialist ideology which held that the Mongols, led by Chinggis Khan and his descendants, had a heaven-given mandate to conquer the world.[34] This traditional Mongol imperial ideal combined with a desire to avenge the defeats at ʿAyn Jālūt and subsequent battles. This having been said, the Mongols in Iran were never able to devote themselves fully to achieving this goal, due to various concerns, mostly their preoccupations with other Mongol fronts. In addition, it would appear that the Ilkhans never developed a coherent frontier strategy, unlike their Mamluk counterparts. This lack of a clear frontier policy, together with the shortage of manpower and other resources devoted to the area, led naturally to the Mamluks enjoying the upper hand there.

In the Jazīra region, whose western part could be considered the main frontier zone of the Mongols *vis-à-vis* the Mamluks, there seem to have been few concentrations of Mongol troops. The garrisons which Mamluk raiders encountered in Qarqisiya (1265) and Ḥarrān (1271) were quite small,[35] and the relative ease with which Mamluk scouts crossed the western Jazīra indicated that the region was not full of Mongol troops.[36] The Mongols maintained some type of formation called *qaraghul*, which combined the function of frontier guards and highway patrol, but little is known of its actual structure and numbers.[37] The location of the closest large concentration of Mongol troops is not known, but this seems to have been somewhat to the north and east. In any event, there is some indirect evidence that at least one *tümen*, a unit of theoretically 10000 troops, was stationed in the Jazīra,[38] but again it would appear to have been placed far away from the frontier *per se*. There are indications that there was a minimal Mongol presence in

Lesser Armenia, but these troops made no attempt to interfere with Mamluk columns which raided in the area.[39] There were of course large concentrations of Mongol forces further north in Anatolia which was under ostensible Seljuq rule.[40] The Armenian forces made an attempt to oppose the first Mamluk raid of 1266, which was partially provoked by their own probes into northern Syria, but the results of their efforts were a disaster. Thereafter, the Armenians made no serious effort to hold the frontier against the Mamluks, who raided the country with virtual impunity.[41]

Effects of the War along the Frontier

One outcome of the border war, together with the effect of the Mongol conquest and continual Mongol misrule,[42] was the demographic and economic decline of their frontier area. One pro-Mongol historian, Rashīd al-Dīn (d. 1318), who also served as wazir to two Ilkhans, wrote:

> The entire population of some provinces, because they were frontier (sarḥadd) [regions] and were traversed by armies, was either killed or fled, such as . . . parts of Abulustayn and Diyār Bakr: thus Ḥarrān, Ruḥā [= al-Ruḥā], Sarūj and Raqqa, as well as most of the cities on this and that side of the Euphrates, were completely uncultivated and abandoned.[43]

At least for the Mongol side of the border this information is confirmed by Ibn Shaddād al-Ḥalabī's geographical survey of Syria and the Jazīra, al-Aʿlāq al-khaṭīra, which provides some additional details: al-Raqqa had been destroyed during the original Mongol invasion, and nobody lived there; after ʿAyn Jālūt, the citadel of al-Ruḥā had been wrecked and its inhabitants had fled; Qalʿat Jaʿbar had surrendered, but the Mongols destroyed it and the surrounding countryside; Qalʿat Najm was ruined by the Mongols, probably soon after they took it in 1260, and its population fled; the inhabitants of Sarūj had been massacred in 1260 and the Mongols abandoned it finally in 1264–65; by the early 1270s Ḥarrān was in ruins and its population decimated.[44] In some cases, as in Ḥarrān, at least part of the population emigrated to Syria, but it is impossible to give either absolute figures or say what proportion fled west or east.[45] Ḥarrān was the one known instance where the Mongols deliberately transferred the population because of sympathies to the Mamluk. It is clear from the above that the western Jazīra suffered extensive depopulation, as well as physical and economic decline; these phenomena appear not to have been limited to the cities.

The situation on the Mamluk side of the Euphrates was not quite so bleak. Again Ibn Shaddād al-Ḥalabī is the main source. On the one hand, Bālis and Manbij had been destroyed during the Mongol occupation of 1260, and their populations had fled, leaving only a few Turcoman. Likewise, al-Ruṣāfa, some 50 kilometres to the southwest of al-Raqqa, had been abandoned by its population, although in 1260 it had been granted a pardon by Hülegü. On the other hand, however, elsewhere there is evidence of settlement and even some prosperity: Ṣiffīn on the river, and al-Bāb and Buzāgha further west.[46] At least initially, the area around al-Bīra was cultivated,[47] although it is unclear if this was maintained in the long run in view of all the Mongol attacks in the area. Mention has already been made of settled towns – some of them with repaired fortifications – in northern Syria, near the border with Lesser Armenia/eastern Anatolia. It would seem then that the active military Mamluk presence in the frontier regions contributed to a partial demographic and economic recovery in the area, which of course only strengthened Mamluk control over it.

There were no Mamluk attempts to depopulate their side of the frontier, and it appears that the Mamluk authorities were interested in maintaining population and agriculture in the frontier areas, understanding that this contributed to their hold on it. This must be seen in the wider context of a concerted Mamluk bid to keep the Syrian periphery within the Mamluk Sultanate. Anything less than a determined effort by Baybars, the founder of Mamluk policy on the frontier (as of so much else in the Mamluk Sultanate), to show the flag as well as maintaining fortifications, garrisons, communication networks, and the rapid deployment of reinforcements, would probably have led to this area turning into a no-man's land, which would then have suffered a similar demographic fate to that of the Mongol side of the border.

The Nature of the Political Boundary and its Permeability

It can be seen then that there was a clear political boundary between the Mamluk Sultanate and the Ilkhanate. Besides obvious geographical delimitations (most importantly the Euphrates), the political boundary was emphasised by different forms of military arrangements on one hand, and demographic and economic conditions on the other. Certainly the political boundary was understood by the Mamluks and the

civilian elite of their state. Mamluk writers continually refer to the
territories of the Sultanate as *bilād al-islām*, 'the land of Islam', in whose
name the Mamluks fought the pagan Muslims for at least the first forty
years of the war.[48] Mongol territory is referred to as either *bilād al-tatar*,
'the land of the Tatars [= Mongols]', or just *bilād al-sharq*, 'the land of
the East'. Even after the conversion of the Mongols to Islam towards the
end of the thirteenth century, the religious dimension of the war did
not disappear from Mamluk ideology, since aspersions were placed on
the quality of the new converts' Islam, and these terms continued to be
used, indicating a clear political and ideological division between the
two states.[49]

However, neither the clear political boundary nor the well-defined
frontier zone were impermeable. There are numerous indications of
trade across the political and military divide, although curiously
enough almost all the evidence points to commerce from Ilkhanid-
controlled territory into the Sultanate. Particularly striking is that
prominently mentioned in this trade are such militarily important items
as young mamluks, horses, iron, and wood. It appears that the major
land route was from eastern Anatolia into northern Syria, but there
was also some movement across the Euphrates. Commerce was also
conducted by sea, certainly from Ayas (Layasso) in Lesser Armenia,
and perhaps also from the Persian Gulf to the Red Sea. Of course the
Mamluk authorities would have been happy to facilitate the arrival of
strategic goods. The Ilkhanids and their representatives at times inter-
fered with this trade, but mostly they seem to have turned a blind eye.
Otherwise, it is difficult to see how the trade could have continued, even
taking into account the difficulties of patrolling a long frontier.[50]

A second type of traffic over the border was composed of religious
scholars, as well as pilgrims. The Arabic sources from the Mamluk
period give numerous examples of the former, mainly from Mongol
territory into Syria, and mostly in order to settle down. There are many
examples of pilgrims from Anatolia and Iraq (and even further east)
passing through Syria on their way to Mecca. It would seem that civilian
traffic over the border, commercial and otherwise, increased towards
the end of the thirteenth century and the beginning of the fourteenth.
This change was probably first a result of a relaxation in the war on the
frontier from the early 1280s, and eventually may reflect a certain
reduction of tensions in the 1310s.[51]

Another sort of movement across the frontier was espionage. From
early on in Baybars's reign, an efficient spy service was set up, with a

director, secret couriers (*quṣṣād*, singular *qāṣid*), and local contacts across the border (most frequently called *nuṣaḥā'*, *nuṣṣāḥ*, *nāṣiḥūn*, all plurals of *nāṣiḥ*). Ibn ʿAbd al-Ẓāhir writes of his patron's espionage efforts:

> The Sultan did not cease to take interest in the affairs of the enemy. He was on guard against their tricks and resolute in all regarding them. His *quṣṣād* did not stop coming from Baghdad, Khilāṭ [= Akhlāṭ] and other places in the eastern country (*bilād al-sharq*) and Persia (*al-ʿajam*). [The Sultan] spent on them much money, because whoever travels for this matter and plays loosely with his life, there is no choice but that he should take his blood money (*diya*). Without this, who would risk his life? When Allah showed the Sultan this good policy, the *quṣṣād* went back and forth, and they recognised [in the Mongol countries] those who could inform them of the [Mongol] secrets.[52]

These agents and their local contacts were used not only to collect information, but also to disseminate misinformation to confuse the enemy and even discredit troublesome characters. This espionage service was to continue its activities throughout the entire 60-year period of the war with the Mongols and beyond; even in a period of real peace, the Sultans were not ready to let down their guard completely. The efforts and resources devoted to gathering intelligence were worthy investments, and repeatedly brought the Mamluks early notice of impending attacks as well as timely political news from the Ilkhan's court. The Mongols also exerted themselves to obtain intelligence and make contact with Mamluk officials and others. Judging from the Mamluk sources, the only ones which report these efforts, the Mongols were not very successful. However, the Mamluk writers would only know about those Mongol attempts which failed and agents who were caught.

An Ideological Frontier?

The subject of espionage ties in with the question of the loyalty of the local population to their political-military elite, both in the frontier zone and in the heartland of each state. As has already been seen, the Mamluk secret operatives found sympathy among Muslims in the Ilkhanate, who provided them with succour and information. These even included some individuals of the political elite who had remained under the new rulers. The basis for this sympathy for the Mamluks was surely derived in part from the belief that the Mamluks were fighting for Islam against the infidel conquerors. The destruction of the Caliphate in Baghdad by the 'infidel', and its resurrection in Cairo by the Mamluks would surely have contributed to this feeling. A clear indication of how the Mamluk writers – representing here both the Mamluks themselves and the literate strata in the Sultanate – saw these sympathisers, was the use of appellations derived from the root N-Ṣ-Ḥ, connoting the giving of good advice, acting truthfully and being beneficial. The Mongol elite itself was aware of the attraction to the Mamluks among their Muslim officials, and developed a certain paranoia which sometimes led them to believe unfounded rumours and even deliberate falsehoods regarding such contacts.[53] This being said, it is clear that the Mongols had no choice but to draw upon the services of Muslim bureaucrats (mostly native Persian speakers) to run their state. These, often less than enthralled with their new masters, generally saw that they had little choice but to perform their tasks as competently as circumstances permitted.[54]

On the other hand, the populace of the Mamluk Sultanate, and certainly the bureaucratic and scholarly classes, seem to have fallen behind the Mamluk rulers in their struggle against the Mongols, and in general supported their rule.[55] There were, however, individual cases of pro-Mongol feelings and even activity. These tended, however, to be isolated examples of disgruntled members and retainers of the previous regime, or local Christians who may have harboured some sympathy towards the Mongols because of their relative religious 'tolerance' and even patronage of eastern Christianity.[56]

On the whole, it should be remembered that the war between the Mamluks and the Ilkhans was carried out by members of the military-political elite. In the Sultanate, the army was composed mainly of professionals, with auxiliary forces drawn from the bedouin and Turcoman tribes of Syria. The role of the urban and rural civilian elements in the fighting was generally negligible, although in the frontier districts, and more likely in the border fortresses, this may have been different.

As for the Mongols, there is no evidence of local Muslim civilians fighting on their behalf. On the other hand, the Mongols employed indigenous Muslim professional soldiers, from Seljuq Anatolia, the

Jazīra, Iraq, and Iran itself. The Mamluk sources sometimes refer to these as *murtadda/murtaddūn*, which literally means apostates, but here perhaps can be translated as renegades. By fighting under the infidel Mongols against the forces of Islam, these Muslim princes, officers, and soldiers had put themselves, in a sense, beyond the pale. It should be remembered, however, that these various Muslim troops were probably enrolled in the Mongol campaigns against their will. One military element which joined the Mongols with more enthusiasm were the Christian Armenian (from Lesser Armenia) and Georgian troops, who fought with the Mongols on several occasions, sometimes displaying great bravery.[57]

Ethnic and Cultural Affinities

Mention was made earlier of a perceived commonality of origin between the Mongols and the Turkish Mamluks. This sense of ethnic affinity or even oneness between Mongols and Turks, both coming from the nomadic milieu of the Inner Asian steppe, was maintained not only by the Arabic writers of the Mamluk Sultanate, but also appears in some traditions held by the Central Asian peoples themselves, as related by Muslim authors.[58] There are examples, albeit from earlier in the century, of both Mongols convincing Turks to abandon their allies because of 'ethnic solidarity' (*jinsiyya*) as well as Turks appealing to Mongols for leniency on the same grounds.[59] This sense of similarity must surely have been accentuated by the large number of Turks who served in the Mongol army, even at an early date.[60] These Turks were initially from Inner Asia, although increasingly, as the Mongols expanded their holdings in the Middle East, they would have included Turks who had been living in the Islamic lands for some time.[61] As we have seen, the Mamluk army in its early years was mainly composed of Turks, primarily from the Qipchaq tribes living north of the Black Sea. At the same time, there was a not insignificant contingent of Mamluks of Mongol origin, including one, Kitbughā al-Manṣūrī, who became sultan for a brief period (1294–96).[62] Both Baybars and Qalāwūn (1279–90) had Mongol wives, and it was the Mongol wife of the latter who gave birth to Qalāwūn's son and eventual successor, al-Nāṣir Muḥammad (ruled three times: 1293–94, 1299–1309, 1310–40).[63] This being said, it is clear today that the supposed Mongol influence – particularly that of the Mongol law (*yasa*) – on the Mamluk Sultanate was minimal or non-existent.[64]

With the above in mind we can better understand the phenomenon of deserters and military refugees. From the Mongol side there are many episodes of groups of tribesmen together with their commanders making their way to the Sultanate, usually in the aftermath of some conflict within the Ilkhanate. These groups, known as *wāfidiyya* ('refugees') ranged in size from 200 families in 1262 to 10 000 (or even 18 000) families in 1295. Some came as Muslims, while the others converted only upon their arrival. There is little doubt that they made some contribution to the fighting power of the Sultanate (3000 are reported to have arrived during Baybars's reign alone), and helped the Mamluks score points in the psychological war. Certainly, the common steppe origin of the Mamluks and the *wāfidiyya* made the absorption of the latter that much easier. At the same time, their impact on the Mamluk regime was not very great. The common soldiers were generally not integrated into the elite Royal Mamluks, or even the units of the individual Mamluk officers, while their leaders almost invariably received only middling commissions at best. The Mamluks were glad to have Mongol deserters come over to their side, but only if they accepted a clear subordinate position. The boundary between the Mamluks and their parvenu ethnic 'cousins' was a very clear one.[65]

The incidents of Mamluks fleeing the Sultanate to the east are many fewer and involve smaller groups. There are basically two important examples: the group led by Qibjaq al-Manṣūrī, who fled in 1298, and that by Qarā Sunqur al-Manṣūrī in 1311. Qarā Sunqur had been one of the senior officers in Syria who had assisted the prince al-Nāṣir Muḥammad b. Qalāwūn in regaining his throne for a third time in 1310 (he ruled until 1341). However, he soon fell foul of the Sultan and fled his governorship in Aleppo into the Syrian desert – along with several associates and a large number of personal mamluks – in order to escape arrest. He continued across the Euphrates, where he was well received by the Ilkhan Öljeitü. Eventually he received the governorship of Marāgha and played a certain role in state affairs in the Ilkhanate until his death in 1327. Al-Nāṣir Muḥammad, however, could not abide the fact that his nemesis was still alive and several times sent assassins over the border to finish him off; this having failed, after the peace with the Ilkhan Abū Saʿīd in 1323 he also tried to have him extradited, again without success.[66]

The other, earlier, instance was that of Qibjaq, governor of Damascus, who found himself involved in a conflict with the Sultan al-Manṣūr Lājīn (1296–98), and with several other officers fled to the court of Ilkhan Ghazan. Interestingly enough, Qibjaq himself was of Mongol origin (he had been captured as a youth in 1260), and found his father and brothers at the Mongol court in various capacities. Qibjaq and his associates were properly feted, and were instrumental in prodding Ghazan into launching his invasion of the following year. In the aftermath of Ghazan's victory at Homs in 1299, Qibjaq was again made governor of Damascus, although under Mongol aegis and with a Mongol general keeping a watchful eye on him. With the withdrawal of the Mongols during the early months of 1300, Qibjaq decided to return to the Mamluk fold, and met the Mamluk army as it returned to retake Syria. Qibjaq's treason was forgiven, and soon afterwards he was awarded a minor governorship in Syria, which he occupied until his death a few years later.[67]

What are the conclusions which can be drawn from these two incidents? The relatively neutral language of the sources, which does not condemn the actions of these two 'traitors', seems to my mind to indicate a certain sympathy with their deeds.[68] Both were forced by circumstances to flee to the enemy in order to save themselves. If anything there is, perhaps, an implied criticism of the Sultans involved. This, in any case, might explain the mercy shown by the Mamluk grandees to Qibjaq in 1300, by which time the offending sultan had been deposed and killed. One thing is clear: in spite of family and ethnic ties, let alone the certainty of a high position, Qibjaq chose to throw in his lot with his erstwhile Mamluk comrades. His Mamluk and Muslim loyalties were to prove stronger than other considerations, weighty as they might have been.

All this being said, it is clear that the frontier, political and military, was maintained until the end of the 1310s. Raids still occurred from time to time through most of the decade, and as late as 1312 there was a major offensive launched against Syria (albeit soon aborted). The fifteenth-century writer Maqrīzī writes that around 1316, when the Sultan al-Nāṣir Muḥammad learnt of the troubles that his neighbours were facing, he was overjoyed, since this would lead to their weakening.[69] Only with the negotiations, which began around 1320 and led three years later to a signed agreement, can we speak of the end of a frontier of war and the beginning of a border of peace. Yet, with the collapse of the Ilkhanid state around 1335, the area of Mamluk influence in northern Syria gradually moved north and northeast, into Lesser Armenia and eastern Anatolia, and over the Euphrates. A new and sophisticated frontier system was eventually established later in the fourteenth century and lasted until 1516, when the Ottomans finally breached this frontier and destroyed the Mamluk Sultanate.[70]

NOTES

1. Some aspects of this topic have been discussed in R. Amitai-Preiss, *Mongols and Mamluks: the Mamluk-Īlkhānid war (1260–1281)*, Cambridge 1995, esp. ch. 9; *idem*, 'The North Syrian Frontier between the Mamluks and Mongols', *Hamizraḥ He-Hadash*, 38 (1996), 17–25.

2. For the early history of the Mongol empire, see D. Morgan, *The Mongols*, Oxford 1986.

3. On military slavery in the Islamic world, see D. Ayalon: 'Preliminary remarks on the Mamlūk military institution in Islam', *War, Technology and Society in the Middle East*, ed. V. J. Parry and M. E. Yapp, London 1974, 44–58; H. Kennedy, *The Prophet and the Age of the Caliphates: the Islamic Near East from the sixth to the eleventh century*, London and New York 1986, 158–60.

4. D. Sinor, 'Inner Asian Warriors', *JAOS*, CI (1981), 133–44.

5. R. Irwin, *The Middle East in the Middle Ages: the early Mamluk Sultanate 1250–1382*, London 1986, chs 2–4.

6. Amitai-Preiss, *Mongols*, ch. 2; *idem*, '"Ayn Jālūt revisited', *Tārīḫ*, II (1991), 119–50; J. M. Smith, '"Ayn Jālūt: Mamlūk success or Mongol failure?', *HJAS*, XLIV (1984), 307–45.

7. *Dhayl ʿalā al-rawḍatayn*, Cairo 1947, 208.

8. Irwin, *Early Mamluk Sultanate*, 26–9, and n. 59 below.

9. R. Amitai-Preiss, 'In the aftermath of ʿAyn Jālūt: the beginnings of the Mamlūk-Īlkhānid cold war', *Al-Masāq*, III (1990), 10–12.

10. Usually translated as 'subject khan'; see R. Amitai-Preiss, 'Evidence for the early use of the title *īlkhān* among the Mongols', *Journal of the Royal Asiatic Society*, 3rd ser., I (1991), 353–62.

11. P. Jackson, 'The dissolution of the Mongol empire', *Central Asiatic Journal*, XXII (1978), 186–244; Amitai-Preiss, *Mongols*, 78–94, 233–5.

12. For the campaign of 1281, see Amitai-Preiss, *Mongols*, ch. 7; for later campaigns: J. A. Boyle, 'Dynastic and political history of the Īl-Khāns', *Cambridge History of Iran*, V, ed. J. Boyle, Cambridge 1968, 387–94, 403.

13. Ibn ʿAbd al-Ẓāhir, *Al-Rawḍ al-zāhir fī sīrat al-malik al-ẓāhir*, ed. ʿA.-ʿA. al-Khuwayṭir, Riyad 1976, 227.

14. Shāfiʿ b. ʿAlī, *Ḥusn al-manāqib al-sirriyya al-muntazaʿa min al-sīra al-ẓāhiriyya*, ed. ʿA-ʿA. al-Khuwayṭir, Riyad 1976, 87.

15. Ibn Faḍl Allāh al-ʿUmarī, *Al-Taʿrīffī al-muṣṭalaḥ al-sharīf*, Cairo 1894–5, 199–201; J. Sauvaget, *La poste aux chevaux dans l'empire des Mamelouks*, Paris 1941, 39–41.

16. Sauvaget, *La poste*, 10–36, 42–77.

17. M. Canard, 'La royaume d'Arménie-Cilicie et les Mamelouks jusqu'au traité de 1285', *Revue des études arméniennes*, IV (1967), 217–59; S. Der Nersessian,

'The kingdom of Cilician Armenia', *History of the Crusades*, II, ed. R. L. Wolff and H. W. Hazard, Philadelphia 1962, 630–59.

18. Amitai-Preiss, *Mongols*, 116–19.
19. P. Thorau, *The Lion of Egypt: Sultan Baybars I and the Near East in the thirteenth century*, trans. P. M. Holt, London and New York 1992, 187–92.
20. P. M. Holt, *The Age of the Crusades: the Near East from the eleventh century to 1517*, London and New York 1986, 104–5.
21. Ibn Taghrī Birdī, *Al-Nujūm al-zāhira fī mulūk miṣr wa'l-qāhira*, Cairo 1930–56, VIII, 112.
22. A.-M. Eddé, 'La description de la Syrie du Nord de ʿIzz al-Dīn ibn Šaddād', *Bulletin d'études orientales*, XXXII–XXXIII (1981), 376, 382, 385.
23. *Ibid.*, 378, 380, 386–7.
24. Ibn Shaddād al-Ḥalabī, *Taʾrīkh al-malik al-ẓāhir*, ed. A. Ḥuṭayṭ, Wiesbaden 1983, 155; Ibn Abī 'l-Faḍā'il, in E. Blochet, 'Histoire des sultans mamlouks', *Patrologia orientalis*, XII, XIV, XX (1919–28), 554–5.
25. See references in n. 17; also Amitai-Preiss, *Mongols*, 133–6, 180; Der Nersessian, 655–8.
26. D. Ayalon, 'The auxiliary forces of the Mamluk Sultanate', *Der Islam*, LXV (1988), 13–37; M. A. Hiyari, 'The origins and development of the amīrate of the Arabs during the seventh/thirteenth and eighth/fourteenth centuries', *BSOAS*, XXXVIII (1975), 509–24; Amitai-Preiss, *Mongols*, 64–71.
27. Amitai-Preiss, *Mongols*, 109, 145–6.
28. Logistical problems may have caused the Mongol withdrawal from Syria: Smith, "ʿAyn Jālūt'; D. Morgan, 'The Mongols in Syria, 1260–1300', *Crusade and Settlement*, ed. P. Edbury, Cardiff 1985, 231–5; cf. Amitai-Preiss, *Mongols*, 225–9.
29. Al-ʿUmarī, *Al-Taʿrif*, 201–3; Amitai-Preiss, *Mongols*, 205–6.
30. For Baybars's reign, see Amitai-Preiss, *Mongols*, ch. 5; for later examples: Ibn ʿAbd al-Ẓāhir, *Tashrīf al-ayyām wa'l-ʿuṣūr fī sīrat al-malik al-manṣūr*, ed. M. Kāmil, Cairo 1961, 134–6; B. Spuler, *Die Mongolen in Iran: Verwaltung und Kultur der Ilchanzeit 1220–1350*, 4th edn Leiden 1985, 84; D. P. Little, *An Introduction to Mamluk Historiography*, Wiesbaden 1970, 114.
31. Amitai-Preiss, *Mongols*, ch. 7.
32. See Baybars's inscriptions in *Répertoire chronologique d'épigraphie arabe*, ed. E. Combe, J. Sauraget, and G. Wiet, Cairo 1931–, XII.
33. M. Bonner, *Aristocratic Violence and Holy War: studies in the 'jihad' and the Arab-Byzantine frontier*, New Haven 1996. The frontier with the Byzantine Empire ran further north than the Mamluk frontier.
34. Amitai-Preiss, *Mongols*, 9–11, 230–3; J. F. Fletcher, 'The Mongols: ecological and social perspective', *HJAS*, XLVI (1986), 19, 30–5.
35. Shāfiʿ b. ʿAlī, *Ḥusn*, 101–2; Ibn al-Furāt, *Taʾrīkh al-duwal wa'l-mulūk*, MS Österreichische Nationalbibliothek, Flügel no. 814, fol. 77b; al-Yūnīnī, *Dhayl mirʾāt al-zamān fī taʾrīkh al-aʿyān*, Hyderabad 1954–61, II, 468–9; Ibn Shaddād al-Ḥalabī, *Al-Aʿlāq al-khaṭīra fī dhikr umarāʾ al-shām wa'l-jazīra*, III, ed. Y. ʿAbbāra, Damascus 1978, 62–3.
36. For example, a reconnaissance raid in 1264–65 traversed the Jazīra and reached the Tigris without encountering Mongol troops; Ibn al-Furāt, MS Vienna, fol. 77a.

37. G. Doerfer, *Türkische und mongolische Elemente in Neupersischen*, Wiesbaden 1963–75, I, 399–403.
38. Amitai-Preiss, *Mongols*, 108–9.
39. *Ibid.*, 117–18, 135.
40. J. M. Smith, 'Mongol nomadism and Middle Eastern geography: qīshlāqs and tümens', *The Mongol Empire and its Legacy*, ed. R. Amitai-Preiss and D. Morgan, Leiden 1998.
41. Amitai-Preiss, *Mongols*, 116–18, 133–4.
42. Morgan, *Mongols*, 100–3, 158–67.
43. Rashīd al-Dīn, *Jāmiᶜ al-tawārikh*, III, ed. ᶜA-ᶜA. ᶜAlīzādah, Baku 1957, III, 557–8. Ruḥā/al-Ruhā is the ancient Edessa.
44. Ibn Shaddād, *Aᶜlāq*, III, 40, 60–3, 82, 98–9, 103, 119; Eddé, 'Description de la Syrie', 292; D. Krawulsky *Īrān – Das Reich der Īlḫāne: eine topographische-historische Studie*, Wiesbaden 1978, 452, 454, 614.
45. Ibn Shaddād, *Aᶜlāq*, III, 62; Al-Kutubī, *ᶜUyūn al-tawarikh*, XX, ed. F. N. Sāmir and ᶜA-M. Dāwūd, Baghdad 1980, 379; Amitai-Preiss, *Mongols*, 126.
46. Eddé, 'Description de la Syrie', 294, 373–5, 394, 396, 397.
47. Abū Shāma, *Dhayl*, 233.
48. P. M. Holt, 'Some observations on the ᶜAbbāsid caliphate of Cairo', *BSOAS*, XLVII (1984), 501–7; S. Heidemann, *Das Aleppiner Kalifat (AD 1261): Vom Ende des Kalifates in Baghdad über Aleppo zu den Restaurationen in Kairo*, Leiden 1994.
49. R. Amitai-Preiss, 'Ghazan, Islam and Mongol tradition: a view from the Mamluk Sultanate', *BSOAS*, LIX (1996), 1–10.
50. Amitai-Preiss, *Mongols*, 207–11.
51. *Ibid.*, 212–13.
52. Ibn ᶜAbd al-Ẓāhir, *Rawḍ*, 135; for espionage in general, see Amitai-Preiss, *Mongols*, 139–56.
53. *Ibid.*, 151–2.
54. D. Morgan, 'Persian historians and the Mongols', *Medieval Historical Writing in the Christian and Islamic Worlds*, ed. D. Morgan, London 1982, 109–24; J. Aubin, *Émirs mongols et vizirs persans dans les remous de l'acculturation*, Paris 1995.
55. On the legitimisation of the Mamluk regime: S. Jackson, *Islamic Law and the State: the constitutional jurisprudence of Shihāb al-Dīn al-Qarafī*, Leiden 1996, 49–52.
56. R. Gottheil, 'An answer to the Dhimmis', *JAOS*, XLI (1921), 411–12; Amitai-Preiss, *Mongols*, 153–5.
57. For example, Ibn al-Furāt, *Ta'rīkh al-duwal wa'l-mulūk*, VII, ed. C. Zurayk, Beirut 1942, 215.
58. Mamluk writers include Abū Shāma, quoted above, and authors cited in Amitai-Preiss, *Mongols*, 45, n. 119. Mongol views: M. Dobrovits, 'The Turco-Mongolian tradition of common origin and the historiography in fifteenth century Central Asia', *AOASH*, 57, 3 (1994), 269–77; cf. U. Haarmann, 'Turkish legends in the popular historiography of medieval Egypt', *Proceedings of the VIth Congress of Arabic and Islamic Studies (1972)*, Stockholm and Leiden 1977, 97–107.

59. Two famous examples are in Ibn al-Athīr, *Al-Kāmil fī 'l-ta'rīkh*, Beirut 1966, XII, 368, 385.
60. Spuler, *Die Mongolen*, 379. His evidence appears problematical; the whole subject deserves a thorough review.
61. Morgan, *Mongols*, 56.
62. For Mamluks of Mongol origin: D. Ayalon, '*Mamlūk*', *EI*, new edn.
63. P. M. Holt, 'An-Nāṣir Muḥammad b. Qalāwūn (684–741/1285–1341): his ancestry, kindred and affinity', *Egypt and Syria in the Fatimid, Ayyubid and Mamluk Eras*, ed. U. Vermeulen and D. De Smet, Leuven 1995, 313–24.
64. D. Ayalon, 'The Great Yāsa of Chingiz Khān, a re-examination', *Studia Islamica*, pt A, XXXIII (1971), 97–140; pt B, XXXIV (1971), 151–80; pt C1, XXXVI (1972), 113–58; pt C2, XXXVIII (1973), 107–56.
65. D. Ayalon, 'The *wafīdiya* in the Mamluk kingdom', *Islamic Culture*, 25 (1951), 89–104; R. Amitai-Preiss, 'The Mamluk officer class during the reign of sultan Baybars', *War and Society in the Eastern Mediterranean, 7th–15th Centuries*, ed. Yaakov Lev, Leiden 1996, 267–300.
66. Little, *Mamluk Historiography*, 100–35; Ch. Melville, '"Sometimes by the sword, sometimes by the dagger": the role of the Ismaʿilis in Mamluk-Mongol relations in the 8th/14th century', *Mediaeval Ismaʿili History and Thought*, ed. F. Daftary, Cambridge 1996, 247–63.
67. Little, *Mamluk Historiography*, 129–30; Irwin, *Early Mamluk Sultanate*, 99–101.
68. Cf. Little, *Mamluk Historiography*, 114–15.
69. Al-Maqrīzī, *Kitāb al-sulūk li-maʿrifat duwal al-mulūk*, ed. M. M. Ziyāda and S. ʿA.-F. ʿĀshūr, Cairo 1934–73, II, 184.
70. S. Har-el, *Struggle for Domination in the Middle East: the Ottoman-Mamluk war, 1485–1491*, Leiden 1995, 27–59.

7

THE ENGLISH STATE AND ITS FRONTIERS IN THE BRITISH ISLES, 1300–1600

Steven G. Ellis

The Problem of the English State and its Frontiers

Frontiers were a natural product of the process of state formation. The problems they posed not only influenced relations in general between different kingdoms and peoples; they also determined the nature of the frontier itself, and conditions on the border. This was true also of the English state's frontiers in the British Isles. This essay considers the English frontiers in their final period before the Union of the Crowns with Scotland and the completion of the Tudor conquest of Ireland in 1603. It argues that these frontiers were powerfully shaped both by England's highly centralised system of government and its problematic relations with the other peoples of the archipelago. In the later Middle Ages, English kings had coped fairly comfortably with this important but routine task of frontier administration, which they also faced in the government of their French possessions. Indeed, of the territories held by medieval English kings, the frontiers in Gascony and Normandy were far more difficult to police and defend because of their length, remoteness, and the greater power of the French monarchy. Thus, one unintended result of their loss in the mid fifteenth century was that later kings faced these difficulties in a much more manageable form. In the sixteenth century, however, the remaining borderlands came to be identified by the Tudors as presenting an acute problem of government as the regime attempted to centralise its control over outlying territories. Beginning in the 1530s a highly distinctive strategy was evolved to deal with this frontier problem. Yet paradoxically, this policy turned a routine task of government into an increasingly intractable administrative headache for the regime.

At first sight, conflict and interaction across the frontiers of the British Isles seemed much more muted than in other marcher regions of late medieval Europe. Admittedly, at the end of our period, divisions between Catholic and Reformed versions of Christianity began to complicate relations across the Anglo-Gaelic frontier in Ireland; but they were far less intractable than rivalry between Christian and Muslim in the Mediterranean world. And, English propaganda notwithstanding, interaction between the English state and the peoples of 'the Celtic fringe' did not reflect the sort of conflict between settled and nomadic forms of society which characterised Russia's frontiers with the peoples of the southern steppes and to the east.[1] Yet, as in other parts of late medieval Europe, the British frontiers were typically whole regions, where different peoples lived in close proximity, rather than clearly delineated boundaries. It is not surprising therefore that the more turbulent conditions in these marcher regions tended to highlight the underlying divisions between nations and states within the archipelago. Even so, these divisions were, in principle at least, far from intractable: despite political, cultural, and social differences, the British Isles were everywhere inhabited by literate, Christian peoples who all held much the same range of ideas concerning order and society as other west European peoples.

In large measure, the frontiers of the English state were defined in opposition to its core region and political centre, southern and central England. This region had formed the original area of the Anglo-Saxon monarchy and, in the context of the British Isles, conditions there were uniquely favourable to the exercise of royal authority. It was predominantly lowland, with rich soil and climatic conditions favourable to agriculture. These geographical advantages had been exploited by successive waves of settlers from Roman to Norman times to build up a heavily manorialised and well-populated kingdom, with a culturally homogeneous people living in small towns and nucleated villages. By the standards of later medieval Europe too, the English monarchy was precocious in the centralisation of its government and the uniformity of its administrative institutions; but the system was well suited to the hierarchical social structures and dispersed patterns of landholding and lordship which had developed in lowland England.[2]

To the north and west of lowland England, however, were a number of territories more remote from London which had been added piece-meal to the English state between the eleventh and thirteenth centuries. Here, conditions differed quite significantly from those in lowland England. The geography of this frontier zone was more typical of the British Isles as a whole, with large stretches of mountain, forest, and bog, interspersed with rich coastal plains and river valleys where pasture farming gave place to agriculture. This was a more desolate, sparsely populated landscape of isolated farmsteads, large parishes, and manors, with few substantial gentry or major towns, where more turbulent conditions and fragmented power structures encouraged the maintenance of extended kinship bonds, and strong, compact lordships. In turn, different conditions obliged English kings to maintain in these regions a more decentralised, quasi-military system of government, with special wardens and lieutenants appointed to control the marches and numerous feudal liberties where judicial and military power rested with the local lord. Wherever this system was supplemented by the normal structures of English shire government, these operated only in attenuated form, if at all. For instance, even where quarter sessions and justices of the peace were introduced, their operation was frequently intermittent or ineffective. Thus, despite the centralised and uniform structures of government geared to the English lowlands, the English borderlands were a highly regional and comparatively disturbed land of many marches.[3]

The Nature of the British Frontiers

Until the completion of the English conquest of Wales by Edward I in 1283, there had been three main frontiers within the British Isles, dividing the subjects of the English crown and independent peoples of predominantly Celtic origin to the north and west of the English state. Perhaps the most salient characteristic which these English frontiers shared, and which posed the greatest challenge to English government, was the coincidence within each of the three regions of different kinds of frontier: political, geographical, social, administrative, and cultural. This coincidence is best exemplified in Ireland, by parts of the Anglo-Gaelic frontier there. Within the space of a few miles between the administrative capital of the English lordship at Dublin and the Leinster mountains to the south, the medieval traveller would have crossed all five of these frontiers. The rich coastal plain on which Dublin lay was a well-populated region of mixed farming whose nucleated villages and numerous market towns imparted a strongly English character. This region, 'the English Pale' of Tudor times, was inhabited by 'the king's loyal English lieges', who were predominantly English-speaking, dressed after the English manner, and were governed by English administrative structures and common law. To the south lay Gaelic Ireland, a much more sparsely populated region of pastoral uplands, inhabited by 'the king's Irish enemies', a clan-based people with their own Gaelic system of administration, law, customs, and language. Sandwiched in between, in some exposed parts of the Dublin-Wicklow borderland, lived semi-autonomous, upland marcher lineages of English descent, who straddled the cultural divide between the 'civil English' of the lowlands and the 'wild Irish' of the mountains.[4]

In the case of the other two frontiers, the pattern was a little less complicated and the contrasts were not quite so stark. By 1400, the military character of the Anglo-Scottish frontier was, if anything, even more pronounced, because the Scottish monarchy was a far more formidable adversary than any Gaelic chief: but England and Scotland broadly shared a common culture and had much in common, too, in terms of administrative structures. By contrast, the political and military importance of the Welsh marches had declined sharply after the completion of the Edwardian conquest in 1283, since they no longer had to be defended from independent Welsh princes beyond. The marches of Wales had now become a closed frontier, a closely defined geographical area, separate both from the realm of England and the principality of Wales, with its own particular customs and institutions, such as the officially sanctioned law of the march.[5] Yet, despite the gradual attenuation of its frontier character, the Welsh marches for long retained many of the characteristic features of a march. For instance, the earlier pattern of English settlement there meant that, as with the marches in late medieval Ireland, a characteristic division of the Welsh marches was between the predominantly Celtic society of the pastoral uplands and English society in the arable lowlands.[6] Indeed, in terms of culture, the Welsh marches remained a frontier until long after 1603, but the frontier also survived in terms of law and administration until both principality and marches were incorporated into England between 1536 and 1543.[7]

Given their common features, one might expect that these three medieval frontiers of the English state would have been the subject of numerous comparative studies. In fact, there have been very few.[8] In part, this reflects the unevenness of the surviving documentary evidence: overall, documentation concerning the English marches towards Scotland is far more plentiful than that relating to the English marches in Ireland. Yet as in the case of other national historiographical traditions, it is in some measure, too, an unfortunate by-product of the historian's practice of dividing the English state into neat national territories – England, Ireland, Wales – which anticipate the rise of modern nations more than they reflect contemporary administrative divisions. The treatment of these frontiers by their respective historians has also been somewhat different. The Anglo-Scottish frontier in particular has also marked a boundary in historiographical terms: it divided those parts of the march which are allotted to 'histories of England' from the more northerly parts which are conventionally assigned to historians of Scotland. By contrast, both English and Gaelic Ireland are traditionally seen as falling within the purview of Irish historians, and also outside the remit of English specialists. Thus, the Anglo-Gaelic frontier has been much less of a frontier in historiographical terms. The tendency among Irish historians has been to focus on interaction and assimilation across the frontier, and on the whole coverage of the Anglo-Gaelic frontier has been much more balanced.

Yet these differences are in many ways also historical as well as historiographical. The more fundamental differences between the three frontiers reflected the particular circumstances in which each had originated. Although English colonisation had influenced the development of all three, it was far more important in the case of Ireland and Wales. For the period to 1300, Wales and Ireland may be described as frontiers of settlement, where 'Englishries' (areas of intensive English settlement) were interspersed with 'Irishries' and 'Welshries' (areas of native rule), so creating multiple, localised frontiers which were fragmented and fluid, rather than consolidated blocs. Both were zones of interaction and assimilation between peoples of quite different cultures – rather like the region east of the Elbe which then formed the frontier between Slavs and Germans.[9] Yet during the period of the Gaelic Revival in Ireland, some of the outlying areas of English settlement in Connaught and Ulster were reconquered by Gaelic chiefs, and English retrenchment in the late Middle Ages led to the establishment of more stable and continuous frontiers in the east and south by 1500. Then, in the mid-Tudor period, the English broke out of their bridgehead in the English Pale and the remaining Gaelic parts were gradually overrun in a new wave of English expansion and settlement.[10]

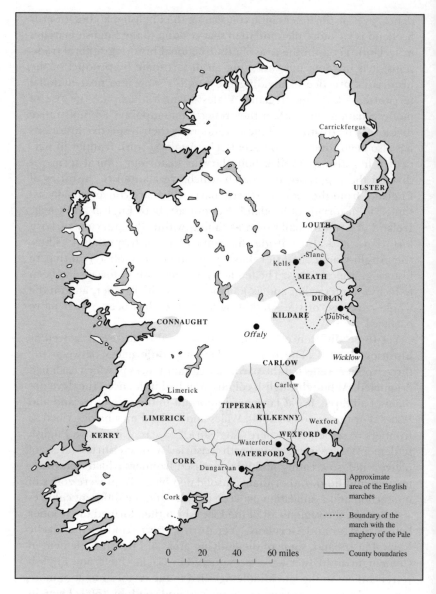

Map 7.1   The Lordship of Ireland, *c*. 1525.
Reproduced by kind permission of Oxford University Press.

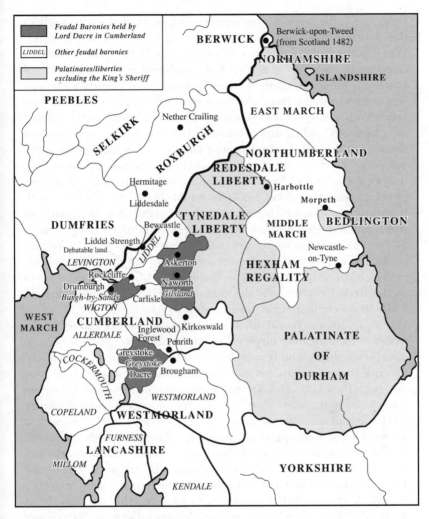

Map 7.2   The Anglo-Scottish border region.
Reproduced by kind permission of Oxford University Press.

By contrast, the Anglo-Scottish borders approximated more closely to the political geographer's definition of a border than a frontier. Whereas the English marches in Ireland and Wales were regions located on the margins of a settled or developed territory, the Anglo-Scottish frontier was more of a clearly demarcated boundary between two sovereign states. Its origins were also rather different. It had been created when English and Scottish kings had divided up the ancient kingdoms of Cumbria and Northumbria between them and annexed these territories into their respective kingdoms. Yet these political developments did not disturb the essential cultural unity of the region, despite the advent of Norman feudalism and colonisation, since these penetrated into Scotland too. The actual line of the Anglo-Scottish border was also more clearly defined and stable than in Ireland or preconquest Wales. Substantially the present border on the Tweed-Solway line had been mentioned in the Treaty of York in 1237. Yet this boundary only survived because subsequent attempts to alter it unilaterally – notably the creation of an English Pale in southern Scotland in the fourteenth century, and the intrusion of English garrisons there in 1548–50 – were in general unsuccessful.[11]

Even so, such technical differences between a border and a frontier were far from clear to medieval officials, and it would be unwise to exaggerate them. The terminology employed by English officials to describe these concepts was quite varied: 'march', 'frontier', and 'border' (with their Latin and Norman-French variants) were all in use, but 'march', or more often 'marches', was the most general term. Henry VIII used all three in the course of a letter with instructions for a garrison 'to be laide vppon our ffronters forayenste Scotelande, aswell for the defense of thesame our borders as also for the annoyaunce of our enemyes', specifying that troops might be recruited 'out of our Westmarches'.[12] The term 'borders' was chiefly used with reference to the Anglo-Scottish frontier: for instance, the inhabitants of Bewcastledale in the west marches were described as living 'in a corner in thextreme partes of the Borders'.[13] It often referred more specifically to the border line, as in the survey in 1542 of the 'wastes & decayes of his graces fronters & borders of his Este & mydle marches of England foranenste Scotland'.[14] The actual boundary – the 'bounder', or 'metes and bounds' – was also described as 'the Marche bank' or 'the Marche dike'.[15] More normally, the 'marches' meant the whole region, and it was in turn divided into the marches of England and those of Scotland.

In 1495, however, an inquisition described lands in the manor of Otterburn in Redesdale in England as lying 'in marchia Scocie'.[16] The 'frontiers' likewise normally meant the area closest to the border line. The military outpost of Calais, for instance, which had agreed international borders like the Anglo-Scottish frontier, was frequently described as 'the marches of Calais', but land close to its western boundary with France was said to be 'bordering on the frontiers'.[17]

In Ireland, by contrast, there was no agreed border line between the English lordship and Gaelic Ireland. Despite the island's division between the Englishry and the Irishry, when it came to describing the location of particular castles or lands, jurors could only state that they lay 'on the borders of the English country in Ireland on the boundary-line of the country (*super limites patrie*) of Offalye', or 'on the outermost part of the English country (*in finibus patrie anglicane*) on the borders of Offalye'.[18] The lordship was traditionally divided into 'la terre de pees, appelle Maghery' [the land of peace, called Maghery], as a statute of 1428 described it, and the marches.[19] And, as on the Anglo-Scottish borders, particularly exposed marchlands lay 'in frontura Marchie' or 'en lez frontures del Marche' ['in the frontiers of the March'].[20]

Beyond these 'frontiers' lay uninhabited wasteland. The 1541 surveys of crown lands in Ireland identified large tracts of land which were now 'uncultivated and for a long time lying waste through the daily spoils and extortions of the aforesaid wild Irish'.[21] The overall extent of these wastelands was also influenced by such factors as demographic change and the general state of Anglo-Gaelic relations, but essentially the struggle for their control reflected the shifting balance of power in each particular march. A statute of Poynings's parliament required each tenant of marchland to make a double ditch 'at thende, syde or parte of the said lande that he doth so occupie that juneth next unto Irishemen' and further ditches 'in the wastes or *fasaghe* landes withoute the saide marcheis'.[22] Thus, it would seem that only the inhabited parts were included in the marches as 'the Englissch grounde' or 'the English contree'.[23] The wastes beyond were a fluctuating no-man's land, to which both English and Gaelic proprietors laid claim.[24] The surviving estate records of major landowners include title deeds of lands which had been conquered during the period of English expansion in the thirteenth century, and subsequently lost during the Gaelic Revival.[25] They also include deeds recording other land grants which had remained purely speculative as medieval English expansion had faltered. Yet during the period of the Kildare ascendancy (1470–1534) successive earls were buying them up in order to secure common-law title to lands reconquered from Gaelic chiefs.[26]

A very similar situation confronted royal officials in the Anglo-Scottish borders, where constant raiding had created great strips of permanent wasteland, abandoned townships, and lands 'unplenyshed ever sythence before the remembraunce of any man now lyvynge'.[27] Inquisitions concerning borderlands were likewise punctuated with such findings as that particular townships 'have for sixty years past lain totally waste and uncultivated through the destruction of the Scots', and that 'no profit can be taken therefrom on account of the Scots and others from Scotland dwelling near' them.[28] Yet in the Anglo-Scottish marches, the earlier stabilisation of the frontier (between 1157 and 1296) at a mutually accepted border line had led to the emergence of rather different concepts of a geographical kingdom and national territory. Whereas Northumbria as far as the Forth had in Anglo-Saxon times been regarded as lying in England, during the fourteenth-century English occupation of southern Scotland the territory under English rule had still been regarded in England as part of Scotland.[29] Thus the treaty line of 1237 retained a jurisdictional significance even when the establishment of an English Pale in southern Scotland deprived it of a political one.

Disputes about what was actually part of England or Scotland were confined to relatively small parcels of land which were 'debatable' – that is, in dispute between the two kingdoms. The border surveys of 1542 and 1550 mention six of these (as well as particular Scottish encroachments on the border);[30] but much the most important was the Debateable Land, a strip of territory in the west marches measuring some ten to fifteen miles by four miles.[31] In 1530–31 the English warden refused redress for outrages committed by Englishmen on Scots in the Debateable Land, because to do so was tantamount to admitting Scottish claims to the territory.[32] Ultimately, English military pressure succeeded at only two points in advancing into southern Scotland the political boundary between the two kingdoms. In the east, Berwick-on-Tweed, which had once been Scotland's chief town and seaport, was finally retaken by the English in 1482, although it was not immediately incorporated into England. In the west, the parish of Kirkandrews, comprising the southern portion of the Debateable Land, became part of England when the Land was finally partitioned in 1552.[33]

The Military Character of the Frontiers

Perhaps the most remarkable feature of the development of the English marches in the late Middle Ages concerned the way in which the Anglo-Scottish frontier was gradually transformed under the impact of war so that it came to resemble much more closely the military frontier in Ireland. The key development was the attempted English conquest of Scotland from 1296, which inaugurated over two centuries of warfare and uneasy truces between the two countries. Although the English occupied large parts of southern Scotland, Scottish armies also raided as far south as Yorkshire in the fourteenth century. After 1388 Scottish armies did not penetrate beyond the River Tyne,[34] but the atmosphere of insecurity affected the whole region. In both regions border lords and gentry continued to live in fortified dwellings; magnates like the earls of Kildare and the Lords Dacre of the North were still building castles in the early sixteenth century, when English nobles elsewhere were abandoning them in favour of country houses. In terms of military architecture, however, the real distinguishing feature of the marches were the towerhouses: free-standing stone keeps, usually three or four stories high, with battlements. Beginning in the far north in the late fourteenth century and in Ireland a generation or so later, towerhouses were built in great numbers, particularly by gentry in the lowland plains; but apart from a few examples in the Welsh marches, these fortified dwellings were almost entirely absent from other parts of the English state.[35]

Frontier defence rested chiefly on the king's subjects in the two regions, and even in Tudor times county levies from as far south as Yorkshire were regularly summoned for border defence against the Scots. From the 1380s the four most northerly shires were exempted from national taxation in return for military service on the borders. For the purpose of defence, the northern border counties and the numerous feudal franchises of the region were organised into marches, with Cumberland and the barony of Westmorland comprising the west marches, and Northumberland and the adjacent franchises the east marches – in turn divided into east and middle marches from the 1470s. Since the crown effectively relied on the numerous tenantry of the region's major landowners for border defence, it aimed to secure the magnates' co-operation by appointing them as wardens of the marches. The wardens supervised and co-ordinated military activity, enforcing in their warden courts the special legal code, known as 'march law', by which border defence and cross-border relations were regulated.[36] Marcher conditions, particularly the needs of defence, placed a premium on strong resident lordship. It also prompted the development on border estates of a special form of land tenure for smallholders, known as 'tenant right' and geared chiefly to military service.[37] Thus a progressive militarisation of the region occurred, and the border line became an extended march.

In Ireland, the Gaelic Revival from the late thirteenth century had created a similar atmosphere of insecurity in the English lordship. Then, between 1315 and 1318 Scottish armies systematically ravaged the lordship during the Bruce Invasion and brought about a permanent weakening of English power there.[38] Everywhere, as frontier defences were undermined, 'the land of peace' shrank and marchlands expanded, leaving embattled English communities eking out a precarious existence on the edge of a wilderness in a land of constant war. In general, the manorial villages of the arable lowlands were easier to defend than the isolated farmsteads of the pastoral uplands. For this reason the frontier was more stable in the south Dublin marches around Tallaght and Saggart and along the northern border of the English Pale in County Louth than it was along the Pale's western frontier in County Meath.[39] Similarly, on the Anglo-Scottish border, the east marches towards Scotland were more easily defended against minor incursions than the west and middle marches, where in the fifteenth century whole districts were left uninhabited after Scottish raids. In Ireland especially, vigorous marcher lordship by resident local magnates was necessary to organise the defence of these borderlands, since the resources of the central government were so slender. Absentee lordship could undermine the defence of entire marches; and in this respect, the crown was the worst offender!

The Social Consequences of Militarisation

The effects of this crisis of lordship were most apparent among the exposed marcher communities of the pastoral uplands, where endemic disorder encouraged a reversion to an earlier form of lineage society. Significantly, these clans, kindreds, and 'surnames' were seemingly peculiar to the frontier regions of the English state, although they were of course indigenous to Gaelic and Welsh society. Not surprisingly, in examining the response of these pastoral English communities to the Gaelic Revival in Ireland and the more disturbed marcher conditions there, the tendency among Irish historians has been to focus on the level of interaction and cultural assimilation between English and Gaelic as the settlers adapted to their new situation.[40] The emergence of English marcher lineages there has been portrayed as a direct borrowing from the Gaelic clan system. No doubt there is some truth in this – interaction and assimilation between two different societies was the essence of the frontier experience – but what is perhaps more significant in the context of the English borderlands is that the phenomenon of marcher lineages was also replicated in the Anglo-Scottish borders.

The northern 'surnames' emerged in response to the endemic insecurity of the region from 1296. They inhabited the poorer, predominantly upland parts of the west and middle marches, and were clan or kinship groups who acted together, collectively seeking vengeance when one of their surname was harmed, and often accepting joint responsibility when charged by the warden officials with reiving and other misdeeds. Across the border, there were similar surnames who frequently intermarried with the English surnames so that under the early Tudors, English branches of Scottish surnames became established in Bewcastledale and Eskdale in the English west marches.[41] Culturally, the English and Scottish surnames were virtually indistinguishable, although the government attempted to classify them as English or Scottish, depending on which side of the border line they resided. In this respect therefore the surnames differed from kinship groups in Ireland, where patrilineal descent and culture, rather than the concept of a national territory, were the primary determinents of nationality.[42]

In wartime, the English surnames constituted a welcome addition to English military might. When the Northumberland surnames were 'booked' by the government in 1528, for instance, they numbered 403 altogether in Tynedale and 445 in Redesdale.[43] And when mustered with the rest of the shire in 1538, the surnames supplied almost one fifth of the shire's most highly prized troops, the mounted spearmen.[44] They could, on the whole, be encouraged to direct their activities northwards in wartime, so long as worthwhile targets of plunder presented themselves in Scotland. Yet essentially the surnames were uncontrollable. Classifying them as English or Scottish, depending on which side of a notional border line they resided, did not make them act any differently, or prevent them from collaborating with each other. The government regarded them as thieves and robbers, and it at-

tempted to control their activities in much the same way as it did those
of Gaelic clans in Ireland. The wardenry officials 'booked' the surnames
to determine responsibility for offences, and they then forced the captains and headsmen of each surname to surrender pledges for their
good conduct.[45]

The Response of Tudor Government

Under the early Tudors, attitudes towards the frontiers and English
marcher society began to harden. This occurred for a number of reasons. In the first place, the loss in 1449–53 of Normandy and Gascony
had eliminated the most important exceptions to the growing domi-
nance of English culture and administrative structures in the late medieval English state. Despite some English settlement in Normandy, the
continental possessions had remained predominantly French in language and culture, and they had been governed by very different forms
of law and administration.[46] Thus, as the Tudors consolidated their
control over lowland England after 1485, the anomalous position of the
English borderlands within the early-Tudor state was increasingly highlighted. The endemic unrest of the frontiers was soon identified as a
serious threat to royal authority and public order. And once the attention of king and council was attracted by the evident lawlessness of the
borderers, the hybrid, quasi-military structures by which they were
ruled automatically came in for scrutiny.

Perhaps the most significant feature of this hardening of official
attitudes towards marcher society was the gap which gradually developed between Tudor perceptions of the nature of the frontier problem
and the realities of the situation on the ground. The continuing disorders of marcher society, in the face of repeated attempts by the crown
to strengthen royal authority and control there, eventually prompted
the Tudors to dismantle the quasi-military system of administration, by
which these regions had traditionally been governed, in favour of the
more centralised and uniform structures of local government operating
in lowland England.

In essence, the identification by Tudor officials of a specific frontier
problem reflected the conflation of two different strands of traditional
English thought. The first concerned English attitudes to the other
peoples of the British Isles. As early as the twelfth century, English
writers were denigrating the Irish, Scots, and Welsh as barbarians, on
account of their alleged 'backwardness' in terms of material culture:

they were primitive peoples living in idleness and brutality in woods and bogs. Depending on the state of Anglo-Scottish relations, the Scots were sometimes given credit for the fostering of towns, agriculture, and commerce in the Scottish lowlands, but tensions were further exacerbated by English claims to empire throughout the British Isles. English kings claimed an overlordship over Scotland and tended to treat their Scottish counterparts as disobedient vassals.

In Ireland, their conduct in dealing with Gaelic chiefs was even more contemptuous: they were usually treated as aliens who squatted illegally on land rightfully belonging to the English crown and its subjects. They were denied access to the king's courts and their titles to land and property went unrecognised. Thus the extension of English rule over 'the Celtic fringe' was presented as the triumph of civilisation over savagery.[47] The second traditional strand of English political thought concerned the relationship between 'English civility' and English government and common law. There was an assumption that the structures of government and society were closely linked, so that the kind of civilised society which had emerged in lowland England reflected the efficacy of England's centralised and uniform system of administration in promoting peace and good government. From these assumptions it was only a short step to the argument that the extension of English administrative structures and the common law over other parts of the British Isles would lead automatically to the establishment there of an ordered civil society on English lines.[48]

In reality, however, the only accurate aspect of this Tudor analysis was the actual existence of a frontier problem. This problem reflected the regime's fundamental inability to understand that special provision had to be made for the rule and defence of the English state's long landed frontiers which could not be governed in the same way as lowland England; and so Tudor attempts to promote law and order in the marches by standardising and centralising local government there without making alternative arrangements for defence only made the problem worse.

On the whole, Henry VII's handling of the borderlands was conservative. Initially at least, he was more concerned by potential challenges to his crown from Yorkist pretenders and disaffected magnates in these regions. Power was therefore diffused in the north, and the financial and military subventions traditionally provided by central government for border defence were reduced both there and in Ireland; reliance on provincial magnates was everywhere curtailed, in part by the creation of special regional councils for Wales and the north; and in Wales the king built up his landed possessions at the expense of the marcher lords. These changes succeeded in their primary aim of reducing the potential of the borderlands as a base for plotters and pretenders.

In his early years Henry VIII simply maintained in office his father's eventual choice as ruling magnates in these regions, so that both the earl of Kildare in Ireland and Lord Dacre in the far north consolidated their power and authority as marcher lords (as did Sir Rhys ap Thomas in Wales), building up powerful local affinities in order to defend the frontiers against the Irish and Scots. Thus, under Henry VIII, frontier rule and defence came to depend more heavily than before upon the private resources of the ruling magnates.[49] Yet, given the sharp reduction in the level of royal subventions and the heavy responsibilities attaching to the offices of warden or governor of Ireland, very few others had the *manraed* or income needed to discharge these offices on the reduced terms now offered. This became very apparent in the 1520s, when Henry found that the earl of Ormond in Ireland and the earls of Cumberland and Westmorland in the far north were unable to rule effectively in the face of opposition from the crown's normal choice as deputy or warden, the earls of Kildare and Lords Dacre. And in turn, the enforced reliance on overmighty subjects – each capable of raising 5000 semi-professional soldiers from among their border tenantry at a time when the general military ethos of English society was in noticeable decline – seemed a serious liability to a government which lacked a standing army. It led to a crisis in 1534, in which the ninth earl of Kildare and William, fourth lord Dacre, were dismissed from office and charged with treason, and a major rebellion ensued in Ireland.[50]

The shortcomings of early-Tudor policy were most visible in the far north, where the external military threat presented by the Scots was much more formidable, and where the sharp reduction of subventions and the exclusion of the Percy earl of Northumberland from power had undermined frontier defence. It is probably no accident that the first specific reference to the northern surnames does not occur until 1498 – at a time when the reduced provision for border defence had greatly exacerbated the government's difficulties in controlling them. In that year, following the murder of Scots in breach of the recent truce, eight surnames were threatened with outlawry for harbouring those charged with the murders and ordered to surrender them within three days.[51] In Henry VII's later years, however, these difficulties were eased by the unwonted Anglo-Scottish co-operation which surrounded the treaty of 1502 – the first formal peace between England and Scotland since 1333. Under Henry VIII, Anglo-Scottish relations soon deteriorated again, leading to periodic war, but the king's response was simply to entrust the defence of all three marches to a minor peer, Thomas Lord Dacre. He even allowed the council in the north to lapse, and paid for a lieutenant and augmented border garrison only during periods of major hostilities.

The result was a serious weakening of the east and middle marches where Dacre had little land, few tenants, and far less following than the disappointed and obstructive Percy earl. Although Dacre built up a much more effective system of defences for the west marches where his principal estates lay, he was forced to develop closer ties with the more disreputable elements in border society, notably the surnames, in order to defend Northumberland.[52] Thus, with military needs now taking priority over law and order, the normal procedures of common law and local government gradually broke down. Sheriffs of Northumberland never accounted at the exchequer and their work was now mainly taken up with policing and defence. Some years there was no sheriff at all. Quarter sessions were kept irregularly because there was a shortage of substantial and reliable gentry for inclusion on commissions of the peace. And even if the annual assizes were not cancelled because of war, those brought to trial were usually acquitted for lack of evidence, since most gentry harboured thieves and were unwilling to convict the servants and tenants of others. The more notorious criminals simply retired to the adjoining liberties for a few days until the king's judges had departed.[53] Much the same comments could be made about English government in parts of Ireland. Eventually, following the peace with France and Scotland in 1525, renewed complaints about disorders in the borderlands attracted the king's attention. In the north, for instance, Thomas Lord Dacre was hauled up before Star Chamber and charged with 'bearinge of theaves'. He was dismissed in disgrace not only from his increasingly unwelcome duties as warden of the east and middle marches, but also from the wardenship of the west marches which he had occupied for forty years, and ordered to compensate all those who had suffered from his maladministration of justice.[54]

Following this, Tudor government in all three regions was reorgan-
ised, notably by reviving and remodelling the provincial councils; but it
was not until the mid 1530s, at the height of the Reformation crisis, that
fundamental changes were attempted on the frontiers. Their thrust was
to extend and consolidate royal control and the normal operation of
English shire government, while curtailing so far as possible magnate
power and the borderlands' traditional administrative structures. The
changes were most far-reaching and effective in the marches of Wales,
where the provincial council was remodelled under a new president in
1534 and where the marcher lordships were abolished in favour of
English shire government and common law after 1536. The comparatively sympathetic response in Wales to this anglicising initiative owed
much to the identification of the Welsh gentry and learned classes with
the Tudor dynasty – in marked contrast to Gaelic perceptions of the
Tudors as mere English! Yet equally important in ensuring success
was the absence of a military frontier in Wales, which might otherwise
have undermined the effective operation of the English system of
government.[55]

A different strategy of state formation in early modern Europe – that
followed by the French and Spanish monarchies – saw the creation of
professional standing armies for the defence of long landed frontiers.
Indeed, this seemed to be occurring in Lancastrian Normandy in the
later 1430s.[56] The nearest the Tudor regime came to adopting this
strategy, however, was the stationing of a substantial English garrison to
rule and defend Tudor Ireland after 1534; but this initiative was pursued very grudgingly and half-heartedly and was not seen as having
any implications for Tudor rule elsewhere. Indeed, after the loss of the
French territories, the English state had no appropriate experience to
draw on, but the Tudor success in assimilating the internal Welsh
frontier supplied a quite misleading precedent for frontier administration, strengthening official convictions that good rule and English civility could be established only by extending to the other frontiers the
same system of administration which operated so effectively in lowland
England.[57] As a result the Tudors embarked on a wholly impractical
strategy which was to have disastrous consequences for the rule of the
frontiers.

In the north, the feudal franchises were effectively incorporated by
statute of 1536 into the adjoining shires and royal control was established over the normal institutions of English local government. Crown
influence was also greatly strengthened by the king's acquisition of

extensive landed estates there, either by confiscation (from the monasteries), inheritance (the Percy earldom of Northumberland in 1537), or
'exchange' (Redesdale and Hexhamshire). Finally, following the major
rebellion of 1536–37, the Pilgrimage of Grace, the king took the
wardenships into his own hands: he recruited three local gentry as
deputy wardens, made them answerable to the king's council there
which was remodelled, and retained sixty-six of the leading borderers
to assist them.[58] In Ireland, lands confiscated from the monasteries and
attainted rebels likewise swelled the royal demesne and crown influence, and in place of the earl of Kildare as ruling magnate, the government of Ireland was much more closely supervised by the appointment
to the governorship and other key posts of English-born administrators, backed by a small English garrison.[59] In short, frontier administration was brought more into conformity with arrangements for lowland
England.

In explaining the Pilgrimage in a letter to his evangelical colleague in
Zürich, Heinrich Bullinger, Archbishop Cranmer offered a revealing
insight into official attitudes to northerners in general, and the borderers in particular. Cranmer described them as:

> . . . a certain sort of barbarous and savage people, who were ignorant
> of and turned away from farming and the good arts of peace, and
> who were so far utterly unacquainted with knowledge of sacred
> matters, that they could not bear to hear anything of culture and
> more gentle civilisation. In its furthest regions on the Scottish border,
> England has several peoples (*populos*) of such a kind, who I think
> should rather be called devastators (*populatores*); in ancient fashion,
> they fight with their neighbouring clans (*gentibus*) on both sides [of
> the border] in perpetual battle and brigandage, and they live solely
> upon the pillage and plunder won from it.[60]

Other reports concerning the border surnames show that the characteristics which evoked most comment from contemporaries were precisely those features which English observers had long deprecated in
Gaelic society – its clans, backwardness, savagery, cattle-rustling, and
feuds. Indeed, by 1560 Irishness and savagery were so closely identified
in the official mind that Archbishop Parker could warn the queen's
secretary that if bishops were not quickly appointed to the northern
sees, the region would become 'too much Irish and savage'.[61] These
reports recalled the traditional complaints of English-born officials

in Ireland concerning the degeneracy of the medieval English of Ireland who forsook English ways and adopted Gaelic customs.[62] Yet unlike the Gaelic Irish, these so-called 'English rebels' in Ireland and the border surnames were at least nominally Englishmen, to whom the benefits of English civility had long been extended. And this in turn prompted the question of why they had degenerated from their earlier civility to their present savagery. In both regions, Tudor officials increasingly identified the problem in terms of moral decline and a defect of justice.[63]

The Consequences of Tudor Policy in the Marches

What this frontier strategy singularly failed to address was the problem of how the new arrangements could be expected to uphold frontier defence. As the British government has recently discovered in Northern Ireland, not even a well-equipped professional army with all the advantages of modern technology is capable of insulating an international frontier entirely from private cross-border raids, even with the full co-operation of the adjoining state. In the sixteenth century, this was far beyond the means of any European state. In both Ireland and the far north petty raiding by neighbouring clans and surnames inevitably spilled across the frontier, even at times of close official, cross-border co-operation, and the more 'civilised' and less militarised English marcher society became, the more tempting a target it presented for cross-border raids mounted from Scotland and Gaelic Ireland. The traditional system of border rule had relied on defence in depth, encouraging marcher lords to hold a battle-hardened tenantry ready to resist invasion. Hence close to the actual frontier, in Northumberland or Kildare for instance, early-Tudor promotion of peace and 'English civility' proved disastrous.

Even before the demise of the Percies, the east and middle marches had been seriously weakened by the non-residence of major landowners. Since they were no longer entrusted with the wardenship, they had less need of border service from their tenants, and they raised their rents and entry-fines in response to inflation. It was thought, for instance, that the fourth earl of Northumberland (1470–89) had been able to raise 1000 spearmen from his tenants in the county, but the sixth earl (1527–37) could raise only a hundred. Other lords' tenants were similarly affected, so that by 1543 only 1000 men in Northumberland were properly harnessed and the county could raise only 300 horse-men.[64] Thus the most obvious result of the crown's emergence as the largest landowner there was the crisis of lordship which followed the replacement of resident lords by an absentee.

A similar development occurred in Ireland following the attainder of the earl of Kildare in 1534. By 1540–41, royal commissioners surveying the crown lands in Ireland painted a sorry picture of decay and destruc-tion in outlying parts of the English Pale; where the earl of Kildare enjoyed a landed income of almost IR£1600 a year by 1534, after the rebellion the king's officers were unable to extract more than IR£900 a year from the same estates, in large measure because of their destruc-tion or seizure by 'the wild Irish'.[65] In contemporary reports on the state of the Anglo-Scottish borders, royal commissioners expressed similar alarm at the failure of leading gentry to ensure that their townships on the border line were properly tenanted and defended or to repair fortresses which had been destroyed by the Scots.[66] In both regions, the commissioners recommended the rebuilding and repair of key border castles and towers;[67] yet once acquired by the crown most of these fortifications were gradually allowed to decay for want of regular re-pairs.[68] In both regions, the crown was gradually drawn in the 1540s into more militaristic initiatives in a bid to stabilise the defence of the frontier which was actually being undermined by its own policies. In the longer term, however, arrangements for frontier defence developed rather differently, reflecting variations in the crown's relations with Scotland and Gaelic Ireland, and the relative magnitude of the military threat which they presented.

In the far north, after war recommenced with Scotland, Henry was forced to appoint southern nobles to the office of warden of the marches in wartime, in the absence of acceptable northern magnates to organise its defence.[69] In Northumberland the local gentry paid black-mail to the thieves in order to protect their property, and since the county was no longer able to defend itself in wartime, a large paid garrison of between 2000 and 3300 men had to be stationed there.[70] Likewise, the promotion of a new group of crown officials and pension-ers and the disintegration of the old Percy connection also fostered 'such envy, hatred, disdain and malice' among the gentry that they refused to rise to assist each other.[71] By 1559, after another war with Scotland, the verdict of Sir Ralph Sadler on the state of the borders was utterly damning:

It is more than xx yeres ago syns I had som understanding of this frontier, and yet dyd I never know it in such disorder; for now the officer spoyleth the thefe, without bringing forth his person to tryall by the law; and the thefe robbeth the trew man, and the trew men take assuraunce of the theves that they shall not robbe them, and give them yerely rent and tribute for the same.

Things had reached such a pass in the last war 'that English borderers were assured by the Scottes from burning and spoyle, and for the same in lyke wise payed the Scottes certen rent and tribute'. Sadler placed the blame for this on 'the lacke of stoute and wise officers',[72] but the basic problem remained the absence of any effective system of border defence.

In fact, after Henry VIII's death in 1547, the English government had briefly tried a different solution to the problem, establishing garrisons in southern Scotland in a bid to protect the region by advancing the border into enemy territory. In the face of substantial military assistance from Scotland's 'auld alliance' with France, this strategy proved ruinously expensive.[73] After the treaty of Edinburgh in 1560, however, the advent of better relations between the English and Scottish courts transformed the problem of the northern frontier. Not needing to guard against a major Scottish invasion, the government had only to police and defend the frontier against petty raids by border surnames until finally, in 1603 England's northern frontier effectively disappeared.[74] Even so, under Elizabeth the state of the borders went from bad to worse. As frontier defences collapsed, the English marches were increasingly destroyed by Scottish reivers. Analysis of recorded complaints of livestock theft between 1510 and 1605 suggests that the English marchers increasingly lost out in cross-border reiving, most especially the inhabitants of North Tynedale, Redesdale, and Bewcastledale, whose growing poverty was reflected in the region's architecture – the building of poorer-quality pelehouses instead of the more expensive towerhouses preferred elsewhere in the Anglo-Scottish marches.[75] The growing incidence of blackmail levied by Scots on English borderers points in the same direction, as does the dwindling numbers of horsemen which the English surnames could muster – in the case of Redesdale, down from 300 in 1558 to 91 in 1580 and little more than 20 in 1586, and 134 from Tynedale in 1580 and only 21 in 1595.[76]

In Ireland, the English government's similar response to the deteriorating military situation had a rather different outcome which, however, proved no more satisfactory in the longer term. Lacking foreign assistance, the isolated and weak chieftaincies of the Gaelic midlands proved much less able to resist when the government proceeded to establish garrisons there in a similar bid to protect the English Pale. Yet advancing the frontier into the Gaelic midlands did not actually solve any of the problems associated with frontier defence. By assuming responsibility for a wider area, by moving the actual frontier away from the standing defences of the English Pale, and by stirring up Gaelic resistance, the strategy actually made the government's immediate problem a good deal more complicated. The result was that, in a destabilising political situation and with Anglo-Gaelic relations becoming increasingly embittered, the Tudor government was gradually sucked further and further into Gaelic Ireland: finally, it was forced to undertake what had never been English policy – a ruinously expensive military conquest of the whole island in the teeth of Gaelic opposition, which almost bankrupted the crown.[77]

Overall, therefore, the government's efforts to promote peace, good rule, and 'English civility' in the far north and Ireland proved spectacularly counterproductive. Tudor policy turned out to be a *pis aller* between medieval English methods of frontier defence and the standing armies built up by contemporary French and Spanish kings. Traditionally, the responsibilities associated with the governorship and the wardenries had encouraged border magnates to tailor their estate-management policies to defence needs and to keep a warlike tenantry ready with horse and harness. The customary fees and perquisites of the office had also allowed the governor and wardens to reward border service. Yet with the exclusion of the magnates from offices which were traditionally theirs, they were less interested in their tenants' military service.[78] In sum, the promotion of 'English civility' undermined border defence. Indeed, under the impact of these policies, by the mid 1540s foreign mercenaries (including Irish kerne) had to be employed to defend the Anglo-Scottish borders.[79] The Tudors had simply exchanged one problem for another: having ensured that great lords with their numerous tenantry were unable to exploit the key border offices to challenge the crown, they now found themselves unable to maintain good rule or defend the marches against wild Irish and Scots. The pursuit of an ordered, civil society and the maintenance of traditional methods of frontier defence proved mutually contradictory goals.

   Thus the highly individualistic Tudor methods of state formation
proved, at best, irrelevant to the problem of the frontiers, which were
solved, in the one case, by a plain, old-fashioned dynastic union, and in
the other, by the equally traditional remedy of military conquest. In this
regard, as in so many other aspects of Early Modern British history, the
real watershed was the dismantling after 1603 of the Tudor state's long
landed frontiers with Scotland and Gaelic Ireland. The Union of the
Crowns with Scotland and the completion of the Tudor conquest of
Ireland finally rendered these military frontiers superfluous and eliminated the need for the kind of territorial marcher lordship by which
they had hitherto been defended. In other respects, however, these
changes destroyed the traditional balance within the English state between the political influence of the richer, more urbanised English
lowlands and the military and strategic value of the semi-autonomous
borderlands. The borderlands were assimilated administratively and
culturally to the centre, but politically they were marginalised. The
regional councils established for these areas were primarily instruments
of central control, not of regional self-government. And by 1603 when,
from a Westminster-centred perspective, English politicians faced the
problem of how to deal with two new borderlands – Scotland, and
Gaelic Ireland – which were even larger, more remote and 'uncivilised',
the Tudor pattern of state-building was so well entrenched that other
methods seemed inconceivable. Thus the new multiple monarchy was
ruled from London through councils in Dublin and Edinburgh in
much the same way that the regional councils ruled Wales and the
north. And neither was there a pan-British parliament to represent the
interests of Scotland or Ireland at the centre of power.[80]
   The fate of England's British frontiers thus provides an important
insight into the wider problem of state formation while also underlining
the basic historiographical inadequacy of traditional nationalist approaches to this problem. Indeed, throughout the British Isles, major
landowners in frontier regions, whether in the Scottish lowlands or the
wider Gaelic world spanning the North Channel, as well as the emerging English state, all faced the same problem in organising the defence
of their estates. Yet because of the nation-based character of modern
British historiography, what was actually a very comparable experience
for these remote marcher communities has been divided up between
English, Irish, Welsh, and after 1603 Scottish historians, and depicted
as the making of the modern nation.

NOTES

1. M. Khodarkovsky, 'From frontier to empire: the concept of the frontier in Russia, sixteenth–eighteenth centuries', *Russian History*, XIX (1992), 115–28. Cf. N. P. Canny, *Kingdom and Colony: Ireland in the Atlantic world, 1560–1800*, Baltimore 1988, esp. ch. 2.

2. For this and the next paragraph, see S. G. Ellis, *Tudor Frontiers: the making of the British state*, Oxford 1995, 4–7, 19–23, 46–8; *idem*, 'Crown, community and government in the English territories, 1450–1575', *History*, LXXI (1986), 187–92.

3. This is to adapt Robin Frame's arresting phrase concerning the medieval lordship of Ireland in his seminal article, 'Power and society in the lordship of Ireland, 1272–1377', *Past and Present*, LXXVI (1977), 32.

4. See especially, R. Frame, *English Lordship in Ireland 1318–1361*, Oxford 1982, 27–46; S. G. Ellis, *The Pale and the Far North: government and society in two early Tudor borderlands*, Galway 1988, 28–30; D. B. Quinn and K. W. Nicholls, 'Ireland in 1534', *A New History of Ireland. III: early modern Ireland 1534–1691*, ed. T. W. Moody, F. X. Martin, and F. J. Byrne, Oxford 1976, 6–7.

5. R. Davies, 'Frontier arrangements in fragmented societies: Ireland and Wales', *MFS*, 81–3.

6. See especially, R. R. Davies, *Lordship and Society in the March of Wales 1282–1400*, Oxford 1978, ch. 14.

7. R. R. Davies, 'The twilight of Welsh law, 1284–1536', *History*, LI (1966), 143–64; Roberts, 'English crown', esp. 118–27.

8. Notably Davies, 'Frontier arrangements'. For the later period, see Ellis, *Tudor Frontiers*. See also R. R. Davies, *Domination and Conquest: the experience of Ireland, Scotland and Wales 1100–1300*, Cambridge 1990; R. Frame, *The Political Development of the British Isles 1100–1400*, Oxford 1990; R. Bartlett, *The Making of Europe: conquest, colonization and cultural change 950–1350*, London 1993.

9. See especially, Davies, 'Frontier arrangements'; Bartlett, *Making of Europe*. The comparisons with German frontiers are suggested by the essays in *MFS*, chs 7, 12.

10. See *A New History of Ireland. II: medieval Ireland 1169–1534*, ed. A. Cosgrove, Oxford 1987, esp. chs 9–10, 12; S. G. Ellis, *Tudor Ireland: crown, community and the conflict of cultures, 1470–1603*, London 1985.

11. G. W. S. Barrow, 'The Anglo-Scottish border', *NH*, I (1966), 21–4; Ellis, *Pale and the Far North*, 6.

12. Carlisle, Cumbria Record Office, MS D/Ay/1/180.

13. York, Castle Howard Archives, MS F1/5/5, fol. 30.

14. Sir Robert Bowes's and Sir Ralph Ellerker's survey of the east and middle marches, 1542, printed in J. Hodgson, *A History of Northumberland*, 3 pts in 7 vols, Newcastle 1820–25, III:2, 171–248, at 193.

15. See 'Of the manner of keeping warden courts', printed in J. Nicolson and R. Burn, *The History and Antiquities of the Counties of Westmorland and Cumberland*, 2 vols, London 1777, I, ch. 3; also in Bowes and Ellerker's survey (1542) (see n.14 above), 171–248.

16. London, PRO, C 142/10, no. 6 (*Cal. I.P.M. Hen. VII*, I, no. 971).

17. Quoted in P. T. J. Morgan, 'The government of Calais, 1485–1558', D.Phil. thesis, University of Oxford 1966, 7, 25–6.

18. London, PRO, SP 65/3/2 (*LP Hen. VIII*, XVI, no. 398); *Crown Surveys of Lands, 1540–41*, ed. G. Mac Niocaill, Dublin 1992, 159.

19. Parliament roll, 8 Henry VI c. 13 (*Statute Rolls of the Parliament of Ireland, Reign of Henry VI*, ed. H. F. Berry, Dublin 1910). 'Maghery' was a transliteration of the Gaelic *machaire*, meaning a 'plain' or 'champaign ground'.

20. D. B. Quinn (ed.), 'Guide to English financial records for Irish history, 1461–1559', *Analecta Hibernica*, X (1941), 24; Parliament roll, 16 & 17 Edward IV c. 24 (*Statute Rolls of the Parliament of Ireland . . . Reign of King Edward IV*, ed. H. F. Berry and J. F. Morrissey, 2 vols, Dublin 1914–39, II, 492).

21. London, PRO, SC 11/934, SP 65/3/2 (*LP Hen. VIII*, XVI, no. 378).

22. London, PRO, E 30/1548, fol. 18 (printed in A. Conway, *Henry VII's Relations with Scotland and Ireland, 1485–98*, Cambridge 1932, 215–16). 'Fasaghe' was a transliteration of the Gaelic *fásach*, meaning a 'waste' or 'desert'.

23. See, for instance, *The Register of Primate John Swayne*, ed. D. A. Chart, Belfast 1935, 108–9.

24. Cf. Quinn and Nicholls, 'Ireland in 1534', 6–7.

25. See the surviving Ormond deeds (mainly in Dublin, the National Library of Ireland), and Kildare deeds (mainly in Belfast, the Public Record Office of Northern Ireland); also *Calendar of Ormond Deeds*, ed. E. Curtis, 6 vols, Dublin 1932–43; *The Red Book of the Earls of Kildare*, ed. G. Mac Niocaill, Dublin 1964; *Crown Surveys*, ed. Mac Niocaill.

26. See especially, the ninth earl's Rental Book, in *Crown Surveys*, 231–357.

27. Bowes and Ellerker's survey (1542), III:2, 184.

28. London, PRO, E 150/112; C 142/10, no. 6 (*Cal. I.P.M. Hen. VII*, I, nos 157, 971).

29. *Calendar of Patent Rolls 1374–47*, 441, 457, *1396–99*, 430, *1399–1401*, 351, *1405–08*, 73; A. Goodman, 'The Anglo-Scottish marches in the fifteenth century: a frontier society?', *Scotland and England, 1286–1815*, ed. R. A. Mason, Edinburgh 1987, 20–5.

30. Bowes and Ellerker's survey, 1542, and Bowes's survey, 1550, in Hodgson, *Northumberland*, III:2, 171–248. See also, *LP Hen. VIII*, III, no. 3286; IV, no. 968.

31. W. MacKay Mackenzie, 'The Debateable Land', *Scottish Historical Review*, XXX (1951), 109–25; T. H. B. Graham, 'The Debateable Land', *Transactions of the Cumberland and Westmorland Antiquarian and Archaeological Society*, new ser., XII (1912), 33–58, XIV (1914), 132–57.

32. *LP Hen. VIII*, V, nos 465, 535, 537, 763.

33. Cf. n. 31 above.

34. A. J. Pollard, *North-Eastern England during the Wars of the Roses*, Oxford 1990, 14.

35. M. W. Thompson, *The Decline of the Castle*, Cambridge 1987, esp. 23 (map showing distribution of towerhouses); P. Dixon, 'Towerhouses, pelehouses and border society', *Archaeological Journal*, CXXXVI (1979), 240–52; C. Ó

Danachair, 'Irish tower houses and their regional distribution', *Béaloideas*, XLV–XLVII (1979), 158–63.

36. R. L. Storey, 'The wardens of the marches of England towards Scotland, 1377–1485', *EHR*, LXXII (1957), 593–615; J. A. Tuck, 'War and society in the medieval north', *NH*, XXI (1985), 33–52; *idem*, 'Richard II and the border magnates', *ibid.*, III (1968), 27–52.

37. R. W. Hoyle, 'An ancient and laudable custom: the definition and development of tenant right in north-western England in the sixteenth century', *Past and Present*, CXVI (1987), 24–55; M. L. Bush, 'Tenant right under the Tudors: a revision revised', *Bulletin of the John Rylands Library*, LXXVII (1995), 161–8.

38. J. Lydon, 'The impact of the Bruce invasion', *New History of Ireland* II, ed. Cosgrove, ch. 10.

39. B. Smith, 'A county community in early-fourteenth-century Ireland: the case of Louth', *EHR*, CVIII (1993), 561–88; S. G. Ellis, *Reform and Revival: English government in Ireland, 1470–1534*, London 1986, 55.

40. For different approaches to this problem, see J. A. Watt, 'Approaches to the history of fourteenth-century Ireland', *New History of Ireland* II, ed. Cosgrove, ch. 11; S. G. Ellis, 'Nationalist historiography and the English and Gaelic worlds in the late middle ages', *Irish Historical Studies*, XXV (1986–87), 1–18.

41. R. T. Spence, 'The pacification of the Cumberland borders, 1593–1628', *NH*, XIII (1977), 60–1; Mackenzie, 'Debateable Land', 117–20.

42. Ellis, *Pale and the Far North*, 19–26.

43. London, PRO, SP 1/48, ff. 117–34v (*LP Hen. VIII*, IV:2, no. 4336 (2)).

44. For the 1538 musters for Northumberland, see J. Hodgson, *Archaeologia Aeliana*, 1st ser., IV (1855), 157–206.

45. Ellis, *Tudor Frontiers*, ch. 2.

46. For example R. Massey, 'The land settlement in Lancastrian Normandy', *Property and Politics: essays in later medieval English history*, ed. A. J. Pollard, Gloucester 1984, 76–96; *England in Europe 1066–1453*, ed. N. Saul, London 1994, chs 8–9, 12–14.

47. J. Gillingham, 'Foundations of a disunited kingdom', *Uniting the Kingdom? The Making of British History*, ed. A. Grant and K. J. Stringer, London 1995, 48–64; *idem*, 'The beginnings of English imperialism', *Journal of Historical Sociology*, V (1992), 392–409. On the status of the Gaelic Irish, see G. J. Hand, 'Aspects of alien status in medieval English law, with special reference to Ireland', *Legal History Studies, 1972: papers presented to the Legal History Conference, Aberystwyth, 18–21 July 1972*, ed. D. Jenkins, Cardiff 1975, 129–35; Ellis, *Tudor Frontiers*, 6, 32–3, 39, 75, 116.

48. Cf. P. Roberts, 'The English crown, the Principality of Wales and the Council in the Marches, 1534–1641', *The British Problem, c.1534–1707: state formation in the Atlantic Archipelago*, ed. B. Bradshaw and J. Morrill, Basingstoke 1996, 131–6.

49. S. G. Ellis, 'Tudor state formation and the shaping of the British Isles', *Conquest and Union: fashioning a British state*, ed. *idem et* S. Barber, London 1995, 40–55; Roberts, 'English crown', 118–22.

50. Ellis, *Tudor Frontiers*, chs 3–6.
51. *Calendar of Documents Relating to Scotland*, 5 vols, Edinburgh 1881–1987, IV, no. 1649; *Calendar of Patent Rolls 1494–1509*, 160.
52. Ellis, *Tudor Frontiers*, ch. 5.
53. *Ibid.*, chs 2, 5; M. James, *Society, Politics and Culture: studies in early modern England*, Cambridge 1986, esp. ch. 2. For the collapse of local government in Northumberland, see S. G. Ellis, 'Civilizing Northumberland: representations of Englishness in the Tudor state', *Journal of Historical Sociology* (forthcoming).
54. Hodgson, *Northumberland*, II:2, 31–40; London, B. L., Lansdowne MS I, fol. 43; London, PRO, C. 85/585 (*LP Hen. VIII*, IV:2, no. 3022); *LP Hen. VIII*, IV, nos 988, 1058, 1117, 1637, 1665, 1700, 1725, 1727, 1762; J. Guy, *The Cardinal's Court: the impact of Thomas Wolsey in Star Chamber*, Hassocks 1977, 122–3, 163 n. 146.
55. See most recently, *The British Problem*, ed. Bradshaw and Morrill, esp. chs 1–5.
56. A. E. Curry, 'The first English standing army? Military organization in Lancastrian Normandy, 1420–1450', *Patronage, Pedigree and Power in Later Medieval England*, ed. C. Ross, Gloucester 1979, 193–214.
57. C. Brady, 'Comparable histories?: Tudor reform in Wales and Ireland', *Conquest and Union*, ed. Ellis and Barber, 64–86; Ellis, 'Tudor state formation', 55–6.
58. M. L. Bush, 'The problem of the far north: a study of the crisis of 1537 and its consequences', *NH*, VI (1971), 40–63; James, *Society, Politics and Culture*, esp. ch. 3; Ellis, 'Centre and periphery'.
59. S. G. Ellis, 'Thomas Cromwell and Ireland, 1532–40', *Historical Journal*, XXIII (1980), 497–519.
60. Quoted in D. MacCulloch, *Thomas Cranmer, a Life*, New Haven 1996, 178.
61. *Correspondence of Matthew Parker, D.D. Archbishop of Canterbury*, ed. J. Bruce and T. T. Perowne, Parker Soc., Cambridge 1853, 123.
62. Cf. Watt, 'Fourteenth-century Ireland', 308–12; B. Bradshaw, *The Dissolution of the Religious Orders in Ireland under Henry VIII*, Cambridge 1974, ch. 1.
63. Ellis, *Tudor Frontiers*, ch. 2.
64. *LP Hen. VIII*, XVIII:1, no. 800.
65. *Crown Surveys, passim*; PRO, SP 65/3/2 (*LP Hen. VIII*, XVI, no. 398); Ellis, 'Thomas Cromwell', 507–18.
66. Border surveys of 1542 and 1550: Hodgson, *Northumberland*, III:2, 171–248.
67. See, for instance, Hodgson, *Northumberland*, III:2, 229; *Crown Surveys*, 63, 118, 152, 157, 159.
68. *Ibid.*, III:2, 244–5; *Crown Surveys*, 152, 160–61, 162, 176.
69. Bush, 'Problem of the far north', 51–2.
70. London, PRO, SP 1/179, fol. 157 (*LP Hen. VIII*, XVIII:1, no. 800); Bush, 'Problem of the far north', 60.
71. *LP Hen. VIII*, XVIII:1, no. 141 (quotation); cf. no. 800.
72. *The State Papers and Letters of Sir Ralph Sadler*, ed. A. Clifford, 2 vols, Edinburgh 1809, I, 444.
73. M. L. Bush, *The Government Policy of Protector Somerset*, London 1975, ch. 2.

74. Ellis, 'Tudor state formation', 58–63.
75. Dixon, 'Towerhouses', 240–52.
76. S. J. Watt, *From Border to Middle Shire: Northumberland 1586–1625*, Leicester 1975, 26, 109; R. Robson, *The Rise and Fall of the English Highland Clans: Tudor responses to a mediaeval problem*, Edinburgh 1989, 215–16.
77. Brady, *Chief Governors, passim*; Ellis, *Tudor Ireland*, chs 8–9.
78. Newton, 'Decay of the borders', 3–5.
79. Bush, 'Problem of the far north', 61; D. G. White, 'Henry VIII's Irish kerne in France and Scotland', *The Irish Sword*, III (1957–58), 213–25. Cf. J. J. Goring, 'Social change and military decline in mid-Tudor England', *History*, LX (1975), 185–97.
80. Ellis, *Tudor Frontiers*, 257–71; Ellis, 'Tudor state formation', 61–3.

8

THE LITHUANO-PRUSSIAN
FOREST FRONTIER, *c*. 1422–1600

S. C. Rowell*

Of its very nature a frontier is duplicitous. For central governments it is a line established in an attempt to display the extent of their power and influence; the further one moves away from its blent air, the clearer it appears to be. For the borderland's inhabitants, however, it is the place where they make their living – farming, peddling, or smuggling – a region, not a line. The boundaries the borderers respect (and exploit), therefore, are not necessarily the ones which distant centres define. From the thirteenth century the wilderness frontier of Lithuania, especially its forests, has occupied a special place on the borders of the European psyche, as a testing ground of moral and physical virtue and a repository of valuable export commodities. Some marvel at nightmare fen and forest, while others praise an idyll of 'fertile meads, honey-drenched; rich in people and strong in soldiery'.[1] The aurochs (wild ox), whose exotic horn so impressed Petrarch, was selected by sixteenth-century Lithuanians as a subject for Latin hexameters celebrating their people's belonging to the same world as the Spanish torero.[2]

Žemaitija (in German *Samaiten*, in Polish *Żmudź*), or northwestern Lithuania, once separated the Teutonic Order's northeastern Prussia from its holdings in Livonia. Between the thirteenth and fifteenth centuries this sparsely populated territory was a buffer zone between two developing military states, the Teutonic Knights' *Ordensstaat* and the Grand Duchy of Lithuania, whose heartlands were reasonably far away in Marienburg and in Upper Lithuania and western Rus'. A decade of Teutonic lordship (1398–1409) was significant for the clear signal it gave a burgeoning Žemaitijan boiarate (see glossary) that its

182

terra had determinable boundaries and might have to look to its own defence. The treaty of Melno (1422), which made peace between the Jagiellionian territories (Poland-Lithuania) and Prussia, established a boundary that survived both the secularisation of Prussia (1525) and the final dismemberment of Lithuania-Poland (1795), and lasted until 1919/1923 when the Klaipėda District was extracted from the German Empire by the Allies and subsequently annexed by the new Lithuanian Republic (see Map 8.1).[3]

Here we will scan four aspects of these borderlands' early history: firstly, how the political boundary was demarcated and enforced; secondly, the economic frontier; thirdly, the colonisation of the region; and finally, the cultural and intellectual boundary represented by Lutheran Prussia, before proceeding to survey a typical fifteenth- and sixteenth-century border dispute, that over Coadjuthen-Katyčiai.

Border Demarcation

The Prusso-Žemaitijan border was reviewable annually, one year on the Lithuanian side at Veliuona, the next in Prussia at Ragnit, with more subtantial discussions every five years should need arise. Representatives of both sides were expected to ride the bounds and confirm the line agreed with Grand Duke Vytautas in 1422.[4] However clear the delineations were, the border could not be sealed hermetically and the existence of permeable borders influenced policy in both Lithuania and 'Prussia' before 1525. After the murder of Grand Duke Žygimantas (1440) and the accession of Casimir (1440–92) the sieve-like frontier, which facilitated communication between Žemaitijan malcontents and a pretender in exile in the neighbouring duchy of Mazovia, indirectly provoked the establishment of a grand-ducal lieutenancy in the province.[5] During the Thirteen Years' War between Poland and the Teutonic Order (1454–66) Lithuania preserved her official neutrality. Žemaitijan forces made incursions into Prussia and the border posts were strengthened, especially at Palanga, in order to prevent Livonian reinforcements from reaching their brethren in Prussia. However, frequent raids on Livonian and Prussian farmsteads seem to reflect local interest more than central policy. An active network of Prussian spies, in the guise of priests or, more commonly, paupers, operated across the frontier, reporting in detail on developments within the Grand Duchy.[6]

Following the secularisation of the *Ordensstaat* in 1525 and the con-

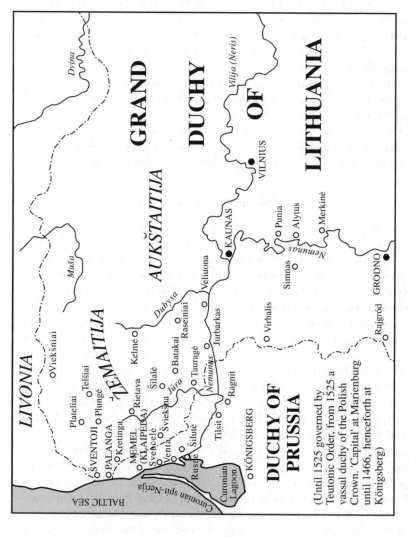

Map 8.1 The Lithuano-Prussian frontier, 1422–1919.

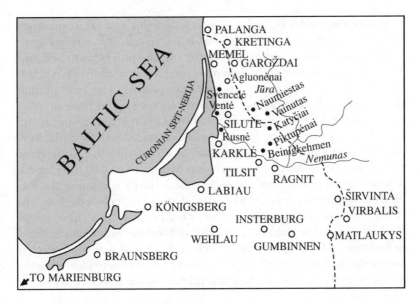

Map 8.2   The Lithuano-Prussian frontier: detail.

version of the last grand master in Prussia, Albert Hohenzollern, to Lutheranism, Prussia became a vassal duchy of the Polish Crown. Thus, the political significance of the same physically constant line changed over the course of a century or so, from a division between two warring parties, through a boundary between two neighbours as mutually trusting as scorpions, to a border between one immense composite monarchy and a vassal state, whose duke needed to secure his position within the bounds of the larger polity.[7] Considering practicalities reveals that, although a stone pillar was erected on the border in 1545, the usual means of marking the frontier was to inscribe trees, especially oaks, on both the Prussian and Lithuanian sides with a sign, dig ditches or cut embankments across the landscape, or prescribe natural landmarks – waterways and woods. Bridges were built to guide traffic across difficult terrain in the way the authorities wished them to be directed, effecting a primitive means of control. The tradition of citing estate or village boundaries as indicators of the limits of political units within the Grand Duchy was more difficult to effect on the western periphery, given the sparse settlement of the area.[8]

Where the border lay was common knowledge and yet its presence could be overlooked should convenience require. Waterways were open to mischievous redirection by the construction of dams and embankments, and the very woods presented a source of livelihood and valuable exports which could be misappropriated. The hand of man not nature, for example, created new obstructions in the course of the Lyck (Ełk) River which separated the Grand Duchy from Prussia and Mazovia.[9] In 1540 Ona, the widow of Stanislovas Kęsgaila, lord lieutenant of Žemaitija, commissioned Jacobus Groloch, a Königsberg merchant with rights to cut timber near Memel, to hew 60 trees on the border. When reprimanded by Duke Albert, the lady, cunning as a fox, denied that the trees were markers and declined to replant the line.[10] In 1542 Albert complained that at Matlaukys a new road had been constructed and the old one blocked with branches and felled trees. Old bridges were knocked down and new ones erected along the illegally revised route. Meanwhile, fields were cleared as far as the trees marked on the Prussian side and grain stores were built by the frontier.[11]

The border was not a curtain of fortresses although both parties maintained administrative centres at major transit points, such as Tilsit, Ragnit, and Memel on the Prussian side, and Palanga, Veliuona, and Jurbarkas on the Lithuanian. These formed the nuclei of new regions. The border came to be signalled more by a ribbon of villages and new towns, not all of which were fully settled even if their plots were measured out. These places denoted ownership and occupation rather than military power. The perpetually reviewed boundary crossed the Wildnis, an area of bog and heathland which was not fully cultivated on the Prussian side until the end of the seventeenth century. Nevertheless, the romantic idea that the wilderness was a disordered desert is erroneous. Negotiation documents clearly distinguish the King's from the Order's wildnis. Hunting, fishing, and settlement were carefully controlled and the land carefully managed.[12] The Königsberg merchant Kasper Lobener was refused permission to burn ashes in a grand-ducal forest in 1531, because previously he had 'harmed many aurochses and hinds'.[13]

The frontier was rife with disputes over political affiliation, taxation, commerce and culture, and settlement and religion, but these were caused not so much by a lack of authority as by a surfeit of it, often ineffectual, with local subofficers on both sides competing to prove their gangster-like power. The venality of such local administrators merited comment in the Protestant divine Jan Łasicki's tract on the Žemaitijan gods. Central control was extremely weak on the borders, but when local officials were threatened by outsiders, the Centre was swift to defend its men – the captains of Tilsit and Jurbarkas were almost permanently on the Königsberg or Vilnius carpet, but very rarely were they punished.[14] The border provided serious obstacles to the smooth running of commerce when local officials chose to tax or impound goods, oblivious to royal charters.[15]

The Economic Frontier

The border zone was traversed by major trade routes running east–west and north–south from Lithuanian Rus' and the Polish Ukraine to Prussia and Gdansk, and from Lublin and Kraków to the Baltic. The strip of coastland belonging to Lithuania between Palanga and Šventoji effectively cut off Livonia from eastern Prussia, contributing to the economic and administrative underdevelopment of the Memel area both before and after the secularisation of Prussia.

The frontier woods, once a nightmarish obstacle hindering crusader armies, were in peacetime a major source of commodities which could be exploited, for a fee, by people living either side of the border, and which could provide a shield for smugglers. Some merchants, such as the Groloch we have already encountered at Memel and in Žemaitija, traded and exploited resources on both sides of the border. Trade in timber products for building, barrelling, burning, and fertilising (*Wagenschos*, *Klapholz*, *Brennholz*, *Nutzholz*) and in potash, furs, honey, and wax was continuous.[16] Attempts were made to manage this resource with the appointment of foresters and other officials from the early sixteenth century.[17] The Lithuanian *Ustava na voloki* (Hide Decree) of 1 April 1557 and subsequent Ducal Forests Decree (27 February 1567) stipulate who may cut timber for what purposes and who may hunt in the forests. As a sporting venue and rich repository of gifts such as falcons, bears, and furs, the woods furnished important means of cementing cross-frontier relationships. In 1561 the grand duke was willing to rent out the Jurbarkas District to Albert of Prussia in return for a contribution to the Lithuano-Polish war effort in Livonia, but he retained full rights over the Jurbarkas Forest. In 1561 forest *matériel* required for the Livonian campaign was shipped by a Prussian merchant, Hans Kopf, along the Nemunas from Grodno to reach Sigismund's troops in the north.[18]

We find the same families involved in trade and trade disputes over generations. Various Pfunffs and Frises appear frequently in the record as timber merchants. Groloch and his wife dealt in timber, salt, and money lending; Andreas Schultz of Kaunas swindled more than one Königsberg merchant out of his purchases. The Prussian duke himself engaged in the import of cattle through his Polish and Prussian factors alongside private citizens such as Henning of Memel and Lauckow of Königsberg. The Toll House at Palanga levied duty on luxury goods travelling between Livonia and Prussia – gold and silver cups and perfumes – as well as foodstuffs and forest products coming from Žemaitija westwards.[19]

The economic hinterland for the garrison town of Memel (Klaipėda) was as much western Lithuania as eastern Prussia. The fact that Memel was not self-sufficient had considerable impact on the region as a whole, rendering borders unsealable given normal circumstances. When refugees came to the town unexpectedly during fifteenth-century food crises, bread had to be requisitioned from Königsberg. In 1443 the local administrator responded to the Grand Master's pleas for increased financial contributions with a plaint to the effect that Memel was an impecunious 'hot spot'. This is hardly astonishing, when one considers its isolation and openness to assault.[20]

When the fortifications of the town were rebuilt in 1539 workmen were sought from Žemaitija in addition to local recruitment at Katyčiai. A parallel is offered on a domestic level by Gallus Klein of Tilsit, whose house-building plans in 1540 required him to import 12 000 bricks from Kaunas. For reasons of convenience or contractual stipulation, merchants dealing across the border had to rely to some extent on hiring a local labour force. We see the dangers involved in such recruitment – of hirelings failing to work or being prevented from working – from Ruckerling's 1535 complaint recorded in the *Ostpreussische Folianten*. Official impediments occurred when excise was changed, as at Plateliai in 1542, when Albert intervened on behalf of the 'poor people of Memel' (*miseris mymelensibus*), and the grand-ducal administrator at Plateliai warned the captain of Memel that if his people continued to evade duty, the captain and not the merchants would be held responsible. The fort at Memel depended on Žemaitijan beef for its rations and when supplies were restricted by the imposition of additional revenue at the Lithuanian customs houses or by official ban on exports, Memel was discomforted. King Sigismund forbade the export of beef to Prussia during the famine of 1544 and again in 1548.

The following year the droves were restricted because of plague in the Memel District. However, during the Livonian wars when Memel was a military station post and contacts between southern Livonia, northeastern Prussia and Žemaitija were strengthened and liberalised (relatively speaking), some prosperity came to the town and its merchants.[21]

Trade embargoes seem to have been imposed rather frequently in order to underscore political points. In 1540 Queen Bona threatened to expel all Germans, especially merchants, from Žemaitija. On occasion Sigismund sought to prevent Prussian merchants from following Lithuanian and Žemaitijan routes as punishment for border violations committed by colonists in eastern Prussia.[22] In 1551 Albert informed the commander of Jurbarkas that although grain would now be sold, sale of forest products remained forbidden. Such policy affected not only merchants and workmen but also other social classes. Žemaitijan lords pleaded for the right to export grain and livestock freely across the frontier without paying duty and so as to be able to reimport the horses and weapons necessary to the upkeep of their noble status and service.[23]

Customs duties could be changed without consultation (at Palanga, Plateliai, Kaunas) and roads closed for no very apparent reason. It is unclear whether this was in all cases in accordance with the will of the central authorities or whether it resulted from a local desire to increase income. In 1542 when Prussian merchants were arrested for travelling along certain 'restricted routes', Duke Albert recalled the case of an Armenian merchant of Lwów, whom his own men had arrested and then released following King Sigismund's intervention. At that time the road was declared open, and now was declared closed by the same king.[24] In theory, specified routes were supposed to be kept open for trade even in time of war and political unrest, and the opportunities for discontented nobles in Žemaitija (or Prussian burghers) to travel freely in search of support went largely uncontrolled. The closure of such routes provoked complaints before the grand duke-king, grand master, and *sejm* (the Polish parliament) almost every year. The trade routes were jealously guarded. The river at Rusnė in the Nemunas delta was blockaded so as to prevent ships from breaking into the Curonian Bay and bypassing the Nemunas customs houses. Žemaitijans took ship at Palanga so as to avoid Memel on their journey south and merchants plied illegal routes along the Curonian Lagoon.[25]

Border violations by raiders in search of chattels, human as well as inanimate, and Žemaitijans who salted fish illegally along the Prussian coast or robbed Norwegian shipwrecked sailors of their cargo were difficult to prevent or bring to justice. Villagers from across the border came to damage their neighbours' fields and pilfer their crops, 'wreaking havoc like bees' as they hunted and fished 'without [official] permission or knowledge', or, like Mastincks of Rajgród, preyed on commercial travellers 'on the open route'.[26] The theft of bees, condemned by the First Lithuanian Statute (1529), and of honey (a due paid by peasants) was difficult if not impossible to prosecute given the indistinct nature of the evidence. However, horse and cattle theft was punished and the stolen goods returned. The Inspector of the Monarch's Forests, Grigory Bogdanovich Volovich, reported in 1559 of Jurbarkas Forest that people from both sides of the border 'shoot game in His Majesty's Wildnis (*pushchi*) and together with the Prussians do great damage to the Wildnis'.[27] The reaction of the Centre(s) to poaching and smuggling was to require (unenforceable) controls on border life: to forbid fishing in border lakes, exploitation of forests directly on the border, and the building of villages or shacks in frontier zones which might be abused by smugglers.[28] At an institutional albeit unofficial level, both Prussian and Žemaitijan officers seem to have regarded selected ravaging as part of policy, as, for instance, when Lithuanian and Žemaitijan soldiers raided Tilsit in 1541, or the Captain of Tilsit attacked Vainutas in 1546. The latter appears to have been directly connected with deliberations over border questions.[29]

Settlement

The consolidation of settlement within Žemaitija intensified after 1441. Grand Duke Casimir's endowments of land do not necessarily represent a case of virgin settlement, but rather the consolidation of land exploitation, as was the case when in 1457 one Gedkantas was endowed with land which had once belonged to Eitortas (now deceased) and Daumantas (now fled to Prussia).[30] At the same time, the surrender of western Prussia to the Poles in 1466 gave an extra impulse to the Order's settlement policy with the creation of new administrative districts, as at Rhein (1468).

In the fourteenth century Lithuanians had received plots of farmland in return for military service, but these were usually far from the recipient's home region. After 1400 not only 'higher level' colonists came to Prussia, but also ordinary land-hungry farmers. Like noblemen, yeomen were liable to change their minds and return home. Some time around 1470–80 the Grand Master and the Lithuanian authorities attempted to establish a procedure for dealing with Lithuanians who came to Prussia to gain a wife and property, but subsequently returned to the land of their birth. Children from such marriages, if left behind in Prussia, were to be recognised as freeborn, whilst those who fled with their family were to lose all rights to Prussian property.[31] Complaints over such tergiversation were a frequent occurrence in both ducal Prussia and Žemaitija. In eastern and central Europe population shortages are much more significant than land famines. It is hardly coincidental that from the late fifteenth century, direct competition between the Order's officers and the lord lieutenant of Žemaitija over border districts and their inhabitants increased. In May 1480, when Lithuania was waking up to the need to form a strong alliance with Livonia and Prussia against Moscow, an outbreak of violence, theft, and murder soured relations on the border as the Order settled Lithuanian subjects in the Ragnit and Memel commanderies there, to the detriment of the grand duke's interests.[32]

Ironically, as competition to settle the region increased and interaction became more strained, correspondence between both sides cast relations increasingly in the mould of good neighbourliness and friendship.[33] Most settlement continued peacefully without royal or magisterial intervention or directive, as in 1510 when the Geverlaukiai forest near Beinigkehmen in southeastern Prussia was purchased by two local Balts, Mikas and Butvilas, from the 'Prussian' village of Lenkininkai. Four years later another local, Tautkus, together with two new arrivals from Žemaitija, Normantas and Milkintas, built a village nearby in Galbrostas wood. Some disputes seem to have developed from practical need rather than planned skulduggery. The peasants who struggled to sow and reap crops in contested areas such as Švekšna (1549) or Šventa (1552) were seeking their daily bread, not the fulfilment of central policy. Bernard Pohibel informed the Prussian duke in July 1547 that paupers living on his land could scrape a living only from collecting wood and making ash from it.[34]

In the course of centuries the region's inhabitants, best summed up by the Polish term *tutejszy* or 'locals' (used in contemporary Lithuanian texts of Prussian ducal decrees),[35] came to define themselves, as one would expect, in relation primarily to locality and prince, rather than race or language: to speak Lithuanian, practise Lutheranism, and call onself 'Lithuanian' did not lessen the population's loyalty to the German duke of Prussia. Mutual service, not blood or language, is the mainstay of political maturity. Denis Hay's comment that 'the [Anglo-Scottish] Borders were a region and remain a region' fits our case too.[36] Preussisch Litauen (Prussian Lithuania), for which an *Amt* was established in 1525, and western Žemaitija maintained their specific regional character as late as the Second World War and its aftermath. Over two centuries or so the local inhabitants strengthened their identity as loyal subjects of the duke (and later king) of Prussia. Prussia provided the press for the first Lithuanian-language imprint (Mažvydas's 1547 translation of Melanchthon's Catechism), and later for illegal Lithuanian books smuggled into the Russian Empire after the 1864 ban on the Latin alphabet. In the eighteenth century, when German artisans and peasants moved to Žemaitija in the wake of economic discomforts in east Prussia they came not from the immediate borderlands, but from deep within the region. The borderers remained on the frontier.[37]

The ethnic composition of that border society is a very thorny issue, not least for the implications it has borne since the racialist foundations of nationhood were stressed in the last century. Lubricious appeals to 'historical ethnic composition' dominate certain discussions of the Kaliningrad (Königsberg) Region's status today as an enclave of Russia between Poland and Lithuania.[38] Given its crusader past, Eastern Prussia could hardly be other than ethnically diverse. Lithuanians, Žemaitijans, Curonians, Skalvians, and Prussians dwelt in the region's villages and border areas, whilst German settlers were commoner in the towns of the western districts. In such places as Mohrungen and Preussich Holland, settlers were invited from the Netherlands. In other words, the colonisation of northeastern districts should be viewed in the light of general resource exploitation and appropriation rather than as the lurid scenario of specifically *anti-Lithuanian* Teutonic skulduggery.

Fifteenth-century sources are reticent on ethnic matters. Letters from the commander of Memel speak of Curonians there and of Skalvians around Ragnit and Tilsit.[39] The ethnic composition of the region was prone to variation on the Lithuanian side too, where, in Žemaitija, the northwestern areas were home to Curonians. In Eastern Prussia we find some Poles and Germans, although it is difficult to distinguish ethnicity clearly from a bare list such as the cadastres of 1540 or the earliest list of Memel District villagers from around 1510–20. It is impossible to tell whether part of this population was indigenous to the region or not. We know little or nothing of the ethnic composition of Wildnis villages mentioned in fourteenth- and fifteenth-century documents.[40]

It is difficult to be precise about the numbers of migrants or even about when migration was most prevalent. This may be due to the sparsity of sourçe material – we rely on general complaints, specific reported incidents, and the irregularly preserved taxation cadastres. The evidence is slanted and leaves room today for fanatical nationalist sketches on both German and Lithuanian sides. The material, as it stands, appears to indicate that a peak was reached around 1540–60. According to Gertrud Mortensen's unpublished, but frequently cited figures there were 5000 peasant families of Lithuanian origin in Eastern Prussia in 1540, making 30000–40000 settlers in all. Since this figure is enormous in relation to the estimated population of western Lithuania at that time, which was by no means emptied by westward migration, it is difficult to accept it. In one of several such districts, the Insterburg Amt, the number of Lithuanians rose from 713 in 1553–54 to 1085 in 1564–65. Naturally enough no figures are available for the number of peasants who *returned* to Lithuania, but that some did so must be borne in mind. Similarly, Prussian subjects chose to settle in the Grand Duchy. In the Memel Region *c.* 1520 there were 384 male villagers liable for taxation, of whom perhaps some 360 had Lithuanian (or Baltic) names, but there is no indication of when or how they came to dwell in the region and to which Baltic ethnic group they belonged.[41]

Taking cadastre evidence for Agluonėnai as an example, it appears that families spread over neighbouring settlements, one such being Pawel 'the Žemaitijan' who also held land at Misyčiai; and that most inhabitants were of Baltic origin with one possible German, Jorgelle Rastenbach. The village seems to have maintained its size over this generation with 18 families in 1510–20 and 18 in 1540. The later cadastre has seven families identical with those in the first list, five possible surnominal convergences, and six which were definitely different.[42]

Village foundation and cross-border migration are similar on both sides of the frontier. It is not a matter of 'poor Žemaitija' against 'enlightened Prussia', a cliché that was common in earlier German studies on this subject. Villages appear to have grown up later on the holdings of local farmers, such as Jodicken-Wittko (owned once by Woytko Judeka) and Szauken-John – the Soucken Erbe mentioned *c.* 1520. This is also typical of new villages in Žemaitija: Kontaučiai, founded on the Kantautas estate, or Tūbausiai near Kretinga. Colonists, free or refugee peasants, passed to and fro across the border. Albert complained in 1539 that Lithuanians had come to him and received land and rights of bequest and subsequently fled back to Žemaitija. He names several fugitive *rustici* and then bemoans the fact that the majority were Lithuanians whose names he does not have at hand. These were tillers of the soil for the most part, but also included a scribe who also dabbled in trade. The Insterburg elder, Alex, reported in 1554 that a Lithuanian boiar had come to him in search of renegades.[43] The Lutheran pastor at Labiau, Johann Bretke, threatened to migrate to the Grand Duchy because he could not make ends meet on his stipend of 60 florins per annum.

Agricultural life was not necessarily easier in Prussia than in the other Jagiellonian territories – judging by refugee peasants and the complaints of Lutheran ministers whose farmland was too infertile to meet their needs.[44] Certain migrants knew enough of competition between various administrative structures to claim that a man had different allegiance when he committed a crime and should therefore be tried by a different (and distant) legislation. In 1542 Stanislav Iushkevich of Kuršuva complained of a serf woman who had robbed him and subsequently fled to Prussia.[45] Workmen were recruited in disputed areas for work on projects elsewhere; they could also be kidnapped and settled across the border by either side. On a domestic level spouses were sought across the border, as the preacher Martynas Mažvydas complained to the Duke in 1551. We might cite a Tauragė woman who married a Tilsit man and quickly fled back to Lithuania abandoning her husband, or a Königsberg youth who dallied with the daughter of a local merchant and then fled to Vilnius in search of a better offer.[46] Mažvydas, who held land in the Lithuanian border village of Virbalis in 1561 and maintained contacts with his kinsmen in Lithuania, was in the habit of employing at Ragnit servants '*ex Samogithia aut Lituania . . . , alios enim habere nequeo*' ('from Žemaitija or Lithuania, for I am unable to keep any others').[47] Whether this was because only Lithuanians would work for the pastor – who was not very popular in Ragnit – or because he could afford only their labour is unclear.

H. Mortensen sought in the 1920s and 1930s to base imperial German claims to the Memelland on ethnicity: he noted that those who migrated knew what they were doing and that they understood that migration meant subjection to the separate state of ducal Prussia.[48] In that the settlers understood that they were moving to a different jurisdiction, Mortensen was correct, as we have seen. Duke Albert himself was even prepared to treat the villagers of Katyčiai as subject to Lithuanian rather than Prussian law while the question of allegiance remained in doubt. However, while migrants also reserved the right to leave if they wished, the density of their arrival seems to have increased after 1525, that is, when ducal Prussia was a fief of the Polish Crown, the sister suprajurisdiction with Lithuania in the Jagiellonian monarchy. Prussia was alien but little more so now than such major centres of Lithuanian and Polish Rus' as Polotsk or Lwów, and the duke himself exploited the legal status of his land very nimbly, arguing that to grant land to Lithuania rather than to Prussia was to rob the Crown of Poland (suzerain of Prussia) of territory.[49]

Religious and Cultural Exchange

Why did Lithuanians come to Prussia? Setting aside accidental factors such as the outbreak of plague or war, and bad lordship, or agricultural conditions which were as yet not so harsh as in Lithuania, some may have decided to live with kinsmen resident in Prussia. Nineteenth-century scholarship focused on the (apparent) confessional division between the two areas, but it is far from clear that Protestantism was doomed in Žemaitija, or, indeed, that Lutheranism was the salvation they sought – as a tendency to disappear across the frontier to Catholic churches in border towns or, indeed, the return of neophyte Lutherans to the Old Faith when back in Lithuania would illustrate.[50] Nor is it entirely clear that on becoming Prussian subjects they lost their previous sense of identity; a sense of *natione Prussicus gente Lithuanus* ('Prussian by political allegiance, Lithuanian by birth'), although not expressed in such terms, appears in Prussian writings.

The border had Lutheran churches on the Prussian side, Catholic ones on the Lithuanian. Such a statement of fact might presuppose religious confrontation, but in reality did not and, in the sixteenth century at least, a religious hotchpotch of Catholic magic and Lutheran preachifying suited the religious needs of a population living in a spiritual structural vacuum. In religious terms, the existence of the western tip of heathen Žemaitija aborted the creation of a practical Catholic ecclesiastical apparatus in northeastern Prussia. The aim of founding a bishopric at Memel, which was first mooted in 1252 when the fort was built, was short-lived. To the north Curonia remained subject to Riga and the Memel Region to the bishop of Ermland at

Braunsberg. The diocese of Žemaitija, founded in 1416, covered territory only within the Grand Duchy. In 1506, as part of his broader plan to increase pressure on the Teutonic Order, Grand Duke Alexander tried to establish a metropolitan see, in what from 1466 was Polish-controlled Ermland, with authority over all Prussian bishoprics. In order perhaps to disguise the size of his teeth where the East Prussian apparatus was concerned, the Lithuanian proposed joining Žemaitija to Ermland too, thereby creating a consolidated church organisation in the southeastern Baltic.[51] The nominal Lutheranisation of Prussia in 1525 made such a reform all the more unrealisable.

Žemaitija itself was only weakly evangelised. Nineteen churches were founded in the fifteenth century, eight built between the turn of the century and 1525, and only 44 in the period 1500–45. There were imposing churches in the major, and older, border posts: Tauragė (1507), Jurbarkas (1522), Veliuona (pre-1430), Švėkšna (1509), and these were visited by migrants during local patronal feasts – which coincided with major market and hiring seasons. In 1535 the Protestant pastor, Jan Tortyłowicz (Jonas Tortilavičius) of Šilalė began preaching at Batakiai. Between 1559 and 1613 28 Protestant communities were founded in Žemaitija.[52] Nevertheless, the infrastructure of the borderlands was too poorly endowed to provide a basis for any active counter-reformatory initiative. A church was founded by Grand Duchess Bona at her new village of Virbalis (1539) in 1555; the village had been settled with people from all over Lithuania, Žemaitija, and Prussia, but in 1561 the land set aside for the use of the Catholic priest was unoccupied. In 1589, according to the list of churches compiled by Bishop Melchior Giedroyc, himself a former student of the Albertina, there were or had been Protestant pastors at Plungė, Gargždai, Tirkšliai, Viekšniai, Švėkšna, Šilalė, Kelmė, Tauragė, Šiluva, and elsewhere. These churches were returned to Roman obedience.[53] In dealing with matters of religious conversion, we must also take into consideration the fact that in the Insterburg Amt in 1544 there was one church and that when the village of Gawaiten was founded in 1558 it provided the second church of the district.[54] Thus swift conversions to Lutheranism or confirmations of Catholicism were unlikely for practical reasons.

It is hardly surprising that in areas distant from the centre, old traditions die hard. When the preacher Mažvydas became pastor at Ragnit, he complained to Albert that his parishioners still practised pagan religious rites (as Catholic bishops and Jesuit missioners also lamented) and that during the great feasts many travelled across the border to the nearest Catholic churches. It is noticeable that the papist rites they were accused of practising were very rudimentary – the churching of women, for example, and the offering of candles. He was perturbed to find that borderers took spouses from Lithuania and Žemaitija, and that they were not sufficiently zealous in strengthening social connections through Protestant spiritual kinship.[55] Later in the century Duke George Frederick noted that Protestants even went across the border to be rebaptised in a Catholic church. His 1578 Visitation Proclamation, which survives in its Lithuanian version, lamented that church attendance by Curonians and Lithuanians in Tilsit, Kaukėnai, Katyčiai, and Piktupėnai was lax and that many had not received Communion for 'several decades', while such 'pagan' practices as the burning of wax candles prevailed.[56]

In Žemaitija the new religion was supported in the main by the upper and middling boiarate. During the first half of the sixteenth century the Starosta (senior provincial administrator) of Žemaitija, Stanislovas Kęsgaila, patronised Protestant preachers like Laurentius Discordia. The Bilevičiai family, like the Kęsgailos, maintained close relations with Albert of Prussia in which neighbourly need was as important as shared confessional allegiance, as when Jonas Bilevičius commended three Lithuanian youths to Albert after they had shepherded a Königsberg professor of divinity during his business visit to Lithuania in 1547.[57]

Albert used his newly founded university at Königsberg to help form and consolidate a new Lutheran society inside Prussia. In 1561 he increased the 1547 provision of scholarships, the majority for non-Germans, from ten for Prussia and seven each for Poland and Lithuania, to twelve, eight, and eight respectively.[58] The first professors of Divinity in the new academy were Lithuanian Protestants from the Grand Duchy who not only wrote – in Lithuanian – with their homeland in mind, but also retained close links with their families still resident in Kaunas, Vilnius, and Žemaitija. Mažvydas, who was probably a Žemaitijan, maintained contacts with his kin within the Grand Duchy and also with his coreligionists – in 1548 he sought assistance from the *tivun* (junior provincial administrator) of Ukmergė and Anykščiai to obtain restitution of a debt owed him by a local Protestant student, Valentinas Buivydas.[59] Mažvydas's translation of a German (Melanchtonian?) Catechism, printed at Königsberg in 1547, is significant more for the light it sheds on the mentality of the Prussian Lithuanian community than for any influence it may have had in the Grand

Duchy at large. Only two copies survive and it is unclear how many were printed. It reflects Mažvydas's sense of belonging to a Lithuanian-speaking community which was to be defined by confessional rather than political allegiance. Similarly the Lutheran minister from Širvinta, Tomas Gedkantas, who took up a post in Prussia and later held land on the other side of the border at Virbalis, was anxious to have his boiar status recognised by the King-Grand Duke when the lord lieutenant of Žemaitija refused to do so. In 1561 this same Lithuanian Lutheran witnessed the royal mortgage to Albert of the Jurbarkas District. Certain people lived successfully with a foot on either side of the border.[60]

The patronage of students and clerics by Duke Albert, himself a former monk, appears to have been a means not only of spreading religion (Lutheran parishes needed Lithuanophone pastors), but also of forming a network of friends inside the Jagiellonian Realm, who might be of use in discussions at a high level in legal suits, trade regulation, or even political boundary negotiations. The Katyčiai dispute appears to have been resolved miraculously (in theory) after the more direct intervention of Nicholas Radvila, the king's brother-in-law, on Albert's behalf.[61]

In 1545 the son of the Žemaitijan lieutenant, Bilevičius, was received at Albert's court; 14 months earlier the duke's intercession had been sought to obtain the boy a place in Vilnius. We find such interchange also at a lower social level: one Mileski was placed with the Königsberg apothecary through the good offices of the captain of Graudenz, Petrus Woynowski (1547–54); Ruprecht Göckell, a Königsberg physician who sought permission to practice medicine in Lithuania, Žemaitija, and points east in 1539, placed his son with Radvila's *prefectus*, Lucas, to learn Lithuanian in 1554; in 1548 George of Grobin (in Livonia) wished to place his boy Eustachius with Bilevičius, to learn languages; four years earlier his other son, Erhard, had studied Polish with the Mazovian official Jan Krotowski.[62] There is also evidence of servant exchange: Nicholas Talwisch, a nobleman who had served at Albert's court, sought a place with the king in 1554; nine years earlier the Prussian retainer Wolfgang Bleyfoller asked for help securing a place with Nicholas Radvila.[63] The notable feature of this migration, as with that of peasant colonists, artisans, and refugees, is that it went both ways – it is not the one-way flight to the golden west of East Prussia which is often stressed in scholarship of a *kulturträger* (chauvinist) hue that assumes German cultural superiority.[64]

The Katyčiai Dispute

The village of Katyčiai (Coadjuthen, Koczyce) provides a good example of border squabbles (Steinford, Crocki, and Beinigkehmen are others).[65] It lies on the Šyša river and was once regarded as held in common. A road from Tilsit via Katyčiai linked up with the main Memel-Libau-Riga route. At the end of the fifteenth century it became an object of bitter dispute between the lieutenant of Žemaitija and the Order's commander at Tilsit. In November 1492 the latter complained officially, to both the Grand Master and Grand Duke Alexander, of Kęsgaila's behaviour two years earlier when the lieutenant had seized the village and forbidden its population to pay service to the Order. We know from a Lithuanian land charter of November 1501 that Stanislovas Jonaitis Kęsgaila had pretentions to legalising his holding, having reported to Grand Duke Alexander that during his father's day (that is before Jonas's death in c. 1485) people from 60 hearths fled to Prussia and were settled on the border.[66] Alexander granted him those 60 hearths, but seven years later the Order was complaining again that in Jonas Kęsgaila's day, Katyčiai had been its possession.

Although Lithuania did not officially take part in the Prusso-Polish Conflict and War of 1516–24, Žemaitijan parties did raid Ragnit and Tilsit and spy in the Memel District. In 1516 Kęsgaila seized Katyčiai and drove 19 peasants from the village to Jurbarkas.[67] The dispute lasted far longer than it needed to, falling victim to various domestic political intrigues, procedures (when and how negotiations should be held), and interim solutions which were in effect little more than delaying tactics. The Grand Master received an astute reply to his queries over border disputes from Alexander in 1503: they were 'unavoidable'.[68] In Albert's own words of 1535: 'We believe it safer to commit a sheep to the care of a wolf than entrust forests to these peasants and colonists, to say nothing of thieving and other clandestine skulduggeries.'[69]

In the summer of 1530 Duke Albert complained that grand ducal officers were exploiting Katyčiai and that his officials had arrested one *minister* of the Žemaitijan *capitaneus* (administrator) who had claimed to be the palatine of Katyčiai![70] From then on until 1554–55 all manner of accusations, diplomatic manoeuvring, and from the royal side, of plain stonewalling came into play. Peasants in the region were subject to tax demands from both sides, from officials with a right to levy dues and

from those merely claiming a right. In 1533 it was agreed that revenue
should be collected and stored in a chest with two locks and with sets of
keys for each party.[71] However, agreements made in Vilnius were
not so readily enacted on the ground. Katyčiai peasants refused to pay
dues other than old established ones (that is, Bona's) and a 1535
compromise reached in the centre, that officers of Prussia and
the Grand Duchy should levy dues alternately (*alternatim*), came to
nought.[72] The village was placed under sequestration. Meanwhile, at
Katyčiai direct action continued: when the Queen's factor found four
Prussians had come and ejected Žemaitijan peasants, he restored the
victims to their land.[73]

The situation at Katyčiai and elsewhere on this interducal border was
aggravated by domestic developments within the Grand Duchy, where
the grand duke-king was seeking to reorder land ownership, especially
where the ruler's lieutenants were attempting to take over grand-ducal
property. Border districts were taken under the personal control of the
grand duke, or rather his mother Queen Bona, who sought to maintain possession of the frontier provinces of Plateliai, Gargždai, and
Jurbarkas (1527). Kęsgaila, the lieutenant of Žemaitija, was deprived of
control of several large estates. Bona's settlement policy aroused the
displeasure of local boiars who saw the new villages as opportunities for
outsiders to gain local office and for serfs to run away despite the
declaration that only freemen would be enfranchised.[74]

In this atmosphere Duke Albert continued his legal argument, claiming that the Order had founded the village. The Queen continued the
official line that she knew nothing of this and that the village belonged
to the Grand Duchy. Albert attempted to enlist the support of Lithuanian nobles (of his acquaintance and affinity) and Lithuanian clergy
whilst pursuing a different line in Poland. He stressed his loyalty to the
Crown as the King's vassal, asking Sigismund as king (not grand duke)
to defend him. To the vice-chancellor of Poland, the bishop of Kraków,
he very carefully noted that he was an obedient vassal and that if
Katyčiai were to be taken from him and given to the Starosta of
Žemaitija, then the Kingdom would lose territory. The differences
between the Kingdom of Poland and the Grand Duchy of Lithuania
were beautifully exploited.[75]

In 1539 when labour was recruited at Katyčiai for building works in
Memel, the Prussians were accused of pressganging reluctant peasants.
Albert complained bitterly that he was misrepresented by Žemaitijan
officials and that the workmen had volunteered, and subsequently fled

the town in fear after one of their number had murdered a local burgher.[76] When it was agreed at last to investigate the dispute with a Commission, the king required the destruction of certain shacks on the border for which Albert claimed he was not responsible except for a night cabin built for use on journeys to Lithuania. The Žemaitijans began to build in the area as evidence of their established presence in the region – a practice which aroused Prussian ire.[77] After much discussion and the intervention of various dignitaries on Albert's behalf very far away from the borderlands, the 'most wretched' plight of the Katyčiai villagers was formally resolved in 1554–55 when the King-Grand Duke recognised the settlement as part of the Duchy of Prussia.[78]

Conclusion

However romantic or ecologically correct our conception of the wilderness may be, we must not allow the archetypal mystery of the forest to blind us to everyday realities. The Baltic frontier, a dual track through the northern woodlands, although not without its perils made by man or nature, was far from unkempt and unknown. The Prusso-Žemaitijan frontier when demarcated marked the proximity of two hinterlands which had not yet been integrated into either the Teutonic *Ordensstaat* or the Grand Duchy of Lithuania. With its annual review and insistence on conformity with a line established superficially on the landscape in 1422, the Lithuanian western border has a clear formulaic nature which exists contrapuntally with the deliberate everyday ambiguity of this frontier's reality. For those living on either the Prussian or the Lithuanian side the border was not a straight line but a region, an intersection or overlap of barely controlled hinterlands.

In subsequent centuries distinct regions developed on both sides of the border, fostered in part by discomforts which the line's existence intensified: Memel did not remedy its lack of a sufficient hinterland in Prussia and Žemaitija remained without access to a good seaport of its own, despite the best attempts of the Lithuano-Polish authorities and an English merchant house to develop Šventoji as a port. Memel remained a port of second rank within the Prussian state, Žemaitija developed as a commercial hinterland rather than a centre in its own right.[79] For many practical needs these two areas remained dependent as much on one another as on distant centres within their own state. Who the local officer and smugglers of varied nationality, language, religion, and political obedience were, in terms of community, became gradually clarified over the course of centuries but remained distinctly regional. The frontier prevented the formation of a geographically unified region on that part of the southern Baltic littoral. Neverthess, it did foster the creation of two separate but closely linked communities in northwestern Lithuania and northeastern Prussia.

NOTES

* Research for this paper was carried out in part with the support of the *Deutsche Forschungsgemeinschaft* and the assistance of the Prussian State Archive at Berlin (Dahlem) to which bodies the author expresses his gratitude.

The following abbreviations are used for manuscript references:

Archive: GSPK: Berlin, Geheimes Staatsarchiv, Preussischer Kulturbesitz, xx Hauptabteilung.

Deposits: OBA: Ordens Brief Archiv.

OrdF: OrdensFolianten.

OstF: Ostpreussische Folianten.

All manuscripts referred to have page numbers unless otherwise indicated.

1. Peter von Suchenwirt, 'Von Herczog Albrechts Ritterschaft', *SRP*, ii, 164; Joannes Vislicius, 'Bellum prutenum', ii. 1–4, in *Corpus antiquissimorum poetarum Poloniae latinorum*, ed. B. Kruczkiewicz, Kraków 1887, 183.

2. S. Schama, *Landscape and Memory*, London 1995; cf. *Von der Angst zur Ausbeutung. Umwelterfahrung zwischen Mittelalter und Neuzeit*, ed. E. Schubert and B. Herrmann, Frankfurt-am-Main 1994, 13–58, 137–56; Nicolaus Hussovianus, *De statura, feritate ac venatione bisontis carmen*, ed. B. Kazluaskas, Vilnius 1977.

3. *LU*, v, no. 2637, cols 877–89; for a general account of border negotiations, see Z. Ivinskis, 'Kovos bruožai dėl Žemaičių ir jų sienų', *Athenaeum*, vi (1935), 54–117.

4. Treaty of Brest, 31 Dec. 1435: OrdF 14, fols 753–68, discussed by Ivinskis, 'Kovos bruožai', 94–5. Riding the bounds: 'widder zcureiten adder zcugehen anhebn und biß an die Memel ken der Swentoy abr und genseyt der Memel bis ken Palangen nach innhaldunge der verschreibung des ewigen fredes', OrdF 16, 1201.

5. On the Duchy of Žemaitijan charter of 1441/2, see S. C. Rowell, 'Karas ruseno Žemaičiuose. Keletas pastabų apie 1442 m. privilegijos genezes', *Žemaičių praeitis*, viii (1998), 5–28.

6. Thirteen Years War: M. Biskup, *Trzynastoletnia wojna z Zakonem Krżyzackim 1454–1466*, Warsaw 1967. Border posts: *LU*, x, no. 379 p. 259 (11 Sept 1447). Raids: OBA 9592, 15247, etc., and *LU*, xi, 123, 386, 446. Examples of spies: GSPK, OBA 6277, 8465, 12035.

7. Cf. borders of 1529 and 1472: *Limites Regni Poloniae et Magni Ducatus Lituaniae ex originalibus et exemplis authenticis descripti et in lucem editi*, ed. M. Dogiel, Vilnius 1758, 206; 207–11 and below, n. 8; on 1525, M. Biskup, *Polska a Zakon*

krzyżacki w Prusach w początkach XVI wieku. U źródeł sekularyzacji Prus krzyżackich, Olsztyn 1983, and E. Joachim, *Die Politik des letzten Hochmeisters in Preussen Albrecht von Brandenburg*, 3 vols, Leipzig 1892–95, I–II.

8. For 'signa in quercubus et aliis arboribus, fossata, colliculum alias kopiec' ('signs on oaks and other trees, ditches, and embankments called *kopiec*'), see treaty of 3 July 1473 in *Lietuvos Metrika (1427–1506). Knyga nr. 5, Užrašymų knyga 5*, ed. E. Banionis, Vilnius 1993, no. 125, pp. 235–8. 1545 pillar: L. Kolankowski, *Zygmunt August wielki książę Litwy do roku 1548*, Lwów 1913, 269–70, 270 n. 1. Estates: *Istorijos Archyvas*, I (*XVI amžiaus Lietuvos inventoriai*), ed. K. Jablonskis, Kaunas 1934, nos 155, 156, cols 561–668.

9. Blocked routes (water): OBA 8458 (9 April 1444). Steinford: OBA 27879 (n.d.).

10. OstF 51, pp. 197–8, 215–8, 219–20.

11. OstF 52, pp. 411–12.

12. Damages caused by factor of Jurbarkas in new settlements: W. Pociecha, *Królowa Bona. Czasy i ludzie Odrodzenia*, 4 vols, Poznań 1949–58, 252 n. 103. Order's *wildnis*: OrdF 16, 329.

13. Letter to Jurbarkas (27 Jan. 1551): OstF 54, 148–9. Lobener: cited in J. Totoraitis, *Sūduvos Suvalkijos istorija*, I, Kaunas 1938, 103.

14. Martin Bybernicks's case succeeded in 1549 after the provision of gifts (OstF 53, pp. 794–5): 'praefectos, quos civonias vocant, non adeunt, quin ipsis aliqua munuscula adferant' ('they do not visit the officials called *tivunai* without taking them some little gift or other'), J. Lasickis, *Apie žemaičių, kitų sarmatų bei netikrų krikščionių dievus*, Vilnius 1969, 39. On the carpet: OstF 52, pp. 243–60; Simnas-Insterburg dispute, 28 Sept. 1453, OstF 52, pp. 482–4.

15. On *tivunai* in general: OstF 54, p. 999 (1555). Mykola Šukaitis, *tivun* of Pajuris, is a good example: OstF 42, pp. 232–4, 238–9, 244–8 (1533); OstF 49, pp. 211–3 (1532); OstF 52, pp. 646–8 (1544).

16. K. Forstreuter, *Die Memel als Handelsstrasse Preussens nach Osten*, Königsberg 1931; M. North, 'The export of timber and timber by-products from the Baltic Region to Western Europe, 1575–1775', *L'uomo e la foresta, secc. XIII–XVII*, Prato 1996, 883–94.

17. F. Mager, *Der Wald in Altpreussen als Wirtschaftsraum*, 2 vols, Cologne-Graz 1960, 166ff.

18. Forest legislation: *Russkaia Istoricheskaia Biblioteka*, XXX, Yur'ev 1914, cols 573–8, 622–8. Forest retained, but the villages mortgaged: *Istorijos Archyvas*, I, no. 156, cols 563–668, esp. col. 662. Kopf: *LM7*, no. 40, p. 61.

19. Frise: OstF 49 (1533). Groloch: OstF 42 (1533), 52 (1544). Schultz: OstF 49 (1539, 1540). Pfunff Fersbach: OstF 49 (1540), 52 (1545), 53 (1547). Albert's steers: OstF 51, pp. 113–15 (1539), OstF 54, pp. 576–7 (1552). Lauchow: OstF 53, pp. 213–14 (1546). Henning: OstF 52, pp. 84–8 (1542). In 1554 Albert asked the chief customs collector at Palanga (the bishop of Žemaitija) to waive tolls on cloth purchased by his brother, Archbishop William of Riga, at Gdansk and transported to Riga via Žemaitija and Palanga (OstF 54, pp. 794–5). Certain customs records are preserved in Riga, Central State Archive F673 Aprl liet 307 'Polongenscher Zoll'.

20. Winter conditions will not be good (OBA 28196, *c.* 1420–40); difficulties

repairing the defences, inundations from the sea and the wildnis (OBA 28200, mid–late 15th century); shortage of materials and suitable workforce (OBA 28189, 28190, and M. Burleigh, *Prussian Society and the German Order. An Aristocratic Corporation in Crisis*, Cambridge 1984, 128, citing OBA 8330 (1 Oct. 1443)).

21. Klein: OstF 51, pp. 341–2. Ruckerling: OstF 49, pp. 710–11. Duty: OstF 52, pp. 200–3. Poor harvests, 1540–44: K. Jablonskis, 'Lietuvos valstiečių priešinimas valdytojams didžiojo kunigaikščio valsčiuose XVI a. pirmoje pusėje', *Istorija ir jos šaltiniai*, Vilnius 1979, 92 and n. 18; *LM7*, nos 40, 49, 55.

22. Germans to leave by 29 Sept. 1540: OstF 51, pp. 356–7.

23. Prosby Zhomoitskoi zemli, 20 Nov. 1551, § 7 and 1554, § 8: *Russkaia Istoricheskaia Biblioteka*, xxx, no. 6, cols 60–6; no. 10, col. 255.

24. OstF 52, pp. 84–8 (26 Feb. 1542), 230–1 (25 Oct. 1542); earlier conflict: OstF 51, pp. 139–40 (15 Oct. 1539).

25. Details of blockade: a letter of 6 June 1541, OstF 51, pp. 405–7; a letter from Burghers of Memel to the Grand Master, *c.* 1511–25, OBA 27669: '. . . nemlich ungewonlicher strasßn halben auff die Rusße, Weywieße, Szwentzell, Wintburgk, Nerige, die uns zcu schaden zein, den inhallts ewigen friedes aus Littawn unnde Samayten nicht meher dan zcwuo strasßen eyne auff die Memmell, die andre auff Ragnett zullen gehalden werden . . . So auch thuen die Samayten vanner Heyligen Aa unde Palangen mitt schieffen durchs hab ins landt . . . ' ('they use unagreed routes via Rusnė, the Veiviržas, Svencelė, Ventė, Neringa, which is to our disadvantage, for according to the perpetual peace treaty there should be no more than two routes from Lithuania and Žemaitija; one should be along the Nemunas and the other via Ragnit . . . also the Žemaitijans take ship at Šventoji and Palanga and sail the Curonian Lagoon to our land').

26. 'das dy euwern, dy an der grenitcz wonen bynnen unsers herren hom-eisters und des ordens grenczen grosen schaden thun, nemlich honigborne weis sy der vil vorterben und jagen und visschen wydder willen und wissen leth', OBA 27945 (n.d.). Mastincks: OrdF 18b, fol. 271r–v.

27. Bees, horses, and cattle: OstF 51, pp. 176–7, 302. Volovich: *Revizia pushch' i perekhodov' zverinykh' v' byvshem' Velikom' Kniazhestve litovskom'*, Vilnius 1867, 61.

28. Fishing: 19 Sept. 1447, OBA XVIa.16. Smugglers: OstF 51, pp. 176–7.

29. Tilsit: OstF 51, pp. 622–4. Vainutas: OstF 53, pp. 352–5, 405–8.

30. *Dokumenty Moskovskogo Arkhiva Ministerstva Iustitsii*, i, Moscow 1897, 27, 37, 39–40; for Gedkantas, see *LM6*, no. 418, §1, p. 277.

31. OBA 27874 (undated, the water mark fits the period 1469/72).

32. OBA 16881 (17 May 1480): 'so . . . unsern große schade gesthaen ist, unnd noch geschit vonn denn salbigenn unnsern eygen layten ap groß dyberey, bluthstorczunge, morderey unnd beneanenn wylt yachte bebern yachte hanntn' ('thus great damage is done to our own people and those same subjects of ours are prey to great robbery, bloodshed, murder and poaching in the wilderness'); the following January (OBA 16938), the Ragnit problem to be discussed by representatives of both sides; 4 February 1481, Kęsgaila

on good terms with the commander of Ragnit (OBA 16948) and preparing for negotiations with the commanders of Ragnit and Memel.

33. OBA 16338 (29 June 1472), 16569 (Sept. 1475), 16948 (4 Feb. 1481); OrdF 18b, fol. 271 r–v (15 July 1490); OBA 17737 (2 Nov. 1492), 20909 (27 June 1516); OstF 42, pp. 250–2 (9 Sept. 1533); 'unneighbourliness' stressed, OstF 52, pp. 202–3 (18 Aug. 1542).

34. H. and G. Mortensen, 'Der Streit um die Beinigkehmer "Lange Wiese" im Jahre 1526 als siedlungskundliches Dokument', *Preussenland und Deutscher Orden. Festschrift für Kurt Forstreuter zur Vollendung seines 60. Lebensjahres* dargebracht von seinem Freunden, Würzburg 1958, 291–9. Peasant activity: Albert's letters to the border *tivuni*, 6 Aug. 1549 (OstF 53, pp. 832–4), 16 Jan. 1552 (OstF 54, pp. 319–20). Paupers and ashes: *Elementa ad fontium editiones (Documenta ex Archivio Regiomontano ad Poloniam spectantia)*, ed. C. Lanckorońska, 75 vols, Rome 1973–91, XLIV, no. 12, p. 11.

35. 22 Sept. 1589: *Prūsijos valdžios gromatos, pagraudenimai ir apsakymai lietuviams valstiečiams*, ed. P. Pakarklis, Vilnius 1960, Plate 1.

36. D. Hay, 'England, Scotland and Europe: The problem of the frontier', *TRHS*, 5th ser., XXV (1975), 87.

37. General history: J. Jakštas, 'Mažosios Lietuvos apgyvendinimas iki XVII a. pabaigos', *Lietuvių katalikų mokslo akademijos Metraštis*, IV (1968), 1–49; V (1970), 359–414.

38. Summaries of the present problem: J. M. Swerew, *Rußlands Gebiet Kaliningrad im neuen geopolitischen Koordinatenfeld* (series: *Berichte des Bundesinstituts für ostwissenschaftliche und internationale Studien*), Cologne 1996; *Potsdamas ir Karaliaučiaus kraštas*, ed. D. Bakanienė, Vilnius 1996.

39. OBA 28156, 28183.

40. Cadastre of 1510/20: OBA 27670, published in S. C. Rowell, 'The population of the Memel District c. 1510–1520', *Acta Historica Universitatis Klaipedensis* (forthcoming). Cadastre of 1539/40: OstF 911a, p. 19. For fifteenth-century negotiations, see above, n. 3; for w*egeberichte*, see *SRP* II, 664–708 and 708–9.

41. Insterburg: O. Barkowski, 'Die Besiedlung des Hauptamtes Insterburg unter Herzog Albrecht und Markgraf Georg Friedrich von Ansbach 1525–1603', *Prussia*, XXIX (1933), 161–243. For Prussians in Lithuania, see the 1561 Jurbarkas census and another document of 1562 which records a settler at Sartyninkai from Prussia with one hide (*valak*) and rights to use the forest, meadow, and moor on the Prussian border: *Akty Vilenskoi Komissii*, XXV, Vilnius 1898, 88, 89.

42. Villagers from Agluonėnai, 1510–20: Peter Jodeycke, Kantwain, Nayssels, Kuslėycka unnd Kebel, Tautzsch Grefuch, Math uff Jan Sutkiß erbe, Maschwille Kyschenn, Beise Kelle, Nantwith, Woitkus kyn Pecher Borner, Grische Nicles bruder, Saugel Marghe, Pawel Samaith, Jorge Jaiske, Jorgelle Rastenbach, Jan Sawgk, Mascheick Narwolle. In 1540: *Grytsch Niclas*, Jutsch Agolon, *Kusseleka*, *Endres Kantweyen*, Meckys Raxill, Grytsch Kagel, Gedemyn Gelschyn, *Woytkus Mergus*, Peter *Marge*, Gerkandt Gytkandt, Endres Wyssgyn, *Mastwyll Kyschmyn*, Woytko *Judeka*, Merten Jockschs, Symon Deutz, Mescheck Strebel, *Jhan Sauck*, Peter Rock.

43. OstF 51, pp. 19–21 (25 March 1539): 'Ihonnel Diacks, Kletinckus scriba et

qui mercaturam exercet, Iohan Petri frater, Schoppen, Peckuss, Iatzus, Ischwilckyas, Ihormellis, Cardiuschkun, filius Stani cum uno servo Iuschka, Martini Aschungern adfinis, Andreas Iudas cum duobus filiis, qui primum hac in parte sedes habuere, postea vero iterum aufugerunt. Reliqui non potuerunt cognosci, *maior tamen pars communes Lythani fuere*. Et hii coloni meę terrę quondam fuere hereditario ad me iure spectantes' ('Ihonnel Diacks, Kletinckus the scribe who also deals in business, Iohan brother of Peter, Schoppen, Peckuss, Iatzus, Ischwilckyas, Ihormellis, Cardiuschkun son of Stanus along with one servant called Iuschka, a kinsman of Martin Aschungern, Andreas the Jew and his two children, who had property first in these parts and then ran away again. The rest are unknown, *but most of them were Lithuanian commoners*. These settlers were at one time subjects of my land belonging to me by hereditable tenure'). For Alex, see Barkowski, 'Die Besiedlung', 235.

44. J. Bretkūnas, *Rinktiniai Raštai*, ed. J. Palionis and J. Žukauskaitė, Vilnius 1983, 320, 323 (letters of 27 March 1587, 17 July 1595).

45. *LM6*, no. 376, pp. 258–9.

46. Mažvydas: *Katekizmas ir kiti raštai*, ed. G. Subačius, Vilnius 1993, 679–80. The Tauragė-Tilsit case: OstF 54, p. 776 (2 Aug. 1554). Königsberg youth, Jacobus Hoffman: OstF 51, pp. 568–9 (12 May 1541).

47. 1558 letter to Albert: *Katekizmas*, 698–9.

48. H. Mortensen, 'Die litauische Einwanderung nach Ostpreußen', *Prussia*, xxx (1933), 136: 'Die Litauen waren sich somit völlig darüber klar, daß sie sich im fremden Land ansiedelten und eine neue Staatsangehörigkeit erwarten' ('The Lithuanians fully understood that they were coming to settle in an alien land and expected a new nationality').

49. See the Katyčiai dispute, below, n. 75.

50. W. Hubatsch, 'Albert of Brandenburg-Ansbach, Grand Master of the Order of Teutonic Knights and Duke in Prussia, 1490–1568', *Government in Reformation Europe 1520–1560*, ed. H. J. Cohn, New York 1972; Bartkowski, 'Die Besiedlung', 192ff; for Giedroyć, see G. Błaszczyk, *Diecezja żmudzka od XV do początku XVII wieku. Ustrój*, Poznań 1993, 70–4.

51. *LU*, I, nos 241 cols 305–8 (19 Oct. 1252), 244 cols 313–20 (8 Feb. 1253); *Codex Mednicensis seu Samogitiae Dioecesis*, ed. P. Jatulis, I, Rome 1984, no. 7, pp. 29–31 (11 Aug. 1416); *Acta Alexandri magni ducis Lithuaniae*, Kraków 1927, no. 311, pp. 520–1 (28 Feb. 1506), in which unsafe routes and proximity to 'Barbary' were cited as reasons for establishing the new see.

52. V. Vaivada, 'Reformacija Žemaitijoje XVI a. II-je pusėje', unpub. Ph.D. diss., Vilnius University 1995.

53. V. Vaivada, 'Bažnyčių tinklas Žemaitijoje (Descriptio dioecesis Samogitiensis duomenimis)', *Protestantizmas Lietuvoje: istorija ir dabartis*, ed. I. Lukšaitė et al., Vilnius 1994, 44–5.

54. Bartkowski, 'Die Besiedlung', 176.

55. In 1551: 'Sancte Annae in opidulo Botoki, S. Jacobi in Schwekschna, Mariae Virginis gloriosae in Schidlowo, Crucis in Jurgenburga, Georgii et Corporis Christi in Tauroga, Assumptionis in Welona et reliqua dum coluntur

sanctorum festa in oppidis certis', *Katekizmas*, 673–4; for marriages, see p. 679.

56. Proclamations of 1578 for the churches of Tilsit and Ragnit in *Senieji lietuvių skaitymai, I dalis, tekstai su įvadais*, ed. J. Gerullis, Kaunas 1927, 56–61, 61–5.

57. OstF 53, pp. 257–8 (12 Jan. 1547), 333 (22 Mar. 1547); on Kęsgailos, see K. Pietkiewicz, *Kieżgajłowie i ich latyfundium do połowy XVI wieku*, Poznań 1982; for Bilevičiai, see E. Songaila, 'Bilevičiai', *Žemaičių žemė*, 1995: 4, 33–8.

58. Königsberg alumni: I. Lukšaitė, *Lietuvos mokykla ir pedagoginė mintis XIII–XVII a. Istorijos šaltinių antologija*, Vilnius 1994, 193. For details, see T. Wotschke, 'Polnische und Litauische Studenten in Königsberg', *Jahrbücher für Kultur und Geschichte der Slaven*, n.s. VI (1930), 428–7; D. Bogdan, 'Studenci z Rzeczpospolitej na Uniwersytecie Królewskim', *Królewiec a Polska*, ed. M. Biskup and W. Wrzesiński, Olsztyn 1993, 73–87.

59. OstF 53, pp. 718–19 (31 Oct. 1548). Buivydas: V. Biržiška, *Aleksandrynas. Senųjų lietuvių rašytojų, rašusių prieš 1865 m., biografijos, bibliografijos ir biobibliografijos*, I, Chicago 1960, 142.

60. Boiar status: OstF 54, pp. 293–4 (12 Dec. 1551). As witness: *Lietuvos Inventoriai*, cols 636, 651, 666.

61. Clerical shortage: OstF 53, pp. 82–3, letter to Bilevićius (8 May 1546). On 'friendship's limits', see Nicolas Nipszyc's letter to Albert (6–14 Jan. 1534): *Acta Tomiciana*, XVI: 1, ed. W. Pociecha, Wrocław-Kraków-Poznań 1960, no. 11, pp. 21–2.

62. Bilevićius: OstF 52, pp. 480–2 (13 Sept. 1543). Chodkiewicz: OstF 54, pp. 606–8 (18 Nov. 1553). Mileski: OstF 54, pp. 835–6 (1 Dec. 1554). Göckell: OstF 54, p. 822 (3 Nov. 1554). George of Grobin: OstF 52, pp. 762–6 (8 Dec. 1544), OstF 53, pp. 741 (25 Dec. 1548).

63. For Talwisch and Bleyfoller, see OstF 54, pp. 852–3; OstF 52, p. 812.

64. G. Mortensen-Heinrich, *Beiträge zu den Nationalitäten und Siedlungsverhältnißen von Preußisch Litauen*, Berlin 1927; *idem*, 'Die litauische Einwanderung'; for the anti-German equivalent, see M. Brakas, *Mažosios Lietuvos politinė ir diplomatinė istorija*, Vilnius 1995.

65. Katyčiai dispute: OBA 17737, 19574, 20909, 20917, 20920, 21013, 21025, 21357, 21368, 21554, 21576, 21652, 21701–2, 21707, 24134, 25972; Simnas (see n. 14), Beinigkehmen (see n. 34), Steinford (OBA 27879), Crocki (disputed meadows to be divided equally: OstF 52, pp. 243–60 (31 Oct. 1542)).

66. *Akty litovsko-russkago gosudarstva (XIV–XVI st.)*, ed. M. V. Dovnar-Zapolsky, Moscow 1899, no. 77, p. 101.

67. OBA 21013 (2 Sept. 1516); OBA 21652, fol. 2 (29 Dec. 1517).

68. *Acta Alexandri*, no. 194, p. 327.

69. *Elementa*, LIV, no. 1204, p. 73.

70. *Elementa*, LII, p. 154.

71. December 1533: *Elementa*, LIII, p. 140, no. 923; cf. *ibid.*, XLVII, nos 104 (p. 120), 107 (p. 122).

72. *Elementa*, LIV, no. 1187, pp. 54–5 (23 Oct. 1535).

73. *Elementa*, XXXV, no. 467, pp. 130–2 (1 Mar. 1536): letter to Nicholas Wolski, Bona's Court magister.

74. Bona's settlement policy: Pociecha, *Królowa Bona*, iii, 144–59.
75. *Elementa*, liii, no. 1019, 199–200 (18 July 1534). The king and queen deny they ever agreed to collect taxes alternately with the Prussians: *Acta Tomiciana*, xvii, ed. W. Pociecha, Wrocław-Kraków-Poznan 1966, no. 559, p. 700 (17 Nov. 1535).
76. OstF 51, pp. 11–12, 15–16, 18, 118–23.
77. OstF 51, pp. 599–602, 622–4.
78. OstF 54, pp. 148–9, 728–9, 939–47, 976–7.
79. A. Groth, *Żegluga i handel morski Kłajpedy w latach 1664–1722*, Gdańsk 1996; E. Meilus, *Žemaitijos kunigaikštystės miesteliai XVII amžiaus II pusėje-XVIII amžiuje (Raida, gyventojai, amatai, prekyba)*, Vilnus 1997.

9

CRUSADERS AS FRONTIERSMEN: THE CASE OF THE ORDER OF ST JOHN IN THE MEDITERRANEAN

Ann Williams

The crusading movement was from the first a frontier activity. The establishment of the 'Crusader States' in Syria and the capture of Jerusalem in 1099 gave the Christians a permanent border with the Muslims which they had to defend with tenuous lines of communication to western Europe for the supply of manpower, horses, and arms.[1] Hence the need for a trained and stable group of warriors to defend the frontiers was apparent early in the twelfth century. The Templars were founded in 1118 as a military religious order in Latin Syria. Five years earlier, Pope Paschal II had granted recognition to the Order of St John of Jerusalem for their role as protectors of the pilgrim routes and carers of sick pilgrims. Even this role implied the use of arms, and it was not long before they joined the Templars as organised holy warriors. The military orders were technically not crusaders; they did not take crusading vows.[2] Their rules discuss their conduct and their organisation rather than their aims and purposes, but nevertheless, the crusading movement provided their *raison d'être*. The Order of St John, the Knights Hospitaller, provide a particularly good barometer for the changes in the idea of crusade because this very 'medieval' institution remained in action until it was overthrown by Napoleon in Malta in

1798. They patrolled the frontier between Islam and Christendom in the Mediterranean for five centuries.

The Knights of St John

The Order, like other monastic bodies, took vows of poverty, chastity, and obedience, and owed direct loyalty to the papacy. Its central administrative body, the Convent, was based in the eastern Mediterranean, first at Jerusalem, then at Acre, then after the loss of that city in 1291, in Rhodes from 1309 to 1522. It regarded its properties in the west as *outre mer* ('across the sea'). However, the frontier command could not have existed without support from the lands the Order held in Europe. The basic unit was a monastic house called a commandery, often consisting of property bequeathed by those who were unable to go on crusade themselves. These commanderies were grouped into priories within *langues* ('tongues') or 'Nations'. There were eight of the latter by the early fifteenth century: Provence, Auvergne, France, Italy, Aragon and Catalonia, Castile and Léon, England, and Germany. Money was collected from the Knights' estates in Europe and dispatched by receivers in Avignon and Rome to the East for the expenses of defending the Knights' base there. This money was needed to build fortifications and galleys and to supply the Knights and their dependants. Much time was spent in chasing up debts, preventing land being alienated, and after the dissolution of the Order of Templars in 1311, fighting legal battles to gain property which had been promised to the Hospitallers.

Individual Hospitallers were expected to go 'on caravan', to do a tour of duty in the east, and it is clear that some preferred to spend their whole career in active combat. Fully fledged knights, increasingly from noble families from the fifteenth century, were supported by serjeants at arms, and a group of priests to provide for their spiritual welfare. The central governing body, the Convent, comprised the main officials and the Council of the Order. The Grand Master was elected in a monastic chapter-general by the members present at the assembly, and could come from any of the Nations. The other important officers of the Order were representatives of the *langues*, for example, Provence provided the Grand Commander, Auvergne the Marshal, France the Hospitaller, and Italy the Admiral. They were supported by the knights currently on duty in the east. The band was small but efficient.[3]

The Expansion of the Crusades

The original destination of crusaders to the Levant was expanded to other regions in the thirteenth and fourteenth centuries, and to enterprises which were not full-scale general passages. Papal indulgence was extended to Spain in 1122, and the expansion of Castile and Aragon against the Muslim south began the Reconquista which lasted until the fall of Granada in 1492, and even had its echoes in the later Spanish fortresses on the North African mainland. Individual crusaders such as Saint Louis of France went to Egypt in 1248 and made preparations to attack Tunis in 1270. The whole Mediterranean had become the field of crusade, creating a vast frontier between Islam and Christendom which was difficult to control.

The Knights Hospitaller in Latin Syria were at first a small military force under the overlordship of the Crusading States, commanding strong points, like Krak des Chevaliers and Margat, against Muslim attack. The weakness of these small states and frequent disputes among their rulers gave the Hospitallers a great deal of independence. As the crusaders were pushed to the coast, the Hospitallers took to the sea, becoming a fully fledged naval power after the loss of Acre in 1291. The military orders had to reassess their position. The Templars, unpopular in France because of their great wealth, were accused of corruption and sorcery. Their trial at the Council of Vienne in 1311 led to the burning of their grand master as a heretic and the dissolution of the Order. The Hospitallers might well have been affected, but they quickly opted to play an active part in the eastern Mediterranean. After a brief period on its lands in Cyprus, an island ruled by the Lusignan dynasty, the Order decided to conquer its own island base, Rhodes, from the Byzantines in 1306–09. This meant that for the first time the Hospitallers ruled a small state of their own. Like other Frankish rulers in the area, for example the Venetians in Crete or the Gattilusi in Lesbos, they became a small alien elite ruling a largely Greek population, a small enclave in an increasingly Muslim world. The west might regard them as a Christian bulwark, but on a day-to-day basis they had to live and trade with their neighbours to survive.

The Knights had necessarily become a naval power with the conquest of Rhodes. The frontiers in Latin Syria had not been clearly defined; the great crusader castles had marked strategic points, but they were not always manned. The crusaders usually lived in towns and moved

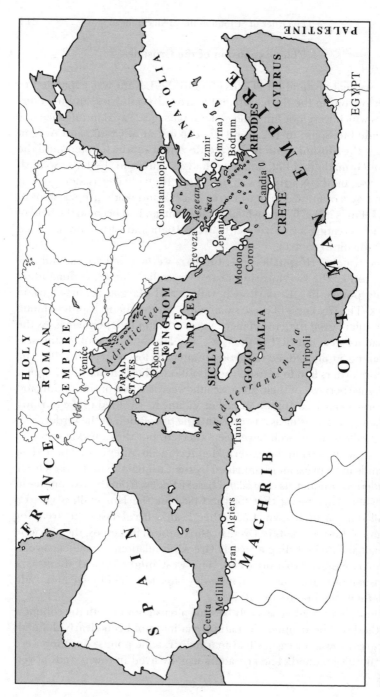

Map 9.1 The Knights of Malta in the Mediterranean, fourteenth to eighteenth centuries.

into the countryside to meet challenges as they arose. The sea frontiers which the Avignonese Papacy expected the Order to patrol were even more amorphous. There was no conception of territorial waters nor limits in which ships were confined. There were very few full-scale naval battles engaging two fleets. Attacks on enemy coastal positions, or the picking off of individual galleys or supply ships, were the most usual events, and they were not decisive. The Mamluk rulers in Egypt and the increasingly active Turkish emirates established on the Anatolian coast pulled the Knights in two directions. A Christian league was proposed by the pope in 1344 to take Smyrna, the most important of the emirates and the centre of important trading interests in the area.[4] Venice and Genoa quickly returned to their economic concerns after the conquest of Smyrna, and the Knights were left holding a tenuous outpost on the edge of the city until Timur's Tartar army overran the area in 1402.

Although individual princes went on crusade, all crusaders sought the pope's blessing as an important part of their enterprise. It meant, among other things, that they might be able to raise crusading taxes for their expedition. The Avignon popes were concerned with the continuation of Holy War against the Muslims, but there was no continuity of policy from one pontificate to another. A change of pope could mean a completely different approach to the defence of Christendom. Gregory XI, the first pontiff to appreciate the danger from the Ottoman Turks, saw the control of mainland Greece as the way to hold back the advance. Juan Fernandez Heredia, who became Grand Master in 1377 as a result of very direct papal provision, was to take Achaea and if the land could be held, to move the Order's Convent there.[5] The attempt failed in 1381 and a later intervention in the duchy of Athens in 1397 was equally unsuccessful.[6] In the more generally preached crusades of Peter of Lusignan against Alexandria in 1365 and in the Danube campaign of Nicopolis in 1396 the Knights also took part.[7] The sea drew them in all directions and they were hopelessly over-extended: the money sent from their western estates had to pay for supplies, fortifications, and equipment.

The Knights in Rhodes

The firm commitment to Rhodes and a steady programme of building in the islands and the mainland fortress of Bodrum in the fifteenth century increased the importance of the small state as an economic centre.[8] The business of ruling the mixed community, now including Venetian, Genoese, and Jewish traders, occupied a growing part of the Grand Master's attention.[9] However, the Order was still able to repulse two determined attacks by the Mamluks in 1440 and 1444.[10] Living in the eastern Mediterranean, the Order's priorities were not always the same as the papacy's. The popes in Rome, involved as they were in the fifteenth century with the rebuilding of their city and their place among the striving states of the Italian peninsula, wanted crusading activities as a boost to their spiritual authority. However, by the 1470s both papacy and Order were agreed that the greatest threat was from the Ottoman Turks. A chapter-general was summoned early in 1475 to discuss the danger and to raise money for a crusade.[11] A year later, Pierre d'Aubusson was elected Grand Master. He was the first of three out-standing leaders that the Order managed to produce in times of great danger, the two others being Philippe L'Isle Adam (1521–34) and Jean de la Vallette (1557–68). His military achievement was the defeat of the Ottoman force besieging Rhodes in 1480. More importantly he proved, once and for all, that the Order was an independent player on the diplomatic stage.

In 1482 Jem Sultan, the younger brother of the Ottoman sultan Bayezet II, fled to Rhodes. Aubusson took the lead in negotiating with Istanbul about Jem's move to the west.[12] His stature enabled the Order to reach the end of the century with a high reputation. This masked the true vulnerability of Rhodes. Palmira Brummett has compared the Ottoman naval strength with that of the Order in the first decade of the sixteenth century and shown how probable a defeat would have been had not the Ottomans been more concerned with the Safavids of Persia and also their closure on the Mamluks.[13] The constant shortage of corn supplies in the eastern Mediterranean at this period preoccu-pied the Knights and made their priority piratical attacks on grain ships. The papacy, for its part, was preoccupied by the internal prob-lems of the Church and the Italian wars and ignored the increasing isolation of Rhodes.

The Ottoman Advance in the Mediterranean

In 1517 the Ottoman conquest of Mamluk Egypt meant that the Turks henceforth required a protected sea route from Alexandria to Istanbul. Consequently, a better-planned and sustained attack against the Knights led to the annexation of Rhodes by Süleyman the Magnificent in 1522. He allowed the Order to leave with full military honour and as much of its moveable property as the Knights could transport. The Order travelled for eight years looking for a new base where its sovereignty would be respected. Meanwhile, the Ottomans, inheriting the sea frontier of the old Byzantine empire in the Mediterranean, gradually took a number of fortresses from the Venetians, such as Modon and Coron in southern Greece, and in 1518 acquired the port of Valona on the eastern coast of the Adriatic. The town became a valuable base for revictualling and the preparation of the Ottoman fleets for activity in the middle and western Mediterranean. The naval campaigns of the 1530s, the attack on Corfu in 1537, and the sorties before Lepanto in 1571 were all supported from Valona.

The conquest of Egypt also drew the Ottomans more deeply into the politics of the North African Maghrib, another border area, where small Muslim city states were encountering Spanish and Portuguese rulers' ambitions. As the Ottomans had taken over the title of Protectors of the Holy Places of Islam from the Mamluks, they gained great influence over Muslim communities in North Africa. In the early part of the sixteenth century three dynasties were predominant, the Hafsids in Tunis, the Zayanids in Tlemcen, and the Wattanids in Fez. These urban-based governments were threatened both by the nomadic rural tribes who could not be brought under control, and by the *presidios*, or fortified settlements on the coast, such as Melilla (taken in 1497), Penon de Velez (1508), Oran (1509), and Algiers and Tripoli (1510). Muslims in Spain had appealed both to the Ottomans and the Mamluks for help in 1492 and their entreaties became more vociferous as the next century progressed.[14]

The Ottomans made use of the corsair leaders, first Kemal Reis and then the Barbarossa brothers, Aruj and Khayraddin. The last became an experienced admiral in the service of the Turks. Matched by the Genoese admiral, Andrea Doria, on the Christian side, he focused attention on the Mediterranean front for over two decades. Beginning with the victory at Prevesa in 1538, through twenty-five years of attacks on the coasts of North Africa, Italy, and the islands, the Turkish fleet took the initiative until the defeats at Malta (1565) and Lepanto (1571). The unexpected raid, known in Ottoman Turkish as *ghazw* (from which they acquired their name as *ghazi* warriors), or *razzia* in Italian, was the Ottoman method of attack in the Mediterrranean.[15] They wanted to keep their Christian enemy on his toes. They did not plan a policy of conquest and systematic reduction of their foes.[16] Indeed, they could not have done so, committed as they were on the Balkan and Persian fronts, and also given the nature of naval warfare. Surprise was the Ottoman weapon, and their seizing of plunder and local inhabitants – men, women, and children – as slaves caused deep apprehension in the coastal communities of southern Italy and the islands. They were not concerned if one enterprise failed. After their unsuccessful siege of Malta in 1565, they turned in the following year to an attack on Genoese Chios. After the loss of their fleet at Lepanto, they quickly bought the services of Venetian shipbuilders to restore their sea power. The Ottomans, under one of their greatest sultans, Süleyman the Magnificent (1521–66) appeared to be unbeatable in the Mediterranean.

The Christian Response

The Christian world was fragmented in its approach to the Ottoman threat. The Order of St John returned to western Europe, eventually being given the papal fortress of Viterbo as a base. There was no debate in their councils at this time about their future role.[17] They saw the loss of Rhodes as a temporary setback which could be reversed by papal support for a general crusade to the eastern Mediterranean. Clement VII was, however, threatened by the rival French and Imperial armies and needed a reliable, permanent army. He hoped to employ the Knights as papal bodyguards, but they, having tasted sovereign power in the eastern Mediterranean, did not want to place themselves directly under the political as well as the spiritual authority of the papacy. They pleaded their reluctance to go to Rome because of the outbreak of plague there, a decision which was justified when the city was sacked by the Imperial army in 1527. The Order's position was a difficult one politically, dependent as they were on the resources of their *langues* at a time when the authority of rulers was increasing. This balancing act was to characterise the rest of their existence as an independent state.

In fact, in the 1520s it was Charles V who kept the ideal of crusade alive. He was attacked on his Balkan frontier by the Ottomans and also on his Mediterranean frontier as ruler of Spain. The Knights fitted into the Spanish idea of a *presidio*, a fortified outpost on the frontier with Islam, supplied and supported by food supplies, and if necessary, armed reinforcements from a Spanish base. From the days of the Aragonese empire before the union of the Crowns of Castile and

Aragon in 1469, the Spaniards had had trading interests in the coastal cities of North Africa and had also provided them with military expertise, but the rulers of these cities, as has been suggested, were turning to the Ottomans for help at the beginning of the sixteenth century. The Spaniards, however, still wanted bases to maintain their interests there, and the devout Charles V also saw these enclaves as footholds in a crusade against the Muslims. So in 1530 he granted the Order the islands of Malta and Gozo for the nominal feudal rent of a falcon, with the commitment to defend Tripoli on the North African coast. His purpose was to ensure that the Knights should '. . . obtain at length a fixed residence, and there [they] should once more return to those duties for the benefit of the Christian community which appertain to their Religion, and should diligently exert their strength and their arms against the perfidious enemies of the Christian religion'.[18] The Ottoman-Christian encounter had moved to the middle Mediterranean, and the Knights' defence of Malta's important harbours was a deterrent against piracy, as well as more formal Muslim attacks. Tripoli proved to be a heavy drain on manpower and resources until its loss in 1551.

The Problems of the Order

The Order was suffering great financial hardship. Rich lands had been lost in the east. Their English lands had been lost to Protestantism; so had part of their German territories. They faced heavy expenditure to fortify the harbour town of Birgu in Malta;[19] they were barely prepared to meet the major onslaught on the island in 1565.[20] The challenge for the Ottomans was to make their presence felt in the centre of the Christian Mediterranean. Sicily and Naples were part of the Spanish empire, administered by viceroys from the mother country, and the Papal States were within easy sailing distance, as was the grand duchy of Tuscany. If the Ottoman Turks controlled the important, well-protected Grand Harbour of Malta as a safe berth for Muslim ships, they would be a constant source of anxiety to all the neighbouring maritime states, and beyond them, to Spain and Europe generally. The Knights' heroic defence of the island from May to September was praised throughout Christendom, even in Protestant England, but it masked many of the realities of crusading efforts from the sixteenth century onwards. Popes and rulers were prepared to talk about support for Holy War, but were slow in providing money and resources.

Like the other *presidios*, Malta found the Spanish reluctant to move quickly to their assistance. Don Garcia of Toledo and the Sicilian squadron did not appear off the island until the battle was already won in September.

The success of the siege did encourage renewed papal interest in crusade, supported by Philip II of Spain. The Holy League, which led to the destruction of the Ottoman fleet at Lepanto in 1571, linked the Spanish fleet with Venice and smaller contingents from Malta, Florence, and the Papal States for a brief effort at Christian unity. This was very much in the spirit of the Council of Trent where the Knights' vice-chancellor, Martin de Rojas, had appeared before the assembly in 1563 to stress the perilous position of the Order and the necessity for money and support. New crusading proposals might strengthen Catholic Christendom and push back the Turks who seemed omnipresent in the Mediterranean.

Papal Initiatives after the Council of Trent

Other attempts were made, however, to build the unity of Christendom. The post-Tridentine popes developed, rather late in the day, a renewed awareness of the implications of the Union of the Eastern and Western Churches in 1438.[21] Christian communities of varying rites existed within the Ottoman empire, Greek, Maronite, Nestorian, and others. In 1579 Gregory XIII set up the Collegio Sant'Atanasio to train Greeks coming to Rome, and also to take Armenian and Maronite candidates.[22] The islands and territories of the eastern Mediterranean also had Catholic bishops and communities. Many of these prelates lived away from their dioceses in safer havens, and it was in accordance with the decrees of the Council of Trent, which required episcopal residence in sees, that the papacy encouraged these men to return to their flocks. Sixtus V, in December 1585, also instituted formal visits to Rome by bishops, the *Visitatio Liminum* (a 'visit of the limits' or 'thresholds'). Bishops from southern Italy, the Greek islands, Dalmatia, and Greece were obliged to send three-yearly reports on their dioceses. The term *limen Petri* ('the threshold of St Peter'), was used to describe the Papal Curia, or papal administration, but here the use of the Latin plural, meaning limits or borders, suggested the idea of the extent of the papacy's spiritual claims over Christians of all rites. The papal claim was reinforced by the sending of papal representatives to the communities within the Ottoman empire. In 1583 Leonard Abela, bishop of

Sidon, a Maltese who spoke Arabic, was sent on an embassy to the Armenians, Jacobites, and Chaldaeans.[23] It was not a success, but it did not end such attempts to support these isolated groups.

The inconclusiveness of Lepanto, the truce between Spain and the Ottoman empire in 1580, and the collapse of the alliance between the Ottomans and the North African states in 1590 did not mark a change in the policies of the Mediterranean powers.[24] There is an argument for looking at a 'long sixteenth century' in Mediterranean as in other aspects of European history. Within the Ottoman empire financial problems and the succession of increasingly feeble sultans were slow to show their effect. What seemed more immediate was the strength of the admiral Uluj Ali (d. 1587), whose career spanned the seventies and eighties. Known also to the Christians as Occhiali or Kilij Ali, he was a Christian renegade from southern Italy who had become a Muslim and was based at Algiers; the opportunities offered by the border lands encouraged movement upwards of the poor but enterprising Christian in socially mobile communities of Islam, whereas Muslims hardly ever did so well in Christian states although slaves did convert to Christianity. Uluj Ali, like the earlier North African corsairs, was supported by the Ottoman sultan and had a prominent position on the Turkish side at Lepanto. In 1574 he won back Tunis which the Christians had held briefly. His fleet patrolled the North African coast and dissuaded the Christians from continuing their Holy League and led to attempts at a diplomatic truce between Spain and the Ottoman empire.

On the Christian side it appeared that the papacy might still have plans for a traditional crusade. In 1582 Pope Gregory XIII wrote to the new Grand Master, Verdala, whom he himself had recommended because the Order had been suffering bitter internal tensions under the unpopular Grand Master La Cassière. He stressed how important it was that the Order should settle down and concentrate on its main role in the Holy War against the Turks.[25] A year later in 1583, on the occasion of summoning the Chapter-General, the pope wrote in great detail about the raising of taxes for a war in the eastern Mediterranean and the possibility of getting money throughout Christendom for the enterprise. The Grand Master ordered a new galley from Naples, and the Chapter General decided to keep five galleys permanently ready for war. Two galleys were sent to help the Venetians off Candia (Crete), but the full-scale war the pope envisaged did not materialise, partly because of the disturbances in Rome at the end of Gregory's pontificate in 1583.[26]

Sixtus V, who succeeded him, was a Franciscan who shared the mendicant orders' interest in missionary activity and the promotion of crusade. He was concerned with more than local acts of corsairing and played with various ideas of land crusade, allying with the Tartars of the Crimea, as well as a Mediterranean naval crusade. The Council of the Order, faced by another papal appeal, pleaded that it had to finish the fortifications of its new city of Valletta, before undertaking any large war. However, there were alarms of Turkish attack again in February 1588 and Ibrahim Pasha was reported preparing a large fleet for the western Mediterranean. In the event, he cruised off Tripoli and went home without threatening Malta or Gozo. The Chapter General of the Order, mooted in 1588, was again exhorted by Sixtus to prepare for Holy War. The Order, whose customary financial difficulties were exacerbated by several years of famine among the people, did not respond.[27]

The Crisis of the 1590s

Historians have recently identified a crisis of the 1590s as a precursor to the deeper and wider malaise of the mid seventeenth century.[28] Certainly this is borne out in the middle Mediterranean. For a decade after 1581, the year the Maltese called 'the year of the flood', there was bad weather and consequently bad harvests which increased competition for the food supply.[29] There was desperate famine in Sicily during the three seasons 1590–92, and inevitably also in Malta which obtained its supply of corn from the larger island. The final calamity was an outbreak of plague in 1592 brought by the galleys of the grand duke of Tuscany. More than 800 people died, including 40 Knights.[30] In the midst of this distress, 60 Turkish vessels sailed from Istanbul in May 1593, and although they eventually turned back because of bad weather, the Council of the Order brought in a reform of their naval command and preparations of the galley fleet.

The pope, now Clement VIII, was uncertain whether or not to urge Christendom to support a land war against the Turks in Hungary or to put resources into naval activities in the Mediterranean, again showing the problems of the lack of continuity in papal policy. At one point in the summer of 1594, the Council of the Order promised to raise 100 000 scudi to help the Emperor at the pope's request, but their enemies were closer at hand.[31] They eventually argued convincingly that they could not afford to send such sums away from the island and so leave them unprotected and their poor to die of hunger. It often seemed that the pope did not understand the financial stresses on the Order at a time when its richest commanderies in France were damaged by the Wars of Religion, and some of their most valuable estates in Italy were being appropriated by the popes themselves for their relations.

The Seventeenth Century

Grand Master Verdala died in 1595 and was succeeded by the Aragonese, Martin Garzes. His short rule was a prelude to the long administration of Alof de Wignacourt (1601–22). The latter's more efficient administration ushered in a period of better living in Malta. At home this meant the organisation of a better corn supply from Sicily, and for operations abroad, an approach to the courts of Europe which raised 12 000 *scudi* in 1598 to build a new large galley. The establishment of a loan fund in Malta raised more money. A pattern of naval expeditions was established, a positive move against the Muslims rather than a reactive one. The fleet was sent to Karamania in 1598 and to the Levant and Barbary in 1599. In the latter episode seven Knights and 50 soldiers and mariners were lost. Money was put into the fortifications of Gozo.[32] The Order, now thoroughly committed to Malta, was patrolling the middle Mediterranean, but was still drawn into raids in the eastern part of the sea.

The Grand Master and Council advocated concentrating on North Africa, and they followed an attack on Tripoli in 1600 with an expedition to Mohammadia in 1602. This gave the fleet security to move to the eastern Mediterranean in 1603, where they attacked the forts of Lepanto and Patras successfully. These threats against Ottoman territory roused the fury of the Turks who prepared a large fleet to come to Malta. Only the outbreak of plague in Istanbul and the death of Sultan Mehmet III prevented their determined retaliation. The early years of the seventeenth century again saw great scarcity in Malta and the Chapters General of 1603 and 1612 were faced with the dual problems of supply and plans for war.

Wignacourt's election as Grand Master was matched by the election in 1605 of Paul V. His pontificate (1605–21) and that of his successors, Gregory XV (1621–23) and Urban VIII (1623–44), ushered in a new generation of post-Tridentine popes committed to the renewing and continuing of the reforms of the great Council. Support of Holy War was an activity applauded by Paul V. He saw the Order as his agent in the conduct of this war and looked to it to command the papal fleet. In 1605 there was another attack on Mohammadia and two years later Cyprus (now in Turkish hands) was the target, followed in 1608 by Bizerta. The Turks sent an armada in 1609 which cruised off St Elmo, in sight of Valletta, but it did not raid, although there were rumours of a conspiracy by the Turks with the slaves in Malta. The Knights' objective was Barbary in 1610, and at home they built a tower and a fort in St Paul's and Marsaxlokk to reinforce the fortifications round the island. In 1611 they went to Navarino and a year later to the Levant.

After a break of only a year the Turks were seen off Malta and anxiety about their strength spread to Italy. The pope demanded a crusade. Preparations were set in motion and Wignacourt built a fort at the southeastern end of the island in expectation of a landing there. In 1615 there was again rumour of a Turkish armada, and in 1616 a Christian squadron went to Alexandria to divert attention away from their own territories. The renewed Turkish preparations were followed by the gathering of a combined Catholic fleet, with squadrons from Sicily, the Order, and the papacy, off Messina. In these years at the beginning of the seventeenth century, a 'Catholic' fleet meant a permutation of ships from the three powers just mentioned, with sometimes help from Naples and the grand duchy of Tuscany.

Renewed Missionary Activity

These activities did not end in the promised crusade. The death of the Sultan, followed by the death of Paul V in 1621, and that of Wignacourt a year later, led to a different emphasis on policy. The weakness at the centre of the Ottoman state was becoming more apparent. On the Christian side Gregory XV took up another aspect of Tridentine interests, that of establishing contacts with the beleaguered Christian communities in the Levant. The Patriarchal Vicar in Istanbul was upgraded to bishop in 1622. In the same year a far-reaching decision was made: the setting up of the Sacred Congregation to Promote the Faith. Thirteen cardinals, two bishops, and a secretary were to collect information and report on their findings. They were greatly concerned with the New World, but the eastern Mediterranean through to Persia was considered an important area of mission too.[33] Urban VIII set up a College of Propaganda in 1627 to train young men for the missions. The papacy was again promoting its universal claims to the leadership of Christendom, and the wide extent of its activities meant that the practical support of the Mediterranean sea frontier was relegated to lesser importance. News of the growing difficulties of the Christian communities were reported by a stream of visitors from the east and the religious orders were also increasing their work in the area. The Franciscans continued to be the guardians of the Holy Places in Jerusalem. The Jesuits established themselves in Istanbul in 1609, in Aleppo in 1625, in Damascus in 1644, in Sidon and Levantine Tripoli a year later, and in Cairo by the end of the century.[34] The Dominicans penetrated further inland, reaching as far as Mosul by the end of the eighteenth century.

The Order's Changing Role

The succession of the aged Antoine de Paule as Grand Master in 1621 led to a prolonged constitutional crisis in the Order, culminating in the Chapter General of 1631. The Knights continued to patrol the sea between Malta and the Barbary coast, but there was no more talk of crusade until Urban VIII, encouraged by the Maltese Inquisitor Fabio Chigi, later Alexander VII, supported the building of new fortifications on the landward side of Valletta.[35] The pope sent his own engineer, Floriani, to draw up plans and supervise the work. The collection of a tax for this building plan led to a revolt of the Maltese in 1637.

However, the feared full-scale attack on Malta did not happen. The next incident was in the eastern Mediterranean. The island of Crete, known then by the name of its chief town Candia, had been held by the Venetians since 1204. In 1660, provoked by attacks on Ottoman shipping, more by the Knights than by the Venetians, the Turks besieged the island and took it after six years. The pope regarded the war as a *res christiana* ('Christian enterprise'), but did not preach it as a crusade. The ambivalent attitude of the papacy towards its old enemy Venice probably accounts for the lack of whole-hearted support. The land war culminating in the siege of Vienna in 1683 certainly was regarded a crusade, and in 1684 Pope Innocent XI organised a Holy League in which the Hapsburg Emperor was joined by Poland and Venice. The cities of Buda and Belgrade fell to these forces. The Venetians, joined by their Mediterranean allies, the Knights, the Tuscans, and the pope, also managed to win back southern Greece, notoriously blowing up part of the Parthenon in Athens when they used it as an ammunition dump.

In these campaigns changes were marked. The long-standing alliance between the French and the Ottoman empire, begun with trading agreements in 1535, meant that the former did not want to take part in the Balkan wars. Danger from Peter the Great's Russia, anxious to proclaim itself the Protector of Orthodox Christian communities, was increasingly a consideration in alliances and treaties. International diplomacy among the larger European states had become too important to be left to papal idealists. The affairs of the smaller Mediterranean states were rearranged by 'great power' discussions; thus Venice, in the Treaty of Passarowitz in 1718, lost the Morea and most of the Greek island bases that she had won.

In the Mediterranean the long centuries of crusade were slowly transformed as the organisation of privateering regulated warfare among the states bordering the sea. The sea frontier, unlike land boundaries which, however difficult to defend, contained the state they were trying to protect, almost pulled the enemy in to raid and devastate the coast. Sea battles were inconclusive and almost impossible to follow up. The Knights of St John, as well as defending their own possessions, first in Rhodes and then in Malta, tried to continue offensive actions from North Africa to the Levant. This diffusion of effort inevitably contributed to its ineffectiveness. There was no great development in naval warfare in the Mediterranean until the larger and more powerful fleets of Nelson and Napoleon met at the end of the eighteenth century. The *razzia* type of attack which both Muslims and Christians practised was destructive but not conclusive. Medieval Crusade disappeared, although the Order of St John remained in Malta and the rhetoric of Holy War remained so strong that it could always be invoked to gain the moral high ground.

Aside from the Christian enterprises in which the Order was involved, it ran numerous corsairing expeditions. The line between the two had always seemed a thin one to its opponents. As the Knights committed themselves more fully to Malta, with the building of Valletta in the latter part of the sixteenth century and the fortified development of the whole of the Grand Harbour area, they exploited its maritime potential more fully. The Chancery of the Order issued 280 privateering licences in the period 1600–24.[36] The increase of revenue from prize money and slaves benefited the Order's Treasury, the Knights, and the Grand Master himself.[37] The Knights, making use of the Order's galleys, went further afield in the eastern Mediterranean, while local Maltese and foreigners imitated the Maghribi corsairs as well.[38] These activities were matched by the success of individual entrepreneurs at the expense of the Ottoman state at the other end of the Mediterranean.[39] Privateering, licensed by governments, with regulations about prizes and captives, became a method of managing naval warfare in the area.

The seventeenth-century Mediterranean continued to provide a fluid frontier between Islam and the west. Its line moved with the ebb and flow of the maritime participants in its trading and warlike activities.[40] The papacy, promoting the doctrines of the Council of Trent, wanted the Crusade to continue, to sustain its own position and the idea of Christendom. The Order of St John seemed the traditional institution round which to organise its promotion, but by the end of the century Pope, Knight, and Sultan were caught up in the diplomatic and naval manoeuvres that Russia's entry into the Black Sea provoked.[41] The frontier between medieval and modern had been crossed, although new ideas of international relations and national maritime boundaries promoted by the Netherlands and England in remoter seas took time to replace the ready justification of conflict between Christian and Muslim.[42] As the eighteenth century progressed and Russia's support of Orthodox Christian communities in the Mediterranean increased, perhaps the Crusading wheel was coming full circle. The final irony was Tsar Paul I's acceptance of the Grand Mastership of the Order of St John after Napoleon had evicted the Knights from Malta in 1798.[43]

NOTES

1. For the early history of the crusades, see J. Riley-Smith, *What Were the Crusades?*, 2nd edn, London 1992, 4–7.
2. The English versions of the two Rules are *The Rule of the Templars*, ed. J. M. Upton-Ward, Woodbridge 1992; E. J. King, *The Rule, Statutes and Customs of the Hospitallers 1099–1302*, London 1934.
3. NLM AOM, 282, Statutes of 1466, xxxviiii [*sic*] (r–v), said there were to be 300 Conventual Knights, 30 *Capellani*, and 20 *Servientes*.
4. N. Housley, *The Avignon Papacy and the Crusades 1305–1378*, Oxford 1986, Appendix II, 'Smyrna under Papal rule 1344–1374', discusses the financing and organisation of this crusade.
5. A. T. Luttrell, 'Gregory XI and the Turks 1370–1378,' *Latin Greece, the Hospitallers and the Crusades 1291–1440*, Variorum, London 1982, xv, 391–417.
6. A. T. Luttrell, 'Intrigue and schism among the Hospitallers of Rhodes 1311–89', *The Hospitallers in Cyprus, Rhodes, Greece and the West 1291–1440*, Variorum, London 1978, xxiii, 32–5.
7. K. M. Setton, *The Papacy and the Levant 1204–1571*, 4 vols, Philadelphia 1976–84, i, 224–55.

8. NLM AOM, 283, LXXX (r) and CXI (r).

9. NLM AOM, 282, XLI (r).

10. M. Ziada, 'The Mamluk Sultans 1291–1517', *A History of the Crusades*, ed. K. M. Setton et al., 6 vols, Madison, 1959–89, III, 497–8.

11. NLM AOM, 283, I (r).

12. L. Balletto, 'Sisto IV e Gem Sultano', *Atti e Memorie di Savona*, nuova serie, XXV, Savona 1989, 153–70.

13. P. Brummett, 'The overrated adversary: Rhodes and Ottoman naval power', *Historical Journal*, XXXVI (1993), 517–41.

14. J. F. Guilmartin, *Gunpowder and Galleys*, Cambridge 1974, 57–122.

15. The Ottomans had built their power as *ghazi* warriors for the faith, and the attacks were to maintain their own alertness as well as to alarm the enemy. See J. F. Guilmartin, 'Ideology and conflict; the wars of the Ottoman empire 1453–1606', *The Origin and Prevention of Major Wars*, ed. R. I. Rotberg and T. K. Rabb, Cambridge 1989, 149–76; also see C. Heywood's essay in this volume (Chapter 10).

16. A. Williams, 'The Mediterranean', *Süleyman the Magnificent*, ed. M. Kunt and C. Woodhead, London 1995, 42, 53.

17. NLM AOM, 84, 33 (r).

18. NLM AOM, 70.

19. D. de Lucca, 'The fortifications', *Birgu, a Maltese Harbour City*, ed. L. Bugeja, M. Buhagiar, and S. Fiorini, II, Malta 1993, 521–34.

20. The best modern account of the siege is in Guilmartin, *Gunpowder and Galleys*, 176–93.

21. The earlier attempts at mission activities are summarised in M. W. Baldwin 'Missions to the east in the thirteenth and fourteenth centuries', *History of the Crusades*, ed. Setton et al., V, 452–518; B. Z. Kedar, *Crusade and Mission: European approaches to the Muslims*, Princeton 1984, 136–203.

22. H. Jedin, 'Origin and breakthrough of the Catholic reform to 1563', *History of the Church*, ed. H. Jedin et al., 10 vols, London 1980–81, V, 506.

23. Leonard Abel, *Une mission religieuse en Orient au seizième siècle. Relation addressée a Sixte-Quint par l'Évêque de Sidon*, ed. and trans. A. d'Avril, Paris 1866; C. A. Frazee, *Catholics and Sultans: the Church and the Ottoman empire*, Cambridge 1983, 74–6.

24. Setton, *Papacy and Levant*, IV, 1011–22, 1054–62.

25. NLM AOM, 291, 1 (r)–42 (v).

26. B. del Pozzo, *Historia della Sacra Religione Militare di S Giovanni Gerosolimitano detta di Malta*, 2 vols, Verona 1703 and Venice 1715, I, 177.

27. *Ibid.*, I, 304.

28. *The Crisis of the 1590s*, ed. P. Clark, London 1985, esp. P. Burke, 'Southern Italy in the 1590s; hard times or crisis?', 177–90.

29. Pozzo, *Historia della Sacra Religione Militare*, I, 195.

30. *Ibid.*, I, 340.

31. *Ibid.*, I, 350.

32. *Ibid.*, I, 422.

33. L. von Pastor, *The History of the Popes from the Close of the Middle Ages*, English edn, 40 vols, London 1923–53, XXIX, 212–17.

34. J. Delumeau, *Le Catholicisme entre Luther et Voltaire*, Paris 1971,132.
35. V. Borg, *Fabio Chigi, apostolic delegate in Malta 1634–1639, Studi e Testi*, CCXLIX, Vatican City 1965, 482–3.
36. M. Fontenay, 'Le rôle des Chevaliers de Malte dans le corso méditerranéen au XVIIᵉ siècle', *Las Órdenes en el Mediterráneo occidental*, Madrid 1983, 377.
37. P. Earle, *Corsairs of Malta and Barbary*, London 1970, 168–91.
38. Fontenay, 'Chevaliers de Malte', 378.
39. R. Murphey, 'The Ottoman resurgence in the seventeenth-century Mediterranean: the gamble and its results', *Mediterranean Historical Review*, VIII (1983), 186–200.
40. J. Revel, 'Au XVIIIᵉ siècle: le déclin de la Méditerranée?', *La France et la Méditerranée: vingt-sept siècles d'interdependence*, ed. I. Malkin, Paris 1990, 348–62.
41. L. Cassels, *The Struggle for the Ottoman Empire 1717–1740*, London 1966, *passim*; F. Venturi, *The End of the Old Regime in Europe, 1768–1776*, trans. R. B. Litchfield, 2 vols, Princeton 1979, II, 772–3, 791.
42. B. Kingsbury and A. Roberts, 'Grotian thought in international relations', *Hugo Grotius and International Relations*, ed. Hedley Bull et al., Oxford 1990, 15–26.
43. E. Schermerhorn, *Malta of the Knights*, London 1929, 283–306. Ferdinand von Hompesch, the last Grand Master of the Order, died in 1805. The Knights offered the title to the Tsar, who had declared himself Protector of the Order. They also handed over their treasures, including the holy icon of the Madonna of Philermo and their most important relic, the hand of John the Baptist.

10

THE FRONTIER IN OTTOMAN HISTORY: OLD IDEAS AND NEW MYTHS

Colin Heywood*

'The frontier in Ottoman history'. It is difficult to overestimate the significance of this phrase as a dominating concept within the limited range of formulations which have shaped the writing of Ottoman history since it emerged as a separate academic discipline nearly a century ago. Why should this be so, and why, after so long an interval, should it still be necessary to adopt a historiographical rather than a historical approach to the subject?

Background

According to contemporary mainstream historiography there is no problem, for there the course of Ottoman history appears fairly straightforward. The period of the Ottoman emirate (or *beylik*) begins with the establishment of the Ottoman state in northwest Anatolia, traditionally in 1299, by its eponymous founder, 'Ghazi' Osman (?1299–?1324). By the time they conquered Constantinople in 1453 the Ottomans had incorporated (by conquest, marriage, or purchase) or had reduced to vassal status not only all the other Turkoman emirates of western Anatolia, but also, from the mid fourteenth century, that part of southeastern Europe known to the Ottoman as Rumeli (literally, 'the land of the Greeks'), comprising the remnants of the Byzantine empire, together with the medieval Slav states of Bulgaria, Serbia, and Bosnia, and the fragmentary territories in the Balkans still under Latin rule. Under Mehemmed II (1444–46, 1451–81), known as 'Fatih' ('the Conqueror'), the Ottoman *beylik* not only reached its final form through

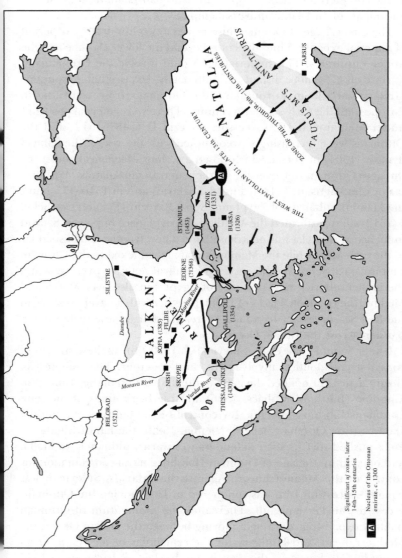

Map 10.1 Pre-Ottoman and Ottoman Islamic frontier zones (*thugūr/uj*) in Anatolia and the Balkans, eighth to fifteenth centuries.

further conquests (the Despotate of the Morea (1460), Trebizond (1461), medieval Bosnia (1463)) but, through the rapid transformation of the conquered Constantinople into Ottoman Istanbul, took on the lineaments of an Islamic universal empire.

The classical age of Ottoman history was a two-hundred-year period of imperial expansion into the lands beyond the lower Danube and the upper Euphrates. This imperial age would involve the Ottomans in warfare on ever more distant and, ultimately, less profitable frontiers. Military setbacks in Europe kept the Ottomans from returning to Europe until the early sixteenth century. There were internal problems under Mehemmed II's successor, Bayezid II (1481–1512) and the Ottomans were increasingly preoccupied with the rise of the Safavid dynasty (1501) in Persia, which posed a serious ideological and social threat to Ottoman rule over the Turkoman tribes in Anatolia. With two major campaigns, in 1514 against the Safavids and in 1516–17 against the Mamluk sultanate of Egypt and Syria, Bayezid II's successor Selim I (1512–20) transformed the Middle Eastern blanace of power. Safavid influence in Anatolia was neutralised and a new frontier established far to the east. Meanwhile the Mamluk sultanate, annexed to the Ottoman Empire, gave Selim and his successors control not only over Syria and the immensely rich new province of Egypt, but also over Mecca and Medina, the two Holy Places of Islam, together with a naval presence in the Red Sea necessary to combat increasing Portuguese seaborne expansion across the Indian Ocean.

Under Selim I's successor, Süleyman I (1520–66), all these strands of conquest and political involvement came together. The conquest of Belgrade in 1521 opened the gates to the destruction of the Hungarian kingdom (Battle of Mohács, 1526) and the beginnings of the long Ottoman-Habsburg struggle for control of the lands of the middle Danube (first Ottoman siege of Vienna, 1529); the fall of Rhodes in 1522 pushed its Christian defenders westwards, ultimately to Malta, and opened up the age of Ottoman-Habsburg naval confrontation for control of the Mediterranean. Against the Safavids, Süleyman was equally successful: Iraq was conquered in 1534, giving the Ottomans access to the Persian Gulf. Thereafter the momentum of Ottoman military expansion continued, moving between the Indian Ocean, the Mediterranean, and Hungary for the remainder of the reign. From around 1550, however, the pace began to slow; setbacks, as in 1552 against the Portuguese at Hormuz and against the Habsburgs in Hungary, may be viewed against disturbing trends farther afield: also in

1552 a Muscovite expeditionary force occupied Kazan, on the middle Volga. This was a major blow against the post-Mongol Turco-Muslim ascendancy in western Asia of which the Ottoman state formed a major part, and was followed in 1556 by the occupation of Astrakhan, which severed the lands of the Ottomans' closest ally, the so-called Khanate of the Crimea, from those of their coreligionaries further east in central Asia.

By the death of Süleyman (1566), problems over the succession, the changing nature of warfare, and growing economic crisis within the administrative structures and in society conspired to place the Ottomans increasingly on the defensive. The conflicts that followed either ended in brief and unprofitable conquests in inhospitable terrain, as in the long war with Persia (1578–90), or ended in diplomatic and military stalemate, as in the 'Long War' in Hungary (1593–1606). The seventeenth century saw both the last conquests (Iraq, Crete, Slovakia, Podolia), and the beginnings of the retreat from empire. Ever more far-flung military adventures in the Ukraine (1677–78), and particularly the disastrous second siege of Vienna (1683), led to a grand alliance of Austria, Poland, Venice, and Russia against the Ottomans, and to the loss, permanent or temporary, not only of Hungary and Podolia but also of lands south of the Danube in the Morea (Greece) which had been ruled by the Ottomans since the fifteenth century. When the Ottomans accepted a peace settlement at Karlowitz in 1699, the age of Ottoman expansion came definitively to an end.

The Ottoman Frontier and the Historians

For present purposes, we may therefore accept as a given that the Ottoman state was a frontier polity which, from 1300 to 1700, possessed an active expansion frontier. The state came into being at the end of the thirteenth century at the interface of two distinct zones of culture and settlement in northwestern Anatolia: the zones of Islamic domination and Turkoman settlement on the one side, and of late-Byzantine rule and Greek Christian civilisation on the other. In terms of microhistory we are looking at the Turkish (and possibly Ottoman) outflanking of the Byzantine frontier defences in Bithynia, on the middle course of the Sangarius river, in the later thirteenth and early fourteenth centuries.[1] In terms of macrohistory, as is less well recognised, we are looking at one of the three great political faultlines which marked the interface (in this context 'boundary' will not serve) between the Ilkhanate and the

Golden Horde, the two westernmost and mutually hostile sub-empires of the Mongols under the imperial authority of the successors of Chinggis (Genghiz) Khan.[2] Neither the local history of late-Byzantine Bithynia, however, nor the world-historical connotations of the Ottomans' Mongol connection, have been seen as relevant for the series of historical formulations which have dominated mainstream historical thought on the Ottoman frontier. In historical terms there have been not one but many Ottoman frontiers. Crucial to them all is a set of general postulations regarding the nature of the Ottoman state and, by extension, the role of the frontier in Ottoman history, formulated by the Austrian scholar and pioneer Ottomanist Paul Wittek (1894–1978). All date, in terms of publication, from his years (1934–40) as a political exile in Belgium.[3]

An examination of the publications of Wittek's Brussels period provides this essay's appropriate point of historiographical departure. Wittek's views concerning the nature of the Ottoman frontier were nowhere brought together within a single article, but may be found scattered throughout a series of wide-ranging articles written during this period. These consist of public lectures delivered in major centres of European learning outside Germany: Paris, Brussels, Leiden, London. Without exception, the lectures were devoted to the interpretation of broad themes in the history of the Seljuks of Rûm and the early Ottomans from the foundation of the sultanate of Rûm to the conquest of Constantinople, that is, from the twelfth to the mid fifteenth centuries. Wittek's elaboration of the frontier element in Seljuk and early Ottoman history, as the second subject of his discourse, is present throughout them all.

Wittekian orthodoxy on the history of the Ottoman frontier – a view currently somewhat embattled, and defended as much by conviction as by reason – has been maintained even in the most recent scholarship on the subject. The Ottoman state is seen as a polity devoted throughout its existence to *ghazā*, or Holy War against the infidel; the Ottomans themselves are categorised as perpetual *ghāzīs*, proponents of and fighters in a sacred enterprise against the forces of polytheism and unbelief. The Ottoman frontier against Christendom therefore must serve principally as the stage on which the *ghāzī* drama is continually played out. As Professor Inalcık, the present doyen of this field, has most recently expressed it: '[The Ottoman Empire's] initial gazi frontier influenced the state's historical existence for six centuries: its dynamic conquest policy, its basic military structure, and the predominance of the military class within an empire that successfully accommodated disparate religious, cultural and ethnic elements.'[4]

These are large claims, and in their essence highly Turneresque, although they have little to do with any transfer of concepts from the writings of F. J. Turner.[5] Instead, they reflect – and to some extent replicate – the formulations and theories developed between the wars by Wittek,[6] arguably still the most influential historian of the first century and a half of the Ottoman state. And yet: in the prolific historical scholarship written during the past three-quarters of a century on the origins and early history of the Ottoman state, one looks in vain for a single article devoted to the early Ottoman frontier as a historical problem.[7]

What then, in the present context, do we mean by 'the Ottoman frontier'? The term in fact encompasses a number of differing phenomena. It was, certainly – or eventually it came to be – a line on the map, a demarcation marking, at least in Europe, the abrupt transition between Christendom and Islam, a point of transfer from one culture-world to another. It has been convincingly argued that the Ottomans' acceptance of a demarcated frontier in 1699 marks the end of the Ottoman Age of Expansion, but this later, European-style demarcated frontier is not considered here.[8] Instead we are concerned with a frontier cast rather in a North American mode, a region of colonisation and settlement involving both military action and proselytisation, and thus both a zone of passage and interaction *and* a political barrier. At the same time, it is a zone in which state control may, at least in the earlier period, be surprisingly incomplete. And although we are dealing here with actions against 'infidels' rather than against Red Indians, if we strip out the respective religious modes of moral judgment, similar attitudes towards indigenous populations may be discerned. Turner's vision of the American frontier as 'the outer edge of the wave – the meeting point between savagery and civilisation' is in its essence not so different from the Ottoman view of the inhabitants of the *bilād al-kufr*, the 'lands of unbelief'.[9]

Ottoman usage was quite capable of distinguishing between the frontier as a *line*, a demarcated or recognised boundary – *hudūd*, or *sınır* in Ottoman legal terminology – and the frontier as a *zone*, in effect as a marchland.[10] The Ottoman term for this marchland was *uj*, with the basic meaning of 'furthest point', 'limit', 'end', 'extremity', and, by extension, 'frontier [zone]'.[11] It was characteristic of the *uj*, as of the earlier Islamic *thughūr*, that they bordered on non-Muslim territory;

they were the borderlands of the legal and social entity known as *dār al-Islām*, the 'abode [= land] of Islām'.[12] Beyond the *uj* lay the 'lands of unbelief'. These were generally regarded in Muslim law as *dār al-ḥarb*, the 'abode of war'. In classical Muslim legal theory, although not necessarily in practice, a permanent state of war existed between the *dār al-Islām* and the *dār al-ḥarb*, except when it was in the interest of the Muslim community to agree a temporary truce, in which case the lands in question acquired the status of *dār al-ʿahd*, 'the abode of the covenant'.[13] In practice, Muslim writers who stressed the primacy of *jihād* (also meaning Holy War) tended to enjoy the patronage of Muslim rulers of Islamic states possessing an expansion frontier against *dār al-ḥarb*. Such were the anonymous author of a north Syrian 'Mirror for Princes' during the mid eleventh century counter-crusade, or Fakhr-i Mudabbar, who wrote a political tract in the following century for the Delhi sultan Iltutmış.[14] The first in particular devotes much space to *jihād*, stressing the ruler's duty to make annual attacks on the unbelievers, 'so that *jihād* should not be interrupted and the enemy not develop designs on Islam'. Fakhr-i Mudabbar, equally, says that 'to make sieges, military expeditions, conquests and raids for the faith' was 'the custom and practice of great kings'.[15]

Political writers could also emphasise the primacy of spiritual *jihād*, with the object of subduing one's own impulses, over 'external' *jihād* against unbelievers. The primacy of 'internal' *jihād* was argued forcefully around 1400 by the Ottoman poet Aḥmedi, as Colin Imber has pointed out, arguing against Wittek who saw in him only a proponent of active *ghazā*.[16] None the less it is worth emphasising that the ruler's duties with regard to *jihād* prescribed by both writers above prefigure later Ottoman practice to a remarkable extent.

Wittek and the Ottoman Frontier

One of Wittek's most important works for our purposes is the article 'Deux chapitres de l'histoire des Turcs de Roum', published in 1936.[17] It supplies the text of two lectures delivered at the Sorbonne in March of that year. The second lecture in particular, entitled 'The ghazis in Ottoman history', demonstrates how closely Wittek's view of the frontier was bound up with his chief preoccupation: the *ghāzīs* and their role as the bearers and transmitters of the collective and corporate ethos of the Ottoman state: 'the emirate of the Ottomans had become the archetypical ghazi state', as he apostrophises it.[18] The frontier was, above all, the domain of the *ghāzīs*. Wittek returned to his theme, restating it in a more compressed and extreme form, in a lecture delivered in Holland early the following year.[19]

Wittek viewed the Ottoman frontier as a dynamic and yet socially regressive zone, an almost living geographical entity, possessed of (or by) a collective will. His view of the frontier in general is reserved for the last paragraph of his '*ghāzī*' lecture: the 'problem of the frontier and of its role, its special culture' was 'a very great historical problem'. As he summarised it:

> [T]here have everywhere and always been similar frontiers, and their situation has often been similar to [that of] the [Ottomans] . . .. A strong frontier is an advantage, as long as the society of the hinterland remains intact. Otherwise, the frontier risks asserting itself everywhere, which can allow of an increase in power, but in general leads to a terrible decline in culture.[20]

His final words are equally significant:

> . . . a frontier culture will be, in most cases, necessarily primitive. It will be a cast-off from the high culture of the interior, mixed to such a degree with the waste products of the enemy's culture, that it will share nothing essential in common with that culture whose defender and champion it vaunted itself as being.[21]

The inhabitants of the frontier zone, the *ehl-i ḥudūd* – which we may translate as 'borderers' – thus remained in Wittek's argument the guardians of the *ghāzī* spirit, now dispersed to the European frontiers of the empire, '[the] distant marches', where the *ghāzī* movement once more became as 'anonymous, as foreign to the central government, to literature and to historiography' as it had been in the days of the Anatolian *thughūr* before the Turkish conquest.[22]

Wittek's concept of the frontier in Ottoman history thus transcends the limits of Ottoman history itself in at least two ways. Firstly, in his view, the Ottoman frontier as an entity predated the Ottomans. They merely came to dominate a sector (but arguably the most politically sensitive sector) of the moving frontier comprising a zone between Islam and a Byzantium that, at the beginning of the fourteenth century, happened to find itself athwart northwest Anatolia. This almost anthropomorphic frontier had begun life as the northern Syrian

or southeast Anatolian *thughūr*, stretching from the Taurus to the
upper Euphrates, and established in the aftermath of the first wave of
Arab conquest in the seventh century. Within the larger process of the
moving frontier, distinct sub-processes may be distinguished. Chief
among these is the recurrent peripheralisation of the frontier in relation to the central institutions and governing ethos of the state whose
territorial limits it defined. Wittek finds the origins of this process in
Khurasān in the ninth century; simultaneously, the phenomenon is
replicated on the Taurus frontier between Islam and Byzantium, where
a frontier sub-culture comes into existence, alien to (and alienated
from) the settled hinterland, and possessing more in common with its
neighbouring Christian frontier society, despite the cultural, religious,
and linguistic divide.[23] This alienation of peripheralised frontier societies by the dominant centre repeats itself, with political and social
consequences of the most serious nature, in the Seljuk sultanate of
Rûm (the revolt of Baba Ishak, 1241), and later with the Ottomans.[24]
Secondly, the mode and imagery of Wittek's discourse draws heavily on
political themes and concepts current in the 1930s and applies them
unquestioningly to the utterly different world of fourteenth-century
Anatolia.[25]

A New View of the Ottoman Frontier?
The Impact of Post-Wittekian Revisionism

To what extent has recent research been successful in re-evaluating
these Wittekian attitudes to the Ottoman frontier? In his last decades
Wittek was predominant in the field, at least in the Anglo-Saxon world.
During the war, in the hidden world of historical scholarship in Turkey,
and also in the remoter intellectual corners of the Third Reich, there
had indeed been criticisms of his work,[26] but after the war, in Britain
and America, and in particular wherever Wittek's students from his
Brussels and London periods and, later, the students of those students,
had filled most if not all of the scanty posts in Ottoman history, hagiog-
raphy largely replaced intellectual criticism, at least in public and in
print.[27]

Subsequently, in the years following his death (in 1978), Wittek's
'*ghāzī* theory' has been the object of radical criticism. The earliest 'new
wave' publication came from North America at the beginning of the
1980s in the form of a short but important article by the Hungarian
scholar Gyula Káldy-Nagy.[28] Rudi Lindner's 1982 article, which con-

cluded that 'zeal for the Holy War had nothing to do with causing the rise of the first Ottomans', but was merely a justification for current and past expansionist policies applied restrospectively by later court chroniclers, followed soon after.[29] The first public criticism of Wittek in British academic circles was made at a somewhat controversial *Wittek-Tagung* held in London in June 1984; in the second half of the 1980s further criticism appeared, by Colin Imber and the late R. C. Jennings.[30] The present writer also published studies on the intellectual background to Wittek's work, modifying and qualifying the criticisms of Lindner and Imber.[31] None of these revisionist approaches, however, gave much attention to Wittek's views on the Ottoman frontier, although the '*ghāzī* theory' was by definition a frontier phenomenon.

To what extent were Wittek's observations on the Ottoman frontier anchored in any form of recoverable historical reality, or how far were they generalised and rather romantic constructs? Two general observations may be made. Firstly, Wittek appears to have confused two distinct sets of historical phenomena. The first was the establishment of military regimes in the settled lands of the Eurasian periphery by Turco-Mongol 'barbarian' invaders from the nomadic-pastoral world of Inner and Central Asia.[32] This process was not peculiar to Islam, to Ottoman history, or even to the preceding establishment of Seljuk rule in Anatolia: analogues can be found in, for example, the fifth-century invasion by the Tabghach (Tuoba/T'o-pa) people – a 'proto-Turkish' tribal grouping from the Mongolian steppe – of north China, a process possessing strong typological resemblance to the Seljuk invasion of the Islamic world five centuries later; or in the 'state' established in the southwest corner of the Pontic steppe and the neighbouring lands of eastern and central Europe in the last third of the thirteenth century by Nogay, the Chinghizid *Heerkönig* and would-be ruler of the Golden Horde.[33]

The second of these phenomena is the institution of *ghazā*, seen as the realised outworking of *jihād*, or the canonical duty of waging war against the external non-believer, and as such one of the major duties of Islam. *Jihād* was also not specific to the Ottomans, but was adopted by Wittek for reasons owing as much to external cultural influences as to his interpretation of the relevant internal sources.[34] For Wittek, the figure of the *ghāzī*, institutionalised and transcendentalised, incorporated the main (in fact, the sole) *raison d'être* and ideological driving force of the Ottoman state throughout its six centuries of existence.

But how valid is this elevated view of the function and achievements of the heroic *ghāzī*? Recent research has demonstrated that '*ghāzī*', as a term, served principally as a 'learned' (*ulemā*-derived) synonym for the Turkish pre-Islamic term *alp*, meaning simply 'hero'.[35] The trustworthiness of Wittek's prime referents for fourteenth-century Ottoman frontier realities, the 1337 Bursa inscription and the verse-chronicle of the late-fourteenth century Anatolian poet Aḥmedī, have both been severely questioned. Wittek leaned heavily on the Bursa inscription of 1337, as what he termed 'the oldest epigraphic document we have from an Ottoman ruler', to support his '*ghāzī*' thesis, mentioning the inscription in several works of the late 1920s and 1930s. Most significantly, in his 1937 London lectures published as *The Rise of the Ottoman Empire* (1938), he gave the inscription considerable prominence, using it in his first lecture to provide clinching evidence for his assertion of the essential *ghāzī* nature of the Ottoman state.[36] Wittek transliterates the relevant section: *Sulṭān ibn sulṭān al-ghuzāt, ghāzī ibn al-ghāzī, Shujāʿ ad-daula waʾd-dīn, marzbān al-āfāq, bahlavān-i jihān, Orkhān ibn ʿOthmān.*[37] His translation, inserted into the body of his lecture, and utilised secondhand by most subsequent commentators, omits the third and the final phrases of his text, as follows: 'Sulṭān, son of the Sulṭān of the *Ghāzī*s, *Ghāzī*, son of *Ghāzī*, marquis of the horizons, hero of the world.'[38] Anything that did not refer to *ghāzī*s as he saw them was omitted.

Clearly, by 1937 Wittek had absolutely no doubts about either his text's integrity, the correctness of his reading, or its specific historical significance as supplying unquestionable proof of his '*ghāzī*' thesis. Raising the question as to whether Aḥmedī's *ghāzī* testimony, previously mentioned, should be dismissed as 'mere literary form', he responds that a glance at the 1337 inscription 'will dissipate all such doubt'.[39] He describes the translated phrases of the inscription as 'an ensemble of titles absolutely unique in the Ottoman protocol', where, as he observes, 'generally the classical and quite different formulas of the Seljuk period are used'.[40] Historically, too, the inscription raises for him no uncertainty, for he asserts that 'we can . . . be sure that this strange formula is the expression of an historical reality, of the same reality which dominates the chapter of Aḥmedī'.[41]

It is also clear how far removed these wild *ghāzī* elements were from the tolerant norms of Ottoman polite society in the mid fourteenth century, as is well illustrated by the experiences of Gregory Palamas. Palamas, a celebrated archbishop of Thessaloniki, was captured in

1354 by the Turks while on a journey. This occurred late in the reign of '*Ghāzī*' Osman's son, Orkhan (?1324–62), with whom, while in captivity, Palamas engaged in theological discussions on the respective merits of Islam and Christianity. It is noteworthy, as a recent study points out, that one of only two examples of less than civil treatment he received from Muslims during this episode was at the hands of a body of *ghāzīs* encountered on campaign near Lapseki.[42] Wittek's view of the *ghāzīs* as exalted Muslim hero-figures, even in contemporary Muslim eyes, was wildly romantic, whereas his view of the border zone's inhabitants as cultural and social barbarians may have possessed an element of truth, a distinction amply confirmed in a recent study of the legacy of the *baba* (dervish) leader Seyyid ʿAlī Sulṭān, who, according to his *Vita*, was active in the first Turkish conquests in Thrace at exactly the time of Palamas's adventures.[43] As the study points out, the tone of Seyyid ʿAlī's *Vita* is violent: in the name of religion the unbelievers' eyes are gouged out, or they are killed, skewered on a stake, and roasted over a fire. There is even a scene of cannibalism – simulated, but in the narrator's eyes an astute piece of psychological warfare against the infidels.[44] What is interesting, in this representation of popular, dervish-led frontier culture in the earliest phase of the 'Ottoman' conquest of Rumeli, is not simply the frontier attitudes which it reveals, but the parallels which may, with some hesitancy, be adduced with patterns of cultural behaviour demonstrated, at least in the popular literature of the time, at earlier stages of the moving frontier.[45]

None the less, Wittek's perception of the Ottoman *uj* as a zone of cultural barbarism seems not to be borne out on closer examination. Recent research has served to emphasise not only what is now becoming generally recognised, namely the great autonomy enjoyed by the Turkish frontier lords (*uj-begis*) in the territories under their control, but also their immediate implementation in the newly conquered districts, for instance of western Thrace in the later fourteenth century, of such measures as founding towns, building mosques, caravanserais, and markets, and encouraging settlement. Ottoman construction work, founding new settlements and establishing caravanserais, baths, lodging-houses for travellers, as well as mosques and other more specifically religious establishments, seems to have begun along the route of the Via Egnatia in Thrace and Thessaly immediately after the first incursions of the *uj-begis* in the 1360s. That these activities could coexist with their continuing raiding and slaving expeditions into territories beyond the *uj*, which were not directly under their control but none the less in nominal vassal status to their Ottoman overlords, points up the complexities of the social situation within the Ottoman *uj* with which the historian must deal.[46]

Old Myths and New Views:
The Ottoman Frontier in a Broader Perspective

It seems remarkable that although it is not difficult to identify frontier institutions or elements in Ottoman frontier society comparable to, say, the Habsburg *Militärgrenze* and its inhabitants, or the Polish and Muscovite zones of Cossack settlement erected against the Golden Horde and its successors, the Ottoman 'institutions of the border' have not been subjected to systematic study.[47] Was there an Ottoman *limes*? Geographically, the Ottoman Empire's boundaries roughly coincided with many of the Roman Empire's, yet there appears to be no state philosophy of a *limes*. Why was that? In any case, recent classical historiography has placed the long-accepted idea of a *limes* in doubt, regarding it at least partly as a by-product of nineteenth-century imperialist mentalities.[48] The Ottomans never appear to have considered the construction of a *limes*: the idea of a wall, serving, much as successive 'great walls' of China may have done, to define the limits of a civilisation and a culture as much as to act as a barrier against the barbarians, appears to have been alien to them.[49] Was this because the 'ever-victorious frontier' (*serḥadd al-manṣūra*) remained in their minds an expansion frontier even after late seventeenth-century events – the defeat under the walls of Vienna, the loss of Hungary, and the effective closing of the Ottoman frontier – had rendered such an attitude dangerously obsolete? Or was it due to the unconscious survival of earlier self-images as 'outsiders', deriving from Ottoman origins in the 'barbarian' lands of Central Asia which lay *outside* the *limes*, actual or mental, of the 'civilised' world – Christian, Muslim, or Confucian – of their time?[50]

Thus, attempting to apply typologising concepts, such as 'expansion frontier', or 'pioneer frontier', hitherto not employed by specialists in this field, may not be accounted an exercise in total futility. It is possible to identify elements of the Ottoman frontier and its society that fit in with such concepts. The Rumelian *uj*, for example, in its successive stages from 1353 to 1453, appears to be an 'expansion frontier' in highly developed form. To what extent Ottoman colonisation in the newly conquered districts of Rumeli also fits the idea of a 'pioneer frontier' is a more debateable question. Certainly there was intense migration of Turkish/Turkoman elements from Anatolia to Rumeli in this period. The role in this process of the Ottoman state, in so far as it can be identified as a prime agent in the earlier decades, makes it difficult to speak of a free peasantry here.[51] Wittek's orthodox interpretation of the Ottoman frontier as a zone of transition is perhaps still not entirely superseded as a fruitful approach, however much his historical formulations may merit re-evaluation.

A re-examination of the frontier in Ottoman history does, however, permit a further stage of discussion in the debate over Wittek's '*ghāzī* thesis'. Recent critics, Imber in particular, have emphasised that the basic epistemological error in Wittek's approach to Ottoman history was his assumption that the existence of a state depended on the active implementation of an ideology – in the Ottoman case, *ghazā* or Holy War against the infidel.[52] Wittek also made the fundamental assumption that, to quote what he termed 'the well-known sentence': 'every state owes its existence to the same causes that created it'.[53] To Wittek the Ottomans' renunciation of the '*ghāzī* idea', in his view a result of their Great War alliance with the Habsburg monarchy, meant the loss of the Ottoman state's *raison d'être*. He wrote that:

> ... by this alliance both the empires of Austria and Turkey broke with their most essential traditions [those of multi-ethnic/multi-confessional empires of marchland origin] and thus showed that they had outlived themselves. It is not surprising that both empires failed the test of the Great War and disappeared for ever[54]

His solemnly intoned and sweeping judgment refers of course to a situation in which Wittek failed to declare his own political and emotional involvement, since he had seen active service in the Austrian army in the First World War.[55]

Criticism of Wittek for these formulations has been severe. A reconsideration of the Ottoman frontier as a historical phenomenon enables us, however, to suggest that he may have been wrong not so much in his judgments but in his periodisation. It was not the Habsburg-Ottoman alliance in the First World War which marked the end of the *ghāzī* state, but Ottoman acceptance of a demarcated frontier at the instance of the selfsame Austrian Habsburgs and their allies in the Holy Alliance, in the treaties signed at Karlowitz in 1699.

It is the merit of Abou-el-Haj's article, referred to above, that it brings out this point so forcefully. With Karlowitz the open frontier, as a zone for irregular military activity – as a *ghāzī* frontier if one must call it that – and as a rallying-ground for the continuous *Kleinkrieg* (see glossary) into enemy ('infidel') territory, was finally closed, through Ottoman official acceptance of the idea of a demarcated frontier, a continuing peace, and respect for the territorial integrity of neighbouring states. Revolts against the Karlowitz settlement prove the point: the unsuccessful attempt fomented amongst the 'wild' Nogay Tatars of the Bessarabian marches by the Khan of the Crimea and the Ottoman grand vizier Dal Taban Mustafa Pasha, documented by Abou-el-Haj, and the successful revolt of 1703, which brought down the sultan Mustafā II and the Ottoman ministers who had engineered the Karlowitz settlement.[56]

In this sense the '*ghāzī* state' mentality endured in the official Ottoman mind until 1699; similarly, Wittek's emphasis on a strict dichotomy between Ottoman history before and after 1453 – the '*ghāzī* state' and the 'Islamic Empire' phases – may be seen to be misplaced: the ideological continuities were much greater than he assumed. Equally, Inalcık's definition of the period 1300–1600 as the 'classical age' of Ottoman history, which has gained wide acceptance, should perhaps be revised.[57] As a political entity dominated by the idea of *ghazā* – a fact tacitly admitted even by so severe a critic of Wittek as Imber[58] – the Ottoman state from 1300 to 1700 possesses a unity hardly affected by the wildly fluctuating episodic elements subsumed under such overworked categories as 'rise' and 'decline', and apparently brought to an end only by the heroic failure of the Köprülü grand viziers' attempt, between 1656 and 1699, to bring about a *sharī'a*- and *ghazā*-based *renovatio imperii*.[59]

Conclusions, Retrospective and Prospective

But was the Ottoman *uj* a unique institution? So far little has been said about it in a comparative context, except within the linear tradition leading from the classical Islamic *thaghr*. Dyschronic parallels, however, keep suggesting themselves. Particularly fruitful is the function or character of the Ottoman frontier as a *refugium* for millenary or messianic movements, the adherents of which migrate *within* a frontier zone in search of a spiritual Eldorado. A paper by the Brazilian sociologist José de Souza Martins on popular religious movements in Amazonia in the first half of the twentieth century raises fascinating parallels with what we know of social conditions in the remoter regions of the Ottoman Balkans in the fifteenth century,[60] and it is tempting to point out some other dyschronic parallels between Spanish expansion in the New World and Ottoman expansion in the Islamic 'new world' in Rumeli. It might be going too far to draw parallels between the autonomous *uj-begis*, laying the social foundations for Ottoman imperial rule in the Balkans, and the conquistadores, operating similarly at arm's length in the New World on behalf of the Spanish crown a century or so later, although the parallels of atrocities against the 'natives', ahead of the formal assumption of central state control, suggests similarities in the mentalities involved. There might not have been all that much difference between the *uj-begis'* view of Balkan native 'infidels', ripe for conversion (if we accept the Wittekian equation of Balkan conversion-zones coinciding with areas of intense *uj-begi* activity), and the conquistadores' view of the benighted – and certainly 'infidel' – 'Indians' encountered in the New World.

Nor are what may be termed the positive aspects of the process entirely dissimilar. Another Latin Americanist, Alastair Hennessy, has remarked that the middle decades of the nineteenth century in the United States saw an unprecedented rise in the estalishment of new towns. He adds that in order 'to find a comparable example we would have to go back to sixteenth-century Spanish America where the extraordinary spate of town founding was due as much to the *pobladores'* desire to achieve fame and the belief that cities were synonymous with civilisation as to functional need'.[61] It has already been emphasised how equally this is an Islamic view of urban life, and how much it correlates with the rash of town foundations across the post-Conquest Ottoman Balkans from the later fourteenth to the early sixteenth centuries. As for the *uj-begis' latifundia* (estates held as *wakf*) and the Balkan mining towns in the *uj*, refounded post-conquest by the Ottomans, such as Novo Brdo and Srebrnica: to what extent do they bear comparison with the great estates in the Spanish New World? And to what extent do the Ottomans' newly founded administrative centres such as Sarajevo equate with Hennessy's observation that 'most Latin American "cities" remained isolated outposts, many remaining static for a century or more, increasing by natural growth rather than immigration from outside'?[62] We may also ponder his further observation that, 'apart from mining cities, they tended to be commercial or bureaucratic centres'. Spanish America and the Ottoman Balkans, when viewed as 'New Worlds', seem to have possessed many characteristic features in common.

It is worth observing in conclusion that the Ottoman frontier also fits the stereotypes of other frontier societies: there exist in it (or appear to exist, following the sources) few women (and those only in stereotypical romantic roles, in the very early period), and no children.[63] Obviously this was not the case in reality. Equally, the Wittekian view of the 'hinterland' is, to say the least, inconsistent. On one hand, this land behind the frontier is the seat of what he defined as 'High Islam': orthodox, urban, civilised; on the other, it is 'Levantine', racially mixed (!), lacking in manliness, and essentially decadent. Similarly, there is an inconsistency between Wittek's view of the clear division between *dār al-Islām* and *dār al-ḥarb*, and his idea of the *uj* as a zone of transition, a 'middle ground', to adopt the most recent concept on the frontier. In this Wittek, following Bartol'd, was perhaps ahead of his time. As Professor Lambton has pointed out, 'the *thaghr* is what divides the *dār al-Islām* from the *dār al-ḥarb*. The Arab authors are very clear in this respect'.[64] She also points out that there is no clear idea of territoriality in the idea of thaghr – a view that would seem not to be supported by the Ottoman acknowledgment of the *uj* as a region capable of being ruled, at least for a time, by its own lords, the *uj-begis*, and of serving as a zone of settlement.

The historical reality of the Ottoman frontier, and what historians have made of it, is obviously in need of further serious (and serious comparative) study. Hennessy's observation that 'only by a knowledge of other [frontier zones] can the unique features of a particular frontier's development be appreciated' would appear to fit the Ottoman case exactly. What John Haldon and Hugh Kennedy term 'the most important conclusion' to their work on the Arab-Byzantine frontier in the pre-Turkish period, that while it need not be doubted that these regions were different in character from the better-protected central territories lying behind them, *we still know remarkably little about them*, also applies equally well to the Ottoman frontier in its expansionist phase.[65] What is clear is that research in this field, in both intensity and depth, lags behind comparable work done on other areas. Whether this is because of, or despite of, the fact that Wittek's concept of 'his' adopted frontier has received less critical attention from a smaller number of historians than that of Turner is a topic with potential for future development.

NOTES

* The published version of this paper reflects the intellectual stimulus afforded by the papers and resulting discussions at the original 'Frontier in Question' conference. My thanks are due in particular to the present editors and to Manuel Lucena Giraldo, Alastair Hennessy, Eduardo Manzano Moreno, José de Souza Martins, and Willard Sunderland.

1. C. Foss, 'The defenses of Asia Minor against the Turks', *Greek Orthodox Theological Review*, xxviii (1982), 145–205, and 'Byzantine Malagina and the Lower Sangarius', *AS*, xl (1990), 161–83.

2. C. Heywood, 'Between the Golden Horde and the Ilkhanate: the emergence of the Ottomans, 1298–1304', paper given at the 11th Congress of the Comité des Etudes Pré-Ottomanes et Ottomanes, Amsterdam, June 1994. Cf. works by Central Asian specialists: Z. V. Togan, 'Die Vorfahren des Osmanen in Mittelasien', *ZDMG*, xcv (1941), 367–73; O. Pritsak, 'Two migratory movements in the Eurasian steppe in the 9th–11th centuries', *Proceedings of the 26th International Congress of Orientalists, New Delhi 1964*, New Delhi 1968, ii, 157–63, repr. Pritsak, *Studies in Medieval Eurasian History*, London 1981, vi; and J. Fletcher, '[The] Turco-Mongolian monarchic tradition in the Ottoman Empire', *HUS*, iii–iv (1979–80), 236–51.

3. C. Heywood, 'Wittek and the Austrian tradition', *JRAS*, 2nd ser. (1988, 1), 7–25, including further references for Wittek's career and publications; Wittek's own bibliography of his works on Ottoman history is in 'Schriftenverzeichnis, 1921–1966', *WZKM*, lxviii (1976), 1–7.

4. The opening words of *An Economic and Social History of the Ottoman Empire 1300–1914*, ed. H. Inalcık with D. Quataert, Cambridge 1994, 11.

5. F. J. Turner, 'The significance of the frontier in American history', *The Frontier in American History*, New York 1920, 1–38.

6. C. Heywood, '"Boundless dreams of the Levant": Paul Wittek, the *George-Kreis* and the writing of Ottoman history', *JRAS* (1989, 1), 32–50, and 'Wittek and the Austrian tradition'.

7. In marked contrast to the history of the Asia Minor frontier between Islam and Christendom in the seventh to eleventh centuries, preceding the Turkish conquest of Anatolia. More recent studies include A. Pertusi, 'Tra storia e leggenda: akritai e gazi sulle frontera orientali di Bizansio', *Actes du XIVᵉ Congrès International des Études Byzantines, Bucarest, 6–12 septembre, 1971*, ed. M. Berza and E. Stanescu, Bucarest 1974, i, 237–84; J. F. Haldon and H. Kennedy, 'The Arab-Byzantine frontier in the eighth and ninth centuries: military organization and society in the borderlands', *Recueil des travaux de l'Institut d'Études Byzantines*, xix (1980), 79–116; C. E. Bosworth, 'The city of Tarsus and the Arab-Byzantine frontiers', *Oriens*, xxxiii (1992), 268–86, and 'Abū 'Amr 'Uthmān al-Ṭarsūsī's *Siyar al-Thughūr* and the last years of Arab rule in Tarsus (fourth/tenth century)', *Graeco-Arabica*, v (1993), 183–95. Cf. Wittek on the Ottoman frontier: 'Die Glaubenskämpfer im Osmanenstaat', Oostersch Genootschap in Nederland, *Verslag van het VIIIe Congres, Leiden, 6–8 jan. 1936*, Leiden 1936, 2–7; 'Deux chapitres de l'histoire des Turcs de

Roum', *Byzantion*, XI (1936), 285–319; 'De la défaite d'Ankara à la prise de Constantinople', *REI*, XII (1938), 1–34; *Rise*.

8. R. A. Abou-el-Haj, 'The formal closure of the Ottoman frontier in Europe: 1699–1703', *JAOS*, LXXXIX (1969), 467–75.

9. Turner, 'Frontier in American history', 3.

10. Arabic *ḥadd*, pl. *ḥudūd*, with a multiplicity of meanings; Greek *sínoron*, 'conterminus' > 'boundary', cf. P. Wittek, 'Zur einigen frühosmanischen Urkunden (VI)', *WZKM*, LVIII (1962), 175, n. 27. The terms were applied mainly in defining local boundaries in Ottoman endowment deeds (*vaḳf-nāme*). On boundaries, legal and physical, in Ottoman usage: K. Kreiser, 'Osmanische Grenzbeschreibungen', *Studi preottomani e ottomani*, Naples 1976, 165–72.

11. G. Clauson, *An Etymological Dictionary of Pre-Thirteenth-Century Turkish*, Oxford 1972, 17–18. Modern Turkish: *uc*.

12. Arabic *thaghr*, pl. *thughūr*: M. Bonner, 'The naming of the frontier: *ʿawāṣim*, *thughūr*, and the Arab geographers', *BSOAS*, LVII (1994), 12–24. The semantic development in classical Arabic of the basic concept of *thaghr*, from 'the front teeth' via 'a gap [in teeth, for example]' and 'a gap [part of a country from which enemy invasion is feared]' to 'the frontier of a hostile country' and 'a place that is a boundary between the countries of the Muslims and the unbelievers' is clear-cut: E. W. Lane, *An Arabic-English Lexicon*, 8 vols, London 1863, repr. Beirut 1968, I, 338–9. For the historical background: E. Hönigmann, '*thughur*', *EI*. Thaghr and *uj* were regarded as synonymous as early as the eleventh century: Maḥmūd al-Kaşgarī defined *u:ç é:l* as *al-thaghr*, 'borderland', *Divanü Lugat-at-Türk tercümesi*, ed. B. Atalay, Ankara 1940–43, I, 44.

13. Under the Ottomans grants of *ʿahd-nāmes* (in effect, peace treaties) to neighbouring tributary princes were almost invariably the first stage in the process of absorption and conquest. H. Inalcık, '*dār al-ʿahd*', *EI*, new edn, with further references, and Inalcık's 'Ottoman methods of conquest', *Studia Islamica*, II (1953), 103–29.

14. Summarised in A. K. S. Lambton, 'Islamic Mirrors for Princes', *Theory and Practice in Medieval Persian Government*, London 1980, VI, 420, 426–36, 438–9.

15. Lambton, 'Mirrors', 428, 438.

16. C. Imber, 'The legend of Osman Gazi', *The Ottoman Emirate (1300–1389)*, ed. E. Zachariadou, Rethymnon 1993, 73–4.

17. *Byzantion*, XI (1936), 285–319, repr. P. Wittek, *La formation de l'Empire ottoman*, London 1982, I.

18. Wittek, 'Deux chapitres', 311.

19. P. Wittek, 'Glaubenskämpfer', 2–7.

20. Wittek, 'Deux chapitres', 318–19.

21. Wittek, 'Deux chapitres', 319.

22. Wittek, 'Deux chapitres', 316. To what extent the social situation in Anatolia before the later eleventh century could (or should) be compared with that on the Ottoman Empire's European frontiers from the later fifteenth century cannot be settled here. See Bosworth, 'Al-Ṭarsūsīs Siyar al-Thughūr'; Y. Dedes, *Baṭṭāl-nāme*, Cambridge, Mass. 1996, I, 13–14.

23. Y. Bregel, 'Turko-Mongol influences in Central Asia', *Turko-Persia in Historical Perspective*, ed. R. L. Canfield, Cambridge 1991, 53–77.
24. C. Cahen, *La Turquie pré-ottomane*, Paris 1988.
25. Heywood, '"Boundless dreams of the Levant"'.
26. Principally by the Turkish nationalist historian Meḥmed Fuʿād (Mehmet Fuat Köprülü), 'The question of the ethnic origin of the Ottoman Empire' [in Turkish], *BTTK*, VII, 28 (1943), 285–303; and by Wittek's former collaborator, the German Ottomanist Friedrich Giese, who wrote a highly critical review of Wittek's 1932 monograph on the fourteenth-century western Anatolian emirate of Menteshe, analysed in my '"Boundless dreams of the Levant"', 46–8.
27. For example, obituary notices by J. Wansbrough and others (references in my 'Wittek and the Austrian tradition').
28. Gy. Káldy-Nagy, 'The Holy War (*jihād*) in the first centuries of the Ottoman Empire', *HUS*, II–IV (1979–80); also in *Eucharisterion: essays presented to Omeljan Pritsak on his sixtieth birthday*, 2 vols, Cambridge, Mass. 1981, 467–73.
29. R. P. Lindner, 'Stimulus and justification in early Ottoman history', *The Greek Orthodox Theological Review*, XXVII, 2 (1982), 207–24, and *Nomads and Ottomans in Medieval Anatolia*, Bloomington 1983, 1–9, where he seeks to re-establish a species of tribalism as a basis for the early Ottoman state.
30. Published versions of critical papers from the *Wittek-Tagung*: Heywood, '"Boundless dreams of the Levant"', and C. Imber, 'Paul Wittek's "De la défaite d'Ankara à la prise de Constantinople', *OsmAr*, V (1986), 65–81. Cf. J. Wansbrough, 'Paul Wittek and Richard Hakluyt, a tale of two empires', *OsmAr*, VII–VIII (1988), 55–70. Imber: see esp. 'Ottoman dynastic myths', *Turcica*, XIX (1987), 7–27; 'Legend of Osman Gazi'; 'Canon and apocrypha in early Ottoman history', *Studies in Ottoman History in Honour of Professor V. L. Ménage*, ed. C. Heywood and C. Imber, Istanbul 1994, 117–37. Cf. H. Inalcık, 'Osmān Ghāzī's siege of Nicaea and the Battle of Baphaeus', *Ottoman Emirate*, ed. Zachariadou, 77–99, and 'How to read ʿAshık Pasha-Zāde's history', *Ménage Festschrift*, ed. Heywood and Imber, 139–56. R. C. Jennings, 'Some thoughts on the Gazi-thesis', *WZKM*, LXXVI (1986), 151–61.
31. Heywood, 'Wittek and the Austrian tradition'.
32. Fletcher, 'Turko-Mongolian kingship'.
33. W. Eberhard, *Das Toba-Reich Nordchinas*, Leiden 1949. On Nogay and his 'state': G. Vernadsky, *The Mongols and Russia*, New Haven 1953, 163–89. The possibility of links between the collapse of Nogay's steppe imperium in 1298–99 and the foundation of the Ottoman beylik are explored in my 'Emergence of the Ottomans'.
34. Lindner, 'Stimulus and justification'; Imber, 'Wittek's "De la défaite"', 68ff; Jennings, 'Some thoughts on the Gazi-thesis'.
35. Imber, 'Legend of Osman Gazi', 73–4.
36. *Rise*, 14–15.
37. *Rise*, 53 n. 27.
38. *Rise*, 15.
39. *Rise*, 14.

40. *Rise*, 15.
41. Recent strong criticism of the historicity of the Brusa inscription: Jennings, 'Some thoughts on the Gazi-thesis', 154–5. Wittek's use of Aḥmedī: Imber, 'Ottoman dynastic myths'. On the nature and function of, *inter alia*, Ottoman epigraphy: R. Ettinghausen, 'Arabic epigraphy: communication or symbolic affirmation', *Near Eastern Numismatics, Iconography, Epigraphy and History: Studies in Honor of George C. Miles*, ed. D. R. Kouymjian, Beirut 1974, 297–317.
42. M. Balivet, 'Culture ouverte et échanges inter-religieux dans les villes ottomanes du xivᵉ siècle', *Ottoman Emirate*, ed. Zachariadou, 2–3.
43. I. Beldiceanu-Steinherr, 'Seyyid ʿAlī Sultan d'après les registres ottomans: l'installation de l'Islam hétérodoxe en Thrace', *The Via Egnatia under Ottoman Rule 1380–1699*, ed. E. Zachariadou, Rethymnon 1996, 45–66.
44. Beldiceanu-Steinherr, 'Seyyid ʿAli Sultan', 50.
45. For instance, the frontier epic or wondertale of the *Baṭṭāl-nāme*, retelling, in unusually violent imagery, the *gesta* of the semi-legendary figure of Seyyid Baṭṭāl *Ghāzī*. Dedes, *Baṭṭāl-nāme*, i, 1.
46. V. Demetriades, 'Vakıfs along the Via Egnatia', *Via Egnatia*, ed. Zachariadou, 90–5; 'Problems of land-owning and population in the area of Gazi Evrenos Bey's wakf', *Balkan Studies*, xxii (1981), 43–57; 'The tomb of Ghazi Evrenos Bey at Yenitsa and its inscription', *BSOAS*, xxxix (1972), 328–32; M. Kiel, 'Ottoman building activity along the Via Egnatia: the cases of Pazargah, Kavala and Ferecik', *Via Egnatia*, ed. Zachariadou, 145–58; 'Yenice-i Vardar: a forgotten Turkish cultural centre in Macedonia in the 15th and 16th centuries', *Studia Byzantina et Neohellenica Neerlandica*, iii (1971), 300–27; 'Observations on the history of northern Greece during the Turkish rule: Komotini and Serres', *Balkan Studies*, xii (1971), 415–62; E. Balta, *Les Vakıfs de Serres et de sa région (XVᵉ et XVIᵉ s.)*, Athens 1995.
47. G. E. Rothenberg, *The Austrian Military Border in Croatia, 1522–1747*, Urbana 1960; O. Subtelny, *Ukraine: a history*, Toronto 1988, 105ff. For the Ottoman-Cossack frontier in the early seventeenth century: V. Ostapchuk, 'An Ottoman Gazānāme on Ḥalīl Paša's naval campaign against the Cossacks (1621)', *HUS*, xiv (1990), 482–521; G. M. Meredith-Owens, 'Kenʿān Pasha's expedition against the Cossacks', *BMQ*, xxiv (1964), 76–82; L. A. Hajda, 'Two Ottoman Gazanames concerning the Chyhyryn campaign of 1678', Ph.D. diss., Harvard University 1984. On Ottoman attitudes to their northern frontier: A. W. Fisher, 'Muscovite-Ottoman relations in the sixteenth and seventeenth centuries', *HI*, i (1973), 207–17; I. M. Kunt, 'An interpretation of 17th-century Ottoman northern policy' [in Turkish], *BÜD*, iv–v (1976–7), 111–16. For the actualities of Ottoman administration on the Hungarian frontier: *Türkische Schriften aus dem Archive des Palatins Nikolaus Esterházy*, ed. L. Fekete, Budapest 1932; G. Bayerle, *Ottoman Diplomacy in Hungary: letters from the Pashas of Buda, 1590–1593*, Bloomington 1972. For Ottoman garrison life on the Hungarian frontier in the later sixteenth century, see the Ottoman documents published by C. Römer, *Osmanische Festungsbesatzungen in Ungarn zur Zeit Murāds III*.

dargestellt anhand von Petitionen zur Stellenvergabe, Wien 1995; and on the remotest Ottoman frontier in Upper Egypt: M. Hinds and V. Ménage, *Qaṣr Ibrīm in the Ottoman Period: Turkish and further Arabic documents*, London 1991.

48. B. Isaac, *The Limits of Empire*, Oxford 1990; 'The meaning of the terms *limes* and *limitanei*', *Journal of Roman Studies*, LXXVIII (1988), 15–47; C. R. Whittaker, *Frontiers of the Roman Empire: a social and economic study*, London 1994. I am indebted to Daniel Power for these references.

49. O. Lattimore, 'Origins of the Great Wall of China: a frontier concept in theory and practice', *Geographical Review*, XXVII, 4 (1937), repr. *Studies in Frontier History: collected papers 1928–58*, London 1962, 98–118. The long-standing view of 'the' Great Wall as tangible reality rather than a mental divide, at least in the pre-Ming period, has also been convincingly deconstructed: A. Waldron, *The Great Wall of China: from history to myth*, Cambridge 1990.

50. For a general discussion of cultural transference from the steppe to the settled lands in terms of government, J. Fletcher, 'Turco-Mongolian king-ship', and I. Ecsedy, 'Nomads in history and historical research', *AOASH*, XXXV (1981), 201–27, esp. 215ff. For steppe attitudes see D. Sinor, 'Inner Asian warriors', *JAOS*, CI (1981), 133–44; 'Horse and pasture in Inner Asian history', *Oriens Extremus*, XIX (1972), 171–83.

51. Ö. L. Barkan, 'Osmanlı Imparatorluğunda bir iskân ve kolonizasyon metodu olarak vakiflar ve temlikler', *VD*, II (1942), 279–386 (French summary, 'Les fondations pieuses comme méthode de peuplement et de colonisation', 59–65, separate pagination).

52. *Rise*, 2–6; cf. Imber, 'Wittek's "De la défaite"', 68.

53. *Rise*, 5.

54. *Rise*, 3.

55. Heywood, '"Boundless dreams of the Levant"' and 'Wittek and the Austrian tradition'.

56. Abou-el-Haj, 'Closure of the Ottoman frontier', 472–4.

57. H. Inalcık, *The Ottoman Empire: the classical age, 1300–1600*, London 1972.

58. Imber, 'Ottoman dynastic myth', *passim*.

59. In fact, on the post-Karlowitz frontiers, *ghāzī* attitudes endured, as in Bosnia: C. Heywood, 'Bosnia under Ottoman rule, 1463–1800', *The Muslims of Bosnia-Herzegovina: their historic development from the Middle Ages to the dissolution of Yugoslavia*, ed. M. Pinson, Cambridge, Mass. 1994, 22–53.

60. J. de Souza Martins, 'The time of the frontier: a return to the controversy concerning the historical periods of the expansion frontier and the pioneer frontier', paper given at the 'Frontier in Question' conference, University of Essex, April 1995.

61. A. Hennessy, *The Frontier in Latin American History*, London 1975, 143.

62. Hennessy, *Latin American Frontier*, 143.

63. P. Wittek, 'The taking of Aydos Castle: a ghazi legend and its transforma-tion', *Arabic and Islamic Studies in Honor of Hamilton A. R. Gibb*, ed. G. Makdisi, Leiden 1965, 662–72. Wittek's analysis of the sources is taken

further in: W. Hickman, 'The taking of Aydos Castle: further considerations on a chapter from Aşıkpaşazāde', *JAOS*, xcix (1979), 399–407.

64. A. K. S. Lambton, *State and Government in Medieval Islam*, Oxford 1981, 13, 18–19.

65. Haldon and Kennedy, 'Arab-Byzantine frontier', 116, my emphasis.

SELECT BIBLIOGRAPHY

Unpublished and published primary sources are listed by article, in the order in which they appear. The secondary bibliography covers the entire work.

Primary Sources

1. Introduction, D. J. Power

Published sources

Anglo-Scottish Relations, 1174–1328: some selected documents, ed. and trans. E. L. G. Stones, Oxford 1965.

2. E. Manzano Moreno, 'Islam and Christianity in the Iberian Peninsula'

Published sources

Ibn Ḥayyān, *al-Muqtabis min anbā'ahl al-Andalus*, ed. Maḥmūd ʿAlī Makki, Cairo 1390/1971.
    al-Muqtabis min fī ta'rīj rijāl al-Andalus, ed. M. Martínez Antuña, Paris 1937.
    al-Muqtabis, ed. P. Chalmeta, F. Corriente, and M. Sobh, Madrid 1979.
Ibn Manẓūr, *Lisān al-ʿarab*, Beirut 1935.

3. N. Standen, '(Re)Constructing the Frontiers of Tenth-Century North China'

Published sources

Cefu yuangui 冊府元龜 [*The Magic Mirror in the Palace of Books*], 1000j., comp. Wang Qinruo 王欽若 et al., 1013. Beijing 1960.
Jiu Wudai shi 舊五代史 [*Old History of the Five Dynasties*], 150j., comp. Xue Juzheng 薛居正 et al., 974. Beijing 1976.
Liao shi 遼史 [*Liao History*], 116j., comp. Toghto 脱脱, Ouyang Xuan 歐陽玄 et al., 1344. Beijing 1974.
Liao shi shiyi 遼史拾遺 [*Anecdotes Not Recorded in the Liao History*], 24j., Li E 厲鶚, 1743. Congshu jicheng chubian 叢書集成初編, Shanghai 1936.

Liao shi shiyi bu 遼史拾遺補 [*Supplement to the* Anecdotes *Not Recorded in the Liao History*], 5j., Yang Fuji 楊復吉, 1794. Congshu jicheng chubian 叢書集成初編, Shanghai 1936.

Qidan guo zhi 契丹國志 [*Kitan History*], 27j., Ye Longli 葉隆禮, 1247? Shanghai 1985.

Quan Tang wen 全唐文 [*Collected Prose of the Tang*], 1000j., Qing. Qinding 欽定 reproduction of 1814 ed, Taibei 1965.

Shuowen jiezi zhu 說文解字注 [*Analytical Dictionary of Characters*], comp. Xu Shen 許慎, *c.* AD 100. Ed. Duan Yucai 段玉裁, 15j., Shanghai 1981, reproduction of 1815 edn.

Song shi 宋史 [*Song History*], 496j, comp. Toghto 脫脫, Ouyang Xuan 歐陽玄 et al., 1345. Beijing 1977.

Wudai hui yao 五代會要 [*Documents on Institutions in the Five Dynasties*], 30j., Wang Pu 王溥, 963. Shanghai 1978.

Wudai shi bu 五代史補 [*Supplement to the History of the Five Dynasties*], 5j., Tao Yue 陶岳, 1012. Chanhua an congshu 懺花庵叢書, n.d.

Xin Wudai shi 新五代史 [*New History of the Five Dynasties*], 74j., Ouyang Xiu, 歐陽修 1073. Beijing 1974.

Zizhi tongjian 資治通鑑 [*Comprehensive Mirror to Aid in Government*], 294j., Sima Guang 司馬光 et al., 1084. Beijing 1956.

4. P. Stephenson, 'The Byzantine Frontier at the Lower Danube'

Published sources

Anne Comnène, Alexiade, ed. and trans. B. Leib, 3 vols, Paris 1937, trans. E. R. A. Sewter, *The Alexiad of Anna Comnena*, London 1969.

Constantine Porphyrogenitus De administrando imperio, ed. G. Moravcsik, trans. R. J. H. Jenkins, *CFHB*, 2nd edn, I, Washington DC 1967.

H. Gelzer, 'Ungedruckte und wenig bekannte Bistümerverzeichnisse der orientalischen Kirche', *Byzantinische Zeitschrift*, II (1893), 42–6.

Historia rerum in partibus transmarinis gestarum, recueil des historiens de croisades, historiens occidentaux, Académie des Inscriptions et Belles-Lettres, Paris 1844, trans. E. A. Babcock and A. C. Krey, *William of Tyre: history of deeds done beyond the sea*, London 1943.

Ioannis Cinnami epitome rerum ab Ioanne et Alexio Comnenis gestarum, ed. A. Meineke, *CSHB*, Bonn 1836.

Ioannis Euchaitorum metropolitae quae in cod. Vat. gr. 676 supersunt, ed. P. Lagarde, Göttingen 1882.

Ioannis Skylitzae synopsis historiarum, ed. J. Thurn, *CFHB*, V, Berlin and New York 1973.

La vie de Saint Cyrille le Philéote moine byzantin (d. 1110), ed. E. Sargologos, *Subsidia hagiographica*, XXXIX, Brussels 1964.

Leonis Diaconi Caloensis historiae libri decem, ed. C. B. Hase, *CSHB*, Bonn 1828.

Les listes de préséance byzantines des IXe et Xe siècles, ed. and trans. N. Oikonomides, Paris 1972.

Le traité sur la guerilla de l'empereur Nicéphore Phocas (963–969), ed. and trans. G. Dagron and H. Mihăescu, Paris 1986.

Liuprand of Cremona, *Opera*, ed. I. Bekker, *MGH SS in usum scholarum*, Hanover and Leipzig 1915, trans. F. A. Wright, *The Works of Liutprand of Cremona*, London 1930.

Michaelis Attaliotae historia, ed. I. Bekker, *CSHB*, Bonn 1853.

Michael Psellus, *Chronographia*, ed. E. Rénauld, Paris 1928, trans. E. R. A. Sewter, *Michael Psellus: fourteen Byzantine rulers*, London 1966.

Historia syntomos, ed. W. J. Aerts, *CFHB*, xxx, Berlin and New York 1990.

Notitiae episcopatuum ecclesiae Constantinopolitanae, ed. J. Darrouzès, Paris 1981, 344–50.

Nicetae Choniatae historia, ed. J. Van Dieten, *CFHB*, xi: 1, Berlin 1975.

Povest' Vremennykh Let, ed. V. P. Adrianova and D. Likhachev, Moscow and Leningrad 1950, trans. S. H. Cross and O. P. Sherbowitz-Wetzor, *The Russian Primary Chronicle*, Cambridge, Mass. 1953.

Suidae lexicon, ed. A. Adler, 5 vols, Leipzig 1935.

Three Byzantine Military Treatises, ed. and trans. G. T. Dennis, *CFHB*, xxv, Washington DC 1985.

5. D. J. Power, 'French and Norman Frontiers in the Central Middle Ages'

Unpublished sources

Rouen, Bibliothèque Municipale:
Y 51 (cartulary of the abbey of Fécamp).
Y 52 (cartulary of the abbey of St-Georges-de-Boscherville).
Évreux, Archives de l'Eure:
H 319 (cartulary of the abbey of Estrée).

Published sources

Cartulaire de la léproserie du Grand-Beaulieu, ed. R. Merlet and M. Josselin, Chartres 1909.

The Charters of the Anglo-Norman Earls of Chester, ed. G. Barraclough et al., Chester 1988.

Chronica Magistri Rogeri de Hovedene, ed. W. Stubbs, 4 vols, London 1868–71.

Chronique de Robert de Torigni, ed. L. Delisle, 2 vols, Paris 1871–72.

Diplomatic Documents 1101–1272, ed. P. Chaplais, i, London 1964.

The Ecclesiastical History of Orderic Vitalis, ed. M. Chibnall, 6 vols, Oxford 1969–80.

Froissart, Jean, *Chroniques*, ed. G. T. Diller, 4 vols to date, Geneva 1991–.

The Historical Works of Ralph de Diceto, ed. W. Stubbs, 2 vols, London 1876.

Layettes du Trésor des Chartes, ed. A. Teulet et al., 5 vols, Paris 1863–1909.

Œuvres de Rigord et de Guillaume le Breton, ed. H.-F. Delaborde, 2 vols, Paris 1882–85.

Patent Rolls (Henry III) 1225–32, ed. HMSO, London 1903.

Recueil des actes de Philippe Auguste, ed. H.-F. Delaborde et al., 4 vols, Paris 1916–79.

Recueil des actes des ducs de Normandie de 911 à 1066, ed. M. Fauroux, Caen 1961.
Rodulfus Glaber, *Opera*, ed. J. France, Oxford 1989.
Rotuli Litterarum Patentium, ed. T. Duffus Hardy, London 1835.
Suger, *Vie de Louis le Gros*, ed. H. Waquet, Paris 1929, trans. R. C. Cusimano and J. Moorhead, *The Deeds of Louis the Fat*, Washington DC 1992.
William of Jumièges, *Gesta Normannorum Ducum*, ed. E. M. C. van Houts, 2 vols, Oxford 1992–95.

6. R. Amitai-Preiss, 'Northern Syria between the Mongols and Mamluks'

Unpublished sources

Ibn al-Furāt, *Ta'rīkh al-duwal wa'l-mulūk*, MS Österreichische Nationalbibliothek (Vienna). Flügel no. 814.

Published sources

Abū Shāma, *Dhayl ʿalā al-rawḍatayn*, Cairo 1947.
Ghāzī b. al-Wāsiṭī, *Kitāb al-radd ʿalā ahl al-dhimma wa-man tabaʿahum*, in R. Gottheil, 'An answer to the Dhimmis', *JAOS*, XLI (1921), 383–457.
Ibn ʿAbd al-Ẓāhir, Muḥyī al-Dīn, *Al-Rawḍ al-zāhir fī sīrat al-malik al-ẓāhir*, ed. ʿA-ʿA. al-Khuwayṭir, Riyad 1396 AH/1976.
   Tashrīf al-ayyām wa'l-ʿuṣùr fī sīrat al-malik al-manṣūr, ed. M. Kāmil, Cairo 1961.
Ibn Abī 'l-Faḍā'il, Mufaḍḍal, *Al-Nahj al-sadīd wa'l-durr al-farīd fīmā baʿda ibn al-ʿamīd*, ed. E. Blochet, 'Histoire des sultans mamlouks', *Patrologia Orientalis*, XII, XIV, XX (1919–28).
Ibn al-Athīr, *Al-Kāmil fī 'l-ta'rīkh*, Beirut 1966.
Ibn al-Furāt, *Ta'rīkh al-duwal wa'l-mulūk*, VII, ed. C. Zurayk, Beirut 1942.
Ibn Shaddād al-Ḥalabī, *Al-Aʿlāq al-khaṭīra fī dhikr umarā' al-shām wa'l-jazīra*, III, ed. Y. ʿAbbāra, Damascus 1978.
   Al-Aʿlāq al-khaṭīra fī dhikr umarā' al-shām wa'l-jazīra, in A.-M. Eddé, 'La description de la Syrie du Nord de ʿIzz al-Dīn ibn Šaddād', *Bulletin d'études orientales*, XXXII–XXXIII (1981), 265–402.
   Ta'rīkh al-malik al-ẓāhir (Die Geschichte des Sultans Baibars), ed. A. Ḥuṭayṭ, Wiesbaden 1983.
Ibn Taghrī Birdī, *Al-Nujūm al-zāhira fī mulūk miṣr wa'l-qāhira*, repr. n.d. of Cairo 1930–56.
Juvaini [= Juwaynī], *The History of the World-Conqueror*, trans. J. A. Boyle, Manchester 1958.
Al-Kutubī, *ʿUyūn al-tawarikh*, XX, ed. F. N. Sāmir and ʿA-M. Dāwūd, Baghdad 1980.
Al-Maqrīzī, *Kitāb al-sulūk li-maʿrifat duwal al-mulāk*, ed. M. M. Ziyāda and S. ʿA-F. ʿĀshūr, Cairo 1934–73.
Rashīd al-Dīn, *Jāmiʿ al-tawārikh*, III, ed. ʿA-ʿA. ʿAlīzādah, Baku 1957.
Shāfiʿ b. ʿAlī, *Ḥusn al-manāqib al-sirriyya al-muntazaʿa min al-sīra al-ẓāhiriyya*, ed. ʿA-ʿA. al-Khuwayṭir, Riyad 1976.
Al-ʿUmarī, Ibn Faḍl Allāh, *Al-Taʿrīf fī al-muṣṭalaḥ al-sharīf*, Cairo 1312 AH/1894–5.
Al-Yūnīnī, *Dhayl mir'at al-zamān fī ta'rīkh al-aʿyān*, Hyderabad 1954–61.

7. S. G. Ellis, 'The English State and its Frontiers, 1300–1600'

Unpublished sources

Belfast, Public Record Office of Northern Ireland, Kildare deeds.
Carlisle, Cumbria Record Office, MS D/Ay/1/180.
Dublin, National Library of Ireland, Ormond deeds.
Dublin, Trinity College Dublin, Red Book of the Earls of Kildare.
Durham, Durham University, Department of Palaeography and Diplomatic, Howard of Naworth MS C/201/4A.
London, British Library, Harleian MS 3756, Lansdowne MS I.
London, Public Record Office, Chancery Lane, C 85, C 142, E 30, E 150, SC 11, SP 1, SP 65.
York, Castle Howard Archives, MS F1/5/5.

Published sources

Calendar of Documents Relating to Scotland, 5 vols, Edinburgh 1881–1987.
Calendar of Inquisitions Post Mortem, Henry VII, 3 vols, London 1898–1955.
Calendar of Ormond Deeds, ed. E. Curtis, 6 vols, Dublin 1932–43.
Calendar of Patent Rolls, 1232–47 [etc.], London 1906–.
Correspondence of Matthew Parker, D. D. Archbishop of Canterbury, ed. John Bruce and T. T. Perowne, Parker Soc., Cambridge 1853.
Crown Surveys of Lands, 1540–41, ed. G. Mac Niocaill, Dublin 1992.
Letters and Papers, Foreign and Domestic, Reign of Henry VIII, 21 vols, London 1862–1932.
Musters for Northumberland, 1538, *Archaeologia Aeliana*, 1st ser., IV (1855).
'Of the manner of keeping warden courts', printed in J. Nicolson and R. Burn, *The History and Antiquities of the Counties of Westmorland and Cumberland*, 2 vols, London, 1777, I, ch. 3.
The Red Book of the Earls of Kildare, ed. G. Mac Niocaill, Dublin 1964.
Sir Robert Bowes and Sir Ralph Ellerker's survey of the east and middle marches, 1542, printed in J. Hodgson, *A History of Northumberland*, 3 pts in 7 vols, Newcastle 1820–25, III: II, 171–248.
The State Papers and Letters of Sir Ralph Sadler, ed. A. Clifford, 2 vols, Edinburgh 1809.
Statute Rolls of the Parliament of Ireland . . . Reign of Edward IV, ed. H. F. Berry and J. F. Morrissey, 2 vols, Dublin 1914–39.
Statute Rolls of the Parliament of Ireland, Reign of Henry VI, ed. H. F. Berry, Dublin 1910.

8. S. C. Rowell, 'The Lithuano-Prussian Forest Frontier, 1422–1600'

Unpublished sources

Berlin, Geheimes Staatsarchiv, Preussische Kulturbesitz.
Ordens Briefarchiv (OBA), 6277, 8330, 8458, 8465, 12305, 16338, 16569, 16881, 16938, 16948, 17737, 19574, 20909, 20917, 20920, 21013, 21025, 21357, 21368, 21554, 21576, 21652, 21701, 21702, 21707, 24134, 25972,

27669, 27670, 27874, 27879, 27945, 28156, 28183, 28189, 28190, 28196, 28200.
OrdensFolianten (OrdF) 14, 15, 16, 18b.
Ostpreussische Folianten (OstF) 42, 49, 51, 52, 53, 54, 911a.
RIGA, Latvijas valsts vestures arhiva:
F673 ap.1 liet.307.

Published sources

Acta Alexandri magni ducis Lithuaniae, ed. F. Papee, Kraków 1927.
Acta Tomiciana, xvi:1, ed. W. Pociecha, Wrocław-Kraków-Poznan 1960.
Acta Tomiciana, xvii, ed. W. Pociecha, Wrocław-Kraków-Poznan 1966.
Akty izdavaemye Vilenskoiu Komisseiu dlia razbora drevnikh aktov, xxv *(Inventari i razgranichitel'nye akty)*, Vilnius 1898.
Akty litovsko-russkago gosudarstva (XIV–XVI st.), ed. M. V. Dovnar-Zapolsky, Moscow 1899.
Bretkūnas, J., *Rinktiniai Raštai*, ed. J. Palionis and J. Zukauskaitė, Vilnius 1983.
Codex Mednicensis seu Samogitiae Dioecesis, ed. P. Jatulis, i, Rome 1984.
Dokumenty Moskovskogo Arkhiva Ministerstva Iustitsii, i, Moscow 1897.
Elementa ad fontium editiones (Documenta ex Archivio Regiomontano ad Poloniam spectantia), ed. C. Lanckoronska, 75 vols, Rome 1973–91.
Istorijos Archyvas, i *(XVI amžiaus Lietuvos inventoriai)*, ed. K. Jablonskis, Kaunas 1934.
Joannes Vislicius, *Bellum prutenum*, *Corpus antiquissimorum poetarum Poloniae latinorum*, ed. B. Kruczkiewicz, Kraków 1887.
Jonas Lasickis, *Apie žemaičių, kitų sarmatų bei netikrų krikščionių dievus*, ed. K. Korsakas et al., Vilnius 1969.
Lietuvos mokykla ir pedagoginė mintis XIII–XVII a. Istorijos šaltinių antologija, ed. I. Lukšaitė, Vilnius 1994.
Lietuvos Metrika (1427–1506). Knyga nr. 5, Užrašymų knyga 5, ed. E. Banionis, Vilnius 1993.
Lietuvos Metrika (1528–1547) 6-oji teismų bylų knyga (Kopija-XVI a. pabaiga), ed. S. Lazutka et al., Vilnius 1995.
Lietuvos Metrika knyga nr. 564 (1553–1567). Viešujų reikalų knyga 7, ed. A. Baliulis, Vilnius 1996.
Limites Regni Poloniae et Magni Ducatus Lituaniae ex originalibus et exemplis authenticis descripti et in lucem editi, ed. M. Dogiel, Vilnius 1758.
Liv- Esth- und Kurländisches Urkundenbuch, nebst Regesten. Abteilung 1, 12 vols, ed. F. G. v. Bunge, Reval-Riga-Moscow 1853–1910, repr. Aalen 1967–81.
Martynas Mažvydas, *Katekizmas ir kiti raštai*, ed. G. Subačius, Vilnius 1993.
Nicolaus Hussovianus, *De statura, feritate ac venatione bisontis carmen*, ed. B. Kazluaskas, Vilnius 1977.
Peter von Suchenwirt, 'Von Herczog Albrechts Ritterschaft', *SRP*, ii, 164.
Prūsijos valdžios gromatos, pagraudenimai ir apsakymai lietuviams valstiečiams, ed. P. Pakarklis, Vilnius 1960.
Volovich, Grigory, *Revizia pushch' i perekhodov' zverinykh' v' byvshem' Velikom' Kniazhestve litovskom'*, Vilnius 1867.
Russkaia Istoricheskaia Biblioteka, xxx, Yur'ev 1914.

Scriptores Rerum Prussicarum, ed. F. Hirsch, M. Töppen and E. Strehlke, 5 vols, Leipzig 1861–74, repr. Frankfurt-am-Main 1965.
Senieji lietuvių skaitymai, I dalis, tekstai su įvadais, ed. J. Gerullis, Kaunas 1927.

9.   A. Williams, 'The Order of St John in the Mediterranean'

Unpublished sources

NLM AOM 70: Donation of Malta.
NLM AOM 280–296, 309: Sacra Capitula Generalia 1330–1631 and 1776.
NLM AOM 73–111: Libri Conciliorum 1459–1633.
NLM AOM 6559: Ordinationes et altre scritture concernenti il governo di Tripoli [*sic*].
NLM LIB: Codici manoscritti II Letter of Gregory XIII on Abela as Papal Nuncio.

Published sources

Abel, L., *Une mission religieuse en orient au seizième siecle: relation addressée a Sixte-Quint par l'Évêque de Sidon*, ed. and trans. A. d'Avril, Paris 1886.
Abela, G. F., *Della descrizione di Malta*, Malta 1647.
Bosio, G., *Dell'istoria della Sacra Religione e illustrissima militia di S. Gio. Gerosolimitano*, 3 vols, Rome 1594–1620.
Pauli, S., *Codice diplomatico del Sacro Militare Ordine Gerosolimitano oggi di Malta*, 2 vols, Lucca 1733–37.
Pozzo, B., *Historia della Sacra Religione di S. Giovanni Gerosolimitano detta di Malta*, 2 vols, Verona and Venice 1703–15.

Secondary Works (All Essays)

Abou-el-Haj, R. A., 'The formal closure of the Ottoman frontier in Europe: 1699–1703', *JAOS*, LXXXIX (1969), 467–75.
Amitai-Preiss, R., 'In the aftermath of ʿAyn Jālūt: the beginnings of the Mamlūk-Īlkhānid cold war', *Al-Masāq: Studie Arabo-Islamica Mediterranea*, III (1990), 1–21.
"Ayn Jālūt revisited', *Tārīḫ*, II (1991), 119–50.
Mongols and Mamluks: the Mamluk-īlkhānid war (1260–1281), Cambridge 1995.
'The Mamluk officer class during the reign of sultan Baybars', *War and Society in the Eastern Mediterranean, 7th–15th Centuries*, ed. Y. Lev, Leiden 1996.
'Ghazan, Islam and Mongol tradition: a view from the Mamluk Sultanate', *BSOAS*, LIX (1996), 1–10.
Anderson, B., *Imagined Communities: reflections on the origin and spread of nationalism*, revised edn, London 1991.
Anderson, R. C., *Naval Wars in the Levant 1559–1853*, Princeton 1952.
Ang, M. Thlick-len., 'Sung-Liao diplomacy in eleventh- and twelfth-century China: a study of the social and political determinants of foreign policy', Ph.D. diss., University of Pennsylvania 1983.
Ardener, E., 'The construction of history: "vestiges of creation"', *History and Ethnicity*, ed. E. Tonkin, M. McDonald and M. Chapman, London 1989, 22–33.

Armstrong, J. A., *Nations before Nationalism*, Chapel Hill 1982.

Arrignon, J.-P., and Duneau, J.-F., 'La frontière chez deux auteurs byzantins: Procope de Césarée et Constantin VII Porphyrogénète', *Geographica Byzantina*, ed. H. Ahrweiler, Paris 1981, 17–30.

Aubin, J., *Émirs mongols et vizirs persans dans les remous de l'acculturation*, Paris 1995.

Ayalon, D., 'The *wafidiya* in the Mamluk kingdom', *Islamic Culture*, 25 (1951), 89–104.

'The Great Yāsa of Chingiz Khān, a re-examination', *Studia Islamica*, pt A, XXXIII (1971), 97–140; pt B, XXXIV (1971), 151–80; pt C1, XXXVI (1972), 113–58; pt C2, XXXVIII (1973), 107–56.

'Preliminary remarks on the Mamlūk military institution in Islam', *War, Technology and Society in the Middle East*, ed. V. J. Parry and M. E. Yapp, London 1974, 44–58.

'The auxiliary forces of the Mamluk Sultanate', *Der Islam*, LXV (1988), 13–37.

Babinger, F., 'J. H. Mordtmann zum Gedächtnis', *MSOS*, XXXV: II (1932), 1–16.

Balon, J., 'L'organisation judiciaire des marches féodales', *Annales de la Société Archéologique de Namur*, XLVI (1951), 5–72.

Baraschi, S., and Damian, O. 'Considerations sur la céramique émaillée de Nufăru', *Dacia*, XXXVII (1993), 237–78.

Barbero, A., and Vigil, M., *Sobre los orígenes sociales de la Reconquista*, Barcelona 1974.

La formación del feudalismo en la Península Ibérica, Barcelona 1978.

Barfield, T. J., *The Perilous Frontier: nomadic empires and China, 221 BC to AD 1757*, Oxford 1989.

Barkowski, O., 'Die Besiedlung des Hauptamtes Insterburg unter Herzog Albrecht und Markgraf Georg Friedrich von Ansbach 1525–1603', *Prussia*, XXIX (1933), 159–243.

Barnea, I., 'Dinogetia et Noviodunum, deux villes byzantines du Bas-Danube', *Revue des Études Sud-Est Européenes*, IX (1971), 343–62.

'Sceaux byzantins inédits de Dobroudja', *Studies in Byzantine Sigillography*, III, ed. N. Oikonomides, Washington DC 1993, 61–5.

Barrow, G. W. S., 'The Anglo-Scottish border', *NH*, I (1966), 21–42, repr. *The Kingdom of the Scots*, London 1973, 139–61.

Barry, T., Frame, R., and Simms, K., eds, *Colony and Frontier in Medieval Ireland: essays presented to J. F. Lydon*, London 1995.

Barth, F., ed., *Ethnic Groups and Boundaries: the social organisation of cultural difference*, Bergen-Oslo 1969.

Bartlett, R., *The Making of Europe: conquest, colonisation and cultural change 950–1350*, London 1993.

Bartlett, R., and Mackay, A., eds, *Medieval Frontier Societies*, Oxford 1989.

Bates, D., *Normandy before 1066*, London 1982.

Benzoni, G., ed., *Il Mediterraneo nella seconda metà del '500 alla luce di Lepanto*, Florence 1974.

Bisson, T., 'The "Feudal Revolution"?', *Past and Present*, CXLIV (1994), 6–42.

Boch Vilá, J., 'Algunas consideraciones sobre el Ṭagr en al-Andalus y la división político administrativa de la España Musulmana', *Etudes d'Orientalisme dediées à la mémoire de Lévi Provençal*, Paris 1962, 23–33.

Bol, P. K., 'This Culture of Ours:' intellectual transitions in T'ang and Sung China, Stanford 1992.

Bonenfant, P., 'À propos des limites médiévales', Éventail de l'histoire vivant: hommage à Lucien Febvre, 2 vols, Paris 1953, 73–9.

Bonner, M., 'The naming of the frontier: ʿawāṣim, thughūr, and the Arab geographers', BSOAS, LVII: 1 (1994), 12–24.

Aristocratic Violence and Holy War: Studies in the 'jihad' and the Arab–Byzantine frontier, New Haven 1996.

Bono, S., I corsari barbareschi, Turin 1964.

Bosworth, C. E., 'Abū ʿAmr ʿUthmān al-Ṭarsūsī's Siyar al-Thughūr and the last years of Arab rule in Tarsus (fourth/tenth century)', Graeco-Arabica, V (1993), 183–95.

Boyle, J. A., 'Dynastic and political history of the Īl-Khāns', Cambridge History of Iran, V, ed. J. A. Boyle, Cambridge 1968, 303–421.

Bracewell, C. W., The Uskoks of Senj: piracy, banditry and Holy War in the sixteenth-century Adriatic, Ithaca and London 1992.

Bradshaw, B., and Morrill, J., eds, The British Problem, c.1534–1707: state formation in the Atlantic Archipelago, Basingstoke 1996.

Brady, C., The Chief Governors: the rise and fall of reform government in Tudor Ireland, 1536–1588, Cambridge 1994.

Brakas, M., Mažosios Lietuvos politinė ir diplomatinė istorija, Vilnius 1995.

Braudel, F., The Mediterranean and the Mediterranean World at the Time of Philip II, 2 vols, London 1972–73.

The Identity of France, trans. S. Reynolds, 2 vols, London 1988–90.

Brummett, P., Ottoman Seapower and Levantine Diplomacy in the Age of Discovery, Albany 1992.

'The overrated adversary: Rhodes and Ottoman naval power', Historical Journal, XXXVI (1993), 517–41.

Bur, M., 'La frontière entre la Champagne et la Lorraine du milieu du Xe siècle à la fin du XIIe siècle', Francia, IV (1976), 237–54.

La formation du comté de Champagne, Nancy 1977.

'Recherches sur la frontière dans la région mosane aux XIIe et XIIIe siècles', Actes du 103e Congrès National des Sociétés Savantes (Nancy-Metz, 1978): principautés et territoires et études d'histoire lorraine, Paris 1979, 143–60.

Burleigh, M., Prussian Society and the German Order: an aristocratic corporation in crisis, Cambridge 1984.

Bush, M. L., 'The problem of the far north: a study of the crisis of 1537 and its consequences', NH, VI (1971), 40–63.

The Government Policy of Protector Somerset, London 1975.

'Tenant right under the Tudors: a revision revised', Bulletin of the John Rylands Library, LXXVII (1995), 161–8.

Cahen, C., La Turquie pré-ottomane, Paris 1988.

Canny, N. P., Kingdom and Colony: Ireland in the Atlantic world, 1560–1800, Baltimore 1988.

Cassels, L. J., The Struggle for the Ottoman Empire 1717–1740, London 1966.

Cavaliero, R., The Last of the Crusaders: the Knights of St John and Malta in the eighteenth century, London 1960.

Cen Jiawu 岑家梧, 'Liaodai Qidan he Hanzu ji qita minzu de jingji wenhua lianxi' 遼代契丹和漢族及其他民族的經濟文化聯係, *Minzu tuanjie* 民族團結, 1963:12, 25–31.

Chalmeta, P., 'Simancas y Alhándega', *Hispania*, xxxvi (1976), 359–444.

'El concepto de Ṭaġr', *La Marche Supérieure d'al-Andalus et l'Occident Chrétien*, ed. P. Sénac, Madrid 1991, 15–27.

Chan, M. K., 'The historiography of the *Tzu-chih T'ung-chien:* a survey', *Monumenta Serica*, xxxi (1974–5), 1–38.

Chédeville, A., *Chartres et ses campagnes*, Paris 1973.

Chénon, É., 'Les marches séparantes d'Anjou, Bretagne, et Poitou', *Nouvelle Revue Historique du Droit Français et Étranger*, xvi (1892), 18–62, 165–211; xxi (1897), 62–80.

Clark, P., ed., *The Crisis of the 1590s*, London 1985.

Classen, P., 'Die Verträge von Verdun und Coulaines, 843, als politische Grundlagen des westfränkischen Reiches', *Historische Zeitschrift*, cxcvi (1963), 1–35.

Combe, E., Sauvaget, J., and Wiet, G., eds, *Répertoire chronologique d'épigraphie arabe*, Cairo 1931–.

Conway, A., *Henry VII's relations with Scotland and Ireland, 1485–98*, Cambridge 1932.

Cosgrove, A., ed., *A New History of Ireland, ii. Medieval Ireland 1169–1534*, Oxford 1987.

Coulson, C. L. H., 'Fortress-policy in Capetian tradition and Angevin practice: aspects of the conquest of Normandy by Philip Augustus', *ANS*, vi (1983), 13–38.

Crossley, P. K., 'Thinking about ethnicity in early modern China', *Late Imperial China*, xi:1 (1990), 1–35.

Curry, A. E., 'The first English standing army? Military organization in Lancastrian Normandy, 1420–1450', *Patronage, Pedigree and Power in Later Medieval England*, ed. C. Ross, Gloucester 1979, 193–214.

Davies, R. R., 'The law of the March', *Welsh History Review*, v (1971), 1–30.

Lordship and Society in the March of Wales 1282–1400, Oxford 1978.

'Kings, lords and liberties in the March of Wales, 1066–1272', *TRHS*, 5th ser., xxix (1979), 41–61.

Domination and Conquest: the experience of Ireland, Scotland and Wales 1100–1300, Cambridge 1990.

Davis, R. H. C., *The Normans and their Myth*, London 1976.

de Moxó, S., *Repoblación y sociedad en la España cristiana medieval*, Madrid 1979.

de Souza Martins, J., 'The time of the frontier: a return to the controversy concerning the historical periods of the expansion frontier and the pioneer frontier', paper given at the 'Frontier in Question' conference, University of Essex, April 1995.

Dedes Y., ed. and trans., *Baṭṭāl-nāme*, 2 vols, Cambridge, Mass. 1996.

Delaville le Roulx, J., *Les Hospitaliers à Rhodes jusqu'à la mort de Philibert de Naillac 1310–1421*, Paris 1913.

Dhondt, J., 'Essai sur l'origine de la frontière linguistique', *L'Antiquité Classique*, xvi (1947), 261–86.

Di Cosmo, N., 'Ancient Inner Asian nomads: their economic basis and its significance in Chinese history', *JAS*, liii:4 (1994), 1092–1126.

Diaconu, P., *Les Pétchènegues au Bas-Danube*, Bucharest 1970.

Diaconu, P., and Vîlceanu, D., *Păcuiul lui Soare, cetatea bizantină*, i, Bucharest 1972.

Dion, R., *Les frontières de la France*, Paris 1947.

'À propos du traité de Verdun', *Annales: Économies, Sociétés, Civilisations*, v (1950), 461–5.

Dixon, P., 'Towerhouses, pelehouses and border society', *Archaeological Journal*, cxxxvi (1979), 240–52.

Dobrovitz, M., 'The Turco-Mongolian tradition of common origin and the historiography in fifteenth century Central Asia', *AOASH*, lvii:3 (1994), 269–77.

Doerfer, G., *Türkische und mongolische Elemente in Neupersischen*, Wiesbaden 1963–75.

Dow, Tsung-i, 'The Confucian concept of a nation and its historical practice', *Asian Profile*, x:4 (1982), 347–61.

Duby, G., *La société aux XIe et XIIe siècles dans la région mâconnaise*, 2nd edn, Paris 1971.

Duffy, P. M., 'The nature of the medieval frontier in Ireland', *Studia Hibernica*, xxii–xxiii (1982–83), 21–38.

Earle, P., *Corsairs of Malta and Barbary*, London 1970.

Eaton, R. M., *The Rise of Islam and the Bengal Frontier, 1204–1760*, Berkeley 1993.

Eberhard, W., 'Remarks on the bureaucracy in north China during the tenth century', *Oriens*, iv (1951), 280–99.

Conquerors and Rulers: social forces in medieval China, 2nd edn, Leiden 1965.

Ellis, S. G., 'Thomas Cromwell and Ireland, 1532–40', *Historical Journal*, xxiii (1980), 497–519.

Tudor Ireland: crown, community and the conflict of cultures, 1470–1603, London 1985.

Reform and Revival: English government in Ireland, 1470–1534, London 1986.

'Crown, community and government in the English territories, 1450–1575', *History*, lxxi (1986), 187–92.

'Nationalist historiography and the English and Gaelic worlds in the late middle ages', *Irish Historical Studies*, xxv (1986–87), 1–18.

The Pale and the Far North: government and society in two early Tudor borderlands, Galway 1988.

Tudor Frontiers and Noble Power: the making of the British state, Oxford 1995.

Ellis, S. G., and Barber, S., eds, *Conquest and Union: fashioning a British state*, London 1995.

Evans, R. J. W., 'Frontiers and national identities in Central Europe', *International History Review*, xiv (1992), 480–502.

Febvre, L., *A Geographical Introduction to History*, trans. E. G. Mountford and J. H. Paxton, London 1932.

'*Frontière*: the word and the concept', *A New Kind of History: from the writings of Lucien Febvre*, trans. K. Folca, ed. P. Burke, London 1973, 208–18.

Ferenczy, M., 'Chinese historiographers' views on barbarian-Chinese relations (14–16th centuries)', *Acta Orientalia*, xxi:3 (1968), 353–62.

Fine, J. V. A., *The Early Medieval Balkans*, Ann Arbor 1983.

Fletcher, J., '[The] Turco-Mongolian monarchic tradition in the Ottoman Empire', *HUS*, III–IV (1979–80), 236–51.

Fletcher, J. F., 'The Mongols: ecological and social perspective', *HJAS*, XLVI (1986), 11–50.

Fontenay, M., 'Le rôle des Chevaliers de Malte dans le corso méditerranéen au XVIIe siècle', *Las Órdenes militares en el Mediterráneo occidental (s. XII–XVIII)*, Madrid 1989, 369–95.

Forstreuter, K., *Die Memel als Handelsstrasse Preussens nach Osten*, Königsberg 1931.

Fossier, R., *L'enfance de l'Europe (X–XII siècles): aspects économiques et sociaux*, 2 vols, Paris 1982.

Foucher, P., *L'invention des frontières*, Paris 1986.

Frame, R., 'Power and society in the lordship of Ireland, 1272–1377', *Past and Present*, LXXVI (1977), 3–33.

Colonial Ireland 1169–1369, Dublin 1981.

English Lordship in Ireland 1318–1361, Oxford 1982.

The Political Development of the British Isles 1100–1400, Oxford 1990.

Franklin, S., and Shepard, J., *The Emergence of Rus 750–1200*, London and New York 1996.

Frazee, C. A., *Catholics and Sultans: the Church and the Ottoman empire 1453–1923*, Cambridge 1983.

Ganshof, F. L., 'The significance of the treaty of Verdun (843)', *The Carolingians and the Frankish Monarchy: studies in Carolingian history*, trans. J. Sondheimer, London 1971, 289–302.

Génicot, L., 'La ligne et zone: la frontière des principautés médiévales', *Études sur les principautés lotharingiennes*, Louvain 1975, 172–85.

Gillingham, J., 'The beginnings of English imperialism', *Journal of Historical Sociology*, V (1992), 392–409.

'Foundations of a disunited kingdom', *Uniting the Kingdom? The Making of British History*, ed. A. Grant and K. J. Stringer, London 1995, 48–64.

Glick, T. H., *Islamic and Christian Spain in the Early Middle Ages: comparative perspectives on social and cultural formation*, Princeton 1979.

Gómez Moreno, E., ed., 'Las primeras crónicas de la reconquista: el ciclo de Alfonso III', *Boletín de la Real Academia de la Historia*, (*c*.1932), 600–27.

Goodman, A., and Tuck, J., *War and Border Societies in the Middle Ages*, London and New York 1992.

Goodman, A., 'The Anglo-Scottish marches in the fifteenth century: a frontier society?', *Scotland and England, 1286–1815*, ed. R. A. Mason, Edinburgh 1987, 18–33.

Goring, J. J., 'Social change and military decline in mid-Tudor England', *History*, LX (1975), 185–97.

Graham, T. H. B., 'The Debateable Land', *Transactions of the Cumberland and Westmorland Antiquarian and Archaeological Society*, new ser., XII (1912), 33–58; XIV (1914), 132–57.

Green, J. A., 'Lords of the Norman Vexin', *War and Government in the Middle Ages*, ed. J. Gillingham and J. C. Holt, Woodbridge 1984, 47–61.

'Aristocratic loyalties on the northern frontier of England, *c*.1100–1174', *England in the Twelfth Century (Proceedings of the 1988 Harlaxton Symposium)*, ed. D. Williams, Woodbridge 1990, 83–100.

Grodzins, M., *The Loyal and the Disloyal: social boundaries of patriotism and treason*, Chicago 1956.

Groth, A., *Żegluga i handel morski Kłajpedyw latach 1664–1722*, Gdańsk 1996.

Guilmartin, J. F., *Gunpowder and Galleys*, Cambridge 1974.

Haarmann, U., 'Turkish legends in the popular historiography of medieval Egypt', *Proceedings of the VIth Congress of Arabic and Islamic Studies (1972)*, Stockholm and Leiden 1977, 97–107.

Haldon, J. F., and Kennedy, H., 'The Arab-Byzantine frontier in the eighth and ninth centuries: military organization and society in the borderlands', *Recueil des travaux de l'Institut d'Études Byzantines*, xix (1980), 79–116.

Han Guanghui 韓光輝, 'Liaodai Zhongguo beifang renkou de qianyi ji qi shehui yingxiang' 遼代中國北方人口的遷移及其社會影響, *Beifang wenwu* 北方文物, 1989: 2, 72–80.

Hartwell, R. M., 'Demographic, political and social transformations of China, 750–1550', *HJAS*, xlii (1982), 365–442.

Hay, D., 'England, Scotland and Europe: The problem of the frontier', *TRHS*, 5th ser., xxv (1975), 77–91.

He Tianming 何天明, 'Lun Liao zhengquan jieguan Yan-Yun de biranxing ji lishi zuoyong' 論遼政權接管燕雲的必然性及歷史作用, *Liao Jin shi lunji* 遼金史論集, iv, ed. Chen Shu 陳述, Beijing 1989, 100–15.

Heidemann, S., *Das Aleppiner Kalifat (AD 1261): Vom Ende des Kalifates in Baghdad über Aleppo zu den Restaurationen in Kairo*, Leiden 1994.

Heiss, G., and Klingenstein, G., eds, *Das Osmanische Reich und Europa 1683 bis 1789: Konflikt, Entspannung und Austausch*, Wien 1983.

Hennessy, A., *The Frontier in Latin American History*, London 1975.

Hess, A., *The Forgotten Frontier*, Chicago 1978.

Heywood, C., 'Wittek and the Austrian tradition', *JRAS*, 2nd ser., 1 (1988), 7–25.
  '"Boundless dreams of the Levant": Paul Wittek, the George-Kreis and the writing of Ottoman history', *JRAS*, 2nd ser., 1 (1989), 32–50.

Heywood, C., and Imber, C., eds, *Studies in Ottoman History in Honour of Professor V. L. Ménage*, Istanbul 1994.

Hiyari, M. A., 'The origins and development of the amīrate of the Arabs during the seventh/thirteenth and eighth/fourteenth centuries', *BSOAS*, xxxviii (1975), 509–24.

Hobsbawm, E., and Ranger, T., eds, *The Invention of Tradition*, Cambridge 1983.

Hodder, I., *Symbols in Action: ethnoarchaeological studies of material culture*, Cambridge 1982.

Hodgson, J., *A History of Northumberland*, 3 pts in 7 vols, Newcastle 1820–25.

Holt, P. M., 'Some observations on the ʿAbbāsid caliphate of Cairo', *BSOAS*, xlvii (1984), 501–7.
  The Age of the Crusades: the Near East from the eleventh century to 1517, London and New York 1986.
  'An-Nāṣir Muḥammad b. Qalāwūn (684–741/1285–1341): his ancestry, kindred and affinity', *Egypt and Syria in the Fatimid, Ayyubid and Mamluk Eras*, ed. U. Vermeulen and D. De Sme, Leuven 1995, 313–24.

Hoppen, A., *The Fortification of Malta by the Order of St John 1530–1798*, Edinburgh 1979.

Hoyle, R. W., 'An ancient and laudable custom: the definition and development of tenant right in north-western England in the sixteenth century', *Past and Present*, CXVI (1987), 24–55.

Hubatsch, W., 'Albert of Brandenburg-Ansbach, Grand Master of the Order of Teutonic Knights and Duke in Prussia, 1490–1568', *Government in Reformation Europe 1520–1560*, ed. H. J. Cohn, New York 1972, 169–202.

Hudson, J. C., 'Theory and methodology in comparative frontier studies', *The Frontier*, ed. D. H. Miller and J. O. Steffen, Oklahoma 1977, 5–35.

Imber, C., 'Paul Wittek's "De la défaite d'Ankara à la prise de Constantinople', *OsmAr*, V (1986), 65–81.

'Ottoman dynastic myths', *T*, XIX (1987), 7–27.

Inalcık, H., with Quataert, D., eds, *An Economic and Social History of the Ottoman Empire 1300–1914*, Cambridge 1994.

Irwin, R., *The Middle East in the Middle Ages: the early Mamluk Sultanate 1250–1382*, London 1986.

Isaac, B., 'The meaning of the terms *limes* and *limitanei*', *Journal of Roman Studies*, LXXVIII (1989), 125–47.

The Limits of Empire, Oxford 1990 and revised edn 1992.

Ivanišević, V., 'Interpretation and dating of the *folles* of Basil II and Constantine VIII – the class A2', *Zbornik Radova Vizantološkog Instituta*, XXVII–XXVIII (1989), 19–42.

Ivinskis, Z., 'Kovos bruožai dėl Žemaičių ir jų sienų', *Athenaeum*, VI (1935), 54–117.

Jackson, S., *Islamic Law and the State: the constitutional jurisprudence of Shihab al-Dīn al-Qarāfī*, Leiden 1996.

Jagchid, S., and Van Simmons, J., *Peace, War and Trade along the Great Wall*, Indiana 1989.

Jakštas, J., 'Mažosios Lietuvos apgyvendinimas iki XVII a. pabaigos', *Lietuvių katalikųmokslo akademijos Metraštis*, IV (1968), 1–49; V (1970), 359–414.

James, M., *Society, Politics and Culture: studies in early modern England*, Cambridge 1986.

Jay, J. W., 'Memoirs and official accounts: the historiography of the Song loyalists', *HJAS*, l, 2 (1990), 589–612.

Jennings, R. C., 'Some thoughts on the Gazi-thesis', *WZKM*, LXXVI (1986), 151–61.

Joachim, E., *Die Politik des letzten Hochmeisters in Preussen Albrecht von Brandenburg*, 3 vols, Leipzig 1892–95.

Jones, S. B., *Boundary-Making: a handbook for statesmen, treaty editors and boundary commissioners*, Washington DC 1945.

Jordanov, I., 'Établissement administratif byzantin à Preslav aux Xᵉ et XIᵉ siècles', *Jahrbuch der Österreichischen Byzantinistik*, XXXII (1982), 35–44.

Kaegi, W., 'The frontier: barrier or bridge?', *17th International Byzantine Congress, Major Papers*, New York 1986, 279–305.

Káldy-Nagy, G., 'The Holy War (*jihād*) in the first centuries of the Ottoman Empire', *HUS*, II–IV (1979–80); also in *Eucharisterion: essays presented to*

Omeljan Pritsak on his sixtieth birthday, ed. I. Ševčenko and F. E. Sysyn, 2 vols, Cambridge, Mass. 1981, 467–73.

Kedar, B. Z., *Crusade and Mission: European approaches to the Muslims*, Princeton 1984.

Kennedy, H., *The Prophet and the Age of the Caliphates: the Islamic Near East from the sixth to the eleventh century*, London and New York 1986.

Khodarkovsky, M., 'From frontier to empire: the concept of the frontier in Russia, sixteenth-eighteenth centuries', *Russian History*, XIX (1992), 115–28.

Krawulsky, D., *Īrān – Das Reich der Īlḫāne: Eine topographische-historische Studie*, Wiesbaden 1978.

Kreiser, K., 'Osmanische Grenzbeschreibungen', *Studi preottomani e ottomani*, [Comité des Études Pré-Ottomanes et Ottomanes, First International Conference, Naples, 24–26 Sept. 1974], Naples 1976, 165–72.

Kunt, M., and Woodhead, C., eds, *Süleyman the Magnificent*, London 1995.

Lambton, A. K. S., 'Islamic Mirrors for Princes', *Theory and Practice in Medieval Persian Government*, repr. London 1980, VI, 419–42 (orig. pagination).

State and Government in Medieval Islam, an Introduction to Islamic Political Theory: the jurists, Oxford 1981.

Lattimore, O., 'Origins of the Great Wall of China: a frontier concept in theory and practice', *Studies in Frontier History: collected papers 1928–58*, London 1962, 97–118.

Inner Asian Frontiers of China, New York 1951.

Lauer, P., 'Une enquête au sujet de la frontière française dans le val d'Aran sous Philippe le Bel', *Comité des Travaux Historiques et Scientifiques: Bulletin de la Section de Géographie*, XXXV (1920), 17–38.

Le Patourel, J., *The Norman Empire*, Oxford 1976.

Feudal Empires: Norman and Plantagenet, ed. M. Jones, London 1984.

Lemarignier, J.-F., *Recherches sur l'hommage en marche et les frontières féodales*, Lille 1945.

'La dislocation du «pagus» et le problème des «consuetudines» (X^e–XIe siècles)', *Mélanges d'histoire du Moyen Âge dédiés à la mémoire de Louis Halphen*, Paris 1951, 401–10.

Lévi Provençal, E., *Historia de la España Musulmana, Historia de España Menéndez Pidal*, IV, Madrid 1950.

LeVine, R. A., and Campbell, D. T., *Ethnocentrism: theories of conflict, ethnic attitudes and group behavior*, New York 1972.

Lewis, A. R., 'The closing of the mediaeval frontier, 1250–1350', *Speculum*, XXXIII (1958), 475–83.

Lewis, A. R., and McGann, T. F., eds, *The New World Looks at its History: Proceedings of the Second International Congress of historians of the United States and Mexico*, Austin 1963.

Lin Ronggui 林榮貴 and Chen Liankai 陳連開, 'Wudai Shiguo shiqi Qidan, Shatuo, Hanzu de zhengzhi, jingji he wenhua jiaoliu' 五代十國時期契丹、沙陀、漢族的政治、經濟和文化交流, *Liao Jin shi lunji* 遼金史論集, III, ed. Chen Shu 陳述, Beijing 1987, 155–86.

Lindner, R. P., 'Stimulus and justification in early Ottoman history', *The Greek Orthodox Theological Review*, XXVII:2 (1982), 207–24.

Linehan, P., *History and the Historians of Medieval Spain*, Oxford 1993.

Little, D. P., *An Introduction to Mamlūk Historiography*, Wiesbaden 1970.

Lot, F., 'La frontière de la France et de l'Empire sur le cours inférieur de l'Escaut du IXᵉ au XIIIᵉ siècle', *Bibliothèque de l'École des Chartes*, LXXI (1910), 5–32.

Loud, G. A., '*The Gens Normannorum* – myth or reality?', *ANS*, IV (1981), 104–16.

Lü Simian 呂思勉, *Sui Tang Wudai shi* 隋唐五代史, 2 vols, Beijing 1959, repr. Shanghai 1984.

Luttrell, A. T., *The Hospitallers in Cyprus, Rhodes, Greece and the West 1291–1440*, London 1978.

Latin Greece, the Hospitallers and the Crusades 1291–1440, London 1982.

The Hospitallers of Rhodes and their Mediterranean World, London 1992.

Ma He 馬赫, 'Liaodai wenhua yu "hua yi tongfeng"' 遼代文化與 '華夷同風', *Minzu yanjiu* 民族研究, 1987: 3, 27–34.

Mackay, A., *Spain in the Middle Ages: from frontier to empire, 1000–1500*, London 1977.

MacKay Mackenzie, W., 'The Debateable Land', *Scottish Historical Review*, XXX (1951), 109–25.

Mager, F., *Der Wald in Altpreussen als Wirtschaftsraum*, 2 vols, Cologne-Graz 1960.

Malamut, E., 'L'image byzantine des Petchénègues', *Byzantinische Zeitschrift*, LXXXVIII (1995), 105–47.

Mallia Milanes, V., *Hospitaller Malta 1530–1798*, Malta 1993.

Manzano Moreno, E., *La frontera de al-Andalus en época de los Omeyas*, Madrid 1991.

'Christian-Muslim frontier in al-Andalus: idea and reality', *The Arab Influence upon Medieval Europe*, ed. D. A. Agius and R. Hitchcock, Reading 1994, 83–99.

Mănucu-Adameşteanu, G., 'Circulaţia monetară la Nufăru în secolele X–XIV', *Peuce*, XXIV (1991), 497–554.

Meilus, E., *Žemaitijos kunigaikštystės miesteliai XVII amžiaus II pusėje XVIII amžiuje (Raida, gyventojai, amatai, prekyba)*, Vilnus 1997.

Melville, C., '"Sometimes by the sword, sometimes by the dagger": the role of the Ismaʿilis in Mamluk-Mongol relations in the 8th/14th century', *Mediaeval Ismaʿili History and Thought*, ed. F. Daftary, Cambridge 1996, 247–63.

Menéndez Pidal, R., 'Repoblación y tradición en la cuenca del Duero', *Enciclopedia lingüística Hispana*, Madrid 1960, I, xxix–lvii.

Meng Guangyao 孟廣耀, 'Shilun Liaodai Hanzu rushi de 'huayi zhi bian' guannian' 試論遼代漢族儒士的 '華夷之辨' 觀念, *Beifang wenwu* 北方文物, 1990: 4, 62–9.

Meserve, R. I., 'The inhospitable land of the barbarian', *Journal of Asian History*, XVI:1 (1982), 51–89.

Moody, T. W., Martin, F. X., and Byrne, F. J., eds, *A New History of Ireland, iii. Early Modern Ireland, 1534–1691*, Oxford 1976.

Morgan, D., 'Persian historians and the Mongols', *Medieval Historical Writing in the Christian and Islamic Worlds*, ed. D. Morgan, London 1982, 109–24.

'The Mongols in Syria, 1260–1300', *Crusade and Settlement*, ed. P. Edbury, Cardiff 1985, 231–5.

The Mongols, Oxford 1986.

Mortensen, H., 'Die litauische Einwanderung nach Ostpreußen', *Prussia*, XXX (1933), 133–41.

Mortensen-Heinrich, G., *Beiträge zu den Nationalitäten und Siedlungsverhältnißen von Preußisch Litauen*, Berlin 1927.

Murphey, R., 'The Ottoman resurgence in the seventeenth century: the gamble and its results', *Mediterranean Historical Review*, VIII (1993), 186–200.

Musset, L., 'Actes inédits du XIe siècle. III: Les plus anciennes chartes normandes de l'abbaye de Bourgueil', *Bulletin de la Société des Antiquaires de Normandie*, LIV (1957–58), 15–54.

Musset, L., 'Considérations sur la genèse et le trace des frontières de la Normandie', *Media in Francia, Recueil . . . K. F. Werner*, Maulévrier 1989, 309–18.

Nelson, L. H., *The Normans in South Wales*, Austin 1966.

Nicolson, J., and Burn, R., *The History and Antiquities of the Counties of Westmorland and Cumberland*, 2 vols, London 1777.

Noble, T. F. X., 'Louis the Pious and the frontiers of the Frankish realm', *Charlemagne's Heir: the reign of Louis the Pious*, ed. P. Godman and R. Collins, Oxford 1990, 333–47.

Ó Danachair, C., 'Irish tower houses and their regional distribution', *Béaloideas*, XLV–XLVII (1979), 158–63.

Obolensky, D., *The Byzantine Commonwealth: Eastern Europe, 500–1453*, London 1971.

'The principles and methods of Byzantine diplomacy', *Actes du XIIe congrès international des études byzantines*, I, Belgrade 1963, 45–61, repr. D. Obolensky, *Byzantium and the Slavs*, New York 1994, 1–22.

Oikonomides, N., 'Presthlavitza, the Little Preslav', *Südost-Forschungen*, XLII (1983), 1–9.

Ostrogorsky, G., *History of the Byzantine State*, trans. J. Hussey, 2nd edn, Oxford 1968.

Ovčarov, D., ed., *Dobrudža-études ethno-culturelles*, Sofia 1987.

Pan Yihong, 'The Sino-Tibetan treaties in the T'ang dynasty', *T'oung Pao*, LXXVIII (1992), 116–61.

Peters, R., *Islam and colonialism: the doctrine of 'jihād' in modern history*, The Hague 1979.

Petrocchi, M., *La politica della Santa Sede di fronte all'invasione Ottomana 1444–1718*, Naples 1955.

Pietkiewicz, K., *Kiezgajłowie ich latyfundium do połowy XVI wieku*, Poznań 1982.

Pociecha, W., *Królowa Bona. Czasy i ludzie Odrodzenia*, 4 vols, Poznań 1949–58.

Pollard, A. J., *North-eastern England during the Wars of the Roses*, Oxford 1990.

Poly J.-P., and Bournazel, E., *The Feudal Transformation 900–1200*, trans. C. Higgitt, New York and London 1991.

Potsdamas ir Karaliaučiaus kraštas, ed. D. Bakanienė, Vilnius 1996.

Power, D. J., 'What did the frontier of Angevin Normandy comprise?', *ANS*, XVII (1994), 181–201.

Prescott, J. R. V., *Boundaries and Frontiers*, London 1978.

Political Frontiers and Boundaries, London 1987.

Pulleyblank, E. G., 'The An Lu-shan rebellion and the origins of chronic militarism in late T'ang China', *Essays on T'ang Society: the interplay of social*, *political and economic forces*, ed. J. C. Perry and B. L. Smith, Leiden 1976, 33–60.

Ragosta, R., ed., *Le genti del mare mediterraneo*, I–II, Naples 1982.

Ren Chongyue 任崇岳, 'Lüelun Liaochao yu Wudai de guanxi' 略論遼朝與五代的 關係, *Shehui kexue jikan* 社會科學輯刊, 1984: 4, 109–15.

Revel, J., 'Au xviiie siècle: le declin de la Méditerranée?', *La France et la Méditerranée: vingt-sept siècles d'interdependence*, ed. I. Malkin, Leiden 1990, 348–62.

Reynolds, R. L., 'The Mediterranean frontier', *The Frontier in Perspective*, ed. W. D. Wyman and C. B. Kroeber, Madison 1957, 21–34.

Richard, J., *Les ducs de Bourgogne et la formation du duché du XIe au XIVe siècle*, Paris 1954.

Robson, R., *The Rise and Fall of the English Highland Clans: Tudor responses to a mediaeval problem*, Edinburgh 1989.

Rodríguez López, A., *La consolidación territorial de la monarquía feudal castellana: expansión y fronteras durante el reinado de Fernando III*, Madrid 1994.

Rossabi, M., ed., *China among Equals: the Middle Kingdom and its neighbors, 10th to 14th centuries*, Berkeley 1983.

Rotberg, R. I., and Rabb, T. K., eds, *The Origin and Prevention of Major Wars*, Cambridge 1989.

Rowell, S. C., 'Karas ruseno Žemaičiuose. Keletas pastabų dėl 1442 m. privilegijos genezės', *Žemaičiupraeitis* (Vilnius, forthcoming).
'The population of the Memel District *c*.1510–1520', *Acta Historica Universitatis Klaipedensis* (forthcoming).

Rowlands, I., 'The making of the March: aspects of the Norman settlement in Dyfed', *ANS*, III (1980), 142–57.

Saddington, D. B., 'The parameters of Romanization', *Roman Frontier Studies*, ed. V. A. Maxfield and M. J. Dobson, Exeter 1991, 413–18.

Sahlins, P., *Boundaries: the making of France and Spain in the Pyrenees*, Berkeley 1989.
'Natural frontiers revisited: France's boundaries since the seventeenth century', *American Historical Review*, XCV (1990), 1423–51.

Sánchez Albornoz, C., *Despoblación y repoblación del valle del Duero*, Buenos Aires 1966.

Sauvaget, J., *La poste aux chevaux dans l'empire des Mamelouks*, Paris 1941.

Schubert, E., and Herrmann, B., eds, *Von der Angst zur Ausbeutung: Umwelterfahrung zwischen Mittelalter und Neuzeit*, Frankfurt-am-Main 1994.

Schwarz-Schilling, C., *Der Friede von Shan Yüan (1005 n. Chr.)*, Wiesbaden 1959.

Searle, E., *Predatory Kingship and the Creation of Norman Power*, Berkeley 1988.

Setton, K. M., *The Papacy and the Levant 1204–1571*, 4 vols, Philadelphia 1976–84.

Setton, K. M., et al., eds, *A History of the Crusades*, 6 vols, Madison 1959–89.

Shepard, J., 'Symeon of Bulgaria – peacemaker', *Annuaire de l'Université de Sofia 'St. Kliment Ohridski'*, LXXXIII (1989) [1991], 9–48.
'Constantinople – gateway to the north: the Russians', *Constantinople and its Hinterland*, ed. C. Mango and G. Dagron, Aldershot 1995, 243–60.

Sinor, D., 'Inner Asian warriors', *JAOS*, CI (1981), 133–44.

Sinor, D., ed., *The Cambridge History of Early Inner Asia*, Cambridge 1990.

Smith, A. D., *The Ethnic Origins of Nations*, Oxford 1986.

Smith, B., 'A county community in early-fourteenth-century Ireland: the case of Louth', *EHR*, CVIII (1993), 561–88.

Smith, J. M., '"Ayn Jālūt: Mamlūk success or Mongol failure?' *HJAS*, XLIV (1984), 307–45.

'Mongol nomadism and Middle Eastern geography: qīshlāqs and tümens', *The Mongol Empire and its Legacy*, ed. R. Amitai-Preiss and D. Morgan, Leiden 1998.

Smith, J. M. H., *Province and Empire: Brittany and the Carolingians*, Cambridge 1992.

'The *fines imperii:* the marches', *The New Cambridge Medieval History, ii (c.700–c.900)*, ed. R. McKitterick, Cambridge 1995, 169–89.

Songaila, E., 'Bilevičiai', *Žemaičių žemė*, 1995: 4, 33–8.

Spence, R. T., 'The pacification of the Cumberland borders, 1593–1628', *NH*, XIII (1977), 59–160.

Spuler, B., *Die Mongolen in Iran: Verwaltung und Kultur der Ilchanzeit 1220–1350*, 4th ed., Leiden 1985.

Standen, N., 'Frontier crossings from north China to Liao, *c*.900–1005', Ph.D. thesis, University of Durham 1994.

'The disappearance of a frontier region: the Liao and the borders of tenth-century north China', *Selected Papers of the 10th Biannual Conference, European Association for Chinese Studies*, Prague 1996, unpaginated.

Stevenson, W., 'England and Normandy, 1204–59', 2 vols, Ph.D. thesis, University of Leeds 1974.

Stokes, A. D., 'The Balkan campaigns of Svyatoslav Igorevich', *Slavonic and East European Review*, XL (1962), 466–96.

Storey, R. L., 'The wardens of the marches of England towards Scotland, 1377–1485', *EHR*, LXXII (1957), 593–615.

Su Tianjun 蘇天鈞, 'Hou Tang Beiping wang Zhao Dejun' 後唐北平王趙德鈞, *Beijing shiyuan* 北京史苑, 1 (n.d.), 166–78.

Suppe, F. C., *Military Institutions on the Welsh Marches: Shropshire 1066–1300*, Woodbridge 1994.

Swerew, J. M., *Rußlands Gebiet Kaliningrad im neuen geopolitischen Koordinatenfeld*, Cologne 1996.

Tanaşoca, N.-Ş., 'Les mixobarbares et les formations politiques paristriennes du XIᵉ siècle', *Revue Roumaine d'Histoire*, XII (1973), 61–82.

Tao Jing-shen, *Two Sons of Heaven: studies in Sung-Liao relations*, Tucson 1988.

Tăpkova-Zaimova, V., 'L'administration byzantine au Bas Danube (fin du Xᵉ–XIᵉ s.)', *Byzantinoslavica*, LIV (1993), 95–101.

TeBrake, W. H., *Medieval Frontier: culture and ecology in Rijnland*, Austin 1985.

Thompson, M. W., *The Decline of the Castle*, Cambridge 1987.

Thorau, P., *The Lion of Egypt: Sultan Baybars I and the Near East in the thirteenth Century*, trans. P. M. Holt, London and New York 1992.

Tietze, K., 'The Liao Song border conflict of 1074–1076', *Studia Sino-Mongolica: Festschrift für Herbert Franke*, ed. W. Bauer, Wiesbaden 1979, 127–51.

Totoraitis, J., *Sūduvos Suvalkijos istorija*, I, Kaunas 1938.

Tuck, J. A., 'Richard II and the border magnates', *NH*, III (1968), 27–52.

  'War and society in the medieval north', *NH*, XXI (1985), 33–52.

Turner, F. J., 'The significance of the frontier in American history', *The Frontier in American History*, New York 1920, 1–38.

Twitchett, D. C., *The Writing of Official History under the T'ang*, Cambridge 1992.

Urvoy, D., 'Sur l'évolution de la notion de Gihād dans l'Espagne Musulmane', *Mélanges de la Casa de Velazquez*, IX (1973), 335–71.

Vaivada, V., 'Bažnyčių tinklas Žemaitijoje (Descriptio dioecesis Samogitiensis duomenimis)', *Protestantizmas Lietuvoje: istorija ir dabartis*, ed. I Lukšaitė et al., Vilnius 1994, 41–7.

  'Reformacija Žemaitijoje XVI a. II-je pusėje', unpub. Ph.D. diss., Vilnius University 1995.

Vatin, N., *L'Ordre de Saint-Jean-de-Jérusalem, l'Empire ottoman et la Méditerranée orientale entre les deux sièges de Rhodes 1480–1522*, Paris 1994.

Viguera, M. J., ed., *El retroceso territorial de al-Andalus. Almoravides y Almohaes, siglos XII–XIII, Historia de España Menéndez Pidal*, VIII–IX, Madrid 1997.

Waldron, A., *The Great Wall of China: from history to myth*, Cambridge 1990.

Walker, D., 'The Norman settlement in Wales', *ANS*, I (1978), 131–43.

Wang Gungwu, 'The *Chiu Wu-tai shih* and history-writing during the Five Dynasties', *Asia Major*, VI:1 (1958), 1–22.

  'Feng Tao: an essay on Confucian loyalty', *Confucian Personalities*, ed. A. Wright and D. Twitchett, Palo Alto 1962, 123–45.

  The Structure of Power in North China during the Five Dynasties, Stanford 1963.

Wang Mingsun 王明蓀, 'Lüe lun Liaodai de Hanren jituan' 略論遼代的漢人集團, *Bianzheng yanjiusuo nianbiao* 邊政研究所年報, XI (1980), 229–69.

Wansbrough, J., 'Paul Wittek and Richard Hakluyt, a tale of two empires', *OsmAr*, VII–VIII (1988), 55–70.

Werner, K. F., 'Kingdom and principality in twelfth–century France', *The Medieval Nobility*, ed. and trans. T. Reuter, Amsterdam 1978, 243–90.

White, D. G., 'Henry VIII's Irish kerne in France and Scotland', *The Irish Sword*, III (1957–58), 213–25.

White, R., *The Middle Ground: Indians, empires, and republics in the Great Lakes region, 1650–1815*, Cambridge 1991.

Whittaker, C. R., *Frontiers of the Roman Empire: a social and economic study*, Baltimore and London 1994.

Wieczynski, J. L., *The Russian Frontier: the impact of borderlands upon the course of early Russian history*, Charlottesville 1976.

Wittek, P., *The Rise of the Ottoman Empire*, London 1938.

  La Formation de l'Empire Ottoman, London 1982.

Wolfram, H., 'The shaping of the early medieval principality as a form of non-royal rulership', *Viator*, II (1971), 33–51.

Worthy, E. H., Jr, 'The founding of Sung China, 950–1000: integrative changes in military and political institutions', Ph.D. diss., Princeton 1976.

Wright, D. C., 'Sung-Liao diplomatic practices', Ph.D. diss., Princeton 1993.

Ximenez de Rada, *Historia Arabum*, ed. J. Lozano Sánchez, Seville 1993.

Xing Yitian 邢義田, 'Qidan yu Wudai zhengquan gengdie zhi guanxi' 契丹與五代政權更迭之關係, *Shihuo yuekan* 食貨月刊, I:6 (1971), 296–307.

Yang Lien-sheng, 'A "posthumous letter" from the Chin emperor to the Khitan emperor in 942', *HJAS*, x (1947), 418–28.

Yang Lien-sheng, 'The organisation of Chinese official historiography: principles and methods of the standard histories from the T'ang through the Ming dynasty', *Historians of China and Japan*, ed. W. G. Beasley and E. G. Pulleyblank, London 1961, 44–59.

Yao Congwu 姚從吾, 'Abaoji yu Hou Tang shichen Yao Kun huijian tanhua jilu' 阿保機與後唐使臣姚坤會見　談話集錄, *Dongbei shi luncong* 東北史論叢, I, Taibei 1959, 217–47.

Yver, J., 'Philippe Auguste et les châteaux normands: la frontière orientale du duché', *Bulletin de la Société des Antiquaires de Normandie*, LIX (1967–89), 309–48.

Zachariadou, E., ed., *The Ottoman Emirate (1300–1389)*, Rethymnon 1993.

The Via Egnatia under Ottoman Rule (1380–1699), Rethymnon 1996.

Zhou Jun 周軍, 'Xu Xuan qiren yu Songchu "erchen"' 徐鉉其人與宋初 '貳臣', *Lishi yanjiu* 歷史研究, 1989: 4, 120–32.

INDEX

272

Index   293